Time, Religion and History

History: Concepts, Theories and Practice

Series editor: Alun Munslow, University of Staffordshire

The New History
Alun Munslow

History on Film/Film on History
Robert A. Rosenstone

Imperialism and Postcolonialism
Barbara Bush

Class
Dennis Dworkin

Time, Religion and History

WILLIAM GALLOIS

Harlow, England • London • New York • Boston • San Francisco • Toronto
Sydney • Tokyo • Singapore • Hong Kong • Seoul • Taipei • New Delhi
Cape Town • Madrid • Mexico City • Amsterdam • Munich • Paris • Milan

Pearson Education Limited

Edinburgh Gate
Harlow CM20 2JE
United Kingdom
Tel: +44 (0)1279 623623
Fax: +44 (0)1279 431059
Website: www.pearsoned.co.uk

First edition published in Great Britain in 2007

© Pearson Education Limited 2007

The right of William Gallois to be identified as author of this work has been asserted
by him in accordance with the Copyright, Designs and Patents Act 1988.

ISBN: 978-0-582-78452-9

British Library Cataloguing in Publication Data
A CIP catalogue record for this book can be obtained from the British Library

10 9 8 7 6 5 4 3 2 1
12 11 10 09 08

Set by 35 in 11/13pt Bulmer MT
Printed in Malaysia   (CTP - VVP)

The Publisher' policy is to use paper manufactured from sustainable forests.

Contents

Preface to the series

*H*istory: *Concepts, Theories and Practice* is a series that offers a coherent
and detailed examination of the nature and effects of recent theoretical,
methodological and historiographical developments within key fields of
contemporary historical practice. Each volume is open to the idea of history
as a historicist cultural discourse constituted by historians as much as it is
reconstructed from the sources available about the past. The series examines
the discipline of history as it is conceived today in an intellectual climate that
has increasingly questioned the status of historical knowledge.

As is well known, questioning of the status of history, indeed of its very
existence as an academic subject, has been seen in several recent scholarly
developments that have directly influenced our study of the past. These
include the emergence of new conceptualizations of 'pastness', the emergence of fresh forms of social theorizing, the rise of concerns with narrative,
representation and the linguistic turn, and a self-conscious engagement with
the issues of relativism, objectivity and truth. All these are reflected in the
appearance of new historical themes and frameworks of historical activity.

In acknowledging that history is not necessarily nor automatically auth-
orized by one foundational epistemology or methodology and that history
cannot stand outside its own genre or form, all volumes in the series reflect
a multiplicity of metanarrative positions. Nevertheless, each volume (regard-
less of its own perspective and position on the nature of history) explains the
most up-to-date interpretational and historiographic developments that fall
within its own historical field. However, this review of the 'latest interpretation
and methodology' does not diminish the broad awareness of the 'challenge
to history as a discipline' reflected in the tensions between referentiality,
representation, structure and agency.

Each volume offers a detailed understanding of the content of the past, explaining by example the kinds of evidence found within their own field as well as a broad knowledge of the explanatory and hermeneutic demands historians make upon their sources, the current debates on the uses to which evidence is put, and how evidence is connected by historians within their field to their overall vision of What is history?

Alun Munslow

Acknowledgements

This book was supported at various points in its life by generous assistance from the American University of Sharjah, the Mellon Foundation, the School of Oriental and African Studies and Roehampton University. I have also been lucky enough to have been able to call upon a number of specialist readers who have offered helpful suggestions regarding drafts of chapters. They are: Alun Munslow, John Tosh, John Seed, Jonathan Rée, Larry Woods, Marzia Balzani, John Fox, Norman Wallwork, Nicholas Swann, Rebecca Niblock, Kate Niblock-Siddle, Ben May, Ramues Gallois, Dina Gillespie, Ruth Hall, Otis Kempinski, Mark Knight, Andy Barnett, Niall O'Flaherty and Barbara Wallwork. I should also like to thank the excellent Mary-Clare Connellan and Christina Wipf Perry at Longman-Pearson.

Chapter 1

Introduction – The enigma of being-in-time

The argument of this book is that we live in different times. This contention is made up of two claims, for it describes our sense that we do not experience time in only one fashion, as well as the idea that the study of different cultures assures us that others have conceptions of time unlike our own. This book follows both of these lines of argument to assert that time is the great *unsaid* in western historical thought precisely because it is more complicated than we might at first think; time is plural in the sense that we experience it in different ways and in the manner that we know that others live in temporal cultures that are not predicated on our basic assumptions about time. The very act of thinking hard about time becomes a form of liberation in which we disabuse ourselves of the idea that our picture of the world is a natural one that is shared by all others.

The declaration that 'we live in different times' seems strange to us, for we are not often in the habit of either thinking about time or questioning whether our own understanding of time is shared by others. 'Time', we suppose, is a given; it is one of the structures of our world that is assured. As a backdrop to our lives, it is one of the categories of things which Wittgenstein (1974: 341) said we 'exempt from doubt', for to trouble such basic building blocks of existence would disrupt the coherence of our lives. Wittgenstein insisted, though, that the assuredness of such concepts should not exempt them from investigation, for the very fact that they were 'the *scaffolding* of our thoughts' (1974: 211) meant that the examination of such things should take precedence over more detailed studies of the world.

This book follows Wittgenstein's epistemological emphasis in order to undertake an investigation into time and history. It describes the temporal cultures of five religions (Judaism, Christianity, the Australian Dreamtime,

Islam and Buddhism) so as to demonstrate the ways in which different peoples created distinct temporal cultures. Most of the world's great cultures cohered around religions and it was through meditations on the sacred and the practices of ritual that they developed distinctive temporal cultures. It is evidently the case that such cultures can be discerned outside of religion – in fields such as literature, art and philosophy – but it is my contention both that the clearest pictures of temporal cultures were found in religion and that religious ideas of time tended to serve as a point of origin for temporal discussion in other social spheres. The study of religion serves, then, as an example here, but I would suggest that it stands as the best example in a comparative study of temporalities.

Studying religious temporalities also allows us to see how particular cultures used ideas about time to make works of history, for it is evidently the case that any idea of history is predicated upon some broader notion of temporality. This book is therefore interested in both theories of time and the manner in which such ideas were deployed in the construction of historical texts and indeed narratives about time more generally. What I think the comparative stress of this book adds here is a very practical illustration of the great variety of modes of time and history-making that have existed in world history. Different religions operated with very different epistemologies of time and as a consequence they produced histories that looked dissimilar to those of other cultures, which served very different purposes, and whose composition relied on very different techniques and senses of the historical craft. It has become something of a commonplace in modern western historiography to stress the range of styles of historical practice found in the profession – evinced in book titles such as *The Varieties of History* and *The Houses of History* – yet my aim in this book will be to show that such diversity is actually expressive of only one branch of a network of historical temporalities and possibilities which has rarely been explored.

The sentence with which I began this book also serves as a means to summarizing some of the key differences in the temporal cultures that will be studied. Slight alterations of its claim reveal the manner in which basic differences in temporal orientation are made plain in language. Christians, for instance, might stress the idea that we will live in different times: a futurity expressive of a redemptive historical philosophy. The Australian Dreamtime contends that we lived in different times, but we must attend to the grammatical uncertainty of the pastness implied by the verb 'lived' in this instance. The Jews of the Old Testament might have said that they were living in different times, as a means of describing the culture of historicity which they developed, whilst an Islamic twist on such an idea would stress that we write our lives in time. Buddhists, in contrast, would at one and the same time see the statement 'we live in different times' as indicative both of karmic cycles and a tragic eventuality to be fought against, given its assumption of an idea of selfhood. Modern science, after Einstein, argued very clearly that we live in different times, for principles of temporal relativity structure much of the universe.

It is not my aim in this book to claim that modern styles of history-writing are inferior to those found in other cultures, for there can be no grounds for suggesting that such histories are better or worse than, say, Zen Buddhist accounts of time or the eschatological history of John's Revelation. They are each simply different examples from the genre of time-writing. It is not all my intention to create a grand narrative of oppositionality to western empiricism in this book, in part because history presumed to be written under that banner can too easily be fetishized into a constricting homogeneity and, more importantly, because my argument depends not on an opposition between a self and an other, but on the presentation of a much more divergent cast of temporal and historical possibilities.

What a comparative stress does, however, emphasize is the difference and the cultural specificity of western empirical history, for when seen from the perspective of other temporalities western empiricism is strange and unique. The acquisition of a sense of estrangement from empiricism can be a great gain to those of us who have grown up in that tradition, especially when one confronts theoretical writing which suggests that there is some innate conceptual, methodological or moral superiority inherent to the empirical tradition. The elision of empiricism with the upper-case disciplinary heading 'History' has simply reflected the intellectual history of the modern world in which a western description of time and history was exported globally at the time of, and through, western imperialism.

In fact, as Marcus (1961: 128–29) observes, the notion of history that was delivered from the west was one that was actually waning in its homeland at the moment of its despatch:

> History delights in irony. During the century when the Western *Weltan-schauung* was decaying at home, it was coming to exert its greatest influence on other societies. [. . .] The last wave of West European expansion manifested itself in the imperialism of the nineteenth century, and naturally the colonists took with them the unconscious assumptions of the then-contemporary mystique: progress, egalitarianism, individualism, control over the environment, and the linearity of time in a world which awaited change and improvement. Subsequently the expansionist influence of Communism has exerted a similar impact upon the non-Western world by those who had inherited the nineteenth-century faith in a line of progress in

'science' even as they were emptying it of its liberal content. Thus in our time, the mystique of progress and the expectation of betterment, retreating in the West, took hold in the non-Western world and revolutionized it.

I hope that this book will offer a thrill in allowing readers to see both the difference of temporal cultures other than the one in which modern western ideas of history were founded and in the developing realization that the heritage of those 'western' ideas of time is rather more complex than modern historiography would lead us to believe. As Marcus notes above, ideas about time and history can change quickly within a culture. This book is not simply a historiographical exercise, but a project of recovery, since I am interested in retrieving the temporal cultures of major world religions as they described themselves and the ways in which these ideas about time led to their take on what might be called histories. Religious texts often offer very clear descriptions of the cultures of time which they expect adherents to adopt in their lives, and it is the richness, complexity and directness of these discussions of time that might surprise many readers today.

Epistemology

The project of modern historiography has displayed an admirable reflexivity in the manner in which it has interrogated the origins of the discipline of history. Yet it has proved curiously unwilling to look carefully at the epistemological grounding of history and, in particular, those ideas of time upon which the discipline is evidently predicated. 'History' after all is a time word; it presumes itself to be about time and an approach to time where there is a radical disjuncture between the past, present and future.

Writing in 1962, Pierre Chaunu expressed well the historian's fear of epistemology (Ricœur 1999: 95):

> Epistemology is a temptation one must resolutely cast aside. Does not the experience of the last few years prove that it can provide a facile solution to those who give themselves up to it with delight – one or two brilliant exceptions no more than confirm the rule – as a sign of research standing still and becoming sterile? At best, it is opportune that a few leading minds dedicate themselves to it – this we in no way claim to do – in order to preserve the robust craftsman who is busy forging a knowledge still under construction.

Chaunu's words are, I think, revealing. First because his talk of 'temptation' reminds us that the historian's fear of epistemology, and philosophy more generally, is based on a strict moral code. To allow historical research to 'stand still' would be a sign of degeneracy, a lack of commitment to the collective construction of knowledge in which historians are engaged and the idea of progress that underpins this enterprise. This work will never be finished and as such it induces constant guilt in the 'robust craftsman', for, although we cannot reach a point where knowledge is no longer 'still under construction', our duty is in following this path. Such ideas are of course based very strongly on particular ideas of Christian culture and morality in which salvation can be found in the practice of good work.

Tosh (2000) speaks of the manner in which 'Historians in general are not much disposed to reflect in public on the nature of their craft', and this lack of philosophical interest in expanded upon by Nagel (1963: 76):

> Like other intellectual workers, professional historians are rarely self-conscious about the organizing concepts or the principles for assessing evidence which they habitually employ in their discipline. To be sure, historians have written extensively on the specialized techniques of their craft as well as on the general problems that arise in the external and internal criticism of documents and other remains of the past. Nevertheless, serious discussions of such broad questions as the structure of historical explanations, the grounds upon which they are warranted, and in particular the logic of causal imputation in historical research, have in the main been carried on by professional philosophers or philosophically minded students in other branches of social inquiry.

Nagel's point is well made when we think of the negligible impact of the work of theorists who work on temporal questions upon the discipline of history, such as Rotenstreich, Adam and Wilcox. Yet we ought also to acknowledge that significant cultural differences with regard to theory exist between national historiographical traditions. As Burke (2000: 403) observes, 'the resistance to theory remains strong in Britain, whereas in Germany the history of historiography is an acknowledged subdiscipline of history.' Such a claim is borne out in the reliance that I will have on Germanic thought in the opening theoretical chapters of this book, for the cast of Germanic thinkers through whom my argument develops includes Friese, Rüsen, Heidegger, Kant, Nietzsche, Müller, Sebald, Fabian, Hegel, Ranke, Buber, Herder, Benjamin, Husserl, Freud, Dada, Marx, Ranke and Iggers. A similar observation could be made with regard to biblical scholarship in Chapters 4 and 5.

This book is, therefore, partly designed to push historians towards questions of epistemology and the manner in which it is structured is designed both to counteract Nagel's justified criticisms and to appeal to a broad historical audience. By this I am referring to the fact that this is not a work of pure *historical theory*, if such a thing could exist, but a consideration of historical ideas and practices. The chapters of this book offer detailed case studies of religious temporalities in a fashion which I think should seem approachable to all historians, though this should not disguise the fact that on a very basic level I am deeply critical of the failure of both historians and historiographers to engage with ideas of time which I contend should be formative of both historical theory and education.

This epistemological stress also draws on the broader aims of the series of which this book forms a part, for two of the central aims of the works in *History: Concepts, Theories and Practice* are the desire to open up new theoretical literatures to historians and the rejection of the assumption that western empiricism's lack of interest in epistemology is a natural state of affairs. As Munslow puts it (2003: ix), the series is premised on the idea that 'history is not necessarily nor automatically authorised by one foundational epistemology or methodology'. My aim in this volume is to show how such a claim operates in practice, through illustrative studies of a series of temporal and historical cultures.

This book does not reshape current interpretations of religion, time and history, but, rather, asks us to see something which has always been present in historical writing and thinking, even if it was not interrogated. As we will see, in Buddhist temporal thought for example, there are instances of historical cultures which have always laid great stress on epistemological concerns, and an interest in time in particular. Such a project derives support from a number of important contemporary theorists of time and of history – Elizabeth Deeds Ermarth, Paul Ricœur and Robert Young – but I hope that the lines of enquiry and the imaginative space that it opens up offer the potentiality for further work in the manner in which I feel such writers opened my eyes to new possibilities in thinking about time and history.

The example of Hayden White's *Metahistory* has been in my mind while writing this book, for White took a set of ideas from philosophy and literary analysis, in order to see afresh the character of historical production in a manner that was both conceptual and deeply practical (in his suggestions for the discipline and his detailed studies of particular nineteenth-century texts). The example of that work has inspired me as I sought to clearly express why our idea of history could be expanded and globalized through a consideration of time and religion. That spatial context forms an important part of the argument of this book, for as a discipline history finds itself in the curious position of claiming to be made up of geographically determined specialisms, and even a branch of 'world history', yet it knows almost nothing of ideas of time and history from outside its space and moment, and cannot conceive of how such things might influence its own practices.

Religion and history: the enigma of being-in-time

The study of religion in this book is both a vehicle and an end in itself. It is a vehicle in that the study of religions serves as an illustration of how different cultures use and create time, slowly building up my case that a variety of modes of history and temporality can be discerned. Yet it is also an end in itself for there have been relatively few works which have explicitly compared temporalities and history-making across religious cultures. This is not to suggest that theological literatures lack an interest in time, for I hope that one of the revealing aspects of this work for historians will be the access they gain to a discipline which sites the study of time at the heart of its enterprise, often with an explicit epistemological stress and always with an openness to the idea that there are plural times and modes of history-making. One of the tasks, therefore, of this book is to open up both the cultures of temporality that we find in primary sources such as the Bible and the Australian Dreamtime and to show how the insights into such works from theologians can aid historians not just in the analysis of religious works but in the study of sources more generally.

The text of the book is supplemented by a long bibliography which is itself added to in a guide to further reading which directs interested readers to the most important secondary literatures in particular theological traditions and disciplines outside history that have been used in writing this book. These two supplements to the text are of great importance because the individual chapters' studies of particular religious cultures are of necessity sometimes exercises in condensing and simplifying complex discussions. I hope, nonetheless, that the body of this book conveys to readers how wonderful an experience it can be to read primary texts such as the Qur'an and the Old Testament from temporal perspectives and that the guide to further reading stresses the depth of pleasure that can be gained from reading D.T. Suzuki on Zen Buddhism, T.G.H. Strehlow on the Australian Dreamtime and Jürgen Moltmann on Christian time. As these three introductory chapters will set out, this book has a number of arguments to make, but it also hopes to serve as a resource for historians in introducing them to religious texts, temporal cultures and secondary works.

There is evidently a confluence of interest, purpose and form between religions and histories, for they are both centrally concerned with time: about belief in and across time, the manner in which time is structured and the status of events in time. Religions and histories can be seen as corporate enterprises and have traditionally been viewed as such by theologians who have sought to understand the development of specific religious cultures through changes in the production of historical narratives as, for instance, in the shifts that take place across the New Testament as we move through a set of biographies, letters, revelations and other temporal representations.

A further connection between religion and history, which provides a rationale for this study, is that they are both driven by mystery, for both seek to explain the nature of being in a totalizing fashion. What is more, both religions and history focus on time as the epistemological basis of answering questions about the mystery of life, for they begin with accounts of time as they seek to account for the world. As orientations towards time, they seek to develop frameworks within which questions of meaning and structure can be resolved so as to come closer to solving essential mysteries. They hope to leave a mark on the world, and in doing this to express a faith in things that cannot be seen by men. We might also mention as an aside that historians and theologians tend to share another trait in common, which is that they are both believers, ardent searchers after truth, so I think it is incumbent on a study such as this, founded as it is on a more ironic moment in historiographical reflection, to also consider the assault on revealed belief and implied truth that we find in modern scientific relativism.

All religious work is therefore essentially about time, as are all histories. Barbara Adam, one of the leading theorists of time, makes this point in a manner with which I cannot wholly agree (2004: 90):

> Impermanent are all created things but underlying them is an eternal atemporal reality. This is the shared belief that underpins all the major religions, where the principle of infinity and timelessness is variably called Brahman, Nirvana, Absolute Tao, Yahweh, God and Allah. Irrespective of how the world is conceived – in terms of cycles of reincarnation or rebirth, of absolute flux rooted in the continuous flow of creation and destruction, as apparent and absolute aspects of the Absolute Tao, as creation with a beginning and an end or as an irreversible progress towards increasing perfection – the purpose of the earthly journey is reunification with the eternal ultimate reality, however this may be defined. Despite their considerable diversity, therefore, the world religions – Hinduism, Buddhism,

Taoism, Judaism, Christianity and Islam – share a belief in an eternal, transcendent principle beyond time and space from which our world emanates and to which we are ultimately to return.

In this book I hope to show that, while Adam is right to make the study of time central to her consideration of religion, it is incorrect to claim that essentially purposive forms of time underlie all the major religions and that a transcendent temporal sphere is universally venerated as the ultimate goal of religious belief. Such commonality can be observed in many branches of major world religions, most especially in more recent times, but I aim to show that analysis of, say, early Christianity and Buddhism leads us to a much more complex cast of accounts of time.

The idea that the very essence of being human is to locate one's sense of self in time is common to both theologies and philosophies. Religions serve to answer what White called 'the enigma of being-in-time', offering believers above all else an account of meaning that is located in a consideration of time. Time is in this sense epistemological since it precedes notions of both being and belief. As Brandon says (1965: 2), time 'may even be described as *the* basic factor, or rather, the very source, of the religious intuitions and aspirations of our race.' Theologians like Brandon are convinced that this centrality of time in being human and making faith comes from man's understanding of his mortality and his (1965: v) 'unceasing quest for security from Time's menace'. I shall hope to show that this is a rather narrow view of man, time and religion, but Brandon's argument is representative of much conceptual thought about time. Let us look, for instance, at Rée's useful summary of Heidegger's ideas in *Being and Time* (1998: 43):

> The moments of authentic temporality are 'ecstatic' in the sense that they 'stand outside themselves'. They are linked to each other by countless pathways of memory and anticipation: they are not positions fixed on a bridge over time, but indefinite fields that reach out into both past and future. Moments are 'futural', but not in the sense of being oriented towards infinite times to come. Each moment is magnetized by finitude, anticipating death like a compass needle pointing to the North Pole.

Heidegger, then, sites death as the key moment in his account of time, and it will not be until we escape European conceptions of time later in this book that we will shake off this particular imputation of ultimate significance to the twinning of time and death, and its assumption that the individual and his or her mortality lie at the heart of all temporal systems. We shall also go on to see the manner in which the apprehension of the startling originality of Paul's picture of time in the New Testament was of fundamental importance to Heidegger in his placing ideas of time at the centre of his philosophical work.

This question of the relationship between often complex theological traditions and simplified religious practices is an important one which needs to be addressed here. In some cultures it may be the case that intricate understandings of time develop which do not necessarily impact upon the broader religion tradition, though they might always be valued at the margins, and, similarly, it may be the case that complex ideas about time may not always have a direct impact upon practice – be it the practice of worship or the practice of historical production. This thought struck me as I saw a group of men leaving a mosque in central London, wondering quite what Maimonides' disquisitions on time might mean in their worship. How could the ideas of a figure born more than eight hundred years ago, whose place in Islamic intellectual history is imperative, yet who was not himself a Muslim, be said to be formative in the temporal world of modern Muslims, and how should this affect my study? The pertinence of such a question seems especially important in the case of Islam, given the visceral promotion of a much less philosophically complex set of ideas of Islamic time in recent decades. My resolution of this question comes in the chapter structure of the book. After this introduction, the first five chapters of the book look at both originary accounts of time in religious cultures, and sophisticated reworkings of these cultures from the medieval world, while the sixth chapter considers the workings of time in modern religions and science.

Similar questions about origins and complexity might also be asked of history, and indeed the relationship between religious temporalities and history. It is a truism to say that western history is based in part on Judaeo-Christian culture, yet what I hope to show in the third and fourth chapters of this book is the manner in which ideas of time in the Bible are more radical, plural and productive than the basic forms of Jewish and Christian thought which are later embedded in many histories.

Structure

Having claimed a certain radical intent in terms of the epistemological and de-westernizing approaches of this book, I think that the broadly chronological structure of the text requires some justification. Following this introduction and two further theoretical discussions, each of the book's chapters is based around the study of a particular religious culture and those chapters begin in ancient times and end in the present. The reason for this approach is to make plain not just the different historical epistemologies of religions and the historiographies of writing upon religion, but major shifts in these areas within religious cultures. Thus, the manifold changes induced in Christian culture after the Reformation, the Counter-Reformation and the Enlightenment will be explored in Chapter 10. The chapters of the book are divided between those that try to piece together the leading ideas of time and philosophies of history of specific religions in their early days (Judaism, Christianity, the Australian Dreamtime) and those that look at the development of temporal cultures in particular faiths (Islam, Buddhism). Such divisions are, however, in some senses arbitrary, for a chapter such as that on Judaism, which concentrates on a reading of the Old Testament, examines the first two thousand years of Jewish history as it is narrated there.

Clearly this book will not be able to discuss all cultures at all times, but, as I have said, what it will aim to do is to point the interested reader in the direction of key texts that will enable them to expand their conception of historical theory and practice. In many cases these texts will come from allied fields such as anthropology, sociology and theology, which have longer traditions of theoretical and cross-cultural enquiry in this area. Part of the originality of this book will, I hope, come in its interdisciplinarity, for the subject of time belongs to no one discipline, and, while I seek to make my main contribution to history, this will partly come from the engagement of that discipline with other fields' debates on time and narrative.

In terms of the texts it analyses, this book endeavours to conceive of the historical narrative in as broad a fashion as possible, inviting the reader to make connections between archival documents such as law codes and collections of correspondence, artistic works such as paintings and buildings, and other forms of cultural texts such as novels and poems. It takes material on time that is scattered across texts and which has not always been seen as a topic of investigation in itself. While this may seem an arbitrary exercise – since this is not necessarily what texts are meant to be talking about or to focus on – one could argue that it is similar to an exercise one might find in a linguistic study. Where linguists look for the grammatical structures underlying our use of words and their content, I look for the grammar of time, which I contend structures religious and historical texts. My analytic focus is on the study of primary texts, with bibliographical introductions offered to secondary literatures, partly as a means of ensuring the originality of my argument, and also to make certain that this is a book which readers can engage with as they too analyse the sources that generate my argument.

This is not a book where I seek to answer a set of questions which have enjoined lively debate, but a book where I seek to find new questions for history. My answers may be scant and provisional in places, but I will have succeeded if some of the questions it asks are genuinely new and if it promotes the idea that different epistemological conceptions of time might lead us to write very different kinds of histories, based not just on modern historical methods but on the temporalities of other cultures and their religions. Those temporalities are presented alongside each other in what I hope is a clear and precise fashion which neither denies complexity nor forgets that this study originates in very simple questions about the nature of time and history. These are some of the ways in which this book serves as a starting point, hopeful that new answers and practices will follow its lead. I also hope to extend this work's scope in the future, for there are obviously a series of religions and themes – Zoroastrianism, the Greeks, African religions, Hinduism, Egyptian religion, Mesopotamian culture, Mayans, Taoism, Jainism, geological time, modernist literature and art – which are as worthy of comparative analysis as those subjects that I have chosen to look at in this book.

Chapter 2

The varieties of time

One way of considering the complexity and varieties of time is to relate our investigation to what we think we know best: our own lives. In doing so we recognize that each of our lives consists of the mediation and the running together of a series of different forms of time – the present, memories, hopes, our knowledge of death, our guesses as to what happens after death, our picture of nature, sleep, and our view of time in others' lives, among others – and their resolution into a more manageable general conception of time, which we tend not to think of too much. This management of time, or the imposition of a sense of order upon the pluralities of time, is evidently one of the chief tasks of religions, though in some cases this is achieved through making time still more complex. In this chapter I want to further explore the notion that there are a variety of times and look at how we might access such temporalities.

If such claims sound as though they privilege the philosophical over the practical, then that is no bad thing, since, as I have said, it can be too easy to skate over questions of epistemology, even in the philosophy of history. In fact, though, my enterprise here is intensely practical, since it is rather the unity and unchallenged clarity of time which is a philosophical conceit, and an uncertainty as to the nature of time which is eminently commonsensical. If we think of our own experience – let us say of our memories of yesterday, and the difficulties we would find in writing a history of our day – we begin to see that a doubting and pluralized approach can be far simpler and more pragmatic than a desire for a narrative that glosses over simple questions about time which it might otherwise seem to be easier to forget.

From our comparative perspective, then, history is not just about the past, but rather concerns itself with the experience of living in time, and the responsibility for understanding the complexity of the human experience of time lies with the historian. No one understood this better than the Anglo-German historical writer W.G. Sebald whose four novels are profound meditations on the varieties of time. In trying to explain how humans come to grips with time, Sebald showed (2002a: 207) that it was its multifariousness which encouraged a sense that man was at home in plural times, as we see in this passage from *The Emigrants*:

> What interests me most are the countless glossy black stag beetles in the Windheim woods. I track their crooked wanderings with a patient eye. At times it looks as if something has shocked them, physically, and it seems as if they have fainted. They lie there motionless, and it feels as if the world's heart had stopped. Only when you hold your own breath do they return from death to life, only then does time begin to pass again. Time. What time was all that? How slowly the days passed then! And who was that strange child, walking home, tired, with a tiny blue and white jay's feather in her hand?

> If I think back nowadays to our childhood in Steinach (Luisa's memoirs continue at another point), it often seems as if it had been open-ended in time, in every direction – indeed, as if it were still going on, right into these lines I am still writing. But in reality, as I know only too well, childhood ended in January 1905 when the house and fields at Steinach were auctioned off and we moved into a new three-storey house in Kissingen, on the corner of Bibrastrasse and Erhardstrasse.

In this short passage it is possible to identify sixteen distinct temporal forms, as Sebald answers his question, 'What time was all that?':

    i. A memory of present continuous being.
    ii. Action in time: we are 'crooked wanderers'.
    iii. The suspension of time.
    iv. Man in God's time.
    v. Time and nature: breathing.
    vi. Time as a metaphysical concept.
    vii. The variety of time: 'What time was all that?'
    viii. The varying speeds of time.
    ix. Memory and mystery (what man can and cannot know of time).
    x. Reminiscence.
    xi. The reading of others' pasts.
    xii. Living the varieties of time.
    xiii. Open-ended time, moving in every direction.

xiv. Seeming time.
 xv. Continuum.
xvi. Historical time.

Sebald had a wonderfully clear view of the way that different times were grammatically embedded in our lives and in this passage he provides a brilliant response of illustrative plurality to Augustine's interrogation of the nature of time. In reading his novel our minds are impelled onwards by the captivation of narrative but if we go back to look at Sebald's writing in detail we find the singularity of time cracking, as seen in this passage. Reading Sebald, we are able to reflect upon the range of temporal experience available to us in our daily lives and once we have been able to accept this pluralization of time it becomes less difficult for us to conceive that other cultures might have very different means of apprehending time.

The emphasis that western empiricists place on a rigid distinction between three temporal forms which move in a linear, progressive fashion is something that we imagine must be very hard to think beyond – for it forms the background of our lives – yet writers like Sebald reveal that such re-imagination is rather easier than it might seem to be. This is not to say that there are not challenges in coming to accept the temporal cultures of religions for what they are, rather than what we might wish them to be. When, for instance, we look at Buddhist time and history, it *is* hard to accept ideas of un-time and un-history as being equal or superior to the pictures of time we carry with us.

A social scientific complement to Sebald's fictional work on pluralizing time is found in the work of writers such as Adam (1995: 12), who contends that 'There is no single time, only a multitude of times which interpenetrate and permeate our daily lives. Most of these times are implicit and, taken for granted, and seldom brought into relation with each other', and Gurvitch (Hassard 1990: 4), in the *The Spectrum of Social Time*, where he offers a typology of eight forms of modern time-being. Elsewhere in the social sciences, work has been undertaken by linguists on the manner in which ideas of time structure languages in different cultures, by psychologists, such as Piaget, who look at the child's acquisition of a sense of time, and by sociologists working on the management of time in modern forms of production.

Yet the conviction of both cultural producers and social scientists in the modern west that time is a complex subject worthy of study has not been matched by an equivalent interest in history, historiography or the philosophy of history. In fact, where the former fields have sought to interrogate time precisely because of its complexity and plurality, historians have tended to either ignore such claims or resent them because of what they seem to imply about both the impoverishment of historical theory and potential lacunae in historical practice.

If, as Michelet said (Corfield 1996: 9), 'l'histoire, c'est le temps', why is the subject of time so absent from historiography and the philosophy of history? Looking at some of the major works in these fields, one finds scant mention of time, if it appears at all. The index (1989: 440) of Arthur Marwick's *The Nature of History*, for instance, reveals entries for *Time on the Cross* (a book), the *Times Literary Supplement* (a newspaper) and *Timewatch* (a TV programme), but not 'time' in a consideration of the nature of history. Harry Ritter's *Dictionary of Concepts in History* (1986) would appear to have an entry on time, but it actually simply leads us to the entry on 'Periodization', which I find emblematic of historians' preference for the discussion of the practices of their craft rather than the theories that underpin it.

In twentieth-century western historical production, there were, however, a series of key figures and movements who did question ideas of time and, most especially, periodization, such as the Annalistes, Braudel, Febvre and Le Goff. There is no doubt that the last writer's consideration of the development of time in his *Medieval Civilization* (1991) and his earlier study of 'Merchant's Time and Church's Time in the Middle Ages' (1980) are classic studies of the manner in which very different kinds of temporality existed in earlier western history, and also of the meaning of time codes in the lives of groups of people and the manner in which such codifications came to change in late medieval Europe. In addition, Le Goff's deployment of the Annaliste division of time into *durées* of varying length served as a contemporary textual illustration of the kind of complex culture of time he described in the medieval world. We might also mention Marxist historians such as E.P. Thompson and the *History Workshop Journal* movement, who had an instinctive suspicion of the kinds of structures and ideas which underlay often calcified narratives which served entrenched interests. I do not seek to diminish the contributions of these writers, for their historiographical discussions of time and theory remain of great importance, though I would note that the comparative task I have assigned myself in this book is very different from their critiques of the west from within.

At this stage, it would also be remiss of me to ignore late twentieth-century discussions of history and time which we find in cultural texts (leaving aside the question of modernism which I come to later). In both painting (Gerhard Richter, William Kentridge, Susan Hillier) and the novel (Italo Calvino, Borges, Primo Levi), we find a common historical theme, which began from the premise that histories were both harder to realize than historians imagined and the assertion that historical narratives had tended to be co-opted for political ends. Yet such producers also insisted on the great necessity of the production of histories of the events, ideas and horrors of the twentieth century. In the case of a number of these producers – most especially Kentridge, but also Borges and later postcolonial literatures – there was a realization that there was an inherent problem in the association of westernness with superiority of method, and a search for idioms and worldviews which might offer a different glimpse on to the west and the non-west (seen also in both the influence of African and Native American forms on art from Picasso to Barnett Newman, and on the wave of interest in eastern religions from the 1960s onwards). In some sense, this book is borne from such movements.

Returning to historiography, more recently McIntire (Woolf 1998: 890) makes the claim that 'Historians invariably make time relations central to their studies and their definition of history. [. . .] Historians from any culture and epoch are specialists in time relations.' This is essentially untrue but I would concede that there is a growing sense that the analysis of time is emerging as a distinct field of study in historiography. This is made plain in Black's recent introduction to historiography (2000: 14–15), where he asks:

> What is time – whether past, present or future? This question is central, on many different levels, to our understanding of what history is. The historian who fails to conceptualise time, its variable speeds in different contexts, and its varying impact upon past or present societies, will be somewhat disadvantaged. Students must not view time as an inflexible or unchanging entity, but as a relative phenomenon.

The interesting aspect of Black's stress on time as central to the historical enterprise is that he sees the question of time as an epistemological one, which was precisely the approach to time that historians traditionally shied away from (Corfield 1996 is arguably moving in the same direction). Instead, when forced to confront questions of time, historians described it in a number of ways which seemed to confirm their own methods and outlook. Time was viewed as social, as subject to a process of modernization, where the mythical time cultures of the past had been superseded by ideas of time which were no longer bound to such obviously religious notions such as eschatology. The modern historian knew that it was foolish to live one's life based around the notion of the world's end, yet he was somewhat reluctant to face the idea that the abandonment of the teleological mode necessarily implied the adoption of another means of thinking about time. At the same time, of course, brands of idealist history, from Hegel and Marx to Spengler and Toynbee, sought to harness the temporal power of religious modes of understanding. Brandon understood this idea well (1965: 210), when he observed that:

From the existential philosophy of life which it thus seems to thrust upon us our instinct still is to turn and seek other and transcendental values. Hence the continuous effort, finding expression in an unceasing series of books, to explain the nature of history or to make sense of mankind's past. [. . .] these works are symptomatic of a deep-rooted need to find some signific- ance in the life of man, both as an individual and as a species. It is probable that this need will never be satisfied, since man's awareness of the challenge of Time may well be the penalty he has to pay for rationality.

Here, then, the philosophy of history becomes a form of substitute religion.

Yet the underlying absence of time from the analytical study of history cannot be excused by recent and idealist tendencies. It can, I think, be explained in a discussion of the place of the historian with regard to history and her status as an intellectual worker. Let us see what Adam has to say about those who work on time (1995: 30):

> Irrespective of their respective disciplines, studies of social time seem to share two interrelated problems: first, time is implicated not only in the subject matter of anthropology, history and sociology but also in the lives, understandings and methods of those who conduct the studies. Second, in spite of its omnipresence, time is curiously invisible and constitutes one of the most taken-for-granted features of our lives. As such it forms the largely implicit base from which studies are conducted and from which the time of 'the other' is explicated. For these reasons I want to suggest that studies of 'other time' are not merely dealing with difficulties of translation between cultures. Rather, the problem extends far deeper to the *unquestioned* understanding of Western time.

It is precisely because anthropologists developed a reflexive culture in terms of the questioning of their own practices that they have been able to think hard about time and to see that their own work unwittingly contributes to an under- standing of western time. I think we could legitimately call this style of work *ethical* because at its heart lies a concern with doing justice to the subjects of anthropology and an attempt to ensure that a potential for dialogue and learning from the other is never blocked out by the desire to understand the other's difference. History, by contrast, has a remarkably poor conception of the ethics of its endeavour and as a consequence it is resentful both of the idea that the form of historical work might be viewed by outsiders as contributing to an understanding of *its* western culture and that it might be possible to learn from its subjects. This is also borne out by the fact that when historians study other historical cultures they are quite happy to say that those works are as interesting for what they tell us about the culture of the writer as for the notional subject of the work (as in Victorian British history's celebration of nation and empire in the guise of constitutional history), yet they are truculent when asked to consider the possibility that such critique could be applied to their own work.

I would also suggest that guilt lies at the heart of the historian's refusal to think of time. Part of the historian's reluctance to engage in 'unproductive' reflective thought comes from the guilt induced by the knowledge that the 'real' work of history will both never be finished (for we can always know more) and never be perfect (for the words of the present cannot mirror the events of the past). So long as history remains bound to nineteenth-century notions of empiricism, it will not be possible to escape this guilt. These themes are well addressed in Munslow's critique (2003: 5) of the 'supposedly "common sense" approach to understanding reality', and works such as *The New History* can be referred to for more detailed considerations of aspects of historical time such as causation which I do not intend to cover in this broad survey of time in historical epistemology.

If further justification that historians ought to think more carefully about time is needed, evidence enough could be found in the work of Richard J. Evans whose book *In Defence of History* (1997) has come to be seen by many western empiricists as a reasoned defence against their critics. Evans begins his call to resist epistemological consideration of time by censuring (1997: 141) Frank Ankersmit for his claim that 'Historical time is a recent and highly artificial invention of Western civilization.' In response to such claims Evans believes that Ankersmit's arguments that the character of temporal cultures changes over time, even in the modern west, collapse in the face of his assertion that (1997: 141) 'A basically linear concept of time continues to be used the world over by people both in the conduct of their everyday lives and in their preference for, say, novels which narrate a story over novels which do not; for John Grisham over Alain Robbe-Grillet for example.' Evans argues therefore that, because a linear sense of time is common across the world, it is necessarily a superior mode of temporalizing and, second, that because genre novels use this form of time, it must therefore be a uniquely powerful description of the world. While there is no doubt that linear conceptions of time are indeed features of most world cultures, and have been so, what Evans does not seem to realize is that writers such as Ankersmit would not deny the prevalence of linearity, but that they would ask that its particular incarnations be studied and that attendance be made to the presence of other modes of time. To take a clear example, it is now recognized by biblical scholars that the time culture described in the Old Testament was one where linearity interacted with cyclical notions of time (to take but the two main examples from those texts). Jews could not in fact live without both kinds of time for they relied on cyclical narratives to stress the continuance of their Abrahamic heritage and in late Judaism they relied upon linearity as a means of structuring apocalyptic thought which described the movement of time towards an ending.

Evans goes on to say that (1997: 142) 'any attempt to deny historical time necessarily presupposes the very thing it denies'. It is such claims which make it very difficult not to caricature western empirical history because Evans' total reliance on a singular notion of time, which ought not to be questioned, is in reality a debasement of the tradition he claims to represent (for thinkers such as Ankersmit also stand as representatives of the development of a modern western discipline of history from the Enlightenment). Evans' claim makes sense only in the context of his own worldview, which denies any form of meaningful difference from other cultures and their senses of time. This is made plain in his suggestion that we cannot impute temporal difference from the fact that different cultures operate with separate forms of measuring time. As he says (1997: 142):

> *How* we count the years – whether we use the Western calendar, or the Jewish, or the Chinese, or whatever – is completely irrelevant to this point, and it is hard to escape the conclusion that postmodernists here are confusing the Western hegemony implicit in the worldwide use of the Western calendar with the culturally neutral, because universal, sequence of time which calendars are designed to count.

In attempting to show off his multiculturalist credentials here, Evans reveals only the narrowness of his point of view and the shallowness of his view of time: as if time consisted only of clocks and calendars and as if all its differences between cultures could be found in such things. Equally significant are both Evans' conflation of 'Western' with 'Christian' (for the Jews are left out of the west here) and the dismissive character of the term 'whatever' as it is applied to all that lies outside his own purview and worldview. We might also mention Evans' questionable belief that, in the abstract, calendars present 'culturally neutral' sequences of time for, as Evans must know full well, there is not a single major calendrical system that does any such thing for all calendars are founded upon pictures of time in which linear sequencing forms but one part of a broader temporal narrative (typically such linearity might be attached to eschatology, a myth of eternal return, cyclical patterns, or may in fact be viewed as the illusory covering of true temporal experience).

A more sophisticated account of the empirical picture of time is offered by Fernández-Armesto. He begins in an epistemological fashion making the claim that (Lippincott 1999: 246), 'For historians, time is the past', but he goes on to acknowledge that (Lippincott 1999: 246):

> In practice, as the concept of time has changed, the way history is written has changed with it. At the risk of over-simplification, we can summarize the state of our knowledge by saying that the history of the concept of time has gone through three phases: a cyclical phase, which encouraged cyclical notions of history; a linear phase, which encouraged teleological history-writing; and a chaotic phase, which has encouraged chaotic history.

While I am obviously supportive of Fernández-Armesto's central claim that a study of other cultures reveals a plurality of understandings of time, which in turn have generated a variety of modes of history, my central problem with his account is its westernness. The move from cyclical to chaotic time, via linearity, is a description merely of time in the western tradition, which bears no relation to the equally interesting development of non-western temporal cultures. It may seem unduly harsh to criticize Fernández-Armesto on these grounds for he is trying to think beyond his own situation, which is far removed from the narrowness of Evans, but in doing so he is still reliant upon a linear narrative which fails to perceive the radical difference of other times and their potentiality as sources for history.

Fernández-Armesto's attempts at the analysis of what we might call the selfhood of western historical thinking are extended in recent work by Rüsen and Burke which has sought to interrogate the particularities of that thought from a global perspective – an approach towards which this book is evidently deeply sympathetic. Their goal has been to begin a history of histories and to identify what is specifically western about western history, so that it can see links, differences and the possibility of dialogue with other historical traditions. The problems involved in such work are outlined by Burke (2002: 15):

> Consider that to discuss what is distinctive in European historical thought it is also necessary to have a good knowledge of other historiographical traditions, such as the Chinese, Japanese, Islamic, African, indigenous American, and so on. No wonder that virtually no one has tried to study historiography in a comparative way.

My hope is that this book adds to Burke's essay and as such constitutes a small step towards the 'new theory of history' which Rüsen (2002: viii–ix) talks of as being the overarching aim of the project on which he is engaged with Burke and others. This theory of history sees itself as 'an interdisciplinary and intercultural field of study'. Burke's attempt to identify the specific contours of

western history are a first step, building on existing historiographical literatures, which need to be accompanied by a simple acceptance that western
historians are as likely to learn about method and theory from the Chinese,
Japanese, Islamic, African and indigenous American historiographical traditions as they are to learn from the western tradition.

Burke's important analysis of the western historiographical tradition sets
out a series of areas of cultural distinctiveness, including the idea of perspective (2002: 12), historicism (2002: 20), the stress on collective agency (2002:
21), an emphasis on causality (2002: 24), putative objectivity (2002: 24) and
the quantitative approach (2002: 25). Western historiography is also characterized by division and segmentation, for as Burke writes (2002: 28):

> For better or for worse, there has not been any consensus (for centuries, at
> least) on major issues such as uniqueness versus the illustration of historical
> laws, progress versus cycles, or causes versus meanings. It is ultimately this
> conflict of systems – or system of conflicts – the particular shifting balance
> between different 'forces' which has characterized historical thought and
> historical writing in the West.

Burke is quite right here but I think he is mistaken in divining from such
conflict the idea (2002: 23) that 'Western historiography is distinctive in its
preoccupation with epistemology, with the problem of historical knowledge.'
It seems to me that such a claim is wrong on two levels: that it overestimates the
epistemological character of the western tradition, mistaking debates about
method and disciplinary structures for more fundamental troublings of the
very bases of history, and, second, that it is precisely through the kind of
intercultural work proposed by Burke and Rüsen that we can find examples of
historiographical cultures which are much more deeply epistemological than
those of the modern west. It may seem unjust to tax Burke with such omissions
but I believe it is what his larger project demands, and it is incumbent on
books like this to try to disprove Burke's assertion through close readings of
other historiographical traditions.

Burke himself has rightly criticized Brown's *Hierarchy, History and Human
Nature: The Social Origins of Historical Consciousness*, which he identifies
as one of the few attempts at a truly comparative historiography, for its assumption that western methods are superior to all others. This is readily apparent
from the first lines of Brown's work (1988: 1):

> Among some literate peoples, historians have flourished; among others,
> they have not. Why should this be so? That a civilization such as India's
> long enjoyed literacy yet gave almost no attention to writing its own or any

other history presents a substantial puzzle to the sociology of knowledge. Of course, Indians wrote much about things *alleged* to have taken place in the past, but these are accounts of gods and supermen: myths and fables, not 'real history.'

The problem with Brown and most other attempts at intercultural historiography is summed up by the quotation marks that bracket the term 'real history'. While they signal some ironic intent – as if they mean to indicate *what people, or our cultural tradition at least, believes to be proper history* – it is quite clear that Brown intends these words to mean *proper history as determined by the gold standard of the modern western tradition*. The rather sad consequence of this is that, even when writing about other traditions, Brown tells us more about his own heritage, for he is never able to concede that the 'myths and fables' of the 'gods and supermen' of the Indians might constitute a historiographical culture with its own internal logic and objective sense of selfhood.

Brown's stance evidently has a series of antecedents, as we can see, for example, in Baillie's claims as to the theoretical superiority of western history's Christian base (1950: 83–84):

> The pattern which Christianity gave to history, and which provided an intellectual frame for Western culture, until at least the time of the Renaissance, is thus an elaborate one. There is enough and to spare of elaboration in such other patterns as the Buddhist and Jainist, but it is elaboration of a different kind, being merely the detailed definition of successive ages within a fundamentally simple cyclic scheme. The orthodox Christian scheme lacks this wealth of mythological detail but is basically more complex than any other.

As we shall see, such a claim is simply false and borne of ignorance of the development of temporal cultures in faiths such as Buddhism and Jainism. I am not interested in suggesting that other forms of time should be deployed merely as correctives to western history, for I believe that they should instead be seen as clear alternatives to the sequential time of absolute history. This is not to say that western history is without virtues and needs to be wholly abandoned; it simply ought to see that it is not alone.

The study of time is evidently spread across a wide variety of disciplines, of which the most significant are probably philosophy, theology, linguistics, anthropology, physics, literary theory and sociology. As a result of this spread of common interest, studies of time are increasingly characterized by their interdisciplinarity and, as Macey (1994: ix) noted, 'The great majority of the publications in the large, interdisciplinary, and dynamic discipline of time studies, which serves in the vanguard of so many areas of modern research, have appeared as recently as the last twenty-five years.'

There are, therefore, limits as to how great an engagement with these many literatures a book such as this one can undertake. In the main, I restrict myself to borrowing from theological and anthropological literatures on time, in part because they tend to address relationships between religion and time which are of direct interest to this book, and partly because the discipline of anthropology has displayed a willingness to engage in critical epistemological reflection of a kind which I think could serve as an example to historians. Indeed, another way of stating my case that history needs to understand and learn from non-western modes of thinking about time is to say that the discipline ought to anthropologize itself.

Unlike its fellow nineteenth-century field of study history, anthropology – and the allied fields of ethnography and sociology – saw the study of time as central to its purpose from its very beginnings. The importance of discussions of time in the work of early anthropologists such as Durkheim and Weber has led later theorists to feel that time is a theme with which they must engage, so anthropology offers a rich heritage of studies of time in the work of Hubert, Evans-Pritchard, Leach, Lévi-Strauss, Fabian, Gell, Whorf, Mbiti, Bloch, Howe, Jenkins and Farriss (these works are discussed at greater length in the guide to further reading). The depth of this research may also partly explain why the topic of non-western time has been ceded to anthropology by other disciplines, which I evidently feel has been a real loss for historians.

Of the key insights established by anthropologists on time, one of the most important was Durkheim's description of 'social time' in his *Elementary Forms of Religious Life* (1960). As Hassard says (Macey 1994: 170):

> Basing his analyses on evidence from studies of primitive societies, he [Durkheim] suggests that 'The foundation of the category of time is the rhythm of social life.' Durkheim was thus the first to focus on the collective social aspect of temporality. Time is not, as Kant argued, a universal category inherent in the mind. Instead, it is essentially a 'collective representation,' arising from the experience of the collectivity.

In a later chapter we will see that there is much to criticize in Durkheim's generation of such a theory from ethnographic studies of Australian culture, but the importance of Durkheim's account of the created, unnatural, social character of time remains, most especially because it punctured the Kantian assumption of the universal experience of time, which we have seen still underpins most western empirical history.

The moral and epistemological doubt displayed by many modern anthropologists may seem unnerving and hesitant to most historians, but the discipline's reconsideration of its forebears' studies of time has, I think, led in some very interesting directions. Fabian's work exemplifies the productiveness of the doubting of the anthropological enterprise (1992: 198):

> Generally speaking, anthropology appears to have been a field of knowledge whose discourse requires that its object – other societies, some of them belonging to the past, but most of them existing contemporaneously in the present – be removed from its subject not only in space but also in time. Put more concretely, to belong to the past, to be not yet what We are, is what makes Them the object of our 'explanations' and 'generalizations.' Everything we ever had to say on the topic from primitive mentality to mythical consciousness, to pre-rational, preliterate thought, feeds on temporal distancing. As it turns out, such denial of coevalness [. . .] is achieved by a number of conceptual and rhetorical devices all of which have in common to neutralize time as a constitutive dimension, constitutive of human action, interaction and, indeed, of the production of knowledge about other societies.

It is this questioning of the lack of coevalness in the anthropological relationship between self and other which has led writers like Fabian to show that the value of much anthropological work comes not only in its account of time in 'primitive' cultures but in what it reveals about the western notions of time on which such studies are predicated. Adam describes this as (1995: 31) 'the assumed backcloth of western time', which emerges as anthropologists' attempt to describe the essential differences of the cultures of others, for which they are forced to rely on a notion of their own culture as a natural and stable body of knowledge. It has even led writers like Müller to argue recently that in anthropology (2002: 33) 'The eurocentric perspective is beginning to fade, falter and could ultimately erode.'

Yet I am not suggesting that dialogue between historians and anthropologists need be a one-way process. As James and Mills have written of Alfred Gell recently (2005: 14):

> The plain 'minimalist' approach to time recommended by Gell fails to capture the rhythm and time-shapes of events; like the plain historical chronology of one-damn-thing-after-another it fails to recognize the collusion of people in the making of material life and events through significant timing. There is still a need to rescue an 'anthropology of time' which can engage with history and the work of historians.

The work of Thomas (1996) on the anthropological project of rethinking time extends such ideas to critique the differences which anthropology claims between its historical time and the ethnographic time of its subjects, arguing that anthropology needs to be historicized, so there is something of an irony in the fact that, while historians might not discuss time much, they are still seen as a community from whom anthropologists might learn. This is also stressed by Fabian (1992: 225):

> Our [anthropologists'] assigned role is to be purveyors of 'comparative' difference. But we cannot deliver different experiences; we can only give accounts of different experiences. Furthermore, constructions of time cannot be accounted for (or recounted) without construing time. There is no way of thinking about chronotypes but chronotypically. Unless we want to accept an infinite regress into relativities, we have, in my view, but one direction in which to move: We must seek a better understanding of a praxis, ours as well as theirs, of giving accounts of difference (and, of course, of sameness; and of 'movements' between difference and sameness) that are constructed 'temporally,' *with* conceptualized experiences of time.

So the task of a book such as this one which aims to recover the conceptualized experiences of time and their praxis is a task that serves as part of a dialogue between history and anthropology.

Thus far I have tried to show that time is a central, yet underexplored dynamic in historical work, that there exists very little awareness of non-western, non-modern theories of history, that western empiricism needs to be relentlessly critiqued for its presumed universalism, as well as celebrated and analysed for its unique picture of time, and that a positive case for a plurality of times in history needs to be made through a detailed study of other temporalities.

This last claim is also made in Wilcox's brilliant study *The Measure of Times Past: Pre-Newtonian Chronologies and the Rhetoric of Relative Time*. Wilcox takes the value of non-western temporalities, and the potential of cross-cultural borrowing, very seriously. He also identifies the potentiality of earlier forms of 'western history' (1987: 13):

> These non-Western narratives by their very nature are hard to incorporate into our own experience. The sense of absolute time seems a distinctive western contribution, colouring our view of the world and shaping our sense of self and society. Absolute time is undeniably a Western contrivance, but most [earlier] Western history is not recorded in absolute time.

He contends that both premodern and non-western modes of temporality (1987: 12) 'have identified a sense of time much closer to that which underlies the Einsteinian universe than the one Westerners currently use in everyday life', and in a sense he sees his project as a means of outflanking 'absolute time' from three directions: from the perspective of Einsteinian relativized time, from non-western modes of temporality, and from the premodern west (1987: 271). In a strategic sense, I am wholly convinced by Wilcox's argument and what I hope to do in this book is to advance Wilcox's thesis by making more concrete the specificities of the forms of time which he suggests exist in addition to absolute time.

On progress

As the branches of the discipline that have been assigned the task of detailing conceptual development and progress, historiography and the philosophy of history have themselves constructed a narrative of some force which underpins the motor of progress in western history. The story of history is one of development and increasing technical sophistication. In relation to a discussion of Vico, Kant, Hegel and Ranke, for instance, Buber makes (Rotenstreich 1958: v–vi) the claim that, 'Only when we come to the end of the 19th century do we find historical knowledge subject to a process of self-reflection.' From within the logic of historiography it is clear how such a claim makes sense, but when set in a broader context of both western and global temporalities such ideas seem absurd. To take only two examples, historical knowledge is subjected to the deepest form of self-reflection in the four Gospels of the New Testament, just as it is relentlessly critiqued in medieval Islamic thought.

Other temporal cultures with rich heritages exist as complex modes of history which can be adopted by people both in and outside those cultures. We might ask, what would the discipline of history look like today if the norm that had been globalized had not been western empiricism but a form of history founded on Hindu conceptions of cyclical time which rejected the idea of there being a radical difference between past and future? Or a history based upon Australian notions of the Dreamtime where the purpose of remembering the past, individual and collective identity formation, and religious belief, could not be separated?

When people talk about histories, plural, they ought not therefore simply to imply methodological and ideological differences, but to stress epistemes and temporal character. At present, we know very little in a comparative historical sense about the variety of temporal cultures. What, then, are the consequences of taking time seriously? Evidently, that we recognize that there are other temporal cultures. The consequence of recognizing that there are other temporal cultures is that we see that our own historical method is founded upon a cultural-specific notion of time, which is not superior to other ideas of time (the reason being that we are talking about aesthetic and moral choices, not about scientific difference). As Fabian says (1992: 225), 'If, to rehearse an ancient argument one more time, experience of time came "naturally" then, nature being one, experience would be one.' What flows from this recognition is the possibility that historians might operate with different ideas of time. Just as I prefer modern Japanese art to modern western art, I might prefer to think and write in terms of ancient Jewish time rather than modern western time. The fact that no one has presented me with this option is merely a reflection of the narrowness of my professional training and its assumption of both cultural insularity and superiority.

Deeply embedded within such discussions are, of course, notions of progress, for the underlying reason why a discipline such as history has not turned to Aborigines for insights into the historical method is that there exists an assumption that such cultures are less progressive than our own, not nearly as far advanced along the linear path of progress as we happen to be. Yet such thoughts are of course conceptually extremely sloppy, for westerners operate with more complex notions of progress than this, even if this is not always acknowledged. The form of progress called upon to disallow the idea that Aborigines might be able to teach us about time and history is that of science and technology. It seems obvious, after all, that our CT scanners prove that we can learn little from a people who relied on plants and grubs as forms of medicine. Yet, if we switch our measure of assessment from science to painting, we begin to complicate our narrative. After all, there are many in the west who would contend that the art of the Renaissance is much superior to that which we enjoy today and that, in the five hundred years since Michelangelo, western art has arguably decayed as much as it has progressed. So western accounts of progress are not quite as plain as they seem. Embedded deep within all such claims is a binary of superiority and inferiority. This book is a celebration of 'inferior' modes of conceiving of time and making history.

Before moving on there are two important potential criticisms of my project that I need to consider. The first is the question as to whether or not it is right for me to claim to be able to see around or through my own western, temporal heritage in order to truthfully describe other cultures of time. Such a concern has been raised on the broader level of the history of religion by Dubuisson, who suggests that the very idea of 'religion' is essentially a western, Christian concept whose presumed universality as a means of conceptualizing belief systems is utterly false, since it really only allows analysts the means to redescribe their own cultural norms. As he puts it (2003: 39):

> From the moment one admits (1) that the notion of religion is a typically Western creation; (2) that it has, moreover, supplied the nucleus about which the West has constructed its own universe of values and representations; and (3) that in this capacity, it has influenced the totality of our ways of conceiving and thinking the world, how can one imagine that the history of religions, inasmuch as it too was born in the West and associated from the outset with this idea of religion, could escape its influence?

The second, related concern is the manner in which I use the term 'time' and the fact that I am not primarily concerned with the extensive philosophical literatures on the subject of time. Here I am not concerned with the general, metaphysical question of time, and of beginning with a conceptual disquisition on time which then leads me to more specific study of particular temporal cultures. I am aware that to move down that track would involve tackling the Kantian argument that (Rée, private correspondence) 'we cannot intelligibly talk about different times (or different spaces) because to think about something as temporal (or spatial) is to think of it as belonging to the same temporal and spatial world that you locate yourself in.'

I am fully aware that, in wanting to skate over this literature, I am in many ways evading precisely the kind of conceptual and epistemological difficulties which I allege characterize the historian's thinking about time. Yet I also think that a fairly robust case needs to be developed that it is possible to come to some understanding of other religions' temporal cultures and to argue that we are not wholly bound up by our own inescapable heritage and identity. There is a distinct logic to the claim of the incommensurability of cultures and peoples, but it is ultimately only one logic among many, for we might just as easily follow a path through the philosophy of language or hermeneutics to arrive instead at more celebratory conclusions with regard to the possibility of human understanding. We ought also to note that if the Kantian position is truly followed then all history is disallowed, for we can know the people of the past no better than those from other places. Even if we allow for the coherence and seduction of such rationalities, most historians, historiographers and indeed philosophers would, I think, prefer to operate in a messier, less conceptually neat field, where acknowledged compromises with logic afford the possibility of more practical work. We might also note that philosophical objections to the prospect of understanding other times rest on notions of identity (and the fixity of those identities, of individuals and cultures) to which many would not want to subscribe, and which are themselves as open to the kind of crumbling logic with which the original complaint was framed.

A second objection, to the claims of Dubuisson in particular, is that I think his argument that the idea of religion is indissociably bound to Christianity and western culture is mistaken. In fact, I think that this is something of a delusion which emerges from a reading of world history which concentrates almost exclusively on late medieval and early modern Europe, where it is certainly true that there existed a Christian worldview which permeated almost every aspect of European culture, to the extent that an Enlightenment could emerge as a means of rooting out this religious basis of society. Yet that coherent Christian culture (even leaving aside its factionalism) did not characterize the west in the first millennia after the advent of Christ, when it is plain that many important intellectual and social structures were formed in western Europe. What is more, I would argue that notions of religion were extremely confused in the west in that period: in part because of the manner in which religion has an ambiguous status in terms of its role as a political force, a theology and as a basis for social organisation, and the fact that there was still competition between religions in the west (with Islam in Iberia, with Judaism and, perhaps most importantly, with folk religions across Europe – from which Christianity often borrowed). While to an outsider the early medieval Christian church may have looked like a place of rigid and fixed doctrines, it was of course nothing of the sort, for it took many centuries after the life of Christ for critical aspects of what was later to become a more or less coherent whole to be formed, such as, for instance, the significance and timing of Easter.

A third, rather more practical objection to my project is that this book is about reading texts. Each of the chapters is framed around the reading of key texts from a particular religious culture and they are quoted in some detail. Those extracts are framed by my thoughts on their significance, but I am also hopeful that readers will look at those readings with their own eyes, and that ideas will be sparked off which I could never have imagined. My aim in each chapter is to tie down something which we can call an 'Islamic philosophy of history' or a 'Buddhist conception of time', but in each case I also have to acknowledge the variety of these things that exist within religious traditions, and in the case of Christianity and Judaism I follow recent theology in suggesting that earlier writers tended to underestimate the complexity and interest of their pictures of time that we find in the Bible. That is understandable as people want an operable account of 'Christian time' which can be used as the basis of a method and as a point of comparison with other religions, but it is precisely the task of this book to be charged with trying to offer both coherent, operable accounts of religions' ideas of time and indications of complexities that underlie those ideas.

Where I would agree with philosophical objections to the treatment of time in studies such as this one is in the need to go beyond the idea that descriptions of time must be presented in pictorial form – time flows, time's arrow, cyclical time – for, as we shall see, visual imagery often cannot convey even the basic structuring ideas of time in a religion like Buddhism, let alone its intricacies, just as pictures more generally have limitations as descriptions of things.

Chapter 3

Theorizing time

This chapter moves on from discussions in the first two chapters to look at the manner in which the 'story of time' has been recounted in the western tradition and to identify three key theorists whose work demands a rethinking of that narrative.

The study of time in history has in part been impeded by the power of a set of narratives which have been told about 'the story of time'. These accounts tend to have been characterized by the following themes:

1. An assumption that ideas of time have, as Fernández-Armesto said, broadly moved from the cyclical (found in ancient Greece and Egypt), through the linear (seen in late Judaism and Christianity) to the chaotic (as evinced by science after Einstein, though this final stage does not appear in all accounts).
2. A presumption that these intellectual shifts sketch out a progressive path towards greater knowledge.
3. The absence of discussions of non-'western' modes of time which, if mentioned at all, tend to be described as belonging to 'myth'-based or 'primitive' cultures.

Certain key figures play important roles in sustaining these narratives to the exclusion – as I show in later chapters – of other writers on time whose thoughts should be of equal interest. The writings of Herodotus, Augustine, Newton and the thinkers of the European Renaissance predominate in most accounts of time.

The first stages of this standard narrative are well articulated by Sherover, who suggests that (1975: 2), 'According to the Greeks, time was a cycle and was pictured as moving around the circumference of a circle. By contrast, in the biblical view, time flows in one direction and can be depicted as an arrow.' Collingwood's influential account of the development of historiography added to this narrative in its claim that (Baillie 1950: 78) the 'three great crises' that generated changes in man's thinking about the past could be found in the work of Herodotus, Augustine's 'remodelling' of history based around a creator God, and the post-Renaissance 'rediscovery' of 'scientific history' in the work of writers such as Herder. The significance of Herodotus, for Collingwood, was that he was able to break with the cyclical idea of time which constituted the worldview of his society (Baillie 1950: 54):

> For ancient Greek thought as a whole has a very definite prevailing tendency not only uncongenial to the growth of historical thought but actually based, one might say, on a rigorously anti-historical metaphysics. History is a science of human action: what the historian puts before himself is things that men have done in the past, and these belong to a world of change, a world where things come to be and cease to be. Such things, according to the prevalent Greek metaphysical view, ought not to be knowable, and therefore history ought to be impossible.

The further development of such ideas in the Renaissance is boldly stated by Quinones who asserts that (Macey 1994: 528), 'If the Renaissance may be credited with having invented the spatial dimensions of art, it may also be credited with having discovered time.' Yet, as Tosh (2000: 2) more subtly observes with regard to the historian's desire to know the past, 'This attitude towards the past became commonplace during the Renaissance, when knowledge about the ancient world of Greece and Rome was highly valued for its own sake. It was elevated into a rigorous scholarly inquiry in the nineteenth century.' So, it was not, as Quinones suggests, time itself which was discovered in the Renaissance, but merely a means of using a particular form of time for the purpose of history-making.

The problem with such ideas is not that they are devoid of scholarly value, but that they support the intellectual project of a group that Baillie approvingly (1950: 88) called 'the votaries of progress', asserting that 'the working faith of recent Western civilization' was a belief in 'the pattern of progress.' One does not need to draw on Foucault, Fanon and Benjamin to observe that this cult of progress, which impelled modern western Europe from the period of the Renaissance until well into the twentieth century, was an idea that was more broadly connected with a form of cultural assuredness whose certainty masked a set of injustices both inside and outside the west.

This progressive impulse and its part in the story of time was of course given great succour by the fact that the period from the European Renaissance onwards saw rapid advances in the measurement of time, most especially in the application of ideas of modern science to clocks and watches. This revolution in chronological measurement is well described in the work of Aveni and Macey. Here Macey describes the social significance of these mechanical advances (1994: 662):

> The clock, in particular, appealed to the optimism of the eighteenth century and the sense of order in the leiocentric universe. The status of the clock as the epitome of mechanical engineering and technology provided a metaphor for many things from the lowest animal to the universe itself. In such a universe, God was seen as the watchmaker who created the cosmic clockwork.

In other words, a combination of the story of time, the impulse of progress and new technologies came more and more to convince western Europeans of the rightness of the directions in which they moved, and the fundamental temporal truths which underpinned their actions.

Such accounts could not wholly ignore other cultures of time, but they displayed almost no willingness to view them on their own terms. Baillie stands as an especially marked example of this trend, also illustrative of the manner in which such ideas have persisted into the contemporary era. As he says (1950: 4):

> It may be said with a fair degree of confidence that the idea of progress from generation to generation is entirely absent from the mind of the ruder cultures. There is here no sense of history, no historical memory, no awareness that things had ever been or even would be substantially different from their present familiar condition.

An idea that should be becoming familiar to us by now re-appears here, which is that the modern western idea of progress is used as the sole arbiter in analyses of other cultures, just as western empiricism is presumed as a norm in terms of the development of historical culture. Those 'ruder cultures' are assigned positions at earlier stages of the flight of time's arrow and are thus of interest only in an archaeological sense. In contradistinction to the stress on coevalness found in anthropology, historians are thus able to say that history which does not look like their own practice is not in fact history, as we saw in the work of Brown.

Such logics encourage something of a contemptuous approach to the complexity of things, as Baillie makes plain in his (1950: 57–58) extraordinary claim that, 'Only twice in the history of thought has the idea arisen that history might be tracing another pattern than the circular one, and in both these cases, it was the same general pattern that was proposed, namely, that of a non-recurrent movement towards the ultimate triumph of good. This is the conception which unites the religion of the Magi with that of the Hebrews and which differentiates them from all other religions and philosophies save those which have drawn some degree of inspiration from them.' What I shall show in this book is that the history of religious cultures reveals far more than two non-circular accounts of time, and that it is by no means the case that these all operate in a linear fashion. Indeed, Baillie points to one of the central weaknesses of the case of the votaries of progress here for, in addition to their lack of comprehension of the non-west, they simplify the history of western time to such a degree that they banalize important differences in temporal debates in Judaism and Christianity. As I shall show in Chapter 4 of this book, it is simply untrue to say that the religion of the Hebrews was characterized by linear accounts of time that were oriented towards 'the ultimate triumph of good'. Such a view can be supported by a very selective reading of the Old Testament, but part of my broader argument is that historians of time have tended to read texts such as the Bible as a means of supporting the progressive story of time when it is in fact far from obvious that it is a narrative which they support.

Modernism

The progressivist story of time has been challenged since the middle of the nineteenth century in a number of connected ways. These include the development of literary and artistic modernism (and the flow of these ideas into fields of academic endeavour), the realities and the rhetorical struggles of 'secularization' in the west, and the social and cultural impact of Einstein and post-Newtonian physics. I address the last of these themes in Chapter 10 of this book, but I should like to consider briefly the place of secularization and modernism in this project here.

The narrative of secularization is in many ways closely linked to themes I have already looked at in other contexts: it formed a part of the story of progress (albeit with an unhappy ending to this story in many thinkers' minds), it represented the totalizing instincts of nineteenth-century theory, as evinced in the work of writers like Durkheim who saw the duty of social science as being the formulation of morals and institutions for a post-Christian world, and it drew its picture of that world from a western European setting. We have since seen that the narrowness of that optic led to a belief in 'the death of God' which was not quite as absolute as those locked into the progressivist narrative had hoped or feared. Instead, more recent studies of secularization (such as Beckford 1989 and Martin 1969) have stressed both the manner in which religions have survived, and in some cases prospered with the advent of the modern world, and the migration of religious ideas, value and language to other social spheres and institutions.

This is not to say that the Enlightenment was for naught. It is clear that a fundamental shift in western intellectual history took place in the eighteenth and nineteenth centuries which led to the ending of the dominance of the twin *anciens régimes* of the Christian church and absolute monarchies. Yet, from the perspective of Islamic thought in, say, the eleventh century C.E. or Zen culture in the fourteenth century C.E., the radicalism of the Enlightenment was hardly original, and in some ways it was rather tentative in the manner in which it addressed some fundamental questions pertaining to knowledge, faith and truth. In fact, as I shall show, from the perspective of that supposed very bedrock of western Christian culture – the Bible – books such as Job and Ecclesiastes describe a radical form of scepticism of a philosophical depth and political menace at least equal to the writings of Voltaire and Hume.

While it too had non-western antecedents, the challenge of modernist cultural production was arguably greater and of a higher degree of originality than that posed by secularization, with Einstein's logic offering a still greater rupture with the old ways of thought. Elizabeth Deeds Ermarth, whom we will look at in more detail later in this chapter, compellingly suggests that there was a set of common intellectual impulses which underlay the thought of Einstein, the development of phenomenology and cultural modernism, for (1992: 8):

> The period of Einstein's papers on relativity and Edmund Husserl's logic, for example, also saw the publication of Franz Kafka's stories, the poetry of Guillaume Apollinaire, Sigmund Freud's papers on the unconscious, the cubism of Georges Braque and Pablo Picasso.

Where Einstein broke down the central premises of Newtonian physics, modernist art challenged the purpose and form of the art-work, while in literature and philosophy writers such as Apollinaire and Wittgenstein broke with the forms of earlier western thought, and in devising new forms they opened fissures on to epistemological groundings of that thought that had lain unchallenged through being unseen.

How, then, did history react to these revolutionary changes in western thought? The answer is that it simply ignored its own moment, for one would struggle to find evidence that the work of Woolf, Dada, Husserl, Heidegger, Picasso and Wittgenstein had any impact whatsoever on the practice or theory of history in the twentieth century.

The consequences of this lack of engagement with the central strands of modern thought have had debilitating consequences for the discipline of history and, as the twentieth century progressed, history became progressively more isolated from the rest of the academy, which had to varying degrees grappled with the challenges of modernism. The confusion that is apparent in exchanges between so-called 'traditionalists' and 'postmoderns' in recent historiographical debates is largely a consequence of the former group's lacking an understanding of the modernist project, and the latter camp's failure to realize that it is this absence of an awareness of modernism that prevents an appreciation of postmodern thought on its own terms. It is not at all my intention to distract my own argument in traversing the strict binaries of the postmodern-traditionalist byways of historiographical debate, for this book is not an attack on empiricism from the perspective of Derrida and Baudrillard, but a questioning of the superiority of the western historical method from the standpoint of Jesus and Buddha.

I think it wholly helpful therefore that writers like Wilcox and Deeds Ermarth have called for a modernist turn in historiography. As Wilcox says, such a move would seem to be necessary in a culture where so much in people's lives and their representations of them is refracted through the modernist lens. Thus (1987: 263), 'To present individuals in ways that seem convincing to their readers, historians will increasingly have to shape personality in terms more like those of Proust and Calvino – and, coincidentally, of Suetonius and Bede – than those of Dickens and Eliot.' It should not seem surprising that what I especially like about Wilcox's ideas here is his recognition that the radical complexity of modernist representation is mirrored by methods and styles that we find in the pre-modern world. In other words, as well as advocating modernism, Wilcox is able to deflate the progressivist story in the very same move, just as readers of Einstein's work on time have often observed that, while his ideas reject the Newtonian picture of the world, they bear a close resemblance to Buddhist and Hindu conceptions of time.

I find these to be an incredibly productive set of ideas, because they suggest that it is not history that needs to be abandoned, but simply the imagined singularity or superiority of modern western, Newtonian history. Where Jenkins (1999) suggests that we must abandon the discipline, Wilcox simply says that we must think about time in history and in the genres of writing about the past.

I agree, and hope to extend this project through the consideration of the plural possibilities of history-writing found in religious cultures. As Wilcox says (1987: 4):

> The new time of the twentieth century poses special problems for historians. Not only are they particularly concerned with events in time, but the practice of historical research in the modern era is closely linked, both conceptually and historically, to Newtonian time. [. . .] Working historians seldom have occasion to think about such metaphysical issues as the implications of absolute time and most often prefer to dismiss them as irrelevant to the practice of history.

The key to Wilcox's thought, as I have suggested, is that his remedy for 'working historians' is that they need not necessarily think that they have to find metaphysical correction in those writers who most perturb them (contemporary modernists), for the answers they need are also made available in Bede and Suetonius.

Another possible response to the question of the absence of modernism from history is simply to broaden the scope of what we call history, for, if we allow figures like Walter Benjamin and Martin Heidegger as historians, then it is clear that history does have a modernist tradition. Benjamin's great work (1989) on the Parisian Arcades of the nineteenth century rejected Newtonian ideas of time with its redemptive Marxism making reference both to earlier religious traditions and to the romantic possibilities in modernist time which Benjamin (1983) found in the work of Baudelaire. What Benjamin hoped to show, in fact, was how the progressivist edifice had been created in eighteenth- and nineteenth-century Europe and how temporal and political oppositions to that narrative lay latent within it despite their having been erased from its early history. Through his work of historical compilation, Benjamin aimed to revive the spirits of the past in the name of a socially oriented historical poetics.

Heidegger's work also reacted strongly against the norms of Rankean historicism, which had come to represent the manner in which the Newtonian figuring of time and representation had become embedded within history. As Rée says (1998: 48–49), for Heidegger:

> Historicism tries to extinguish our essential conflict between destiny and fate by reducing history to a mere chronicle of an inert past – an unfolding sequence of unambiguous realities that are now over and done with. Authentic history, in contrast, is a constant struggle to keep past existences open to the future. The motor of history, for Heidegger, is not 'the tremendous power of the negative' but the 'quiet force of the possible'.

So, like Benjamin, Heidegger conceived of history as a field of human possibility and duty, which was centred on a consideration of time. Thinking about the absence of time in modern historiography, we might speculate on the connection between that invisibility and the stress on Rankean norms which are conceived of as opposed to the work of history as an engaged social act. We might also note that the question of the Rankean reception of the ideas of the Enlightenment is one that merits further enquiry. A case can certainly be made that the scientific legacy claimed by Ranke and empirical historians was deeply selective in its adoption of the Enlightenment legacy, for, while it advocated a natural scientific approach to time (against the old theological mode of invisible time of destiny and faith), it abandoned the questioning spirit of the Enlightenment while retaining the strident insistence of absolute facticity of the old regime of truth. A powerful critique of historicism that runs along similar lines is offered by Iggers (1968: 285–86) when he writes that:

> The German historical school maintained that in its concern with the particular, it fulfilled a philosophical as well as a scientific function, because it saw in the historical fact a phenomenal reflection of transhistorical truth and regarded the concrete mores, values and policies of existing institutions as expressions of a higher morality. With the collapse of this metaphysics of identity, German historicism was forced to draw nihilistic conclusions for both knowledge and ethics and to see a world exclusively of volition, struggle, and chaos. Too deeply bound to its origin in the eighteenth-century conservative revolt against the forces of modernity represented by the Enlightenment and the French Revolution, historicism was unable to come to grips with the great social transformations that have occurred in the modern world.

There are a number of features of this remark that deserve to be reflected upon. First, there is Iggers' observation that the empirical historian's belief in facts depends upon a set of philosophical and epistemological presuppositions, and, while it may now be seen as a natural and obvious state of affairs to historians, this emerged as one very distinct and new position in debates within the history of ideas. Second, Iggers makes the point that German historicism emerged as much from the Counter-Enlightenment as it did from the Enlightenment. This is an important claim because there tends to be a rather lazy assumption among historians that, because their discipline emerged at the time of the spread of Enlightenment thought within European culture, history was a product of the Enlightenment. In certain specific ways this was the case, but, as Iggers and later Foucault, Said and Fanon more obliquely observed, history also depended on modes of thinking which came from those who opposed the scepticism and free-thinking of the Enlightenment tradition. We will explore this theme further in Chapter 10.

Ricœur

Let us now move on to look at the work of Paul Ricœur, the first of three recent writers we will consider whose work interrogates ideas of both time and history. If one were seeking for a perfect representative of twentieth-century interdisciplinarity it would be hard not to seize upon the work of Ricœur for his writing draws together philosophy, religion, literature and history in order to investigate a set of problematics relating to ethics, humanism, phenomenology and hermeneutics. The manner in which this work draws deeply on the history of both ancient and modern thought is suggestive of a thinker who, to use Wilcox's idea, connects the ideas of Bede to Proust, and whose learning testifies to the philosophical illiteracy of most historiography. From early in his career (1965: 63) Ricœur expressed the idea that investigations in philosophy were of broader import for history, posing the question: 'Are not the difficulties which the historian of philosophy encounters and actually resolves revealing of the difficulties inherent in history in general?' His intellectual heritage allowed him to ask new questions of history and, as importantly, to emerge with answers to those questions which can be seen both to disorient and validate the empirical method.

More than perhaps anything else, Ricœur's great three-volume work *Time and Narrative* is associated with the position that the study of narrative reveals not just powerful commonalties between histories and fictions but also the deep narrative structures that in fact determine our very being. According to Ricœur, we live our lives as stories and it is not therefore surprising that the genres which humans have conceived to capture their lives in writing have the shape of stories, both in texts which they designate as factual (histories) and those which they see as imaginative (fictions). In Ricœur's scheme the underlying truth of human narrativity actually suggests that the grand differences we see between the form, content and purpose of histories and fictions are illusory, and that we are better served by trying to come to understand the connections between these two forms of life writing, through (Ricœur 1990: 180), 'the actual refiguration of time, now become human time through the interweaving of history and fiction.' Ricœur therefore calls (Fleischman 1990: xiii) 'upon historiography and literary criticism to join together in forming "a grand narratology" in which equal place would be given to historical and fictional discourse.' As Ricœur himself puts it (1990: 181), 'By the inter-weaving of history and fiction I mean the fundamental structure, ontological as well as epistemological, by virtue of which history and fiction each concretize their respective intentionalities only by borrowing from the intentionality of the other.'

The manner in which we expect to make our mark on time is therefore by inscribing our narratives on to the world. In this way, as White notes (1991: 145), there is symmetry between living and making histories, or novels for that matter:

> The creation of a historical narrative, then, is an action exactly like that by which historical events are created, but in the domain of 'wording' rather than that of 'working'. By discerning the plots 'prefigured' in histor-ical actions by the agents that produced them and 'configuring' them as sequences of events having the coherency of stories with a beginning, middle and end, historians make explicit the meaning implicit in historical events themselves.

If Ricœur's chief observation is that we live our lives in a narrativized fashion, his principal claim is perhaps that we make narratives to serve as means of showing our being-in-time; that our sense of being alive is constantly depend-ent on the narrative structures we build in our lives. As White puts it (1991: 142), 'Historical narrative is assigned a specific task in the representation of a reality that presents itself to human consciousness, in one aspect at least, as an insoluble but ultimately "comprehensible" mystery. This mystery is nothing other than the enigma of being-in-time.'

The act, for Ricœur, of writing history is the act of being human for (1984: 52): 'Time becomes human to the extent that it is articulated through a narrat-ive mode, and narrative attains its full meaning when it becomes a condition of temporal existence.' The narrative is a mode of escape from both death and inconsequentiality of a kind with which a theological critic like Brandon could identify. The apprehension of time is therefore of critical importance in Ricœur's picture of things, for it is what connects, and holds together, men and their narratives. We should not be surprised that many of the texts which are of greatest interest to Ricœur are religious narratives, for in his schema it is obvious that such stories would focus on questions of time as a means of explaining the act of being human. Religions deploy narrative forms in order to teach humans lessons about time (and to aid in their emplot-ment of their lives) and this is nowhere more evident than in the Bible or the Australian Dreamtime. It also helps us to understand how religions used their differentiated ideas of time as a means of attempting to derive a competitive advantage over other faiths, and, indeed, why we find such complex debates over the meaning of time within faith communities (most especially Christianity and Judaism).

In the key third volume of *Time and Narrative*, Ricœur (1990: 4) goes on to suggest that:

> The problem of the reconfiguration of temporal experience can no longer be confined within the limits of a psycho-sociology of the influences of narrativity on human behaviour. We must assume the much greater risks of a specifically philosophical discussion, whose stake is whether – and how – the narrative operation taken in its full scope, offers a 'solution' – not a speculative one, but a poetic one – to the aporias that seemed inseparable from the Augustinian analysis of time. In this way, the problem of the refiguration of time by narrative finds itself brought to the level of a broad confrontation between an aporetics of temporality and a poetics of narrativity.

So here essential questions of the nature both of time and of being – which we have already noted are bound together in the thought of Ricœur – are taken away from science and social science, for the potential resolution of these essential epistemological and phenomenological questions (what are things? what is being?) can only be found by the humanist philosopher who has come to understand the importance of narrative structures and the implicit temporal theme of all narratives. If Ricœur is correct this reinforces the importance of the comparative study of modes of time-being and history-making in religious cultures.

What we cannot of course also ignore in Ricœur's words here is his expression of hope that the difficult enterprise he envisages may indeed be undertaken and completed. This expression reminds us that across his work narratives such as the Bible served not just as subjects of study but as emblems of hope. When Ricœur described what he meant hermeneutics to be he called it (1981: 43) 'the theory of the operations of understanding in their relation to the interpretation of texts', which worked against 'the opposition, disastrous in my view, between explanation and understanding' and which 'puts us on guard against the illusion or pretension of neutrality.' In other words, the goals which Ricœur sought were so great that it was necessary to adopt a mindset as a reader which was that of a believer. His rejection of distinctions between explanation and understanding contrasts the way the Bible tells its readers to approach texts with the scientific assumption that we are able to think outside problems, of a philosophical exteriority and a neutrality which Ricœur believed had led historians, philosophers and the academy more generally down a critical path which entailed a loss of the task and the goal of being human. He had expressed such ideas in an earlier essay in which he wrote (1965: 82): 'We have used three words which will serve as guides for our inquiry: progress, ambiguity and hope. They stand for three stages in the flux of history, three ways of understanding and recovering meaning, and three levels of interpretation: the abstract level of progress, the existential level of ambiguity, and the mysterious level of hope.' It was this last level which was to drive the rest of his life's work which, while it may have been seen to come from a series of disciplinary perspectives, actually addressed only a limited number of simple and connected questions.

If indeed we move from such early writing to late work such as *Oneself as Another* (1994) we find a reiterated commitment to these questions. The locus of his discussion in this book is the individual and (1994: 113) 'the fact that the person of whom we are speaking and the agent on whom the action depends have a history, are their own history.' The duty of the historian is therefore an ethical one, for (1994: 164):

> The historian brings back to life ways of evaluating which continue to belong to our deepest humanity. In this history is reminded of its indebtedness to people of the past. And in certain circumstances – in particular when the historian is confronted with the horrible, the extreme figure of the history of victims – the relation of debt is transformed into the duty never to forget.

So it is quite clear that in one sense Ricœur's work offers support to the essential belief of historians of the possibility of recovering the past. In fact, such work is not simply a professional obligation but it is a form of moral duty to mankind, for the specificities of the narratives of people's lives serve as the basis for our study of being human. Yet Ricœur is simultaneously making the point that we ought not to distinguish between outwardly historical and fictional texts in this enterprise, which he understands will be problematic for many. As he says (Wood 1991: 186):

> If we do not resolutely maintain the difference between history and fiction, how do we answer people like Faurisson, in France, who declares: 'In Auschwitz, however, nothing *real* has happened; there is only what is said about it'. Roland Barthes' idea of the 'effect of the real' could, dangerously, support this kind of discourse which is an insult to the dead: they are killed twice. Now, with regard to them we have a debt, I would say of restitution. There comes to my lips the very beautiful word *rendre* in French, 'to render' in English. We must 'render' what has happened, that is to say, figure it at the same time as returning it to the dead. Just as in Nicaea's *Credo* mention

is made of the communion of saints; thus, by means of history, a communion established between the living and the dead. If we are unable to 'fictionalize' the dead we would have to return their 'having been' to them. No simple capitulation before 'being no more'. The past is not just what is absent from history; the right of its 'having been' also demands to be recognized. This is what the historian's debt consists in.

This more conscious sense of moral purpose and 'doing justice to the world' (Wood 1991: 187), then, understands that it is more of an insult to the persecuted to imply that there is but one narrativization of their lives than it is to look at the manner in which historical and fictional modes draw upon one another. Why is it that the empirical history claims a moral superiority as compared with photographs of the camps or a novel such as Primo Levi's *The Periodical Table*? All are driven by the attempt to explain the horror of the Holocaust and to render justice to its victims, for whom Levi's truthful poetics may be as meaningful as the historian's truthful record.

What Ricœur's work takes us back to are basic considerations about the relationship between religions and histories, providing the strongest kind of backing to the idea that it is the study of the temporal character of religious cultures that will provide us with the most profound answers to the question as to how they differ in explaining being human. I have, nonetheless, a fear with regard to Ricœur's project here, for it seems to me that one of its predicates is an idea of the self which is very distinctly associated with the modern west; a self which is rational, self-directed and ultimately concerned with expressing its temporalness through the generation of a series of narratives about its being-in-the-world-in-time. To take one of the more extreme oppositions to such an assumption, Ricœur's account of being and time here is antithetical to what we find in Mahayana Buddhism. There the task of being human is not the creation of narratives that make sense of the self, but the dissolution of such stories that promote the illusion of selfhood and thereby deny the possibilities of *nirvana* which are open only to those who abandon the structures of temporality and selfhood that operate the endless cycle of *samsara* or suffering. In the Mahayana, narrative is not what makes us human but what prevents us from coming to know our potential humanity. When Ricœur writes (Fleischman: 311) that 'We have no idea of what a culture would be like where no one knew any longer what it meant to narrate things' he believes himself to be describing a nightmare for man, but for a Zen Buddhist he seems to be taking the first steps towards enlightenment.

It is not only from a Buddhist perspective that we might critique Ricœur's universalism. There are, for example, powerful psychological objections to

Ricœur's narrativization of experience (seductive though that idea is), while Fabian and Carr (David Carr 1987: 182) implicate his thought within a broader post-colonial critique of western universalism and the manner in which it situates other places as (David Carr 1987: 182) *'precursors* of the Western world'. Of greater concern to me, though, is Ricœur's conviction that there is (White 1991: 152) 'a universal human need to reflect on the insoluble mystery of time.' In this book I hope to show precisely how religious cultures believed that they had solved that mystery in very different ways, some of which were not driven by Ricœur's conviction that human culture is centrally concerned with the act of making sense of things in narrative, or indeed of making sense of things at all. White offers a third objection to Ricœur, which is that (Munslow: 29, 17) it is the historian's narrativization of events that emplots the past, rather than the intrinsic narrative structures of those events.

Deeds Ermarth

A further criticism made (White 1991: 144) of Ricœur has been that his account of narrative coherence is such that he excludes the possibility of history's moving to a modernist moment, whereby its narratives might reflect the new psychological and formal claims of modernists. For Deeds Ermarth, by contrast, the need for an engagement with literary modernism is central to her project. In *Realism and Consensus in the English Novel: Time, Space and Narrative* (1983) and *Sequel to History: Postmodernism and the Crisis of Representational Time* (1992), Deeds Ermarth's achievement has been to construct a new and wholly beguiling narrative account of the manner in which distinct and evolving ideas of time have underpinned the culture of the modern west. Like Ricœur and Young, her disciplinary heritage is in literary studies, and for this reason there has until now been insufficient acknowledgement of the scale of her historiographical achievement.

In her first book, Deeds Ermarth set out the distinctiveness of 'historical time' (which we might equally call western or empirical time) and the manner in which it both drew on and contributed to western modernity (1992: 26):

> The medium of historical time is a construct and itself a representation of the first magnitude. This 'history' may be one of the most specifically modern achievements. Without the production of history, modern culture, that is, without the production of neutral time analogous to the neutral space evident in realist painting, we would be without that temporal

medium that makes possible an activity unknown in classical times: the mutually informative measurement between widely separated events that underlies modern empirical science, modern cartography, and exploration, certain forms of political and artistic organization such as representational government and tonal music, and certain habitual conceptions of identity, simple location, structure, consciousness, the subject, and social 'laws' that govern our metaphors of psychic as well as corporate existence. It is demonstrable that 'history' belongs to the same descriptive conventions that made possible the painting and architecture of the Renaissance and the empirical science of the sixteenth and seventeenth centuries.

History is therefore utterly dependent upon a new means of picturing time which emerges in western Europe at a distinct moment. It conceives of itself as neutral and progressive because it is self-evidently different from earlier conceptions of time, and because it is part of a complex of ideas about space and time which enabled huge advances in productivity, in making histories as much as in making paintings or machines. As a human creation, this idea of historical time is just as subject to critique and innovation as any other invention.

The subject of Deeds Ermarth's second book is the manner in which time has changed in the post-Newtonian world, and the failure of the academic discipline of history – understandably wedded to its own account of time – to adapt to this new picture of time. For Deeds Ermarth this new temporality lies at the very heart of postmodernism, for like Ricœur she believes that orientations towards time constitute the central differences in systems of thought. Postmodernism should then be of especial importance to history, for it offers a new understanding of time in the world which historians could adopt in the manner in which its temporal innovations have been made and taken up by painters and poets. Just as the painters of the Renaissance pointed the way to a new temporal world in the fourteenth and fifteenth centuries, it is the new temporalities seen in modernist culture that point to new ways of life in the twentieth and twenty-first centuries. As Deeds Ermarth puts it (1992: 31–32):

> Like the redefinition of space in painting since cubism, the redefinition of time that has occurred in postmodern narrative literally takes us from a medium that has been vital to Western empiricist culture and with it various important constructs, including that all-important changeling, the individual subject.

The forms of change she is talking about here are then fundamental: of form, time and selfhood (we might recall Sebald as an exemplar of these changes). There is no reason to suppose that history would be immune from such change, not least because of its dependence on Renaissance-era constructions of time, self and narrative. As Deeds Ermarth says (1992: 15), 'We face interesting questions in the history of consciousness now that the discourse which has supported historical thinking turns out itself to be discourse-bound like every other habit and belief.'

Evans misunderstands the implications of such ideas when he writes that (1997: 354), '*Sequel to History* [. . .] is one of the most radical of postmodernist texts on history, arguing for the abolition of historical concepts of time.' Deeds Ermarth is evidently doing no such thing. She is merely observing that we are living in the dog days of historical time, and she is concerned with setting out an archaeology of the coming into being of postmodern time, which she sees around her in scientific, cultural and social forms. This is not to say that the norms of historical time have utterly disappeared, merely that they are being replaced as the ruling premises of western society. Myth-based culture and time did not disappear with the advent of historical time – it simply slowly waned in terms of its influence as a mode of underpinning systems of politics, art, science and history. Deeds Ermarth simply says that she is witnessing a similar process taking place in our moment, and she suggests that historians ought to understand their own time as a means to reconfiguring their enterprise. They are welcome to ignore her observations and advice, but the risk they then run is of becoming viewed in the manner that antiquarians and religious tractarians were viewed in the coming into being of the historical age.

Robert Young

Young's work *White Mythologies: Writing History and the West* undoubtedly begins from some of the same premises as Deeds Ermarth. He concretizes her arguments as to the radical alteration of the character of selfhood in the postmodern age to suggest that one of the central illusions of the historical era was an idea of being human which excluded difference and complexity. The unified self of the rational agent was a description of the idea western cultural producers had of themselves, and built into it was an assumption of human hierarchies in which any who did not conform to the new norms of historical man were necessarily deficient. Young is therefore interested in imagining what a form of history or temporality appropriate to a post-colonial moment might look like.

Before looking at such new times, let us first consider Young's account of western historical culture in more detail. A prefatory note might remark that

Young's investigation into history operates from very different premises from most work on the past (for he sees history as an important point in battles between French Marxism and Anglo-Saxon post-structuralism) and with rather different personnel (Hegel, Marx, Sartre, Said, Jameson, Spivak) from debates in historiography, let alone history. His contention is that an analytical study of history leads us to look at the manner in which ideas of history and the historical method were bound up into the discourse and fabric of colonialism. This is evident in a naked form in nineteenth-century texts, even those that are associated with political progressivism; in fact, as Young asserts, it is precisely history's connectedness to progressivism that causes problems. The assertion that questions of history lie at the heart of the moral justification of imperialism is evident in Hegel (Young 1990: 175) – 'at this point we leave Africa, not to mention it again. For it is no historical part of the World; it has no movement or development to exhibit.' – and Marx (Young 1990: 176):

> Indian society has no history at all, or at least no known history. What we call its history is but the history of its successive intruders who founded their empires on the passive basis of that unresisting and unchanging society . . . England has to fulfil a double mission in India: one destructive, the other regenerating – the annihilation of the old Asiatic society, and the laying of the material foundations of Western society in Asia.

Such accounts of time are based on three interwoven delusions: the notion of pure races and nationhood (which leads directly to racist histories), a lack of consideration of the self (in this case, the true nature of English history and that of the west), and a failure to recognize that places like India had not only histories but also modes of temporalizing which were completely missed by writers like Marx and Hegel.

Such clear racism would evidently not be tolerated in the contemporary academy, but Young suggests that, sometimes in hidden ways, disciplines like history are still living in a nineteenth-century world, which serves as a means for the reproduction of the same premises that informed the historical judgements of Hegel and Marx. As he says with regard to the issue of the relationship between colonial discourse and racism (1990: 175):

> These are difficult political questions. They emerge from the analysis of colonialism because it combines its critique of Western history with one of Western historicism, showing the enactment of the links between the two in the colonial past and the neocolonial present. The effect of this has been to produce a shift away from the problem of history as an idea towards an examination of Western history's and historicism's contemporary political

ramifications. For that history lives on: its effects are operating now. It is those events that the new logics of historical writing must address.

History, then, must find 'new logics' as a means of interrogating the subtler links that exist today between western ideas of temporality and selfhood and forms of neo-colonialism. Young looks to writers like Fanon and Aimé Césaire as figures whose central interest in the psychology and character of western colonialism might produce a broader dividend for students of the past (1990: 118):

> But how to write a new history? When, as Césaire observed, the only history is white? The critique of the structures of colonialism might seem a marginal activity in relation to the mainstream political issues of literary and cultural theory, catering only for minorities or for those with a specialist interest in colonial history. But although it is concerned with the geographical peripheries of metropolitan European culture, its long-term strategy is to effect a radical restructuring of European thought and, particularly, historiography.

This book evidently has similar aims to Young's project, for it too seeks to de-occidentalize history and it suggests that the only means of doing this is to illustrate the forms of temporality and history which writers like Hegel and Marx missed, and in doing so to deepen Young's project of revealing the cultural specificity of western history. This is by no means a negative exercise, for what I suggest in this book is that a study of other temporalities takes us to places of beauty and complexity, and it also reveals productive possibilities in earlier western forms of temporality – especially in Judaism and Christianity – that may be used as a means of further diminishing the claimed universality of the colonial historicism identified by Young.

Conclusion

I hope that the theoretical discussions of the first three chapters have made a case for the value of a comparative study of religious temporalities. It is now time to try to deepen that case by looking in detail at the development of temporal and historical ideas in five religious cultures. We begin with Judaism which illustrates both the centrality of discussions of time in religions and the difficulties and opportunities with which we are presented when we try to use a text such as the Old Testament to piece together a coherent picture of the ancient Jews' philosophy of history. The difficulties entailed come in the main from the history of the production of the Bible, especially the disparate character of this set of texts written by authors from a range of geographical locations over a period of more than a thousand years, yet this complexity also provides us with opportunities as it enables us to see how the ancient Jews debated questions of time, where they disagreed with one other, and how new ideas about time became entrenched at different points in the history of the first millennia of the Jews.

C h a p t e r 4

In the beginning . . . Jewish contestations of time

The absence of time in ancient Judaism is particularly salient and conspicu-
ous when compared to later Jewish sources from the medieval period.

Sacha Stern

Introduction

A ncient Judaism, as it is described in the Old Testament, struggled with
the concept of time. My aim in this chapter runs counter to Stern's claim
(2003: 4) that time is absent from the literature of ancient Judaism, for what I
shall argue is that the culture of ancient Judaism was utterly dominated by
debates on time. Such discussions analysed its character, the manner in which
it functioned, the question as to how it might be recorded, and its place in the
dialogue between man and God. In making this argument, I am contesting the
view not only of Stern, but of other scholars, such as Gunnell who notes that
the Old Testament contains (Whitrow 1988: 53) 'no numbered dates, despite
its concern with an intricate historical record' to argue that (1988: 52), 'unlike
the Greeks, the Hebrews never tried to analyse the "problem" of time as such.
They seem neither to have conceptualized their experience of time nor formed
an abstract idea of history.' I find myself much more in agreement with
Heschel's view (1976: 200) that 'Judaism is a religion of history, a religion of
time', while Barr's key linguistic study (1962) would certainly lend support to
a reading of the Bible that questioned the rigidity of Hebrew/Greek divisions.
Indeed, as Wenham argues (1976: 21), 'Biblical theology may be crudely
described as a theology of history.' In this chapter I hope to show how the

'story of time' in the Old Testament is based around an orientation towards particular forms of time.

For hundreds of years it was not clear as to whether Judaism's account of time would go beyond that blend of circularity and linearity characteristic of the world into which it was born: where the seasons convinced man that time was in some way cyclical, and the ageing process indicated that it was also linear. What I show in this chapter is the manner in which ancient Jews grappled with God's proposed alterations to this temporal order. My overriding argument is that the Judaism of the Old Testament was riven by a temporal battle between the instincts towards 'natural time' held by the Jewish people and the teachings of their God, who asked them to abandon this commonsensical approach towards time in favour of a more complex temporal order founded on faith in his omniscience. The remnants of this debate lie across the Old Testament in a series of discussions of time based more on doubt and free-thinking exploration than dogmatism or an easy acceptance of God's description of the world.

Reading the Bible

Before looking at the temporal culture of ancient Judaism and the manner in which it produced particular views of history, I need to step back from some of the broad claims made above in order to address the character of the Bible and the many different interpretative strategies that have been adopted by its readers. A central tension exists in writing about the Bible between those who see it as a unified text and those who see it as an arrangement of primary and secondary sources compiled from more than a thousand years of human history. In truth the text of the Bible tends to defy a critical drive towards simple views of its disparate or united character. Those who begin from a historical–critical position, stressing the very different cultural and geopolitical circumstances in which, say, Genesis and Ecclesiastes were produced, tend to find themselves drawn to connections between what they would logically see as separate, while theological readings which stress the unity of an encounter of God across the Old and New Testaments are forced to set out a list of caveats which acknowledge the forms of glossing that allow such a critical position to be reached.

My own view is that there is perhaps too great a temptation not to view the Old or the New Testaments as coherent visions. While it is true that things changed over time we shall see that just as early Judaism displays a struggle with the competing temporal culture of Baal and the nature-cults, late Biblical Judaism is still focused on the articulation of the distinctive characteristics of Jewish time, history and identity, though now the competition of ideas, which we see in Job and Ecclesiastes, is with Greek thought. The Old Testament tells the story of a set of struggles over time and as a textual unity it serves as an invitation to its readers to think through these struggles as a means of coming to understand what it meant to be Jewish. This Biblical culture lies in stark contrast to the development of post-Biblical medieval Judaism where, in the years 200–600 C.E., Jews began to reject distinctions between past and present and to move away from the Biblical culture of 'historical time' (Neusner 2003: 2).

It is true, nonetheless, that such a view evidently found conceptual antecedents in the world of ancient Judaism for it was not simply a product of medieval Judaism's adaptation to its particular cultural circumstances. This leads me to an important and awkward interpretative observation, which is this: given the plurality of positions offered in the Old Testament corpus it is quite understandable that later Jewish cultures adopted parts of the text which accorded with the intellectual character of later cultures, but critics need to be in a position to argue that such later facets of the religion (such as the temporal culture of the medieval Dual Torah set out above) do not derive from the mainstream of Biblical Judaism and in fact are a rejection of the dominant culture of ancient Judaism. In the case of both Judaism and Christianity, the later critic needs to show how the two Testaments offer a set of different paths that might be taken, and to ensure the visibility of those paths that come to be ignored in the medieval and modern world. This is important not because it is imperative to recover true and original sets of beliefs from the Bible, but because later religious cultures have an understandable tendency to simplify and to impose coherence where no such certainties may have characterised the early development of the religions. It would be hard to argue that the deepest and most complex pictures of Jewish and Christian culture, especially with regard to time and history, come from anywhere other than the Bible.

The particularity of this complexity of sources is explored by Burrows (1976: 101) in his comparison of ancient Judaism in its comparative context, for:

> Our sources for the Hebrew idea of history are not firsthand, contemporary records like the innumerable cuneiform texts on clay tablets or the inscriptions and pictures on the walls of Egyptian and Assyrian temples and palaces or on the cliff at Bisitun. They are literary documents which have themselves gone through a long history of compiling, editing and copying.

He goes on to consider what holds together this collection of sources, noting (1976: 102) that:

> In this literature the idea of history plays an extraordinary part. It is a religious literature, of course, and history was of basic importance to the religion of Israel. The literature consists very largely of historical narratives, all presented under a dominant conception of the meaning of history. Yet it is not a single, uniform idea. Rather, we have in the Old Testament many ideas of history.

Burrows, it seems to me, is wholly correct in his neat distinction of a Biblical historical culture in which a dominant conception of time lies over a series of alternate visions of history. This chapter will try to set out both the dominant Jewish picture and its variants.

A textual illustration of Burrows' point can be seen in the adjoining books of Chronicles and Esther. Berg reveals that history acquired a very particular resonance in this post-exilic moment and that (1980: 119–20) 'Both accounts reveal that historical events assume a meaningful and orderly direction, and that divine guidance may be discerned in the pattern and nature of events', yet both also reveal very different roles for human agency in the production of history (1980: 120):

> In Chronicles, Yahweh's control of history dominates the account and appears manipulative. Chronicles thus suggests that anything less than total dependence upon the deity is idolatrous. In Esther, an opposite position is taken. Because Yahweh's control of history is neither overt nor easily discerned, the narrator stresses the importance of human initiative.

In Burrows' terms, the dominant view of history in ancient Judaism lies somewhere between these two representative extremes: admitting of man's duty to make history in accordance with the wishes of his God, but certainly not in a world where historical development was as independent from the will of God as it is portrayed as being in Esther.

Burrows' work leads me to a more general point about the characteristics of theological writing about the Bible and the value such work might have to historians. In many ways the tasks, methods and motivations that lie behind history and theology are similar, but a central difference in theology has been the concentration of discussions, especially those of method, on a tiny number of texts. While historians may share common methods and goals, they share no text comparable to the Bible, which for almost all theologians of Judaism and Christianity is ultimately the text on which they will work for the whole of their lives.

The stakes in such work are high, for theologians tend to be advocates not just of critical positions, as might be the case in history, but of visions of their faith as seen through their critical readings of the Bible, and this has led to a competition of ideas and of modes of interpretation which arguably dwarfs the scale of critical debate in a field such as history. Where, for instance, I have argued that it is difficult to find long-running and clear-thinking debates about time in history, it is hard to avoid such discussions in biblical theology. We find them in discussions of eschatology, the quest for the historical Jesus, debates on genre and the literary construction of the Bible, frank expositions on the nature of the historical method and truth across the two Testaments and so on. What is more, where historians have traditionally been reluctant to engage with philosophy and with leading conceptual traditions in the academy, theologians have displayed a constant openness towards such modes of thought. This is of course unsurprising given the place that theology traditionally had in post-classical western culture, first as the chief academic discipline and then as the central repository for intellectual debate in that culture. I certainly believe that the hermeneutic approach to texts in theology has much to teach historians about their own reading strategies and this observation ought to be recalled across the following two chapters as the work of writers such as Bultmann, Moltmann and Braaten could be reimagined as though it was written for historical audiences.

Modern biblical theology, by which I mean the work of the nineteenth and twentieth centuries, which had its origins in the Reformation, has made a set of moves very different from those that we find in the mainstream of the western historical tradition. If both traditions began from the same places – in a belief in the capacity of primary source documentation to reveal the truth of the past – they moved apart in the nineteenth century where the historical method in history came to be seen as a greater validation of that essential truth, while in theology the historical critique of the Bible led to a widespread doubting of the central truths which it had been believed underpinned Judaism and Christianity. While historians came to believe that they could come 'to see things as they actually were', historical critiques of biblical sources led theologians to wonder if they would ever know 'the historical Jesus', let alone Moses or Qoholeth. As Tillich remarked (Braaten 1968: 33–34):

> The historical approach to Biblical literature is one of the great events in the
> history of Christianity and even of religion and human culture. It is one
> of the elements of which Protestantism can be proud. It was an expression

of Protestant courage when theologians subjected the holy writings of their own church to a critical analysis through the historical method. It appears that no other religion in human history exercised such boldness and took upon itself the same risk.

In looking at the Mahayana tradition in Buddhism we shall see that Tillich rather overstates his case here, but his valorisation of the risk and courage of the historical approach is quite correct with regard to the Judaeo-Christian tradition. A consequence of that tradition, now very much associated with the nineteenth century, has been the slow shift to a new paradigm of truth in theology, or rather a complex manifestation of a set of different and underlying truths, for I would argue that one of the implicit goals of twentieth- and twenty-first century theology has been its desire to find and express truth in texts where no assumption of historical accuracy is presumed. As Braaten remarks (1968: 34), a consequence of this is that 'The historical method is proving to be like a football which bounces for and against both sides', providing succour for liberals, conservatives, Protestants and Catholics. In this sense, while it remains interested in historical and archaeological research, theology might be said to have moved beyond history.

This methodological and interpretative pluralism has arguably been heightened by the manner in which new theological traditions have emerged through borrowing from cognate disciplines such as anthropology, literary studies and philosophy, with the development of a colossal range of approaches to questions of language, textuality and social development accompanying differences of faith. A desire for a common belief nevertheless underpins such diversity, as we see in North's remarks on ideas of history in the Old Testament (1946: xiv–xv):

> There may be truth in all the several stages of the development of the Hebrew interpretation of history. The 'higher critic' may be right in his analysis of the documents and in his presentation of the course of Hebrew history and religion as based upon his analysis. At the same time the 'funda-mentalist', who takes the Old Testament in the completed form in which it has been handed down to him, may also be right in his broad conclusions.

Reading the Old Testament

Let us move now from a more general consideration of biblical theology to the question of reading the Old Testament. As we have seen, biblical scholars have shown that more than a thousand years lay between the composition of what is regarded as the earliest biblical text (the Song of Deborah) and the latest, the book of Daniel from the second century B.C.E. (Brettler 2004: 112; North 1946: x).

I have intimated that the Old Testament is best approached as something like an encyclopaedia or archive, to which we can look for distinct and sometimes divergent ideas and truths. It is one of the richest collections of genres, styles, poetics, narrative forms and ideas that we possess, important in itself and as the basis of much in Mediterranean and western cultures. It is, above all, a history, for it tells the story of the journey of the Jews in the period from the beginnings of the earth to 200 B.C.E., setting out a series of expectations as to what histories ought to contain and how they might be constructed. I am evidently interested in this chapter with these questions of form in the Old Testament – as well as its descriptions of time – that we need to consider if we are to be able to reflect critically on the nature of Jewish ideas of history.

We need to recognize that in its totality the Old Testament is less a book about community and cohesion of the faith than it is a history of its continual splintering and near extinction. It is a book of struggles, of the battle to resolve things and an invitation to readers to follow that path. This notion of belief coming through an engagement with doubt, struggle and scepticism is apparent across the Old Testament, but most evident in the books of Job and Ecclesiastes which will play an important role in this chapter.

In terms of its structure we can divide the Old Testament into five groups of books: (1) the early books of the Torah, which offer God's vision of a new orientation towards time, nature and history, (2) the histories and counter-histories of the early Jewish communities from Samuel to Chronicles, (3) the philosophical doubts of Job, and the story of Esther, which attempt to re-imagine the Jewish faith, (4) the archive of Jewish culture found from Psalms to Lamentations, and (5) the later, exilic, books of the Bible, which, in the light of the splintering of the faith, return to the time of David in order to make moral claims as to the desirability of the unity of Judah and Jerusalem. As we shall see, debates and teachings about time constitute many of the central differences in these blocks of the Old Testament. Yet, in seeing this order we need to recognize its artificiality, for, although broadly chronological, it does not reflect the order in which the books of the Old Testament were written, nor the manner in which the Hebrew Bible is compiled, in which the modern translated order of Law, Histories, Poetry and Prophecies differs markedly from the Hebrew distinctions between Law, Prophets and Writings (North 1946: xi).

Referring back to the pluralistic interpretative culture of modern theology, let me now briefly enumerate the character of the main traditions which have been used to understand the Old Testament, beginning with seven general methods (Wenham 1976: 34, 35, 40–42, 55–62) and moving on to four distinct schools of writing (Braaten 1968: 118, 120–21, 125, 127):

1. Textual criticism, which aims to locate 'the original text of a document.'
2. Source criticism, which attempts 'to discover and define the literary sources used by biblical writers.'
3. Form criticism, which uses literary methods as a means of identifying formal similarities between biblical writings that might otherwise not have been seen to be connected.
4. Tradition criticism, which is 'primarily concerned with the history of traditions before they are recorded in writing and incorporated into literary sources.'
5. Redaction criticism, which studies the mode of editing of texts and the manner in which biblical editors can be seen as authors of the text.
6. Historical criticism, which looks at the dating of documents, the 'verification of information about past events contained in such sources', and the study of 'the writing of history, the reconstruction of events and their explanation.'
7. Archaeology, which is increasingly used by many of these interpretative traditions.
8. The Christological interpretation of the Old Testament, often associated with Karl Barth and Wilhelm Vischer, which looks there for intimations of Christ.
9. The existential interpretation, seen especially in Bultmann, which, in contradistinction, contends that faith 'has no use for historical evidences that Jesus Christ is the goal of the prophetic history of Israel.'
10. The typological interpretation, found in the writings of Wolff and von Rad, which 'seeks to discover a relation of correspondence between certain types in the Old Testament, such as persons, institutions, or events, which foreshadow similar realities, or antitypes, in the New Testament.'
11. The *Heilsgeschichte* of Zimmerli and Pannenberg, which concentrates on the particularities of biblical understandings of history.

In fact, there are many more reading strategies for the Old Testament, but I have included this list as a set of exemplars of approaches that see the Old Testament as a text in itself and those that see it as a biblical text which should be read as part of the story of Christianity. It is important to see that in terms of both method and intent many of these approaches are centrally concerned with the question of how history and time are represented and made in the Old Testament.

This stress on temporality was noted by Georges Pidoux who contended (Wilch 1969: 2) that 'Every study of the Old Testament confronts the same great difficulty: namely, the idea of time held to by the authors of the Bible.' Scholars such as von Orelli, Pedersen and R.B.Y. Scott have based their readings on the text on considerations of time, and one clear reason for this focus has evidently been the difference of the overriding picture of time we find in the Old Testament from that of its civilizational neighbours. As Patrides notes (1972: 2–3), the temporal cultures of Hinduism, the Aztecs, the Greeks and many of the Jews' neighbours were cyclical, yet Israel displayed an urge to move away from or beyond such visions of time. We shall in fact see that modern theologians have shown that cyclical structures played an important part in the composition of the Old Testament, but it is certainly true that there was a distinctly Jewish aspiration to think of other kinds of time, in addition to or outside the cyclical. My own suggestion is that the central arena in which this is played out in the text is in the opposition between nature and ritual, for God's gift to the Jews, and his request of them, was that they try to abandon their faith in nature, which was visible and seen to move in a cyclical fashion, and instead live in faith to leap to a belief in an invisible protector and a higher order of temporal organization which could be shared by both God and man.

The discussions in this chapter have to lead us to the point where we can move on from discussions of temporality to answer also the question: what was the Jews' philosophy, or philosophies, of history? Such a question is important in itself, but it also has a broader world historical significance, for its answer will tell us much that informs our interest in the development of Christian and Islamic ideas of time. In order to impose a structure upon the Old Testament which allows me to concentrate on its account of time, this chapter is divided into four sections which address its principles of time (I), the context for the formulation of those principles (II), the practice of time in Jewish culture (III), including the troubling and exploration of the tenets of Jewish time which we find in later books such as Ecclesiastes, and (IV), the many forms of historical narrative we find in the text.

I: Context

The Jews as a nation

A tension exists through the Old Testament as to whether the Jews constitute a separate nation, and indeed what level of separateness they can claim more generally. Such questions are not, of course, always ones that Jews themselves can pose, for they depend on both the will of God and the political circumstances in which the Jewish people found themselves (such as those times when they were enslaved or exiled). These questions are somewhat complicated by our exegetic knowledge which leads us to the stories and mythic archetypes that formed the narrative basis of some key moments in the early history of the Jews, such as the account of Moses in the bulrushes (Freud 1967: 8), which draws on the Sumerian tale of Sargon of Agade.

The Torah tradition sets out very plainly the view that the Jews were a special people whose national history was to be laid out by God (Genesis 18:17–18):

> The Lord said, 'Shall I hide from Abraham what I am about to do, seeing that Abraham shall become a great and mighty nation, and all of the nations of the earth shall be blessed in him?

We see here that there is an actualization of history in the figure of Abraham, which serves to connect traditional, tribal understandings of genealogy and legacy with a broader view of time which we might call historical. We also see intimations of interpretative space in the mentioning not only of other nations, but also the manner in which they too might be blessed, albeit through the Jews.

That genealogical description of time is often understood to be the dominant form of temporal understanding in the Old Testament, for long parts of the text are devoted to accounts of family lineages and the connectedness of the twelve tribes of Israel through time. It is this that causes consternation to Bathsheba, the wife of David, when Adonijah tries to usurp the throne from David's rightful heir, Solomon (1 Kings 1:20–21):

> But you, my lord the king – the eyes of all Israel are on you to tell them who shall sit on the throne of my lord the king after him. Otherwise it will come to pass, when my lord the king sleeps with his ancestors, that my son Solomon and I will be counted offenders.

Here the punishment for man's failing to continue the historical line ordained by God will not be borne by David, but by his ancestors, who will lose not only their power but also their standing before God. The incentives towards communal purity and the maintenance of a distinctly Jewish history were therefore great.

Yet, there is equally powerful textual evidence which suggests that genealogical and national purity was not a driving force in Jewish theology, leaving aside the ample sociological evidence which militates against any ideas of the singularity of the Jews as a people. God, after all, is often shown to interact with other peoples: at times, in order to influence their behaviour towards the Jews, and at times because they too are in some sense his charges. In Jeremiah we read that the Jews serve not only King Nebuchadnezzar of Babylon, but also the kings of Moab, the Ammonites and Tyre. As God says (27:5–7):

> It is I who by my great power and my outstretched arm have made the earth, with the people and the animals that are on the earth, and I give to whomsoever I please! Now I have given these lands to King Nebuchadnezzar of Babylon, my servant, and I have given him even the wild animals of the field to serve him. All the nations shall serve him and his son and his grandson.

Such ideas are taken even further in the book of Isaiah (19:24–25):

> On that day Israel will be the third with Egypt and Assyria, a blessing in the midst of the earth, whom the Lord of hosts has blessed, saying, 'Blessed be Egypt my people, and Assyria the work of my hands, and Israel my heritage.'

It is interesting here that, of the three lands, Israel is identified with the idea of history; indeed it is constituted as a history in the mind of God, and this is suggestive of the early part that it may be destined to play in a greater drama which God will enact in the world. Patrides has recently even suggested that the genealogical genre can be read as universalist rather than particularistic, stressing the importance of re-imagining the context of the production of such writing, for (1972: 5):

> In the chapter following the account of creation in Genesis, we are given in outline the Jewish theory of how, out of the first man, arose the various nations of the world. The seemingly endless lists of names, so tedious to us, were of fundamental importance to the compilers themselves. As we pass through the generations of Adam to those of Noah and his three sons, and on through Abraham and Isaac and Jacob to Joseph, we realise that the roll-call of names is included to stress the essential unity of mankind, that under the one Lord of the universe there exists but a single family of nations, divided at various points in history, yet still retaining their unity under God.

Such universalist ideas are readily apparent in books such as Ruth, which tells the story of a Moabitess within the Jewish community, and one of Solomon's sermons makes this universalism especially plain (1 Kings 8:41–43):

Likewise, when a foreigner, who is not of your people Israel, comes from a distant land because of your name – for they shall hear of your great name, your mighty hand and your outstretched arm – when a foreigner comes and prays towards this house, then hear in heaven your dwelling-place, and do according to all that the foreigner calls to you, so that all the peoples of the earth may know your name and fear you, as do your people Israel, and so that they may know that your name has been invoked on this house that I have built.

Burrows uses such remarks to argue (1955: 129) that 'At the heart of the Hebrew idea of history is the assurance that Israel is God's chosen people, but this involves not merely privilege but obligation' for the Jews serve as the first exemplars of the working out of God's (1955: 128) 'sovereign purpose for the good of his creatures, first for his chosen people, and through them for the rest of mankind.'

This universalist idea is reinforced in Psalm 110 (5–7):

The Lord is at your right hand; he will shatter kings on the day of his wrath. He will execute judgement among the nations, filling them with corpses; he will shatter heads over the wide earth. He will drink from the stream by the path; therefore he will lift up his head.

So although the Lord will wreak vengeance on the nations, there is a contradiction here because those nations were not a part of him and his plan, if you believe most of the Old Testament. Yet the image of the stream is a powerful one – the movement of that stream is the movement of the Jewish people in history, but this is not to say that the stream is all there is, for God is able to look up from the stream and he is able to see aspects of life and time that are not accessible to the Jewish people. This makes reference to God's lordship of time, a theme we will pick up later, in a particularly appealing way.

It is only later in the history of the Jews that we might say that a reinvention of orthodoxy takes place after the splitting of the Jews into exilic and non-exilic communities. This recasting of orthodoxy arguably stresses ideas of race and purity which are absent from the Torah, in a manner akin to Benedict Anderson's descriptions of the ways in which newly organized nation states of the nineteenth century began to constitute themselves as 'imagined communities'. When Ezra (9:2) discovers that the Jews left behind in Jerusalem have inter-married with other tribes, he articulates such views well, arguing that 'the holy seed has mixed itself with the peoples of the lands, and in this faithlessness the officials and leaders have led the way.'

Miscegenation is associated with sin, and the writers of Ezra and Nehemiah (13:1–3) go on to invoke supposed practices of the early history of the Jews as a means of justifying these invented traditions:

> On that day they read from the book of Moses in the hearing of the people; and in it was found written that no Ammonite or Moabite should ever enter the assembly of God, because they did not meet the Israelites with bread and water, but hired Balaam against them to curse them – yet our God turned the curse into a blessing. When the people heard the law, they separated from Israel all those of foreign descent.

Yet the chronicler of Nehemiah (13:23–25) also reveals just how far post-exilic Jewry was from any sense of singular and pure nationhood:

> In those days I saw Jews who had married women of Ashdod, Ammon, and Moab; and half their children spoke the language of Ashdod, and they could not speak the language of Judah, but spoke the language of various peoples. And I contended with them and cursed them and beat some of them and pulled out their hair.

Such things are emblematic of both the history of the Jews and their theology, for they are expressive of the fact that the Old Testament as a record is riven by the tensions that existed in ancient Judaism; tensions which were not at all resolved, but which underlay Jewish civilization for centuries. If such ideas contradict the popular notion that religions are framed around certainties, then they are also revealing of Judaism's commonalty with other world faiths which are as much about the negotiation of choices and uncertainty as they are about absolutes.

Whether the nationalism of the post-exilic period accorded with the Torah or not, what is undeniable is the sense in which the texts that came to make up the Old Testament were regarded by Jews as narratives of immense import for their presents. As DeVries remarks (1975: 31), 'We need to be impressed by the fact that the Hebrews had a very special awareness of their presence in time and in history. For them time was no empty form or meaningless continuum: it was a factor in their experience that – even more than space – gave definition and quality to their existence.' To take one example from the scholarship of this sense of the Jews being a people living in and through history, let us look briefly at McConville and Millar's recent study of *Time and Place in Deuteronomy*. Their contention (1994: 16–17) is that the book of Deuteronomy is emblematically formed around ideas of time and place which are constitutive of the identities of the Jews in their texts and their lives. As the authors explain (1994: 31–32):

> The prologue to the book presents two foundational concepts. The first is that Israel is a nation on the move – engaged on a journey with Yahweh. This journey began in Egypt and is still in progress at Moab. It involves every member of the Mosaic community, and the community's faithfulness to the covenant of Yahweh is mirrored by its course. The second concept cannot be separated from the first, since it asserts that the past experience of Israel holds the key to enjoyment of their covenant relationship. If Israel is to enter the land and live in peace in it, then the lessons of the past must be absorbed into the national consciousness. [. . .] It seems that what we have here is not only salvation history, but an exposition of the *way* of salvation in the present and the future, based on the national experience of the past. The events of the past and the places of the past coalesce with those of the present, *so that Israel might walk in the ways of Yahweh.* This 'journey' means more to the Deuteronomist than a simple transition from the life of the wilderness to the paradisal agrarian existence set before them in Canaan. The journey is a pregnant metaphor for life with Yahweh.

Through this modern theological perspective we gain an important sense here of the importance of the texts of the Old Testament not just in the biblical period, but also in the time of the ancient Jews, for their lives were to a very significant degree determined not just by the word of God and their free will, but by the textual historical descriptions of their ancestors which served to mediate between obedience and independence.

Monotheism?

Just as there exist significant debates surrounding the singularity of the Jews as a people, the Old Testament also presents a series of different pictures of the numbers of gods present in the ancient Jewish world and, indeed, the question as to whether God saw himself as uniquely divine. To raise such things may seem to question the world historical status of Judaism as the first of the great monotheistic religions, though it is better viewed as a means of describing the social world in which Judaism emerged, where it competed with other gods, faiths and sects.

In the Torah, God appears as a somewhat needy and hardly omnipotent figure. He fears the influence other gods might have on the Jewish people and constantly desires thanks for the manner in which he saved the Jews in the flight from Egypt. In Exodus (32:7–14) he wants to punish the Jews for their worship of a golden calf, but is persuaded by Moses that this is not godly behaviour, for we learn (32:14) that 'the Lord repented of the evil which he thought to do to his people', leaving Moses to enact revenge upon those who had strayed, but also betraying a certain insecurity in his relationship with Moses, as a representative of man.

Later the punishments that God invokes for the Jews straying towards the worship of other deities are fearsome (Leviticus 26:27–30):

> And if in spite of this you will not hearken to me, but walk contrary to me, then I will walk contrary to you in fury, and chastise you myself sevenfold for your sins. You shall eat the flesh of your sons and you shall eat the flesh of your daughters. And I will destroy your high places, and cut down your incense altars, and cast your dead bodies upon the dead bodies of your idols; and my soul will abhor you.

The viscerality of God's reaction here acts as a summation of the tensions that exist between him and the Jews in the period out of Egypt. There seems little doubt that at that time, and indeed for all the period described by the Old Testament, many Jews worshipped a basket of gods, many of whom were venerated by the communities among whom they lived. Thus in Judges (8:33–35) we read that:

> As soon as Gideon died, the Israelites relapsed and prostituted themselves with the Baals, making Baal-berith their god. The Israelites did not remember the Lord their God, who had rescued them from the hand of all their enemies on every side; and they did not exhibit loyalty to the house of Jerubbaal (that is, Gideon) in return for all the good that he had done to Israel.

God's admonishment is very specifically temporal here, for the sins the Israelites have committed are as follows: the failure to continue the genealogical line which passed through Gideon, the loss of a sense of loyalty, to God and Gideon, which embodies God's idea that the Jews were his heritage, their refusal to remember the God who was theirs, and their erasure from their history of the key moment in their past, the rescue which God effected in Egypt. Later (Numbers 25:1–3) we read that the Israelites living among the Moabites began to worship those people's gods, notably the Baal of Peor, a figure called Molech worshipped in the form of carved images (2 Kings 17:41), and that even Solomon's heart was turned away from God and towards other deities by his foreign wives (1 Kings 11:1–4). More specific fears emerge in Isaiah (44:13) and Jeremiah (7:18) where the danger of human idols (the 'queen of heaven' in Jeremiah's case) is described, suggestive perhaps of ideas of the over-extension of prophets, kings or God's confidants latent within Judaism, that were later actualized in the life of Christ.

In 2 Kings (17:16–17) we learn more about the specific rites associated with other gods, reading that the people:

> Made for themselves cast images of two calves; they made a sacred pole, worshipped all the host of heaven, and served Baal. They made their sons and their daughters pass through fire; they used divination and augury.

We can thus see that the particularity of the threat of such faiths was their impingement on Jewish temporality. Here the people are described worshipping nature, implying as we shall see that it was the basis of time, rather than God's will. Additionally, they praise 'all the host of heaven', which implies a polytheistic universe beyond man's imagination. This revealed a major fault-line in ancient Judaism's cosmology since the writers of the Old Testament were unsure as to how wholly the heavens were the domain of their God. In many books the implication is that the heavens contain but one God, though in others we read of figures such as angels or of the primacy of God among the 'assembly of the holy ones' (Job 89:5–7). In the extract from 2 Kings we also read that the construction of the sacred pole implied a holy calendar that must have been a direct challenge to Judaism, with its own developing sense of time being broken up into series of festivals and rites. Worst of all, these people 'used divination and augury', implying that man, and not God, might be the master of time. Such ideas are testing ones to deal with, for prophecy was far from unknown in ancient Judaism, but it was usually sanctioned and framed by the words and the will of God.

Addressing the question of monotheism therefore reveals to us God's great struggle to make the Israelites a historical people who would revere tradition and prophecy more than the immediate world of worship and relations with the tribes with whom they lived. The slow take-up of the faith was in part the result of God's strategy to trust that people would give up their lives for his offer of culture; yet the people showed that they did not want to abandon their nature-based culture, which leads us to question the (temporal) distinctiveness of Judaism's early theology. It certainly faced spatial and temporal problems in terms of the difference of its offer, for we know that God resorted to making himself visible to a few, and to miracles, simply because of its lack of differentiation in this world of faiths.

II: Principles

God and man

Man's relationship with God was therefore to be one of obedience. The template for such behaviour was established by Abraham when he showed through his willingness to sacrifice his son that his allegiance to God was greater than his sense of self and his natural instinct to protect his kin (Genesis 22:15–18):

> Because you have done this, and have not withheld your son, your only son, I will indeed bless you, and I will make your offspring as numerous as the stars of heaven and as the sand that is on the seashore. And your offspring shall possess the gates of their enemies, and by your offspring shall all the nations of the earth gain blessing for themselves, because you have obeyed my voice.

Yet, as we know, man's early deference towards God was soon shattered, and God could in no way rely on the transmission of the Abrahamic/Mosaic settlement, with its rituals, beliefs and history, to later generations of Jews (so this story of Abraham and his son needs to be replayed, with different characters, in later books such as Deuteronomy 20). Instead, God needed to engage in a constant dialogue with their leaders in order to chide them towards lives approaching orthodoxy. Such ideas are especially well conveyed in the 'history books' of the Old Testament, notably Samuel and Kings, where the place of God as a director of man's affairs is set in the context of discussions of kingship (with implicit comparison between the suitable status of earthly and celestial kings).

Samuel finds himself caught up in these struggles when the Jews rejected his call for them to look not towards him for leadership, but towards God (1 Samuel 8:19–20):

> But the people refused to listen to the voice of Samuel; they said, 'No! but we are determined to have a king over us, so that we may be like other nations, and that our king may govern us and fight our battles!'

The dangers of kingship were set out by God in the exemplary case of Saul, who broke God's commandments and established rule based around a cult of personality. His behaviour divided the Jews and reached an end-point when Saul faced a climactic battle against the Philistines, who were aided by David. Before going to war Saul sought contact with God or the spirit world in order to have his enterprise blessed, but he found that he had forfeited access to any holy tools that might afford him a broader view of time than that which he had as a man. In desperation, Saul then conjured up the dead Samuel, who told the disobedient Saul that he and his sons would die the next day, which they did, so that the idea of the relative status of man and God could be reinforced.

A more cynical take on this relationship is articulated in Job as he suffered the indignity of his abandonment by God in the desert (14:18–22):

> But the mountain falls and crumbles away,
> and the rock is removed from its place;
> the waters wear away the stones;
> the torrents wash away the soil of the earth;
> so you destroy the hope of mortals.
> You prevail for ever against them, and they pass away;
> You change their countenance, and send them away.
> Their children come to honour, and they do not know it;
> They are brought low, and it goes unnoticed.
> They only feel the pain of their own bodies,
> And mourn only for themselves.

The difference between God and man is expressed temporally, for Job notes that God prevails whilst men die. What is more, God's cruelty towards man is framed by a description of change in nature, for Job contends that the destruction of hope is akin to the manner in which 'the waters wear away the stones.' Although negative, this account of the completeness of God, in time and in his rule over men, represents an affirmation of the Mosaic settlement, as opposed to the account of God which saw him as one figure among many in the political history of the diasporic Jews.

When Job rejects God's offer of life he sees it in relentlessly temporal terms (3:3–6):

> Let the day perish on which I was born, and the night that said, 'A man-child is conceived.' Let that day be darkness! May God above not seek it, or light shine on it. Let gloom and darkness claim it. Let clouds settle upon it; let the blackness of the day terrify it. That night – let thick darkness seize it! Let it not rejoice among the days of the year; let it not come into the number of the months.

Job does not ask for death, but he asks to have not lived. In other words, he asks not for something achievable within the temporal grammar of his own life, but for something that could only be achieved by a god who was able to operate in time in ways that went beyond our own human capacities. Life here is seen as a statement in time, written by a narrator. What is more, Job appeals to nature (darkness, light, clouds) in order to challenge God as the author of time, for only through the potential of an alternative view of temporality might God's plans be scuppered.

God and time

The Bible opens with a description of the coming into being of the world which centres on time (Genesis 1:1–5):

> In the beginning when God created the heavens and the earth, the earth was a formless void and darkness covered the face of the deep, while a wind from God swept over the face of the waters. Then God said, 'Let there be light'; and there was light. And God saw that the light was good; and God separated the light from the darkness. God called the light Day, and the darkness he called Night. And there was evening and there was morning, the first day.

In other words, before he made anything God made the idea of time, embodied by the day and the night, the morning and the evening. In this account of the origin of things, nature is very much subservient to the will of God for it is through the wind and the light that God is able to actualize time in the shape of days and nights. A system of measurement and of understanding the world is therefore put into place in which time has a central position. This ecology of time is further emphasized in God's division of time into weeks (2:2–3):

> And on the seventh day God finished the work he had done, and he rested on the seventh day from all the work he had done. So God blessed the seventh day and hallowed it, because on it God rested from all the work that he had done in creation.

The temporal construct of the seventh day thence became one of the bases of the organization of the world and man's society in it.

In this *ur-time* in which the archetypes of life were being established, men lived for hundreds of years (Adam lived to be nine hundred and thirty), but a new, non-mythical era was destined to quickly come into being (6:1–3):

> When the people began to multiply on the face of the ground, and daughters were born to them, the sons of God saw that they were fair; and they took

wives for themselves of all that they chose. Then the Lord said, 'My spirit shall not abide in mortals for ever, for they are flesh; their days shall be one hundred and twenty years.

As human society develops in the idealized world of the Torah, God's plans for his people are relentlessly described in temporal terms, for his people must come to see that an appreciation of his picturing of time is akin to faith in Him. Readers of the text are also guided by the clarity of the chronology that underpins these books. In Numbers (9:1–3), for instance, we read that:

> The Lord spoke to Moses in the wilderness of Sinai, in the first month of the second year after they had come out of the land of Egypt, saying, 'Let the people of Israel keep the passover at its appointed time. On the fourteenth day of this month in the evening, you shall keep it at its appointed time; according to all its statutes and all its ordinances you shall keep it.'

This passage is not an important one in terms of Jewish theology, but it is revealing in the ordinariness of its stress on time. Here we see both chronological reckoning meshed with an account of the rites that were required of Jews in their nascent faith – and it is arguable here that the timing of these rites is not just a means of structuring their significance, but it, as much as the ritual, is what is significant: that the practice of Passover is a means of actualizing a belief in God's account of time and of connecting the present moment with the heritage of the Jews.

It seems significant that these first books of the Bible are not recast, revised and critiqued in the Old Testament, in the manner we find in the later books of the Jews' history. The time of the Torah is very much immutable as compared with the time of the Jewish kings, yet while such books do not necessarily contain as many conceptual discussions of time, temporal allusions throughout the text reinforce the model of the Torah, in which (1 Chronicles 16:36) the Lord is 'the God of Israel, from everlasting to everlasting.'

What God is able to offer in these books is the everyday evidence of his godhood through time, as in the case of Hezekiah. When this loyal servant asked a prophet when he was to die, the answer that death would come soon alarmed Hezekiah, so he appealed to God to offer him mercy in the shape of extra time on earth. We then read of the manner in which the warp of time is altered, for, when Hezekiah is sent to pray on a particular day, he sees shadows retreating rather than advancing (2 Kings 20:11): 'The prophet Isaiah cried to the Lord; and he brought the shadow back the ten intervals by which the sun had declined on the dial of Ahaz.' Time here is cast as conceptual and malleable in

God's hands; it is the underlying logic of time which determines the character and quality of the life of Hezekiah.

The philosophical character of such remarks is made still plainer by Job, who attempts to describe the manner in which humans live in a relativized universe in which their understanding of time must be radically different from that of God. As he knowingly asks God (10:4–5), 'Do you have eyes of flesh? Do you see as humans see? Are your days like the days of mortals, or your years like human years?', Job understands full well the answers to such questions and it is imperative that we see again that his interrogation of God is centred on his temporal power. As Psalm 90 (1–6) more fully describes this:

> Lord, you have been our dwelling-place in all generations. Before the mountains were brought forth, or ever you had formed the earth and the world, from everlasting to everlasting you are God. You turn us back to dust and say, 'Turn back, you mortals.' For a thousand years in your sight are like yesterday when it is past, or like a watch in the night. You sweep them away; they are like a dream, like grass that is renewed in the morning; in the morning it flourishes and is renewed; in the evening it fades and withers.

There is much to unpack here: from the rare invocation of the creation time of the early Torah, to the revival of the idea that God and time came before nature, and the notion that God is in effect time, signalling the difference between man and God. There is also the beauty of the Psalm's characterization of the different times of man and God, which is founded upon the relativist idea that God's millennia are like our memories or moments (it is notable that these descriptions of time are embedded within this account of the nature of time).

Questions of agency and omniscience

If God, then, is the Lord of time, how much agency do men have beneath his omniscient gaze? If we concentrate on the book of Exodus, for instance, we find that this history of the account of the Jews' life and escape from imperial bondage is merged with a metaphysical tale of redemption and God's gift, in which the escaping Jews evidently play a role which has been plotted by their narrator God. Similarly, the behaviour of the Pharaoh is determined by God so that he might play his assigned role in this narrative structure: (Exodus 9:12) 'the Lord hardened the heart of Pharaoh' even in the face of the suffering of the plagues he wrought upon the Egyptians, so that Pharaoh would not allow the Jews to leave his kingdom of their own accord.

Yet, soon after the escape from Egypt, it is clear that many of the Jews reject the teachings of God and his emissary Moses (Exodus 32:30–35):

> On the morrow Moses said to the people, 'You have sinned a great sin. And now I will go up to the Lord; perhaps I can make atonement for your sin.' So Moses returned to the Lord and said, 'Alas this people have sinned a great sin; they have made for themselves gods of gold. But now, if thou wilt forgive their sin – and if not, blot me, I pray thee, out of thy book which thou hast written.' But the Lord said to Moses, 'Whoever has sinned against me, him will I blot out of my book.'

In the early Torah therefore the idea of God's 'book', which contains within it the narrative of time, is a very powerful one. This idea is revived in Psalm 139 (16), where we read, 'In your book were written all the days that were formed for me, when none of them as yet existed.' Yet the impact of such Psalms and the book of Job is that in spite of God's authorial control of the lives of men in the world, human existence consists of a mixture of agency and destiny. In the face of abandonment by God and his relinquishment to Satan, Job proves his humanity not by a rigid adherence to the word and the will of God, but by a deeper faith that is only achieved through a questioning of his beliefs and the motives that lay behind his desertion. In the sophistication of his exploration of doubt, and the offering of this typical struggle as a legacy for later generations, Job is himself an author whose psychological understanding of man seems to go beyond that of God (or at least the God of the Torah).

Jeremiah also sets out a similar set of tensions, when he says that (10:23) 'the way of human beings is not in their control, that mortals as they walk cannot direct their steps.' Yet he also describes (23:16) God castigating the people for following the teachings of prophets, for 'They speak visions of their own minds, not from the mouth of the Lord.' What we see here, therefore, is a familiar opposition between God's will that men follow his book and men's choice to make their own world. In order to re-assert his primacy in this debate, God announces that it is He (31:35) 'who gives the sun light by day and the fixed order of the moon and the stars for light by night.' In other words, his trump card is the fact that he is Lord of nature and time – these being the variables with which he believes men cannot argue.

Time and nature

As will already have become clear, resolving the question as to how the natural world fits into God's temporal schema is critical to an understanding of Jewish time and history. It also forms a crucial part of my own argument, for I join those who contend that the Old Testament is essentially the story of a battle between a people and a god in a dispute over who is able to interpret the natural world in the more convincing fashion. Since God is the Lord of Time, the natural world is as subservient to him as the human world, and man's engagement with the natural world should be a hierarchical one: where men are superior to nature but inferior to God. Yet across the Old Testament it is clear that men are not so willing to accept these distinctions: both that they are inferior to God and that they live beyond nature. Nature, the world around them, reveals itself on a constant basis, while God is uncovered only rarely. It is for this reason that God needs to structure a holy calendar around events from the mythical history of the Jews of the Torah, such as the Passover, so that people's deepest ideas about time and belief do not draw on nature in the manner of earlier and competing faiths and cults. As Terrien says of the work of De Vries (1975: 9):

> The historicization of agricultural feasts which had been inherited from the Middle Bronze Canaanites constitutes the most eloquent witness to the power of the Hebraic notion of time. In the ancient Near East in general and in the Fertile Crescent in particular, feasts had been almost exclusively seasonal celebrations of nature myths. This book suggests that in almost every feast of the covenant people, the category of nature had been displaced by that of time. In her holy seasons, Israel celebrated not the deified forces of nature but the transcendence of her God over the forces of nature and his ultimate sovereignty over the nations.

More than perhaps any other battle, the struggle over time and nature is critical to an understanding of the Jews. It is in the Torah that the templates for this new time are established.

God's power over nature is made plain in the story of the flood, which allows him to re-establish his original template for the world, with archetypal animals and men upon the earth (Genesis 8:21–22):

> And when the Lord smelt the pleasing odour [of Noah's sacrifice], the Lord said in his heart, 'I will never again curse the ground because of humankind, for the inclination of the human heart is evil from youth; nor will I ever again destroy every living creature as I have done. As long as the earth endures, seedtime and harvest, cold and heat, summer and winter, day and night, shall not cease.'

Interestingly what takes place here is that God vows never again to act as the potential destroyer of nature and time, for he is grateful for the manner in which Noah asserts His dominance over nature in the form of a sacrifice which recognizes that the structure of time is God's and no other. In return for this sacrifice, man and nature will live, and for this to happen 'day and night, shall not cease.'

The relationship between these things is also made plain in the ways in which God describes rites surrounding the death of men. In Leviticus (9:4–8) we read that:

> Moses told the people of Israel that they should keep the passover. And they kept the passover in the first month, on the fourteenth day of the month, in the evening, in the wilderness of Sinai; according to all that the Lord commanded Moses, so the people of Israel did. And there were certain men who were unclean through touching the dead body of a man, so that they could not keep the passover on that day; and they came before Moses and Aaron on that day; and those men said to him, 'We are unclean through touching the dead body of a man; why are we kept from offering the Lord's offering at the appointed time among the people of Israel?' And Moses said to them, 'Wait, that I may hear what the Lord will command concerning you?'

This dialogue takes place while the Jews are in the wilderness, a place without natural goodness or temporal signifiers (where often the people rely on the will of God to eat and drink, for we hear little of their foraging). The sacrality of time is stressed in the way in which the unclean are denied entry into ritualized time celebrations. Why, we might ask, are those who have touched the dead excluded? The answer would seem to be because the activity in which they have been taking part is one that focuses their attention on questions of time and human mortality, a world apart from the temporal world which their God occupies. Similar ideas are expressed in 2 Kings (23:14), where God reacts to the people's abandonment of his temporal rituals and their adoption of those of other nature-based cults. God, we learn, 'broke the pillars in pieces, cut down the sacred poles, and covered the sites with human bones.' In other words, he invited men to reflect on the hierarchy of God–man–nature, where men ought to realize the greater sophistication of ritual based on heritage and memory, rather than on an engagement of equals with the natural world.

While the Jews are in the wilderness after their flight from Egypt, they do seem to live a curious life beyond nature, as God provides for them. Camped at the base of Mount Sinai (Numbers 9:15–18), God sits over them in a cloud, demonstrating his mastery over nature. Wherever they go, this cloud follows the Jews, and they come to realize that ultimately they must follow this cloud, camping safely beneath the protection it offers on their journey to the lands that God will give them. This story therefore presents an emblematic account of how a belief in God might supersede a trust in the order apparent in the visible natural world. The cloud is a miracle from God; and what is a miracle but a work beyond nature? As Duméry remarks (1975: 6), 'The principal discovery of the Jewish people was that history is revelatory. For all pagan civilizations it is nature and not history that reveals God and expresses the divine.' He is mainly correct when he writes (1975: 9) that:

> Judaism is a deliberate humanism, a humanism that attests that the world has not been given to man as a *natural* entity but as a *cultural* entity. As soon as nature presents itself to man, it is grasped in a human manner and is oriented towards humanity. Man appears as the great maker of sense and meaning, and the universe, so humanized, becomes the most radical, vast, and fruitful of institutions. No longer is history merely that which takes place on the world's stage; rather it is that which makes the world properly a human world.

My objection to Duméry here is that by any standards there seems to be a radical over-extension of the concepts of human agency and history, in contrast to God's will and destiny, for, while he correctly identifies the Old Testament's establishment of man's superiority over nature, the absence of God from his picture is striking.

This new relationship between man and nature is well summed up in the book of Deuteronomy (22:6–7):

> If you come on a bird's nest, in any tree or on the ground, with fledglings or eggs, with the mother sitting on the fledglings or on the eggs, you shall not take the mother with the young. Let the mother go, taking only the young for yourself, in order that it may go well with you and you may live long.

Our instinct would be to imagine that God might not allow man to take the bird, or at least to preserve its young, but man's duty is to show his place in the earthly realm. The continuation of the natural world is God's responsibility, not man's, so, while man should respect the natural world in saving the adult bird, he is required to assert his temporal mastery over nature in taking what would continue the life of the birds into the future.

As the Jews meet other people one very obvious sign of God's temporal innovations is the castigation he requires of those whose religious worship is centred on the sun and the moon. This is a faith in visible nature, but the Jews will have to develop a faith that is founded on invisibility. The notion of invisibility is of course symbolized in the use of time as the structuring mechanism in Judaism, for time is conceptual and unseen, and the Lord's use of time as this form of structuring is similarly oblique, if ever present, in the scriptures (so the use of time is like time). Such conceptualism lies in direct opposition to the claims of writers like Stern with which this chapter began.

Deuteronomy (28:12) continues to set out in great detail the manner in which the Jews can lead lives beyond nature:

> The Lord will open for you his rich storehouse, the heavens, to give the rain of the land in its season, and to bless all undertakings. You will lend to many nations, but you will not borrow.

Here we see that the Jews can rely on God's mastery of nature and his promise to them that they would be able to ignore questions of politics and economics which surrounded agricultural production, for no longer would the Jews be dependent on the harvests of others. The punishment that would face the Jews if they did not place their faith in God's mastery of nature would emerge through nature, in the form of plagues and droughts (28:24). What is more, such punishment would come in the form of nature as folk memory, as God invoked the subservience of the Jews in the past to the natural world and imperial masters, for God would bring back (Deuteronomy 28:60) 'all the diseases of Egypt.' An even greater punishment is referred to in Jeremiah (19:9), where an angry God announces that he will make the Jews 'eat the flesh of their sons and the flesh of their daughters, and all shall eat the flesh of their neighbours in the siege . . .' So, during the siege of [Judah] God will remove the natural world from the Jewish people, forcing them to resort to what is least human – the consumption of their families and their peers – as a sign that man must always recognize his place in a hierarchy determined by God.

For Bultmann it is self-evident that the forging of a new relationship between man and nature, or rather a hierarchy of man over nature, would imply a new orientation towards history, for the essential distinction he makes between truly historical cultures and mythical cultures is this dominion over nature. He writes (1957: 12) that:

> *Mythology* originated in the peoples of prehistoric times and is still alive today in primitive tribes which have no real history. Imagination is still occupied only with observation of nature in its order and regularity as well as in its astonishing and frightening consequences. Only when a people becomes a nation through its history does historiography appear.

It is for this reason that the Jews are regarded by scholars such as Bultmann as being the first people who lived in history, though, as we shall see in the Australian case, the dichotomy established here between myth/prehistory/

nature and history/historiography/man is too rigid, for historiographical consciousness is not incompatible with a faith framed around nature.

Job on time

As we have already seen, the deepest exploration of many of these ideas about time takes place in the book of Job, which is some jump in time and ethos from the world of the Torah. The final lines of his book (42:17) – And Job died old, full of days – refer to time, but they give no hint of the systematic fashion in which Job interrogated Jewish conceptions of time, questioning God's account of time and His place in it. Job's consideration of time comes in part because he is placed in a situation unlike other figures in the Old Testament, for he is tested in his battle with Satan in the wilderness, and this generates a meditation on time which questions as much as it answers. Job's anguish at God's control of the mystery of time is poetically expressed (14:5–14):

> Since their days are determined,
> and the number of months is known to you,
> and you have appointed the bound that they cannot pass,
> look away from them, and desist,
> that they may enjoy, like labourers, their days.
> For there is hope for a tree,
> If it is cut down, that it will sprout again,
> And that its shoots will not cease.
> Though its root grows old in the earth,
> And its stump dies in the ground,
> Yet at the scent of water it will bud
> And put forth branches like a young plant.
> But mortals die, and are laid low;
> Humans expire, and where are they?
> As waters fail from a lake,
> And a river wastes away and dries up,
> So mortals lie down and do not rise again;
> Until the heavens are no more, they will not awake
> Or be roused out of their sleep.
> O that you would hide me in Sheol [hell],
> That you would conceal me until your wrath is past,
> That you would appoint me a set time, and remember me!
> If mortals die, will they live again?
> All the days of my service I would wait
> Until my release should come.

We see here a summary of God's ideas of Jewish time, which then goes on to question the bases of this picture of the world. In a systematic fashion, Job sets out the connectedness of the following claims:

    i. That God is the Lord of time
   ii. That man is bound by time
  iii. The contention that God ought to leave people be in their time
  iv. That nature can be reborn
   v. Which leads us to imply that perhaps men might be reborn too
  vi. That men die, but we know not where they go
 vii. That there is perhaps a telos built into the universe, at whose end-point the meaning of life, or life after life, might be made plain: 'until the heavens are no more, they will not awake'
viii. That such ideas also imply the existence of hell
  ix. That Job might crave life after death.

As Job begins to challenge God's intellectual supremacy in questions of time, the Lord responds by asking him (38:4–8, 38:12, 39:1–2):

> Where were you when I laid the foundation of the earth? Tell me, if you have understanding. Who determined its measurements – surely you know! Or who stretched the line upon it? On what were its bases sunk, or who laid its cornerstone when the morning stars sang together and all the heavenly beings shouted for joy? Or who shut in the sea with doors when it burst from the womb?

> Have you commanded the morning since your days began, and caused the dawn to know its place?

> Do you know when the mountain goats give birth? Do you observe the calving of the deer? Can you number the months they fulfil, and do you know the time when they give birth?

In other words, in the face of Job's expression of a human agency which dares to question the post-natural miraculous settlement of time that God bestowed on the Jews, God returns to his control of natural time as a means of reasserting his dominance over Job, and over man. The hierarchy of time needs to be reclaimed, for without it the idea of God and of Judaism no longer exists. It is thus through Job that we understand how central questions of time are to the Jews. Job leads us to a set of questions which also lead us to ask how much of the new temporal offer of Christ was based on an extension of the epistemological critique of God's time provided by Job and, later, by the writer of Ecclesiastes.

As we have seen, Job acknowledges the relativity of time in the universe, for he recognizes that God and men know time in different ways (as indeed the natural world fails to know time in its lack of a conceptual understanding of things). Yet, Job conspires to turn this insight, which would suggest an acceptance of the hierarchical ordering of the universe, into a critique of God's time (24:1):

> Why are times not kept by the Almighty,
> and why do those who know him never see his days?

Where the Judaism of the Torah was built upon the certainty of God's word and a faith in his time, Job distrusts both God's word and his account of time. It is part of the gift of Job to show that these two ideas are inextricably linked.

It is not surprising that this late Jewish fundamental re-evaluation of the character of the core beliefs of the Jews has been one of the most discussed books of the Old Testament. Nineteenth-century writers such as William Henry Green were keen to see the scepticism and sophistication of Job as a foreshadowing of the themes of an immanent Christianity, noting that (1999: 165):

> It is, however, on the side of the gospel that the lessons of the book of Job chiefly lie. These are all in the direction of the ampler disclosures to be subsequently made, though of course they do not in any case pass the bounds imposed on the knowledge of God's grace for the time then present, nor do they ever anticipate in its fullness what was reserved for a brighter future.

More relevant perhaps than Green's final remark is the fact that, while Job's doubts might not be seen to wholly anticipate Christ's teachings, they anticipated in an especially full sense a sceptical Judaism in which the intellectual tools granted by God to man could be used as a manner of loosening the intellectual underpinnings of the faith. Such a view of epistemological untying is not shared, though, by recent theological accounts of Job such as that of Williams (2002) which see it as a book about the triumph of faith over questioning.

A wholly different perspective is proposed by Wilson (2006), who, with an intertextual approach which seeks to imagine the reception of Job at the time of its writing, contends that writers like Green, and indeed Williams, fail to see that Job is essentially a book driven by a double narrative. In Wilson's eyes, Job is a commentary on the popularity of messianic Jewish sects in the second century B.C.E. environment in which it was composed. For strategic and political reasons, Wilson (2006: 3) believes that the author offered general readers a 'politically and religiously correct story of a man whose perfect piety and righteousness enabled him to overcome the worst of adversities', while at the same time 'the informed reader would decipher the code and engage in a discourse based on the philosophic knowledge of his day.' This coded narrative essentially applied Aristotelian logic to the most basic principles of Judaism and it depended on a reworking of the narrative of Genesis being woven into the story of Job, so that informed readers could recognize that a fundamental questioning of Judaism, as well as messianism, was at work in the text. According to Williams (2002: 3–4), the end-points of these discussions seemed to be of great seriousness for the basic principles of the faith, for the book of Job promoted the idea of the engendering of an eternal 'tension between humanity and the Divine', though, as the author notes, even this idea could actually be reasonably comfortably recuperated into a fairly traditional version of Judaism.

In fact, the formal structure of Job invites these kinds of multi-valent interpretations of the text, as the book's narrative is structured around a series of different conversations between Job and God, Job and his companions, and a set of three epilogues in which different conclusions to essential questions are offered. As Wilson (2006: 248) notes of these epilogues:

> First, there is the monologue of the intolerant 'Elihu, a fundamentalist theist, who can brook no criticism of the Divine. [. . .] Second is the reply of YHWH to Job 'from the whirlwind' and Job's unrelenting counter-attack and rejection in response. Third is what we refer to as the 3rd Epilogue in which YHWH and Job come to a compromise of mutual recognition of each other's imperfections and their mutual need for co-existence.

Such complexities recall Newsom's remark (2003: 3) that 'Reading the book of Job has never been easy' for, as she notes, it 'lends itself well – perhaps too well – to being read in the light of shifting philosophical and hermeneutical assumptions. Its complex and elusive nature allows interpreters to see mirrored in it perspectives congenial to the tenor of their own age.' Her own recent work on Job concentrates on questions of authorship and the status of Job as a literary text. The difficulties entailed in such a study lead Newsom (2003: 16) to a fairly radical conclusion, which is that Job is essentially a book about books: a discourse on reading, genre and style, which is about both substantive questions of belief and the manner in which such questions are framed by the language that is used to describe them. In a sense, then, Newsom identifies another potential counter-text within Job that can be set alongside that of Wilson. Both seem equally convincing and the fact that this is the case serves as something of a validation of Newsom's case for, if she is correct that Job is about interpretation, then it is inherent in its very openness that it lays itself open to later interpretative strategies of very different characters (as we have seen also in Green).

Wolfers offers yet another allegorical reading of the text in which he connects modern theological reading strategies to a return to the kind of optimism found in traditional scholarship such as that of Green. Wolfers believes that Job was composed as a response and (1995: 14) 'an alternative to the existential nightmare of Ecclesiastes' in which the covenants of Exodus, Leviticus and Deuteronomy were both incorporated and reimagined for a late Jewish audience. In other words, rather than its being a case of Greek learning being deployed against Jewish tradition, Wolfers sees Job as a sophisticated attempt to revalidate the basic tenets of Judaism in the face of the Ecclesiastical tendency to imagine that new forms of learning were serving to invalidate such basic truths. The book, then, (1995: 15) 'is the veiled story of national disaster, the rupture of Covenants between the tribal desert God and His chosen people, and the trial of faith of Israel in exile which is the true theme of the book, while the superficial layer, treating of personal disaster, betrayal and temptation, is merely an exceptionally effective and compelling disguise and vehicle.' According to Wolfers (1995: 15):

> The purpose of the author in writing the Book of Job was, I believe, to redraw the nature of the relationship between the people of Israel and their God by demonstrating that the Covenants were no longer in operation, that they had been unilaterally abrogated by the Lord, or in the alternative, so transgressed by the people, that they had become inoperative. We can easily see, on reading the story with this thought as a considered possibility, that Job representing the Israelite nation, believed the betrayal to have been the Lord's, while the Lord was equally convinced that His people had deserted Him and His ways.

In fact, as I have tried to argue, if this really is the purpose of Job then it is deeply traditional in both message and form, as this contestatory description and the form in which it is relayed are after all found over and over again in the books of the Torah. My own instinct is that the purpose of the writer or compiler of Job was somewhat more radical in intent, but the critical point to make here is that all critique focuses on Job as a form of historiographical instrument, driven by new modes of thought, to re-investigate the senses of time and history that had come to represent Judaism.

III: Cultures of time

Measuring and celebrating time

Having seen the manner in which Job critiqued the Jewish temporal settlement, let us look now at the ways in which Jews embedded that settlement into their lives through the ways in which they measured time and the manner in which it was made and re-made through their rites and cultural texts.

First we might note just how time-bound everything seemed in the world of the Torah; for instance, slaves were freed after six years of service, every third year's harvest was stored in the towns (Deuteronomy 14:28), and debts were remitted every seven years (Deuteronomy 15:1). God's moral teachings were enshrined in Jewish law, and that law was framed by such time-bound distinctions. The consequences of breaking God's law were also explicitly temporal, as seen in the case of David, after he had sinned, when he was given a choice by God of three years of famine, three months of flight with foes on his tail, or three days of pestilence.

This culture of measured time included very distinct ideas of the short-, medium- and long-run. This was evident in the rites which God insisted would hold together the Jews' new calendar. The short-run was represented by the weekly sabbath, for God said to Moses (Exodus 12:14): 'This day shall be for you a memorial day and you shall keep it as a feast to the Lord; throughout your generations you shall observe it as an ordinance for ever.' The permanent duty of respecting the sabbath also meant that it could be viewed as a rite for the long-term, and one might argue that it was this dual focus of the sabbath that gave it its temporal force. Its enactment, after all, signified not only the giving of thanks in the moment, but both the recollection of times past and the assured knowledge of the continuance of the sabbath in the future, partly ensured by its present performance. As God said (Exodus 31:12–13), 'You shall keep my sabbaths, for this is a sign between men and you throughout your generations, that you may know that I, the Lord, sanctify you.'

A similar function was fulfilled on an annual basis by the month of Passover, with an even more explicit recognition of the need to keep alive the miraculous early history of the Jews (Deuteronomy 16:1): 'Observe the month of Abib by keeping the passover to the Lord your God, for in the month of Abib the Lord your God brought you out of Egypt by night.'

Where before, as we know from the descriptions of life in Egypt, the year was primarily divided by the visible changes in the natural world (with accompanying festivals and rites associated with moments such as harvests), God was determined to impose a set of rites which depended upon a faith in that which was not visible (Him, and also the past), rather than that which could be immediately perceived by man. The importance of these things to God is made plain when the Jews rebel against his order and return to the nature-based rites of the past (2 Kings 17:7–11):

> They had worshipped other gods and walked in the customs of the nations whom the Lord drove out before the people of Israel, and in the customs that the kings of Israel had introduced. The people of Israel secretly did things that were not right against the Lord their God. They built for themselves high places at all their towns, from watch-tower to fortified city; they set up for themselves pillars and sacred poles on every high hill and under every green tree; there they made offerings on all the high places, as the nations did whom the Lord had carried away before them. They did wicked things, provoking the Lord to anger.

The questions put were these: which was to be more powerful, the people's loyalty to (local) tradition or to (God's) history, to (immediate) society or to (the gift of God's) culture? The stress on the importance of the invisibility of God at work here is revealed in the claim (Deuteronomy 29:29) that 'The secret things belong to the Lord our God, but the revealed things belong to us and to our children for ever.' Judaism is a faith based on these 'secret things'.

Perhaps as a result of the element of confusion that must have arisen as to the distinctiveness of Judaism, the later books of the Old Testament also show the faith moving away from sacrificial rites. In the Torah it does seem remarkable that, for a religion that disdains the rituals and magic of other faiths, early Judaism is based more or less solely on a complex sacrifice system which binds together all the descendants of the twelve tribes as a community. Yet, by the time of Isaiah (1:11), we hear from God that he has 'had enough of burnt-offerings of rams.' Other rites based on the natural world are similarly disdained (1:13–14): 'Your new moons and your appointed festivals my soul hates.'

In terms of the playing out of God's plans for the Jews, much of this was revealed through prophecy and dreams. In part this was because it was important to God that his people's relationship with him was as an abstraction, rather than with a realised living figure (akin in many ways to his insistence that time was an abstraction). The exception to this rule was Moses, for God said (Numbers 12:6–8):

> When there are prophets among you, I the Lord make myself known to them in visions; I speak to them in dreams. Not so with my servant Moses; he is entrusted with all my house. With him I speak face to face – clearly, not in riddles; and he beholds the form of the Lord.

Prophecy and dreams are therefore kinds of riddles. They are not things that can be taken at face value and understood in an immediate fashion. They are understood when God's interlocutor is in an altered state: one of sleep or one of rapture. History itself is prophetic in this scheme of things, for all shall work towards the plans for the Jews which God has written in his book. Such ideas also lead us to qualify our description of Jewish law, for such codes could be trumped by the need for prophetic fulfilment. In Deuteronomy (20:10) the Jews learn that 'When you draw near to a town to fight against it, offer it terms of peace', yet there is an exception to this rule (20:16–17):

> But as for the towns of these peoples that the Lord your God is giving you as an inheritance, you must not let anything that breathes remain alive. You shall annihilate them – the Hittites and the Amorites, the Canaanites and the Perizzites, the Hivites and the Jebusites – just as your Lord God has commanded.

Life, death and the end

As we have seen in Job, the question of what happens at death begins to be questioned in the later stages of ancient Judaism. We have also seen the manner in which questions of burial were of great importance in the moral world of early Judaism, for their ritualization of death was critical in a religious system in which time was central. Here I want to further explore the manner by which Jewish ideas of life and death move from a didactic position that life is merely life, a gift from God, to later Jewish ideas that there is perhaps a life beyond this earth. Such ideas were logical in many ways since, although they went against the teaching of the Torah, they drew on the central features of ancient Judaism: its abstraction and its stress on time, for what could be a greater conceptual unknown than the notion of a life beyond our visible, corporeal existence?

The Torah offers a very clear articulation of the idea that life will be ended by death (Genesis 3:19): 'By the sweat of your face you shall eat bread until you return to the ground, for out of it you were taken; you are dust and to dust you shall return.' The most that men can hope for is a long life, and many exemplars are offered of those whose moral goodness led to an extension of their days on earth (1 Chronicles 29:28, Deuteronomy 6:2 and Proverbs 9:11):

He [David] died at a good old age, full of days, riches, and honour.

Keep all his decrees and his commandments that I am commanding you, so that your days may be long.

For by me your days will be multiplied, and years will be added to your life.

In addition to the hope for a long life, Jews were also able to aspire to offer their descendants good lives through their behaviour on earth. Rectitude could lead to knowledge of the continuance of the Jewish legacy, which was one of the greatest gifts that God could bestow upon man, since it showed God's willingness to use his lordship of time to promise men a kind of assured, if delayed, futurity. Such ideas are very well expressed in Psalm 103 (15–18):

As for mortals, their days are like grass; they flourish like a flower of the field; for the wind passes over it, and it is gone, and its place knows it no more. But the steadfast love of the Lord is from everlasting to everlasting on those who fear him, and his righteousness to children's children, to those who keep his covenant and remember to do his commandments.

Jews also had to be aware that such incentives were twinned with the potential wrath of God, which might be wrought upon their descendants (Exodus 20:5–6):

I the LORD your God am a jealous God, visiting the iniquity of the fathers upon the children to the third and the fourth generation of those who hate me, but showing steadfast love to thousands of those who love me and keep my commandments.

Something of a debate exists across the Old Testament as to the justice of God's punishment of children for the sins of their fathers, for books such as Chronicles (2 Chronicles 25:4) and Kings (1 Kings 21:28–29) seem to contradict God's contention that all men are responsible for the morality of their own lives:

But he [Amaziah] did not put their children to death, according to what is
written in the law, in the book of Moses, where the Lord commanded, 'The
parents shall not be put to death for the children, or the children be put to
death for the parents; but all shall be put to death for their own sins.'

Then the word of the Lord came to Elijah the Tishbite: 'Have you seen how
Ahab has humbled himself before me? Because he has humbled himself
before me, I will not bring the disaster in his days; but in his son's days I will
bring disaster upon his house.'

The construction of Deuteronomy (30:19) – Choose life so that you and your
descendants may live – in a way resolves this contradiction by suggesting that
individual behaviour leads to the judgement of God now and in the future.

The books of Job and Psalms, meanwhile, offer a range of temporal positions, in part as a means of critiquing the Mosaic picture of time and death in
Judaism, and suggestive to us of the plurality of Judaisms that must have
existed by this time. On first viewing, parts of the book of Job seem to offer a
traditional conception of Biblical time (7:7 and 10:20–22):

Remember that my life is a breath.

Are not the days of my life few? Let me alone, that I may find a little comfort
before I go, never to return, to the land of gloom and deep darkness, the land
of gloom and chaos, where light is like darkness.

Yet looked at more closely these lines are expressive of a considerable ambiguity as to the unique veracity of the traditional picture of life and death. This
uncertainty is taken further in Job's idea that he would (29:18): 'die in my nest,
and I shall multiply my days like the phoenix . . .' Leaving aside the way in
which this idea suggests the possibility of eternal life for men, Job seems to be
suggesting something of an equivalence between men and God, for it is his
agency here that creates the possibility of his days as a phoenix. The anger that
drove Job to this position is neatly complemented by a more measured line of
argument we find in Psalms (49:5–15):

Truly, no ransom avails for one's life, there is no price one can give to God
for it. For the ransom of life is costly, and can never suffice, that one should
live on for ever and never see the grave. When we look at the wise, they die;
fool and dolt perish together and leave their wealth to others. Their graves
are their homes for ever, their dwelling-places to all generations, though
they named lands their own. Mortals cannot abide in their pomp; they are

like the animals that perish. Such is the fate of the foolhardy, the end of those who are pleased with their lot. Like sheep they are appointed for Sheol; Death shall be their shepherd; straight to the grave they descend, and their form shall waste away; Sheol shall be their home. But God will ransom my soul from the power of Sheol, for he will receive me.

Here we find an exercise in logic where a central proposition, of the Bible as well as this passage, is broken down in order to be rejected. Here that proposition is the idea that men are mortal, and this is challenged in two complementary ways: first, the undermining of such ideas in the comparison of men with animals, which therefore draws upon the Bible's wider aim of establishing differences between men and nature, in the chain God–man–nature; and, secondly, the contention that it is men who cannot distinguish themselves and their culture from nature who are destined to a mortality that is a victory for the devil. Those who gamble on the transcendent qualities of man's relationship with God accept a promise of the reality of eternal life for they are willing to abandon their sensory instincts to the belief in such an idea.

Ecclesiastes

Late in the Old Testament, Qoholeth, the writer or so-called Teacher, of the book of Ecclesiastes, offers a sceptical picture of the world which is even more doubting than that of Job. It is of great value for my argument that this uncertainty is focused on questions of time. The character of the thought of the Teacher reveals tensions that had developed in Jewish thought, most especially over the influence of Greek thinking which had been absent from earlier, eastern Judaism. Indeed, the broader question of the value of the opposition of Greek cyclical views of time with Hebrew linearity and eschatology is challenged by writers such as Van Seters (Rudavsky 2000: 192). The practicalities of this struggle in late Judaism are well articulated by Whitrow (1988: 56) when he writes that:

> It is of particular interest to us today that the rivalry of Pharisees and Sadducees extended to their differing views concerning the way that time should be measured. For, whereas the Pharisees adhered to the lunar year (with intercalary months so that the agricultural year kept pace with the sun), the Sadducees adopted the luni-solar year used by the Greeks. Each sect accused the other of wishing to observe the prescribed religious festivals at the wrong times, although in practice they had to keep the same dates.

The Teacher displays both doubt and anger as to the meaningfulness of life and the manner in which people choose to find meaning in the world through the assurance of their sense of time. Such facets of (human) culture are but vanity according to the Teacher for they impute significance to that which is ephemeral and without cosmic resonance. As he says (1:2–4), 'What do people gain from all the toil at which they toil under the sun? A generation goes and a generation comes, but the earth remains for ever.'

In other words, the fatal error of men has been the construction of the idea of culture's superiority to nature, and the generation of a set of abstractions to account for the simpler truth of man's inferior position in the world of nature (1:8–11):

> All things are wearisome, more than one can express; the eye is not satisfied with seeing, or the ear filled with hearing. What has been and what will be, and what has been done is what will be done; there is nothing new under the sun. Is there such a thing of which it is said, 'See, this is new'? It has already been in the ages before us. The people of long ago are not remembered, nor will there be any remembrance of people yet to come by those who come after them.

The essence of time here is, therefore, merely a function of nature, rather than a structural gift from God. Men delude themselves in two ways in their approach to time, for they believe both that an understanding of time was given to them by God, as a means of distinguishing men from the natural world, and that their rites and temporal culture, such as the construction of histories, constitute appropriate forms of thanks to their God. The Teacher describes a determinist universe, somewhat akin to the view of time we might find in modern science, in opposition to the cosmos where God opens up the possibility of agency that we find elsewhere in the Old Testament.

The centre-piece of the Teacher's critique of Judaic conceptions of time merits being quoted in full (3:1–15):

> For there is a season and a time for every matter under heaven: a time to be born, and a time to die; a time to plant, and a time to pluck up what is planted; a time to kill, and a time to heal; a time to break down, and a time to build up; a time to weep, and a time to laugh; a time to mourn, and a time to dance; a time to throw away stones, and a time to gather stones together; a time to embrace, and a time to refrain from embracing; a time to seek, and a time to lose; a time to keep, and a time to throw away; a time to tear, and a time to sew; a time to keep silence, and a time to speak; a time to love, and a time to hate; a time for war, and a time for peace.

What gain have the workers from their toil? I have seen the business that God has given everyone to be busy with. He has made everything suitable for its time; moreover, he has put a sense of past and future into their minds, yet they cannot find out what God has done from the beginning to the end. I know that there is nothing better for them than to be happy and enjoy themselves as long as they live; moreover, it is God's gift that all should eat and drink and take pleasure in their toil. I know that whatever God does endures for ever; nothing can be added to it, nor should anything be taken from it; God has done this, so that all should stand in awe before him. That which is, already has been; that which is to be, already is; and God seeks out what has gone by.

The Teacher's appraisal of God's use of time is therefore both positive and negative. It is positive in that all should stand awestruck before God since he truly is the master of time, even if the reality of this mastery is somewhat different in its true character from the manner in which it is understood by men. God is eternal. He is time, and, while we cannot know the universe as he knows it, we can see the outlines of the principles by which he operates and arrive at some kind of conceptualization of his control of time. More negatively, the Teacher asserts that the basic ideas of time that God has given to men are only vague approximations of the kind of understanding that God could offer his followers. Men are given a sense of linear time, which offers an illusion that they live contextualized lives, yet, set against the sense of context possessed by God, it is clear that the mysteries which they will never know, let alone solve, are far greater than their narrow perception of the world understood through a local, linear sense of time. Linearity is in fact a kind of drug that dulls men's senses, allowing them to live lives of pleasure, with an illusory sense of agency seeming to mesh neatly with the discovery of linearity. In many ways these ideas – where the temporal scope of men is revealed as minuscule compared with the world of the gods – are reminiscent of the forms of chronology that we find in other religious cultures such as Buddhism.

The Teacher's picture of the world seems to draw heavily on Stoic and Cynic ideas about the logical inferences that men should draw about their behaviour after they have truly confronted questions about time and their place in the universe (3:19–22):

The fate of humans and the fate of animals is the same; as one dies, so does the other. They all have the same breath, and humans have no advantage over the animals; for all is vanity. All go to one place; all are from the dust, and all turn to dust again. Who knows whether the human spirit goes upwards and the spirit of animals goes downwards to the earth? So I saw that there is nothing better than that all should enjoy their work, for that is their lot; who can bring them to see what will be after them?

The life of pleasure to which men should aspire is very different from that described in the Torah, where much greater emphasis is placed on dutiful living, for there men are responsible through their deeds for the actualization of God's plan for the Jews on earth. They are active participants in the generation of a narrative which the Teacher views as pre-determined. Unlike Job, however, the Teacher seems unwilling to explore ideas of an afterlife as an alternative temporal possibility for men (11:8): 'Even those who live for many years should rejoice in them all; yet let them remember that the days of darkness will be many. All that comes is vanity.'

It is unclear, perhaps intentionally so, in Ecclesiastes as to whether the Teacher's encouraging men to develop a realistic appreciation of time might in fact lead to religious scepticism, for one might ask why men should devote such great resources to the construction of religious culture if such acts were essentially meaningless. It would clearly be possible to argue that the Teacher's description of a life of rejoicing militated against such an idea. The legacy of Ecclesiastes was certainly a difficult one for later Christian thinkers such as Augustine. Baillie (1950: 75) suggests that Augustine was torn in his reading of the Teacher, for he found himself unable to approve of what he believed was its cyclical, Greek account of time, yet he believed the work to have been written by Solomon and valued its status as a part of the 'Old Testament canon' (modern scholarship has ruled Solomon out as the text's author).

Later readings of the text find as wide a set of uses for its ideas as those we saw that drew on the book of Job. Let us take for instance John Cotton's 1654 *Brief Exposition with Practical Observations upon the Whole Book of Ecclesiastes*. Cotton was a Protestant minister in the American colony and saw Ecclesiastes as a powerful tool for preaching to his own exilic community, noting (1654: 3) that:

> This whole book is a Discourse not unreasonable for this Countrey, wherein men that have left all to enjoy the Gospel, now (as if they had forgotten the end for which they came hither) are ready to leave the Gospel for outward things; which are here lively and clearly demonstrated to be *vanity*, yea, *vanity of vanities*.

For Cotton, then, Ecclesiastes offered a picture of the value of pure faith and an abnegation of worldly wealth and pursuits.

More recent work has concentrated on the degree of determinism and Stoic thinking in the text (Rudman) and the question as to whether literary readings of the texts undermine or support the idea of Ecclesiastes as a sceptical text. This latter theme is a central concern of Longman III. In part, his work serves as a useful summary of existing debates on issues such as the authorship of the text, but the most interesting aspects of his work are his discussions of time and the textual comparisons with Job.

In terms of time, he notes that (1998: 33) 'As we read his reflections, we are struck by two inescapable facts of human existence that are the source of his anguish: (1) death and (2) the inability to control and know the appropriate time to do anything.' He goes on to say that (1998: 33), 'In terms of the latter, it must be remembered that it was of crucial importance for a wise teacher to know the right time. The book of Proverbs does not give a list of truths that are always, everywhere appropriate, but a series of principles that are to be applied at the right time.' Finding 'the right time' will be a means to pleasing a hard God, whose character seems as it was in the Torah, though in Qoholeth's picture of this relationship much less hope is proffered by God.

Of greater interest are Longman's speculations on the relationship between Ecclesiastes and Job. He sees the books as a pair, for, while they both engage with scepticism and appear to question the central tenets of Judaism, he believes that the structure of the two texts reveals an ultimate meaning which is much more canonical and in line with the other books of the Old Testament. Specifically, where Job (1998: 37) is structured around a dialogue between Job and his friends, in which Job's doubting can be collapsed and rejected in conversation and through the appearance of God, Longman believes that Ecclesiastes is an instructive text (1998: 38) 'concerning the dangers of speculative doubting wisdom in Israel.' In his mind, it is important to concentrate on the rejection of such doubting in the final lines of the book, where we read (12:13–14): 'The end of the matter. All has been heard. Fear God and keep his commandments, for this is the whole duty of humanity. For God will bring every deed into judgement, including every hidden thing, whether good or evil.' These, according to Longman, are the words of a teacher who has used Qoholeth as a case study in the dangers and consequences of certain kinds of thought and a valorization of the superiority of orthodoxy. To my mind there is, however, a certain amount of wishful thinking in believing that the sustained attack on ancient Jewish certainties can be so easily dismissed through the assertion that this was a textual strategy and through a reliance on marginal voices from this particular work.

IV: Histories

Historical modes

So what does this long and detailed account of time in the Old Testament tell us about the text as a history and about the narrative modes it describes for exploring the past? We have already seen that there is a great variety of historical styles found in the text, from the stress on genealogies and chronology in the early part of the Torah, to the philosophies of history and time that we find in later books such as Job and Ecclesiastes. We have also seen the manner in which such narratives were in some ways connected to the specificity of the situation of the Jews at the time when they were written, whether they served as forms of social assurance and cohesion in books such as Chronicles or doubting of Jewish society in Ecclesiastes.

There are also at least six other distinct forms of historical/temporal narrative in the text that I should like to enumerate briefly.

First, in Deuteronomy (25:17–19), history is described as being akin to a form of erasure:

> Remember what Amalek did to you on your journey out of Egypt, how he attacked you on the way, when you were faint and weary, and struck down all who lagged behind you; he did not fear God. Therefore when the Lord your God has given you rest from all your enemies on every hand, in the hand that the Lord your God is giving you as an inheritance to possess, you shall blot out the remembrance of Amalek from under heaven; do not forget.

Here God seems to be saying that history is not just a process of remembering, but for the Jews it must also entail forms of systematic forgetting. Amalek's story needs to be kept alive to perform a religio-social function while God takes the Jews to their promised land, but once there they have a duty to forget Amalek. Interestingly, God shows no capacity to make the Jews forget this, for he demands that they make this forgetting themselves as a part of their culture.

Secondly, the Old Testament offers what could be considered to be emblematic forms of colonial and post-colonial history. Such narratives are played and replayed in different historical circumstances, and often explicitly connected together by the writers of the Old Testament. In Joshua (23:12), for instance, we read the following admonition to the Jews:

> For if you turn back, and join the survivors of these nations left here among you, and intermarry with them, so that you marry their women and they

yours, know assuredly that the Lord your God will not continue to drive out these nations before you; but they shall be a snare and a trap for you, a scourge on your sides, and thorns in your eyes, until you perish from this good land that the Lord your God has given you.

The Jews therefore are encouraged by God to become as the Egyptians were to them, necessarily demonstrating their superiority and ethnic singularity in order to keep the motor of God's linear design running.

Thirdly, there are many examples of cyclical forms of historical patterns throughout the text, as seen in the above example and also in the books focusing on kingship where there is evidently a cyclical logic to the order in which poor, disobedient kings are followed by kings who seem to understand God's will and his word.

This is also seen in the manner in which seminal and mythical events in the Jewish past are replayed in the later books of the Bible or, we might say, the narrative structures and framing of those events are deployed as a manner of understanding very different events in time. In Isaiah (11:1) we read that 'there shall be a highway from Assyria for the remnant that is left of his people, as there was for Israel when they came up from the land of Egypt,' while Jeremiah's vision (4:23–27) of a cleansing apocalypse is very much akin to that described in the story of Noah:

I looked on the earth, and lo, it was waste and void; and to the heavens, and they had no light. I looked on the mountains, and lo, they were quaking, and all the hills moved to and fro. I looked, and lo, there was no one at all, and all the birds of the air had fled. I looked, and lo, the fruitful land was a desert, and all its cities were laid in ruins before the Lord, before his fierce anger. For thus says the Lord: the whole land shall be a desolation; yet I will not make a full end.

Here it is not simply the idea of a civilizational end that is recuperated from Exodus but also the notion that the Jews' God does not believe in the idea of a full telos but a form of purge that is not a 'full end'.

Fourthly, we find the idea of revisionist history and counterfactuals, for, as the editor of the NRSV says (1995: 495):

The purpose of 1 and 2 Chronicles, like that of 1 and 2 Kings, is theological and idealistic. There is practically no attempt to present history as we understand the word. The Chronicler wishes to advocate a certain pattern of religious life for his own day, and to indicate what a proper kingdom of his people under God would be like. He does this by describing the reigns of

David and Solomon in particular, not as they actually had been, but as they ought to have been. David, especially, is highly idealized, and becomes the real founder of the temple and its ritual.

Some might argue that what we in fact find here is a template for History *per se*.

Fifthly, and relatedly, many narratives of the past have performative and literary functions, for they constitute a rich part of Jewish culture. The valorization of such culture was well expressed by David (1 Chronicles 16:7–18):

> O give thanks to the Lord, call on his name, make known his deeds among the peoples.
> Sing to him, sing praises to him, tell of all his wonderful works.
> Glory in his holy name; let the hearts of those who seek the Lord rejoice.
> Seek the Lord and his strength, seek his presence continually.
> Remember the wonderful works he has done, his miracles, and the judgements he uttered, O offspring of his servant Israel, children of Jacob, his chosen ones.
> He is the Lord our God; his judgements are in all the earth.

In other words: recount his history, in narrative and performance, remember the miracles of history, you chosen people, for he is universal, while our history is a pact, which comes from his word, and will go on forever. Later in the Book of Job we read that one of Job's greatest longings is for his trials to be captured for later generations (19:23–27) – O that my words were written down! O that they were inscribed in a book! – for it is absolutely clear that for Job's message to have resonance in Judaism it must be recorded and disseminated.

Sixthly, the Old Testament also includes descriptions of the practice of history, most especially the ways in which archives and sources were used in the production of narratives of the past. Debates exist, indeed, as to whether it was truly figures such as the (NRSV Bible 1995: 330) compiler of 1 Samuel who merits the title 'the father of history', rather than Herodotus, who wrote five hundred years later. As Brandon says (1965: 106):

> Among the sacred literatures of mankind that of the Hebrews is distinguished by its concern with what purports to be historical fact. Not only does a large part of the constituent documents take the form of a historical narrative, but in almost every other writing of the corpus reference is constant to certain notable events of the nation's past.

We see something of the mechanics of historical production in books such as 1 Kings (16:5) where readers are advised that their knowledge of the lives of particular kings can be supplemented by looking at 'the Book of the Annals of the Kings of Israel', which served as a source text for books such as 1 Kings. The variety of texts that could be available to the historian are described in the following passage, which follows the death of Josiah (2 Chronicles 35:25–27):

> Jeremiah also uttered a lament for Josiah, and all the singing-men and singing-women have spoken of Josiah in their laments to this day. They made these a custom in Israel; they are recorded in the Laments. Now the rest of the acts of Josiah and his faithful deeds in accordance with what is written in the law of the Lord, and his acts, first and last, are written in the Book of the Kings of Israel and Judah.

So the chronicler of the life of Josiah has access to a variety of sources, which includes specific, recorded versions of speeches by named figures and oral traditions, as well as a compendium text where Josiah's life is recorded along with those of other kings.

More detailed accounts of historical processes can be found in Ezra and Nehemiah. In Ezra (4:11–16) something which purports to be a primary source is included in the text, and this itself cites other sources as a means of establishing its authority. This is the letter from the Samarians and others to the Persian king:

> To King Artaxerxes: Your servants, the people of the province Beyond the River, send greeting. And now may it be known to the king that the Jews who came up from you to us have gone to Jerusalem. They are rebuilding that rebellious and wicked city; they are finishing the walls and repairing the foundations. Now may it be known to the king that, if this city is rebuilt and the walls finished, they will not pay tribute, custom, or toll, and the royal revenue will be reduced. Now because we share the salt of the palace and it is not fitting for us to witness the king's dishonour, therefore we send and inform the king, so that a search may be made in the annals of your ancestors. You will discover in the annals that this is a rebellious city, hurtful to kings and provinces, and that sedition was stirred up from within it from long ago. On that account this city was laid waste. We make known to the king that, if this city is rebuilt and its walls finished, you will then have no possession in the province Beyond the River.

Here the Jewish text includes the Samarian source, which itself demands that the Persian king consult the sources to be found in his own annals, so that he might establish the cyclical qualities of history, which will lead him to take action against the Jews. The Persian king agrees to the Samarian demand, once he has consulted the historians at his court, for (Ezra 4:19) 'someone searched and discovered that this city has risen against kings from long ago, and that rebellion and sedition have been made in it.'

The only means by which the Jews can counter the legitimacy of this proxy attack on their rebuilding of Jerusalem is by recourse to the same methods as the Samarians. They, therefore, also call on the Persians to search through their archives to discover whether the Jews' actions are legitimate or not (Ezra 5:17 and 6:1–3):

> And now, if it seems good to the king, have a search made in the royal archives there in Babylon, to see whether a decree was issued by King Cyrus for the rebuilding of this house of God in Jerusalem.

> Then King Darius made a decree and they searched the archives where the documents were stored in Babylon. But it was in Ecbatana, the capital in the province of Media, that a scroll was found on which this was written: 'A record. In the first year of his reign, King Cyrus issued a decree: Concerning the house of God at Jerusalem, let the house be rebuilt.'

The truth of the archives is the trump card for the Jews, for the Persians are unwilling to challenge the legitimacy of the past. Even in a case of politics and diplomacy, history serves as a form of contract that cannot be broken.

When Jerusalem is being rebuilt it is again necessary for the Jews to return to their historical texts in order to understand how it ought to be reconstituted (Nehemiah 8:13–14 and 7:5):

> On the second day the heads of ancestral houses of all the people, with the priests and the Levites, came together to the scribe Ezra in order to study the words of the law, which the Lord had commanded by Moses, that the people of Israel should live in booths during the festival of the seventh month.

> Then my God put into my mind to assemble the nobles and the officials and the people, to be enrolled by genealogy. And I found the book of the genealogy of those who were first to come back . . .

Here there is a very clear sense that the new Jerusalem must be a form of reimagination of the old city, which, in spite of the radically different political and social circumstances of these new times, must be re-made according to the old laws and genealogies, as though now was then.

We should not assume that all such appeals to archival truth are necessarily straightforward. In the Book of Esther, which is something of a template for myths, fairytales and other fictional forms, we read (6:1–2) of the night when:

The king could not sleep, and he gave orders to bring the book of records, the annals, and they were read to the king. It was found written how Mordecai had told about Bigthana and Teresh, two of the king's eunuchs, who guarded the threshold, and who had conspired to assassinate King Ahasuerus.

Here the annals and book of records referred to are not texts of the distant past, as was the case in Ezra and Nehemiah, but writing contemporaneous with this narrative in which King Ahasuerus finds himself threatened by court rivals. What the king finds in the text is a vindication of one of his courtiers, who had saved his life. Yet, no indication is given as to why the king could only discover this information through a historical search, nor why a narrative was being written in the midst of this crisis.

What the passage provides is an interesting metaphor relating to historical production, nonetheless, which applies to the Old Testament more generally, for what we see is the manner in which actions and chronicling coincide temporally, as the narrative significance of events is being constructed as those events are lived (where they may not seem to have the coherence and sense of structure that we find in their literary representations). The text we read of here is a text, we might assume, that is written by God, for it is God whose narration accompanies our every deed and idea in the world. The sanctity of this particular narrative is ensured by the creation of the new festival of Purim as a means of remembrance of what happened in the Book of Esther – the only major Jewish festival that is not derived from the time of the Torah.

Jewish linearity and Greek cycles

One of the areas in which modern Biblical scholarship has most shifted our view of the Old Testament has been in the area of the reputed divide between Jewish linear time and Greek cyclical time. Detailed studies, such as that of Brettler, have revealed a series of cyclical ideas that run through and across the books of the Old Testament. For example (2004: 118):

Cycles predominate in the book of Judges, appearing in all sections of the book. The book's author clearly believed that history repeats itself and in that sense believed in cyclical time. Events are like the seasons and times of Ecclesiastes, like the weather of ancient Israel noted in Jeremiah, which has a clear structure, though it is open to internal variation. Similarly, the judges are all depicted in a similar fashion, though they do not all behave in exactly the same manner or defeat the same enemy.

Given my stress on God's desire that the Jews see history as a settlement beyond the time of nature, I would regard such cycles (and there are many more) as indicative of the central temporal tension I have described as structuring the text of the Old Testament, in which the Jews struggle to accept the more abstract and conceptual notion of linearity when faced with neighbouring peoples and their own practices, which stress a more understandable sense of cyclical and natural time.

In some senses, then, the attempt to break free from nature is God's insistence that the Jews break away from cyclical time, yet this is also present in ritual and genealogy which appear to be very important in God's definition of Judaism. We must also be careful not to assume that Jewish borrowing from Greek culture was ineluctably drawn towards its cyclical picture of time, for if we take, for example, the books of Job and Ecclesiastes, we certainly find a challenge to the traditional Jewish picture of time but not one that is dependent on the idea of cycles' superiority over linearity.

Bultmann (1957: 18) has stressed that one of the great differences between the historical cultures of the Greeks and the Jews was that the former was primarily concerned with things that were seen and the latter with the imagination of God's plan of time. For the Jews (1957: 18):

> The experiences of men are understood as divine ordinances, as blessings or punishments of God, and their deeds as obedience or disobedience to the commandments of God. Israelite historiography is therefore not science in the Greek sense. It is interested not in knowledge of the immanent powers working in history but in the intention and plan of God who as creator is also the ruler of history, and leads it to a goal. As a result the idea of the organisation of history grew up. History as a whole is understood as articulated in periods or epochs which each have their importance for the whole structure. [. . .] If there is an interest in knowledge, it is in self-knowledge, and the historian calls his people to self-knowledge in reminding them of the deeds of God in the past and of the conduct of the people.

The immanence of Bultmann's picture of time is extended in his work to suggest that the Bible also contains intimations of eschatology. In early Judaism this eschatology, such as that we find in Daniel and the many (1957, 27–28) 'predictions of salvation and doom', is in effect 'ornamental' for it describes God's judgement for the Jewish people rather than for the world as a whole. In later Judaism, however, cosmology, according to Bultmann (1957: 29), 'was historicised by substituting the destiny of humanity for that of the world.' Relying especially on a reading of Ezra, Bultmann asserts that late Jewish thought was directed towards the coming of a Messiah and a prefiguring of a Christianity whose dominant temporal motif was eschatological.

This view is, however, strongly rejected by scholars such as Brettler, partly on the basis of the translations which are accorded to 'eschatological' remarks, which Brettler suggests rest upon an etymological confusion in which the finality of 'ending' is not as great as writers such as Bultmann suggest. In fact, given this confusion, Brettler claims (2004: 123) that, when Bultmann and others see eschatology, what is really being described is a form of cyclical thought in which texts 'that describe the future often do so in terms of the past', suggesting forms of recurrence or cycles.

Conclusion

As we have seen, the Old Testament is a rich source of temporal language, genres and tropes. While it is apparent that there are certain key structures in Jewish time – such as the privileging of cultural over natural understandings of time – it is also evident that there is a huge variety of temporalities in the text, in part because aspects of Judaism evidently changed over time. In this conclusion, therefore, I intend to open out my discussion rather than closing it down, by looking at warped and psychoanalytical temporalities in the Old Testament.

By warped temporalities, I mean descriptions of time whose strangeness seems to deny rational explanation, or where understanding now seems impossible at our distant remove from the time of the Bible. The first comes from Job (8:8–9), the second from Isaiah (21:11–12):

> For inquire now of bygone generations, and consider what their ancestors have found; for we are but of yesterday, and we know nothing, for our days on earth are but a shadow.

> The oracle concerning Dumah. One is calling me from Seir, 'Sentinel, what of the night? Sentinel, what of the night?' The sentinel says: 'Morning comes, and also the night. If you will inquire, inquire; come back again.'

In the first of these verses Bildad's ideas seem to accord with Job's cynicism, for he contends that the life we live now is but a parodic recreation of lives lived in the past: those of bygone generations, and the ancestors who came before them. The idea that we are but the people of yesterday can be interpreted in at least two fashions, for it could mean that God's plan for the world is a cyclical one where men are denied individuality and originality, or it could suggest that, far from negating natural ideas of time, God's world is utterly predicated on biological determinism, for we find ourselves constrained by the limits of our nature. Yet the idea that 'our days on earth are but a shadow' is a mysterious one. Does it mean that we are destined to live shallow, inconsequential lives or does it hint at a truer existence in a life to come? Is this ambiguity intended to be productive in the minds of its readers?

In the verses from Isaiah, a potent set of terms associated with forms of time are run together: the oracle, the night, and the morning. The oracle seems to be in the process of explaining the mystery of time as it relates to the making of days and nights, but there is a poetic lack of clarity in the words here, for we are unsure if the structuring of such things is played out in the words of the passage, or whether the reader/interlocutor really is invited to come back again, perhaps after a period of reflection, to learn more of this mystery.

There are strong elements of mystery and the fantastic in what I call the psychoanalytical temporalities of the Bible. Reading the Old Testament, one can only express surprise that it was not until the twentieth century that a science of psychoanalysis came into being, for the raw materials for such a study of man are apparent throughout the text. On a simple level this is evident in many of its complex family stories, such as 1 Samuel's account of the relationship of Saul and David, along with its accompanying cast of sons, daughters, grooms and brides who come to belong to the families of both men – leaving aside the dynamic in their relationship that derives from their respective attempts to be close to God.

It is the emotions of God, and the manner in which his emotions direct his behaviour towards the Jews, that offer the most compelling case for a distinct genre of psycho-history being found in the Bible (for I am not simply arguing that the Old Testament is a rich resource for psychoanalysts, but that it itself contains such modes of temporal analysis). This is best seen in the books of Jeremiah and, here, Job, where we learn of God that (12:23): 'He makes nations great; then destroys them.' In Psalm 106 (40–41) we read descriptions of the faithlessness of the Jews who rejected God's offer: 'Then the anger of the Lord was kindled against his people, and he abhorred his heritage; he gave them into the hand of the nations, so that those who hated them ruled over them.' How, we might ask, can the Lord abhor his own heritage? What does this say about God's relationship with the Jews, about the idea of the Jews as a family, and indeed about God's selfhood, and the question as to why that selfhood is so intimately tied to the heritage of the Jews (when it is made plain here that the fates of other nations also lie within God's dominion).

The language of betrayal used to describe the behaviour of the Jews becomes more clearly sexual in the Book of Jeremiah (3:6 and 3:8–9):

> The Lord said to me in the days of King Josiah: Have you seen what she did, that faithless one, Israel, how she went up on every high hill and under every green tree, and played the whore there?

> Yet her false sister Judah did not fear, but she too went and played the whore. Because she took her whoredom so lightly, she polluted the land, committing adultery with stone and tree.

In the second of these passages, it is remarkable that Judah's infidelity is described as being 'with stone and tree.' What we will have guessed is that this refers to the people's betrayal of God's sense of time being dependent upon his will and the culture he has given to the Jews. The Jews have reverted to the temporal system of the nature-worshipping tribes among whom they lived, and they have now ceded their right to be seen as the children of God. It is noteworthy that this discussion takes place at the level of concepts and generalities – the nation, nature, time – for the importance of the lesson is revealed in this manner. Such lessons are stressed throughout Jeremiah, where we learn (3:23) that 'Truly the hills are a delusion, the orgies on the mountains'; in other words, the behaviour of the Jews was worse than we might have first thought for it is not just the case that they engage with the realities of nature as a means of communing with actualities, as opposed to the concept of God, for they also show a willingness to delusionally venerate the concept of nature itself.

If Christianity was to be a religion that deployed forms of dialectical ambiguity in order to take its adherents to a position of convinced belief, in events, ideas and things that needed to be cast from the imagination and from faith, then Judaism was arguably a faith whose great strength lay in its failure to resolve its central debates about time. The depth of questioning that we find in Job, Psalms and Ecclesiastes comes from a dynamic within Judaism very different from that of Christianity, for where Christian dialectics could be resolved in the life of Christ, Jews pushed their debates about faith, nature and time ever onwards into deeper and more sceptical logics. The intellectual ambition of Judaism ensured that for more than a thousand years, in which the books of the Old Testament were written, its uncertain social and political status was mirrored in a set of debates about time which also embraced uncertainty and never sought an easy accommodation with their god and with dissent.

The new times of Christianity

Introduction

This chapter looks at time and history in Christianity. It concentrates on a close reading of the New Covenant, better known as the New Testament, of the Bible. The chapter begins by looking at the manner in which time is key to Christian epistemology, before moving on to look at the ways in which the Bible describes Christianity as struggling to both attach itself and release itself from its Jewish past. We shall then look more closely at the way in which the New Covenant proposes an 'end of days' and the status of this eschatological theory within the variety of temporal assertions found in the text.

A central problem that we find in Christian theology is that the importance of questions of temporality was so great that it is sometimes relatively easy to lose sight of the particularities of the New Testament's pictures of time, as compared with, say, the formation of early medieval Catholic orthodoxy or the hermeneutic revolution in twentieth-century Christian theology. Probably the best known Christian disquisitions on time are those of Augustine – 'What is time? When nobody is asking me, I know what it is, but when I try to explain it to somebody who asks me, then I don't know?' (Pannenberg 1970–71: 62). While these remarks are often admired for their mysteriousness I aim to show that a much clearer picture of time and history, or set of pictures, can be recovered from the New Testament. These later obfuscating factors were enhanced by the fact that the central question that different branches of the Christian church have posed is this: what time? What time, in terms of the arrival of the Parousia, what time with regard to the relationship between the times of the world and the times of heaven, and what time in terms of the moment of the history of the faith on which good practice should be modelled.

Reading the New Testament

Before moving on, it is important to say a few basic things about the act of reading the New Testament, for it can be too easy to gloss and to find coherence where what one actually sees is ambiguity and disjunction. First, the New Testament is a compilation of texts written by a series of authors over a period of around a hundred to a hundred and twenty years. Secondly, the text is divided into a series of twenty-seven books, the purpose and style of which vary greatly. These books can be grouped into five sets of writing: the four Gospels which consist of descriptions of the life of Jesus by his disciples, the letters of the disciple Paul to fellow believers in the early Church, the letter to the Hebrews which attempts to resolve the nature of the connection between Christianity and Judaism, the letters of other early believers, and, lastly, the 'Revelation to John'. Thirdly, not only were these texts written at different times by different people, but they also appear in a number of genres – letters, histories, revelations, biography – and were evidently written with diverse audiences in mind.

The raising of such questions leads us to a very important basic truth about the New Covenant: it is a book written for readers, or listeners, and those readers are encouraged to construct a truth from the narrative which – in its experience in space, time and the physical act of reading and turning pages – is mirrored in the manner in which, it is hoped, that a truth emerges in the reader as the Word fills them. John offers a rare moment of self-referentiality which makes this point well (20:30–31):

> Now Jesus did many other signs in the presence of his disciples, which are not written in this book. But these are written so that you may come to believe that Jesus is the Messiah, the Son of God and that through believing you may have life in his name.

John asks the reader here to recognize that the New Testament is not the sum of Christian knowledge, but to appreciate the exemplary quality of its narratives, their generic purpose, and the effect which they ought to have on the reader.

Wittgenstein (1980: 31e) argued that this was the purpose of the writing of the Gospels, for

> God has *four* people recount the life of his incarnate Son, in each case differently and with inconsistencies – but might we not say: It is important that this narrative should not be more than quite averagely historically plausible

just so that this should not be taken as the essential, decisive thing? So that the *letter* should not be believed more strongly than is proper and the *spirit* may receive its due. I.e. what you are supposed to see cannot be communicated even by the best and most accurate historian; and *therefore* a mediocre account suffices, is even to be preferred.

Reading the Bible was therefore intended to be a dialectical process whereby contradictions in the text were resolved in the mind of the reader, who became the synthesis of these textual theses. In a range of areas – on the relationship between Jesus and God, between Judaism and Christianity, between Jesus' church and that of Paul – the reader of the Bible is required to find a position which they themselves *believe* and it is this belief that they take from the text that then constitutes their faith. Such constructive ambiguity is not unknown among other religions which also possess holy books that demand a certain dialectical spirit of reading, but no faith remains as wedded to this method as closely as Christianity. I hope that this chapter manages to convey something of the intricacy and complexity of ideas of time in the New Covenant, for it is arguable that one of the great diminutions of western culture has been the too easy acceptance of accounts of time and history from the Bible which reflect later critics' and institutions' need for simplicity, clarity and teaching, when the temporal achievement of Christianity lies beyond such virtues.

Compared with the millennium covered by the Old Testament, the century or so in which the books of the New Testament was composed – from the First Letter to the Thessalonians written in 50 C.E. to the Second Letter of Peter from about 150 C.E. – was a relatively curtailed time-period, as was the relative brevity of the historical moment described, beginning with the life of Jesus, and moving through the times of Mark, John, Paul and the early Hellenistic Christians. Given that many fundaments of the church were not yet founded or construed in this period, and given the doubts, gaps and ambiguities that lay within what would later be called 'Christianity', it is not surprising that many theologians' accounts of Christian history, time and culture are determined to stretch the phase of early Christianity to, at the very least, the fourth or fifth centuries C.E. My view is that what such approaches gain in their increased capacity to describe a faith that appears whole and coherent, they lose in terms of their ignoring of the choices and ambiguities of the New Testament that were eventually superseded in the teachings of the Church. Similar arguments have of course been made from the earliest Christian moment to the present, beginning with the Gnostics who tried to shift Christianity away from institutional ritual to a mysticism founded on the figure of Christ, and existing right up to the present day with the revisionist Gospels movement which seeks equal status for many of the other lives of Christ written in the early years of the religion.

In all these discussions we need to remember that compared with the Torah there are great omissions in the formation of early Christian culture: things about which we know little, where speculation would obviously be needed to fill gaps in the faith. There is, for instance, no use of the term 'history' in the New Testament, yet we do not hesitate to attempt to reconstruct its picture of history. Conversely, as I have intimated, there is much that is present in the New Testament that was later ignored in institutional Christianity.

The modern movement of Christian hermeneutics has been centrally concerned with such questions and with the enterprise of affording a set of connections across time so that the words of the New Testament might be read as they were intended to be understood. The problem with such an enterprise is revealed, I think, when we read O'Donnell's remarks (1983: 26–27) on understanding: 'How are we to understand this "bridge" between what has been said in the past and what must be said today if Christian faith is to be adequately expressed? Certainly it is inadequate merely to repeat past formulas.' Why, we ought to ask, is it 'inadequate to merely repeat past formulas?' Such a response is based upon notions of anthropology and progress that would be utterly alien to most religions (the Australian Dreamtime and Buddhism come particularly to mind), though an analogous case can be found in the strictures on reconstruction in Wahhabi Islam. O'Donnell goes on to explain that (1983: 27) 'the conviction commonly held in the science of hermeneutics is that dogmatic texts do not speak for themselves but rather must be seen as answers to questions', so the task of the theologian is the recreation of the culture in which original questions were formed, so that he can extrapolate in order to find answers that are temporally appropriate to his own moment. Yet what this method and its theory of the manner in which culture and texts operate in time ignore is both the rich culture of time described in the New Testament and what God and Jesus had to say about understanding and working in time. Is it because they had so much to say about time that easier orthodoxies needed to be found? Better, it seems to me, to follow Begbie (2000: 272) in his conclusions as to the lessons that music has taught him about the interpretation of the text:

> The temporal wave-patterns of music not only provide a singularly powerful resource to uncover and understand the multi-levelled momentum of promise and fulfilment in the biblical narrative, they also deliver us from pernicious single-levelled, single-line modes of temporality which obscure this momentum.

This is not to say that modern Christian theology has not added a great deal to our understanding of the value of the New Testament as a book about time and history, particularly, as we shall see, in the case of German scholarship of the twentieth century. There is, for instance, the hugely productive dialogue that took place between writers such as Barth and Bultmann and their nineteenth-century forebears who saw it as their mission to use the new science of history in order to definitively uncover the story of 'the historical Jesus'. In doing so, Braaten remarks, they (1968: 55) 'wanted a kind of photographic replica of Jesus which could be had, it was assumed, by wiping away the filmy coatings that later tradition had placed upon him', and the failure of that quest led dialectical and existential theologians to ask the more radical question as to how much historical knowledge they need to still see Christianity as a religion built on faith. For Bart (Braaten 1968: 55), 'there is no good reason why historical research should go chasing the ghost of a historical Jesus in the vacuum behind the New Testament'. This is extended still further in the work of Bultmann for whom, as Käsemann remarked (Braaten 1968: 70), 'Jesus Christ has become a mere saving fact and has ceased to be a person. He himself has no longer any history.' For Bultmann a faith in the *kerygma*, in the Easter faith and the truth of the resurrection was a far more compelling tool for Christians than setting themselves up in a competition of historical facticity in which the revelatory truth of Christ was ignored or dissipated.

Temporal grammar

The New Covenant is a text with an epistemological purpose. It is a foundation for things to come, and as such it articulates very particular claims regarding basic questions about the world: Who are we? Who am I? Why are we here? What is meaning? What has been? What will come? The text sets out answers to these questions in the form of assertions which, once learnt, and embedded in a culture, can always be relied upon and thus lie unquestioned. The answer to the first of these questions, for instance, is that we are human. We are human in contradistinction to being animals or being God. When we wake up in the morning we do not begin by questioning our humanness, for we know that we are human. This is a given that allows us to engage in other activities in our lives.

Assertions, then, become assumptions, and it is often difficult for later cultures to come back to rediscover assumptions when they were unfixed, when they competed with other choices as possible truths. The job of the epistemologist is a hard one, as Wittgenstein (1972: 56e) observes, for it involves unlearning some of our most basic assumptions:

> What we have to mention in order to explain the significance, I mean the importance, of a concept, are often extremely general facts of nature: such facts as are hardly ever mentioned because of their great generality.

The New Covenant aims to develop a rich epistemology whose complexity and scale later become forgotten, for so many of the questions that it answers then blend into the basic beliefs that we all have about ourselves and the universe (and thus hermeneutics seeks to recover that culture of questions). Children, of course, need to be taught these things, for there is no doubt that epistemological presumptions are culturally inculcated, and indeed there are times when even these claims find themselves open to challenge, as we shall see was the case in the Enlightenment, or, in an analogous case, in the Islamic philosophy of Ibn Rushd.

The centre-piece of Christian epistemology is time, and westerners perhaps owe their lack of interest in the concept of time to the depth that Christian temporal ideas penetrated their culture. Later we will look in more detail at specific ideas of time in the New Covenant, but let us now consider the place of time in epistemology and the manner in which it can serve as the core of the Christian ideology, setting it apart from competing approaches to the world. One could just as easily frame an epistemology around a conception of being or space as one could around time, but there is no doubt that the New Covenant is centred on ideas of time. Man is, man is in a particular space, but this is given meaning by the idea that men and things change, through time. God's world is not one of stasis, but one of change, where it is of critical importance that durations are measured: God made the world in seven days, Jesus, and earlier Elijah, went to the wilderness for forty days and forty nights, and three days after his execution Jesus rose from the dead.

As we have seen in the previous chapter, the writers of the Bible took an aspect of life that in many ways was perceived as being natural – time, given its intimate connections to agricultural production and the sanctification of such production in myth-based religions – and framed their faith around what might be called the grammar of human life. I use the term 'grammar' intentionally for it was through language that systems of time had become so rooted in human culture. However, the writers of the New Testament not only adopted this temporal grammar, which they knew in Judaism, as the foundation of their faith – for all potential believers were already naturally fluent in its forms – but they also extended and created new ways of describing time.

In many ways the Christian approach to time was wild and exuberant in its originality. While it could operate in wholly conventional ways, it also twisted and reimagined ideas of time through notions of prophecy, reincarnation, pre-destination and an end of days. It was the simplicity of these new formulations that partly generated their appeal. Let us consider Jesus' statement in John (8:59) that 'Very truly, I tell you, before Abraham was, I am.' Another way of putting this would be to say 'I am the Son of God', but it is through the rupturing of conventional temporal grammar that this claim gains its meaning. We know that it is not possible for the present to be before the past. We could accept Jesus saying 'I was before Abraham', but the message conveyed through temporal grammar here is that believers need to recalibrate their sense of time so that they can truly accept the Christian offer of faith. In terms of its use of language to induce a new way of seeing the world, it is as revolutionary as later philosophical claims, such as Rimbaud's 'je est un autre', which rupture conventional uses of language to claim new, basic truths about the human condition.

The New Testament is full of such reimaginings of time through grammar. The effectiveness of this strategy is enhanced in parts of the text that combine both conventional grammar and new castings of time. Thus in Romans (8:28–30), Paul says:

> We know that all things work together for good for those who love God, who are called according to his purpose. For those whom he foreknew he also predestined to be conformed to the image of his Son, in order that he might be the firstborn within a large family. And those whom he predestined he also called; and those whom he called he also justified; and those whom he justified he also glorified.

Here the language of time begins in the present, switches to the idea of pre-destination, moves to a simple past, and then intertwines predestination with an account of what actually happened in the past. We are also introduced to the idea that there is not a universal experience of time in Christianity, for here God's understanding of time is described as being omniscient. Elsewhere that of Jesus is cast as all-knowing, with clear distinctions also established between the understanding of time available to believers (faithful readers) and non-believers.

A centre-piece, a godhead if you like, of Christian epistemology is its continuation and development of the Jewish valorization of spiritual time over biological time. Biological death is constantly challenged across the New Testament: through miracles, in the life of Jesus and his resurrection, and through the stress on the offer of life after death that is open to all believers. Christian life and time operates in the future conditional, as James (4:13–15) suggests:

> Come now, you who say, 'Today or tomorrow we will go to such and such a town and spend a year there, doing business and making money.' Yet you do not even know what tomorrow will bring. What is your life? For you are a mist that appears for a little while and then vanishes. Instead you ought to say, 'If the Lord wishes, we will live and do this or that.'

The words 'If the Lord wishes, we will live' do not of course refer to our earthly existence, but to a promised, future, life after death. Christian life, then, is not truly concerned with biology and materiality but with the moral world of our earthly behaviour and its connection to our future life after death. What we see therefore is and is not, for it has meaning in terms of its future judgement, but it cannot be said to be what really is, for that is the predicated time (and life) to come.

In this sense, Christian time is deeply anti-linear in its opposition to biological time, and it is also suggestive of the operation of a very fluid sense of history as compared with the empirical brand of thinking about the past that dominates in the modern world. It is critical, therefore, that throughout the Bible proofs are offered that biological time is not superior to other ways of conceptualizing temporality. The superiority of the Christian method in terms of conceiving of both time and space is strongly asserted by Jesus in John (8:14–15 and 8:23):

> Even if I testify on my own behalf, my testimony is valid because I know where I have come from and where I am going. You judge by human standards.

> He said to them, 'You are from below, I am from above; you are of this world, I am not of this world.

History, then, also acquires meaning as destiny and as a form of judgement. Its purpose is the judging of souls to assess whether they are deserving of eternal life, of living beyond human history. Jesus and God's mastery of time enables them to move between old days and new times in a manner which assures men that their immediate apperception of time (from, for example, the changing of the seasons around them) is but one of the modes of time that exist in our lives. Faith is the belief in that which is not obvious, and a belief in the otherness of God's time is one step towards a life of faith: in other words, the Jewish valorization of the invisible over the visible.

In order to un-pick the complexities of temporal representation in the New Testament, I now want to discuss nine specific forms of temporal grammar found in the text:

1. Christianity's connections to Jewish time and the Old Testament
2. Moltmann and the Trinity
3. Ritual and time
4. Prophecy
5. Miracles and the resurrection
6. The end of time
7. Historical writing in the Gospels
8. Paul's history in his letters
9. Metaphors and dreams.

Christianity and Jewish time

As I have already intimated, the New Covenant offers different answers to what might be regarded as foundational questions. With regard to the question of whether Christianity should be considered as a new religion or a reformist Jewish sect, let us compare the first lines of the books of Matthew and Mark. Matthew describes his book (1:1) as being 'An account of the genealogy of Jesus the Messiah, the son of David, the son of Abraham', whilst the first lines of Mark (1:1) announce 'The beginning of the good news of Jesus Christ, the son of God.'

In temporal terms, the difference between these two visions could not be greater. Matthew's account not only attempts to situate Jesus in a line of Jewish prophets, but he announces that the mode of writing he will deploy to establish this claim is genealogy, the archetypal historical mode of analysis of the Torah, with its obsession as to lineage and a route to the origins of the faith. Mark, on the other hand, stresses not the past and continuity but a 'beginning' in which Jesus is not situated in a line of Jewish prophets, but directly referred to as the Son of God: the advent of a new beginning for a soteriological history.

It is not my intention here to offer resolution as to which of these visions offers the truer path for Christianity, but simply to explore in more detail the differences between these two temporal stances. In many ways, of course, this discussion offers another example of the productive ambiguities of the Bible which afford plural understandings of the text. This will also inform my discussion of Paul's history later in this chapter.

The genealogical idea is followed by a number of the writers of the New Testament. Luke, for example, launches into a long account of Jesus' provenance that begins (3:23–25): 'He was the son (as was thought) of Joseph son of Heli, son of Matthat, son of Levi, son of Melchi, son of Jannai, son of Joseph, son of Mattathias, son of Amos, son of Nahum, son of Esli, son of Naggai . . .' Such writing expresses a very particular inclination towards time for it suggests that Jewish history is being invoked so that it can be made clear that Jesus will fulfil Jewish time, that he will take his rightful place in the line of prophets whom God sent to the Jews and he will thus make good the lives of the Jews as other prophets such as Moses did (and as is intimated in Hellenistic readings of later books of the Old Testament). It is for this reason that Mark (11:10) reports that people greeted Jesus with cries of 'Blessed is the coming kingdom of our ancestor David!'

Jesus himself articulates a still more sophisticated version of this idea of his place in a line of Jewish prophets and his role in continuing Jewish history (John 5:45–47 and Luke 24:27):

'Do not think that I will accuse you before the father; your accuser is Moses, on whom you have set your hope. If you believed Moses, you would believe me, for he wrote about me. But if you do not believe what he wrote, how will you believe what I say?'

Then beginning with Moses and all the prophets, he interpreted to them the things about himself in all the scriptures.

In the first of these extracts, what Jesus expresses through metaphor is the idea that religious belief comes from the individual's faith in the ability of prophets to live and act beyond conventional understandings of time. Not only this, but there is also a conflation of self and text in the idea that belief in the written word of Moses equates to the believer's apprehension of the spoken word of Jesus. In some senses, then, this is not just a statement of the idea that the time before (of Judaism) was a preparation for the time that was to come (that of Jesus), but also that, in future days, believers ought to recall that reading the word of the text (the New Covenant) should be seen as equivalent to hearing directly the words of Christ. On a simpler level, these extracts also express the idea of predestination, with intimations that happenings in time amount to the playing out of the plans of God. Moses and the other prophets wrote of the life of Jesus before he was to come, for this was destined through the will of God.

We will go on to consider in more detail the question also raised here as to whether either Jesus (as described in the Gospels) or Paul saw Christianity as being a faith distinct from Judaism, but let us look briefly at a description of the New Covenant. This comes from the Book of Hebrews (8:7–13), which is an especially significant part of the Bible for it serves as a form of intertext between the Old and New Testaments, interpreting each in the light of the other (its authorship is unclear, though I agree with those who contend that Paul was most certainly not its author):

> For if that first covenant had been faultless, there would have been no need to look for a second one. God finds fault with them when he says: 'The days are surely coming, says the Lord, when I will establish a new covenant with the house of Israel and the house of Judah; not like the covenant that I made with their ancestors, on the day when I took them by the hand to lead them out of the land of Egypt; for they did not continue in my covenant, and so I had no concern for them, says the Lord. This is the covenant that I will make with the house of Israel after those days, says the Lord: I will put my laws in their minds, and write them on their hearts, and I will be their God, and they shall be my people. And they shall not teach one another or say to each other, "Know the Lord", for they shall all know me, from the least of them to the greatest. For I will be merciful towards their iniquities, and I will remember their sins no more.' In speaking of 'a new covenant', he has made the first one obsolete. And what is obsolete and growing old will soon disappear.

This covenant, then, is clearly one which is connected to Jewish history, yet it amounts to God's desire to rupture the first narrative of man's redemption, which is now considered to be 'obsolete' and will thus disappear. Instead, God proposes a new pact with man, or rather with 'the house of Israel', which will combine God's forgetting of his earlier pact with the Jews with a jettisoning of the memory of the sins of the living people with whom God will now be enjoined. Christian history in this model, in contradistinction to Jewish genealogical thinking, is not a question of recording the legitimacy of lines of familial and national descent, but instead of conceiving of the life of the individual as a new start, neither blessed nor burdened by the memories of past times.

Interestingly enough, this new beginning offered in the exemplary life of Christ itself must recede into a past, even if it is available afresh to future generations. Baillie takes this idea as a means of arguing (1950: 68) that Christianity borrows from the Hebrew model of time, but with the key difference that:

> The turning point of history, which had hitherto been in the future, is now in the past – a fact soon to be signalled by a new system of dating which counted all earlier years backwards from Christ's advent, and all later years forwards from it. The new age of which the prophets had spoken had now actually dawned, and the Christian church was living in it.

Yet, I think that the flow of Christian time was of a slightly more complex order than Baillie perceives, as had been that of Judaism. Jewish time had, after all, referred in one and the same move to a story of origins and genealogies oriented towards the past and a coming day of judgement, whilst Christianity was able to look back to the life of Christ in comfort only because the spirit of that life was to be made available in future times.

Such questions of time also have a profound influence on the question of who can be a Christian. If the New Covenant is read following the line that it proposes new times that run counter to the Jewish history of the Old Testament, then it can also be seen as the offer of a view of time that is universal and therefore open to all across the world. As Peter says (Acts 10:34–35), 'I truly understand that God shows no partiality. But in every nation anyone who fears him and does what is right is acceptable to me.'

Old Testament distinctions between the Jews and the Gentiles are therefore undone, for, as Acts (11:18) says, 'they praised God, saying "Then God has given even to the Gentiles the repentance that leads to life".' As the New Testament unfolds, the geographical scope of the religion represented expands towards Asia, Arabia, the Balkans, north Africa and southern Europe, and it is often the Gentiles of Rome and Greece who become most committed to the new faith. At one point Paul and Barnabus conceive of Christianity as marking a distinct split with the Jewish people, saying (Acts 13:46–47):

> It was necessary that the word of God should be spoken first to you [Jews]. Since you reject it and judge yourselves unworthy of eternal life, we are now turning to the Gentiles. For the Lord has so commanded us, saying, 'I have set you to be a light for the Gentiles, so that you may bring salvation to the ends of the earth.'

Such rhetoric also of course accords with our understanding of the life of Jesus recounted in the Gospels and, in particular, the role that is played by the Pharisees and the narrow-minded leaders of the Jews who clearly fail to see Jesus' light and his offer of eternal life. Yet, elsewhere in the New Covenant, there is a more flexible approach to the place of the Jews in this new world. In Romans (3:29–30) Paul asks:

> Or is God the God of Jews only? Is he not the God of Gentiles also? Yes, of Gentiles also, since God is one; and he will judge the circumcised on the ground of faith and the uncircumcised through that same faith.

Ultimately Christian universalism does need to be absolute (as indeed some have argued was the case with Judaism). While Christians' lack of adherence to Jewish law does not preclude them from God's gifts, nor are Jews completely lost to God in spite of their failure to abide by his covenants, and the preordained role that they play in the death of his son.

Similarly, it is not the case that the Jewish prophetic heritage is utterly abandoned by the writers of the New Testament. Books such as Acts are full of references to the Old Testament and the idea of intertexts between the Old and the New was clearly of great importance to many of the early Christian writers. Often these references are of course directed at potential Jewish converts. Let us set beside each other two verses from Acts (3:22–24 and 17:11–12):

> Moses said, 'The Lord your God will rise up from your own people a prophet like me. You must listen to whatever he tells you. And it will be that everyone who does not listen to that prophet will be utterly rooted out from the people.' And all the prophets, as many as have spoken, from Samuel and those after him, also predicted these days.

> These Jews [in Beroa] were more receptive than those in Thessalonica, for they welcomed the message very eagerly and examined the scriptures every day to see whether these things were so.

Here, then, we read that the New Covenant is the fulfilment of what had been prophesied in the Old Testament, and that potential Jewish converts to Christianity looked precisely for such textual forewarning in their assessment of the validity of the claims of Christians. As Bultmann remarks (1957: 35), 'The Old Testament was read in the first place not as a historical document but as a book of revelations, as a book of the promises now fulfilled. It is now possible for the first time to know the meaning of Israel's history and the words of the Old Testament.' Indeed, reading the Gospels' life of Christ seems at times like an exercise in Ricœurian repetition since so many key aspects of the life of Jesus had earlier been plotted in the story of Elishah, from his miraculous feeding of large groups of the hungry, his healing of the leprous, his itinerant life, the miracles of the creation of life, his disciples, his descriptions of something akin to a heaven on earth (Isaiah 60:18–22), and his being referred to as 'the man of God' (2 Kings 6:6).

Moltmann and the Trinity

This relationship between the early Christians and the texts of the Old Testament has been of great importance to Moltmann and other scholars of the

Trinity, for such theologians stress the comparative lateness of the formulation of definitive ideas of the Trinity – in the fourth and fifth centuries C.E. – and its being foreshadowed by intimations of such ideas in the Old Testament. In O'Donnell's words (1983: 29), what such Christian thinkers seek to show is that while 'Judaism' was 'radically monotheistic' God himself may have been 'by no means monistic'. Moltmann's 'messianic dogmatics' see the Trinity as (O'Donnell 1983: 109) 'the path from history to freedom' (O'Donnell 1983: 109), in which God moves beyond a portrayal of his simplicity and perfection to a more nuanced Trinitarian perspective in which he is able to know and love man.

For Moltmann, the Old Testament needs to perform this function as a forerunner to the New Testament because it hints at the ultimate meaning that Moltmann imputes to the moment of the crucifixion, the event around which all time, human or divine, is centred. As O'Donnell explains (1983: 111–12):

> We have seen that the context of Moltmann's thought is the suffering of the world. Man finds himself over against a world which appears to him godless and unredeemed. But an adequate anthropology cannot contend itself merely with these two terms, man and world, for precisely what mediates the relationship of man and world, subject and cosmos, is history. If then there is any answer to the cry of man in the face of the unredeemed character of the world, it must be found in history. And this is precisely the key to the Christian understanding of God. The Christian account of God has its origins in an historical event, more precisely in the event of the cross. In this slice of history God encounters man in his suffering and death, even in his God-forsakenness. Moltmann contends that when this history is adequately interpreted – and that means theologically interpreted – it is seen to be nothing less than the history of God himself. And in this historical event God shows himself to be the trinitarian God, i.e. this history is itself the event involving Father, Son and Holy Spirit.

Time is made meaningful in the actuality of the crucifixion, which also reveals the truth of the Trinitarian relationship that God is able to offer man. History in this sense is not a process or a form of progress but a precise location of an event which serves as a form of ultimate meaning for man. It is extraordinarily similar to Australian beliefs about the rupturing moment of the Dreamtime, and one suspects that Moltmann and other Trinitarian thinkers would be deeply impressed with the manner in which Australian cultures have constructed the whole of their faith around this moment in time and the modes of ritual and thinking which can recreate and re-reveal its significance.

In some senses, though, (O'Donnell 1983: 130) 'the radicality of Moltmann's position' of 'God in history and history in God' is not quite as extreme as O'Donnell believes, for we may well recall that in the Old Testament God was by no means always a figure of stasis and otherworldliness: at times his actions bore the marks of precisely the kinds of human emotions that could drive him to anger and revenge, and there is a constancy across the Old Testament, from the Torah to the doubts of Job and Qoholeth, in which Jewish thinkers conceived that they could have a personal dialogue with God, not simply as servants or tools of his will, but as interlocutors entitled to challenge and question God's picture of the universe.

In Moltmann's thought, however, the moment of the revelation of the Trinity through the crucifixion is actually a stage in the fulfilment of Christianity (for it not to be might be a more radical move, I would suggest), since the Trinity is bound to a literalist eschatology. As O'Donnell explains (1983: 136):

> The goal of history then coincides with the completion of God's own history, that is, the eschatological glorification of the Trinity. This will come to pass when the mission of the Son and the Spirit is accomplished and the kingdom is handed over to the Father. In this moment the seeking love of the Father which begot the replying love of the Son finds its completion in the replying love of the whole of creation through the Son and the Spirit. In this sense the fulfilment of the mission of the Trinity *ad extra* is not only a functional completion but the ontological completion of the persons of the Trinity themselves, and thus the completion of the life of the Trinity *ad intra* as well.

Yet, if the doctrine of the Trinity really is critical to the distinctiveness of the Christian offer, it is arguable that a consideration of its incompleteness – which was after all what first recommended it to Moltmann as a message for men – possesses as great an ontological value as the neatness of this eschatology. This incomplete Trinity addresses the question for Christian theology identified by Peters (1997: 263), namely: 'how can an eternal God act, and be acted upon, in a temporal universe?' As he remarks, 'What makes this problematic within Christian theology is the habit in the classical tradition of understanding eternity to be the polar opposite of time. Eternity is said to be timelessness. In time, things pass.'

Ritual and time

Ritual and time are intimately connected in almost all religious cultures since organized rituals give sense to the meaning of time and the place of both the individual and the collective in time. Yet, in most parts of the New Testament there is a fairly clear rejection of the place of ritual in faith and the construction of temporal meaning through rites. In most cases, this is justified on the grounds that ritual often tends to serve as a substitute for true faith, because a special temporality is accorded to moments of ritual that supersede the acts of everyday time.

Thus it seems significant that Jesus rejects the particularity of the Jewish Sabbath and this is accorded a critical place in the case made against him, as John (5:15–16) says after one of Jesus' miracles, 'The man went away and told the Jews that it was Jesus who had made him well. Therefore the Jews started persecuting Jesus, because he was doing such things on the sabbath.'

The rite of circumcision and its place in Judaism is a subject which Paul returns to time and time again (Romans 2:25 and 2:28–29):

> Circumcision indeed is of value if you obey the law; but if you break the law, your circumcision has become uncircumcision.

> A person is not a Jew who is one outwardly, nor is true circumcision something external and physical. Rather, a person is a Jew who is one inwardly, and real circumcision is a matter of the heart – it is spiritual and not literal. Such a person receives praise not from others but from God.

This is suggestive of a powerful idea of privacy within Christianity, whereby the truth within the individual and their relationship with God is prized over public protestations of faith or ritual worship. As Paul also says (Romans 2:16), 'God, through Jesus Christ, will judge the secret thoughts of all' (though this could be seen as making reference to the Old Testament claim in Deuteronomy 29:29 that 'The secret things belong to the Lord our God').

This also leads Paul (1 Corinthians 8:7–10) to oppose food offerings as a form of idolatry, and in Galatians 4:8–11 there is a very revealing set of criticisms of pre-Christian ritual:

> Formerly when you did not know God, you were enslaved to beings that by nature are not gods. Now, however, that you have come to know God, or rather to be known by God, how can you turn back again to the weak and beggarly elemental spirits? How can you want to be enslaved to them again? You are observing special days and months, and seasons, and years. I am afraid that my work for you may have been wasted.

What is especially interesting here is Paul's condemnation of rites that associate faith with natural cycles and biological time. He describes this as a form of enslavement and is emphatic that this bondage is made evident through the construction of systems of temporal understanding: 'special days and months, and seasons, and years.' In his letter to the Galatians he displays an understanding of the powerful hold that such sanctification of natural time had on people, and it was not therefore surprising that the later Church would develop a calendar and a set of rites which also borrowed such concepts in their construction of an everyday architecture of time for believers.

The beginnings of such developments are indeed apparent in Paul's letters, most especially in his valorization of the act of communion (1 Corinthians 10:14–17):

> Therefore my dear friends, flee from the worship of idols. I speak as to sensible people; judge for yourselves what I say. The cup of blessing that we bless, is it not a sharing in the blood of Christ? The bread that we break, is it not a sharing in the body of Christ? Because there is one bread, we who are many are one body, for we all partake of the one bread.

The act of communion is therefore contrasted favourably with 'the worship of idols', yet it is not quite clear how this rite of anamnesis is intrinsically superior to those rituals rejected by Paul. Communion enacts the universal cosmology of Christianity, and is therefore not as centred on the local individual as previous practices, but communion is nevertheless hard to distinguish from all that Paul rejects most fiercely.

It should not then surprise us that the pivotal rite adopted for new entrants to the church – baptism – is also focused on the idea of time. The idea of baptism had of course already existed in Jewish culture, but it was invested with new significance by John and Jesus who extended its meaning from the marking of time in the life of a newborn to an avowed statement on the part of believers that they rejected a time of sin (their old life) and embraced a time of repentance (after baptism). The first of these times of course meant that man was locked on to the path of biological time, but baptism gives man access to everlasting, spiritual time.

Prophecy

Prophecy also forms a key part of the New Covenant's cosmology. In essence prophecy describes a mastering of time, for the prophet is able to describe the future as well as they can depict the past or the present. Time operates in a continuum for the prophet since notions that time is divided make no real sense in this state of knowledge.

The life of Jesus was one that was full of prophecy of different kinds. First, there were Jesus' references to the Jewish prophets who had described his life and the way he would be treated on the earth. These were prophecies that were destined to be fulfilled through him – 'the plan of the mystery hidden for ages in God who created all things' (Ephesians 3:9) – and they serve to show the productive relationship between the Old and New Testaments. Peter extends even this intertext saying (1 Peter 1:20): 'He was destined before the foundation of the world, but was revealed at the end of the ages for your sake', claiming that the prophetic destiny of Jesus was ordained even before the events described in Genesis at the start of the Old Testament.

The complexity of this sense of fulfilment is made plain in the final verses of Luke's Gospel (24:44–46) which describe Jesus' return from the dead:

> Then he said to them, 'These are my words that I spoke to you while I was still with you – that everything written about me in the law of Moses, the prophets, and the psalms must be fulfilled.' Then he opened their minds to understand the scriptures, and he said to them, 'Thus it is written that the Messiah is to suffer and to rise from the dead on the third day . . .'

A whole variety of forms of prophecy that warp conventional understandings of time are made apparent here. First, there is Jesus' referencing of his own prophecies of how things would come to pass; secondly, there is his assertion that he was right to invoke the prophecies of the Old Testament; and third there is his living embodiment of the claim that the Messiah would rise on the third day. We should also note that these claims are framed in a text that also serves as an exemplar of the routine disruption of temporal grammar in Christian writing, as evinced in the statement: 'Then he said to them, "These are my words that I spoke to you while I was still with you",' which moves from a description in the simple past to a present-tense articulation of past events that defies logic, since the past he describes is also one the disciples see standing before them in Christ's body.

The second form of prophecy is seen in the way that Jesus' life was full of predictions where he announced things that would come to pass, such as Judas's betrayal of him (John 13:21) and Peter's denial of him (John 13:38, John 6:71). This shaping of events through Jesus' understanding of his destiny often, of course, needed to be explained to his disciples. Thus in Matthew (16:21) we learn that:

> From that time on, Jesus began to show his disciples that he must go to Jerusalem and undergo great suffering at the hands of the elders and chief priests and scribes, and be killed, and on the third day be raised.

The sense in which Jesus is also an author of time comes across even more strongly in Matthew's (3:13–15) account of the meeting of Jesus and John the Baptist:

> Then Jesus came from Galilee to John at the Jordan, to be baptized by him. John would have prevented him, saying, 'I need to be baptized by you, and do you come to me?' But Jesus answered him, 'Let it be so now; for it is proper for us in this way to fulfil all righteousness.'

The critical word in this passage is of course 'would', for in its incongruity it demonstrates very clearly to us the manner in which Christ's notion of 'fulfilment' trumps all other conceptions of time.

This idea of fulfilment, and of Jesus living in a world of the fulfilment of time among men without his innate understanding of such things, comes across in John 7:30–31 where we read that 'they tried to arrest him, but no one laid hands on him, because his hour had not yet come.' This duality of fulfilled time is made still more plain in Jesus' own words, where he said (John 7:6–8):

> My time has not yet come, but your time is always here. The world cannot hate you, but it hates me because I testify against it that its works are evil. Go to the festival yourselves. I am not going to this festival for my time has not yet fully come.

There is something enigmatic about the first sentence of this passage. The first clause is readily understandable, but the idea that man's time is 'always here' could be interpreted in a number of ways: it could simply mean that men live on the earth and will continue to do so, it could mean that the offer of spiritual time is always available to men on earth, or it could also be read as meaning that man's destiny is fulfilled on earth, and not in the place that Christ will go to when his time comes.

The third mode of prophecy in the New Testament is that found in the Revelation to John, the book which closes the Bible. Here we learn that the art of prophecy does not end with Jesus, but is found after his life on earth as it was before, and can thus be expected to play a part in later Christian cultures. John's Revelation gives us greater access to the work of God as opposed to the rest of the New Testament's concentration on the life of Christ. Thus we learn (16:12) of God's power in fashioning the world so that the story of his son might be told: 'The sixth angel poured his bowl on the great river Euphrates, and its water was dried up in order to prepare the way for the kings from the east.'

The character of God and the reality of a life among angels in Heaven are also vividly described in this book whose tone is much more akin to the Old Testament than the rest of the New Covenant. It combines a claim (16:4) to the timelessness of God – You are just, O Holy One, who are and were – with the idea that earthly time will come to an end (22:7–13):

> 'See I am coming soon! Blessed is the one who keeps the words of the prophecy of this book. I, John, am the one who heard and saw these things. And when I heard and saw them, I fell down to worship at the feet of the angel who showed them to me; but he said to me: 'You must not do that! I am a fellow-servant with you and your comrades the prophets, and with those who keep the words of this book. Worship God!'
>
> And he said to me, 'Do not seal up the words of the prophecy of this book, for the time is near. Let the evildoer still do evil, and the filthy still be filthy, and the righteous still do right, and the holy still be holy.
>
> 'See, I am coming soon; my reward is with me, to repay everyone according to everyone's work. I am the Alpha and the Omega, the first and the last, the beginning and the end.'

In John's prophecy we encounter a much more personal God who, as a being, serves as a master and lord of time, being 'the first and the last, the beginning and the end'. This strand of prophecy is one that unites all previous prophetic declarations – in the Old Testament, in the Gospels and Paul's letters – to point to an imminent end in which judgement is arguably already pre-ordained, for the evildoer is to be allowed to continue to do evil and it is only the righteous and the holy who will be saved.

Miracles and the resurrection

What we might call a family relation of prophecy is the miracle, whose chief purpose also seems to be the demonstration that Christian time supersedes or defeats biological time. The life of Christ, after all, begins with the miracle of Mary's pregnancy and Jesus' birth, where the will of God is shown to trump what would otherwise be seen as the 'laws of nature'. And just as Christ's life begins with a miracle that defeats nature, his life also ends, through the resurrection, in just such an event.

The Gospels are full of stories of Jesus miraculously bringing the dead back to life, and it is clear that this was one of his chief means of describing the message of Christianity. The bringing back to life of an individual served a wider purpose in symbolizing the life after death that would be open to all those who followed Jesus' teachings. As the New Covenant says (Matthew 16:24–26, John 8:51, 2 Corinthians 4:11–12):

> Then Jesus told his disciples, 'If any want to become my followers, let them deny themselves and take up their cross and follow me. For those who want to save their life will lose it, and those who lose their life for my sake will find it. For what will it profit them if they gain the whole world but forfeit their life? Or what will they give in return for their life?'

> Very truly, I tell you, whoever keeps my word will never see death.

> For while we live, we are always being given up to death for Jesus' sake, so that the life of Jesus may be made visible in our mortal flesh. So death is at work in us, but life in you.

Christians therefore must live their lives counter-intuitively, understanding that 'life' is not that which is seen and is related to the biological world, but is in fact that which comes through death. What is conventionally understood to be the end of life is in fact its beginning. The leap of faith that Christians need to make to believe in this is provided through the analogous miracles performed by Christ through his life, in which he showed that he and his father had a power over earthly lives which revealed such lives as beginnings.

The true life that is available to those who reject death is of course heaven, which as I have said is principally described in the book of Revelation. This realm is also mentioned by Paul in the letter to the Romans (8:18), where heaven is contrasted with earth in the way that Jesus compared life with death: 'I consider that the sufferings of this present time are not worth comparing with the glory that is about to be revealed to us.'

This stoic attitude towards the sufferings of the present, in the knowledge of the goodness that is to come – seen also in Christ's suffering on the cross – was especially articulated by Paul, and would arguably become one of the most controversial aspects of Christian theology and politics. If, for instance, life on earth has little meaning compared with the life that is to come, should Christians simply accept the injustices and hardships of their earthly existence, confident that such travails, if endured with grace, only increase their chances of true life after death?

This question was clearly a critical one in the early church since it appears in many forms across the New Covenant, mostly in relation to the question as to whether slaves should suffer their bondage on earth, or whether they should seek their freedom. Paul and Peter are adamant that slaves ought to take the first of these options, and that in doing so they are increasing their prospects of eternal life (1 Corinthians 7:21–24, 1 Peter 2:18–21):

> Were you a slave when called? Do not be concerned about it. Even if you can gain your freedom, make use of your present condition now more than ever. For whoever was called in the Lord as a slave is a freed person belonging to the Lord, just as whoever was free when called is a slave of Christ. You were bought with a price; do not become slaves of human masters.

> Slaves, accept the authority of your masters with all deference, not only those who are kind and gentle but also those who are harsh. For it is to your credit if, being aware of God, you endure pain while suffering unjustly. If you endure when you are beaten for doing wrong, where is the credit in that? But if you endure when you do right and suffer for it, you have God's approval. For to this you have been called, because Christ also suffered for you, leaving you an example so that you should follow in his steps.

Bultmann's vision of eschatology (1957: 36) very much follows this line, with his assertion that because '*The new people of God* has no real history, for it is the community of the end-time, an eschatological phenomenon', 'no social programme can be developed but only negative ethics of abstinence and sanctification', for 'the Old Testament commands remain in force, along with additional commands of Stoic philosophy.'

Yet many theologians have argued that such claims in this regard need to be interpreted in the light of the political environment in the Mediterranean world in which Christianity emerged. Christianity, it needs to be recalled, was a revolutionary sect that faced an array of powerful enemies in the form of the Jewish religious hierarchy, the Roman empire, and local political leaders such as Herod of Judea. Given the appeal of Christianity to many of the poorest in that world, with its universal promise of salvation which seemed to negate the value of riches accumulated on earth, it was necessary for the early church to also adopt a quietist politics that sought accommodation with authoritarian political rule so as to ensure the continuation of the greater good, which was the spread of the message of Jesus through the church.

Yet, this was not a view that was universally held within the church, nor later theology, and was attacked on the basis that it contravened the ethics of justice, freedom and care which were articulated in the life of Jesus, which emphasized that a form of liberation ought also to be promoted on earth as it would be in heaven. As John says (1:13–14), 'Do not be astonished, brothers and sisters, that the world hates you. We know that we have passed from death to life because we love one another. Whoever does not love abides in death.'

Quietism also, of course, contradicted one of the central themes of the Old Testament, which was God's desire to free the Jews from slavery, and for his chosen people to live unburdened by the yoke of political control by forces directly analogous to those which Paul and Peter would encourage subservience. There is also a case that such advice encouraged men away from a life like that of Christ for it implied that a form of perfection could be aspired to on earth, which seems both unrealistic and unlike the life of Christ as described in the Gospels, which is not one without human emotions of anger, bitterness and pride.

When the resurrection is described, great emphasis is placed on the interpretation of this event that will come in the future, and the role that will be played by the texts written by those who witnessed Christ's return from death. Perhaps more than any other event in Christ's life the resurrection is described as an experience which is a message, which needs to be understood individually by believers. Thus, while Thomas sees the resurrected Christ, Jesus offers a special blessing to those 'who have not seen yet have come to believe' (John 20:26–29):

> A week later his disciples were again in the house, and Thomas was with them. Although the doors were shut, Jesus came and stood among them and said 'Peace be with you.' Then he said to Thomas, 'Put your finger here and see my hands. Reach out your hand and put it in my side. Do not doubt, but believe.' Thomas answered him, 'My Lord and my God!' Jesus said to him, 'Have you believed because you have seen me? Blessed are those who have not seen and yet have come to believe.'

In this sense Christianity seems a rather different faith from Judaism, for where Jews were oriented towards a series of events that were to come in the future (the last prophet, the day of judgement), Jesus understood that in many ways his church would be a historical institution, where believers had to have faith in an event that had taken place before they were born. Christian history, then, must be a narration of truth, and special praise is offered to those who believe without seeing, and what we really witness here is a summation of one of the temporal innovations of Christianity: namely the idea that Christian belief is to surrender one's material apperception of the world, which offers plural temporalities, in favour of a continuum of time in which that which is not seen in either the past or the future is as real as that which the individual sees in their present. As Cullmann puts it (1962: 32–33) in his soteriological study:

The unique element in the Christian conception of time as the scene of redemptive history is of a twofold character, and we desire to distinguish the two sides by treating them separately [. . .] In the first place, salvation is bound to a *continuous time process* which embraces past, present and future. Revelation and salvation take place along the course of an ascending time line. Here the strictly straight-line conception of time in the New Testament must be defined as over against the Greek cyclical conception and over against all metaphysics in which salvation is always available in the 'beyond,' and we must show how according to the Primitive Christian view revelation and salvation actually 'occur' in a connected manner during the continuous time process. In the second place, it is characteristic of this estimate of time as the scene of redemptive history that all points of this redemptive line are related to the *one historical fact* at the mid-point, a fact which precisely in its unrepeatable character, which marks all historical events, is decisive for salvation. This fact is the death and resurrection of Jesus Christ.

Yet this continuum of time, as experienced by the believer, must also coexist with an understanding that God and Jesus are masters of time (1 Corinthians 15:20–26):

> But in fact Christ has been raised from the dead, the first fruits of those who have died. For since death came through a human being, the resurrection of the dead has also come through a human being; for all die in Adam, so all will be made alive in Christ. But each in his own order: Christ the first fruits, then at his coming those who belong to Christ. Then comes the end, when he hands over the kingdom to God the Father, after he has destroyed every ruler and every authority and power. For he must reign until he has put all his enemies under his feet.

It is also worth noting that the spirit of the description of Christ and earthly political powers, and their fate, is remarkably unlike the tentative attitude towards such powers earlier described in Paul and the other Fathers' attitudes towards slavery.

The idea of a temporal continuum also emerges in the story of Lazarus, whose metaphorical power is of a high order (John 11:20–27):

> When Martha heard that Jesus was coming, she went and met him, while Mary stayed at home. Martha said to Jesus, 'Lord if you had been here [conditional], my brother would not have died. But even now I know that God will give you whatever you ask of him.' Jesus said to her, 'Your brother will rise again'. Martha said to him, 'I know that he will rise again in the

resurrection on the last day.' Jesus said to her, 'I am the resurrection and the life. Those who believe in me, even though they die, will live, and everyone who lives and believes in me will never die. Do you believe this?' She said to him, 'Yes, Lord, I believe that you are the Messiah, the Son of God, the one coming into the world.'

What is of great significance here is that Martha uses the present continuous form of the verb 'to come' to describe Christ's life and his resurrection. Again the essential message of Christianity – that Christ was, is and will be, for he is a continuum – is articulated through the temporal grammar of the text. What is more, it is the conditional tense of earthly, biological existence and history ('if you had been here') that is so easily vanquished by the master of spiritual time.

The end of time

It should already be clear that to be an early Christian was to believe in a complex set of beliefs about time. Taken individually, these ideas may not have seemed at such a variance with Jewish or pagan cultures, but considered together they amount to a new worldview. A critical part of this stance was the idea that time would end and that there would be a day of judgement for all men – the temporal schema described as eschatology. However, Christian eschatology as it is described in the Bible is a rather more complex and ambiguous phenomenon than it may have seemed to some later Christian cultures.

The theme of eschatology has been central to the modern theological enterprise. In the 1950s von Balthasar described (Hayes 2000: 11) it as the 'storm center' of theology in acknowledgement of its importance and the variety of positions held by different theologians as to its significance. More recently (Hays 2001: 115) Käseman declared that 'apocalyptic is the mother of all Christian theology.' Braaten and Jenson write (2002: vii) that 'The twentieth century will be remembered in the history of theology for its rediscovery of the centrality of eschatology in the message of Jesus and early Christianity. But it reached no consensus on the shape and meaning of eschatology.' They note that this process began with Schweitzer's *The Quest of the Historical Jesus* of 1910 and Barth's remark that 'Christianity that is not entirely and altogether eschatology has entirely and altogether nothing to do with the life of Christ.' In 1957 Bultmann (31) felt certain enough of the accepted centrality of eschatology to write that:

Today it is commonly accepted that the reign of God which Jesus pro-
claimed is the eschatological reign. The only point in dispute is whether
Jesus thought that the reign of God was immediately imminent, indeed
already dawning in his exorcisms, or whether he thought that it was already
present in his person – what today is called 'realised eschatology'.

Such a claim stressed the radical shift that Protestant theology had initiated
with regard to traditional understandings of eschatology (Braaten: 1968), for
it proposed to replace Kant's idea of the kingdom of God as 'an ethical commonwealth gradually coming to perfection in history through love and moral
actions' with a return to a much more literal idea of a cataclysmic end and a day
of judgement. In tracking this shift, Braaten has identified five distinct schools
of modern Protestant eschatological thought. The first (1968: 162) is that of
consistent eschatology, seen in the work of Schweitzer and Werner, in which
Christian thought was seen as a continuation of late Jewish intimations of
ending. Second (Braaten 1968: 163), realized eschatology, as seen in Dodd
(1963), saw Christ describing not a future event but 'introducing the Kingdom
then and there.' Third (Braaten 1968: 165), there were the Heilsgeschichte
eschatologians, such as Jeremias, Kümmel and Cullmann, who combined 'the
present and future elements in the teaching of Jesus about the Kingdom.'
Fourth (Braaten 1968: 166), the existential position of Bultmann develops
realized eschatology to argue that 'To the eyes of faith any moment could
be the fullness of time', for all authentic decision-making on the part of the
individual is eschatological. Finally (Braaten 1968: 172–73), the dialectical
eschatology of early Althaus and Barth contended that 'Eschatology has nothing to do with the end of history, only with the eternal transcendental meaning
of each moment in history.'
     What is clear from Braaten's helpful parsing apart of these positions is that,
while some stand in opposition to each other, some are intimately related differences of interpretation. Indeed, if one were to look at the development
of the work of a number of the theologians mentioned, one would find shifts
between positions across their careers. My task here is to set out a comparison
of their claims through a consideration of the texts of the New Testament,
but also to offer some sense of comparative perspective which might come
from my stress on historiography and the comparative history of religion. It is
remarkable, for example, how Bultmann's existential emphasis sites Christianity in a position that might be regarded as finding itself in the foothills of
the Buddhist journey towards the annihilation of a sense of self.
     In contradistinction to such modern scholarship, it is easy to see how it
might seem more apt to describe the end envisaged in the New Testament as

the end of an age and not as an end of time or the earth. Such a view would seem to be supported by the explicit choice of writers like Luke and Jude to compare the coming end with similar moments in Jewish history, which, while ends of sorts, did not constitute the end of time or of the earth. The existence of narratives of ending within Jewish culture and the popularity of what would come to be called millennarian ideas in radical Jewish sects at the time of Christ's activity encourage the idea that Jesus' followers would have expected his faith to be built around an ending. As Matthew says (24:3):

> When he was sitting on the Mount of Olives, the disciples came to him privately, saying, 'Tell us, when will this be, and what will be the sign of your coming and of the end of the age?'

Memories of such earlier, discrete, ends are invoked in Luke's Gospel (10:10–12) where Jesus deploys popular knowledge of, for instance, God's punishment of Sodom, to encourage people to his side:

> But whenever you enter a town and they do not welcome you, go out into its streets and say, 'Even the dust of your town that clings to our feet, we wipe off in protest against you. You know this: the kingdom of God has come near.' I tell you, on that day it will be more tolerable for Sodom than for that town.

Later in Luke (17:26–30) Jesus invokes not only the end of Sodom but also the story of Noah, where all life was destroyed apart from Noah and his charges:

> Just as it was in the days of Noah, so too it will be in the days of the Son of Man. They were eating and drinking, and marrying and being given in marriage, until the day Noah entered the ark, and the flood came and destroyed all of them. Likewise, just as it was in the days of Lot: they were eating and drinking, buying and selling, planting and building, but on the day that Lot left Sodom, it rained fire and sulphur from heaven and destroyed all of them – and it will be like that on the day that the Son of Man is revealed.

The implication of such passages seems to be that God will soon judge the peoples of the world a third time, and that this ending will be rather more like that of Sodom than that of Noah, for in the case of Sodom people were offered a choice of repentance, whereas in the case of Noah the peoples of the world were destroyed without being offered a chance of redemption.

Peter (2 Peter 3:3–8) places great emphasis upon the reception of the idea of a Christian end, and the manner in which such notions have come to be rejected as impossible by people:

First of all you must understand this, that in the last days scoffers will come, scoffing and indulging their own lusts and saying, 'Where is the promise of his coming? For ever since our ancestors died, all things continue as they were from the beginning of creation!' They deliberately ignore this fact, that by the word of God heavens existed long ago and an earth was formed out of water and by means of water, through which the world of that time was deluged with water and perished. But by the same word the present heavens and earth have been reserved for fire, being kept until the day of judgement and destruction of the godless. But do not ignore this one fact, beloved, that with the Lord one day is like a thousand years, and a thousand years are like one day.

So the world in which the disciples found themselves was one in which many people saw the stories of Sodom and Noah as apocryphal myths that bore little relation to the material realities of life, where time was measured by the natural passing of time and human lives ('For ever since our ancestors died . . .'). It is for this reason that Peter needs to stress that God is the master of time, and he does this with one of the most beautiful evocations of the Christian idea of the continuum of time, urging people to understand that 'with the Lord one day is like a thousand years, and a thousand years are like one day.' This is accompanied by a metaphorical invocation of the standard Christian dictum that visible and material conceptions of time should not be given greater credence than invisible and spiritual understandings of time, in the contrast that is set up between the doubter's perception of time through the natural world of life and death he sees, and the believer's understanding of time from its unseen point of origin in God's unfolding creation.

Having mentioned the twentieth-century revival of eschatology it is equally important to understand the other critical moment in the history of the apocalyptic in the time after Christ: namely the centuries after Christ's death, in which the non-appearance of a final ending needed to be explained within Christian culture. As Bultmann writes (1957: 37), 'Obviously the fact that the expected coming of Christ failed to take place gave rise to disappointment and doubt'. This is indisputable and the point at which I offer some divergence from Bultmann is his insistence in seeing clear distinctions between New Testament writings which tried to adapt to these new realities and time, and the early gospels which were not forced to confront such things. As he puts it:

> The problem of Eschatology grew out of the fact that the expected end of the world failed to arrive, that the 'Son of Man' did not appear in the clouds of heaven, that history went on, and that the eschatological community could not fail to recognise that it had become a historical phenomenon and

that the Christian faith had taken on the shape of a new religion. This is
made clear by two facts: (a) the historiography of the author of Luke and the
Acts of the Apostles, (b) the importance which tradition gained in the
Christian community. Whereas Mark and Matthew wrote their Gospels not
as historians but as preachers and teachers, Luke, as a historian, undertakes
in his Gospel to represent the life of Christ.

It seems to me that, while Bultmann is absolutely right to stress the increasing
importance of the development of a coherent eschatological picture as time
went on, the stark differences he sees between the early Christian culture of
Matthew and Mark and the later one of Luke and Acts overstates the manner
in which a new Christianity develops across the New Testament. It is as possible to find support for literal eschatology in the early part of the text, as it is to
find metaphoric, emphatically non-literal accounts in later books, as I hope to
show through the selection of Biblical passages cited in this section.

What is very clear in the New Covenant's descriptions of an end of time is
that the purpose of such an event is the division of the world into believers and
unbelievers, and their despatch to their rightful fates. The end of the age is a
metaphor for the central Christian orientation towards time as judgement. It
expresses the pivotal choice man faces. It is eschatological in that in this view
of things ultimate meaning is made at the end of time, when the past is viewed
as leading inexorably to an end-point. It is the decisions made by individuals
as they traverse towards the end of the age which define their experience at that
moment. As Matthew (24:13–14) and John (5:28–29) say:

> But anyone who endures to the end will be saved. And this good news of the
> kingdom will be proclaimed throughout the world, as a testimony to all
> nations; and then the end will come.

> Do not be astonished at this; for the hour is coming when all who are in their
> graves will hear his voice and will come out – those who have done good, to
> the resurrection of life, and those who have done evil, to the resurrection of
> condemnation.

Quite when this day would come is a rather more uncertain question. Different writers of the New Testament suggest different answers, and all are of
course relegated to talking in the language of clues, for the day of judgement
only truly makes sense if its coming represents a surprise. As both Paul (1
Thessalonians 5:2) and Peter (2 Peter 3:10) say: 'the day of the Lord will come
like a thief in the night.'

It is quite clear that a number of these writers believed the end of the age was
imminent and would take place in their own lifetimes. Paul, in particular,

preaches to believers a message which implies an imminent ending (1 Corinthians 7:25–26 and Romans 13:11–14):

> Now concerning virgins, I have no command of the Lord, but I give my opinion as one who by the Lord's mercy is trustworthy. I think that, in view of the impending crisis, it is well for you to remain as you are.

> Besides this, you know what time it is, how it is now the moment for you to wake from sleep. For salvation is nearer to us now than when we became believers; the night is far gone, the day is near.

This idea of the imminent end was an essential aspect of the Pauline church and the cause of a great deal of anguished debate in later Christianity, for many theologians argued that Paul's belief in a looming apocalypse led him to encourage the development of a particular Christian culture that was wholly oriented towards this day of judgement. Others have argued both that Paul was mistaken in encouraging a belief in an end of time in the lifetimes of the early believers, and that this led to his failure to develop a church that engaged more with social questions rather than hunkering down in the face of the end of the age. This second view bases itself primarily around the words and ideas of Jesus articulated in the Gospels, such as Luke (17:20):

> Once Jesus was asked by the Pharisees when the kingdom of God was coming, and he answered, 'The kingdom of God is not coming with things that can be observed; nor will they say, "Look, here it is!" or "There it is!" For, in fact, the kingdom of God is among you.'

In contrast then to the literalism of the Pauline end, we find here a symbolic end that contrasts the idea of a cataclysmic day of judgement with a notion which combines the everyday with an understanding of the Christian continuum of time: the end of the age was always around, for people were always judged and would gain their rightful end just as the peoples of the past and future did and would do. The contrast between this approach and that of Paul is made in his second letter to the Thessalonians (2:1–3):

> As to the coming of our Lord Jesus Christ and our being gathered together to him, we beg you, brothers and sisters, not to be quickly shaken in mind or alarmed, either by spirit or by word or by letter, as though from us, to the effect that the day of the Lord is already here. Let no one deceive you in any way; for that day will not come unless the rebellion comes first and the lawless one is revealed, the one destined for destruction.

Although Paul seems to be tempering his idea of the imminence of the end of the age, he also directly contradicts Jesus' assertion that 'the day of the Lord is already here'. Bultmann (Braaten 1968: 167) has suggested that what Paul was trying to express in his words was a form of eschatology that combined the existentialist and the Heilsgeschichte approaches, for his sense of ending was on the one hand a literal one pointing to the crucifixion, and also existentially focused on the duty of the individual in their present moment. Paul's admonitions are seen by Bultmann (1957: 44–45) as a call to Jews to understand that a pious following of the law 'is in reality a way of escaping from the genuine call of God, from decision', stressing the difference of the Christian offer. Heidegger (Philipse 1998: 174–75), meanwhile, saw Paul's writings as an attempt to reject Greek notions of God as 'an eternal substance' in valorizing Christianity as an immanent faith which saw 'human existence as a preparation for a life of becoming'.

Bultmann (1957: 49) makes the important point that the eschatological thinking of both Paul and John shared a key structural similarity, which was the idea of the present as a 'time-between'. For Paul this was the moment 'between the resurrection of Christ and His expected Parousia at the end of the world', while for John it was that time between 'the glorification of Jesus through his crucifixion and the end of the earthly life of the individual believer.' Bultmann shows that the temporal structuring of these two seemingly different ideas was of critical importance in the development of a Christian church culture for it came to serve as the basis for the development of sacramentalism as a set of practices for this waiting period. Under the influence also of Hellenistic and Gnostic thought (1957: 53), the 'Church is changed from a community of the saved into an institution of salvation.'

In opposition to Paul and the modern stress on the central importance of literalist eschatology has been the Jesus Seminar. For those thinkers, as Hays writes (2001: 118), 'wherever the Gospels portray Jesus as using apocalyptic imagery, such passages are resolutely classified by the Seminar as creations of the early church, those pedestrian blunderers who "reverted, once Jesus was not there to remind them", into their bad old Jewish apocalyptic ways of thinking and retrojected on to Jesus the naïve apocalyptic ideas taught by John the Baptist.' The views of Hays here are driven by his hostility to the Seminar as symbolic of (2001: 118) an 'affluent liberal Protestant church in North America seeking some way to reconnect with a kinder, gentler Jesus who will offer them new spiritual stimulation without threatening them with God's final judgement.' Such a claim is revealing both of the degree to which literal eschatology became undisputed in modern theology, not only in the virulence of Hays' reaction but also in his characterization of the Jesus Seminar as having to go outside the existing Gospels in order to find 'a non apocalyptic Jesus', which belies the fact that precisely such a figure had been known from readings of the Gospels for most of Christianity's history.

These two visions of the timing and nature of the end are also apparent in other descriptions of the character of the end of days. Let us compare, for example, the visceral physical chaos envisaged by Mark (13:7–8) and the more contemplative, spiritual approach taken by Paul in his first letter to the Corinthians (15:51–52):

> When you hear of wars and rumours of wars, do not be alarmed. This must take place, but the end is still to come. For nation will rise against nation, and kingdom against kingdom; there will be earthquakes in various places; there will be famines. This is but the beginning of the birth pangs.

> We will not all die, but we will all be changed in a moment, in the twinkling of an eye, at the last trumpet.

At first sight, the account of the day of judgement offered in Revelation (11:17–18) would seem to be akin to that described by Mark:

> We give thanks, Lord Almighty, who are and who were, for you have taken your great power and begun to reign. The nations raged, but your wrath has come . . .

The Revelation of John is one of great physicality and exuberant descriptions of devils, angels, crowns, serpents, sickles and eagles. There are good reasons for feeling somewhat tentative in comparing its description of the end of the age with that of the rest of the New Testament, for its tone and style do set it apart from earlier books. As Bauckham writes (1993: ix), 'among the major works of early Christianity included in the New Testament, it remains the Cinderella', and only now in scholarship such as that by Bauckham is a fuller understanding of the book's 'intertextual relationship with the Old Testament' becoming understood. Bauckham sees the text as a political one in its call to its readers to recognize the (1993: xii–xiii) 'political idolatry and economic oppressions intrinsic to Roman power in the late first century', framed within John's reading and revelation (1993: xvi) of the Old Testament as a text that discloses the appropriate Christian response to life in such a culture.

It is clear that aspects of the eschatology of Revelation have been of colossal influence in Christian cultures, and of great importance to the theology of figures such as Moltmann. Most of the ideas present in its end, as opposed to its literal descriptions, chime with ideas already discussed, such as the notion of a day of judgement (14:14–16):

> Then I looked, and there was a white cloud, and seated on the cloud was one like the Son of Man, with a golden crown on his head, and a sharp sickle in his hand! Another angel came out of the temple, calling with a loud voice to the one who sat on the cloud, 'Use your sickle and reap, for the hour to reap has come, because the harvest of the earth is fully ripe.' So the one who sat on the cloud swung his sickle over the earth, and the earth was reaped.

It is interesting, however, that the metaphor of harvesting is used here. While effective, the notion that God sees time in terms of seasons seems an anathema to those other descriptions where spiritual time is described as being a polar opposite of natural time. However, it is not the case that Revelation simply deploys commonplace ideas of time for its readers' easy consumption. It also contains some striking and strange descriptions, such as this one (12:14–15):

> But the woman was given the two wings of the great eagle, so that she could fly from the serpent into the wilderness, to her place where she is nourished for a time, and times, and half a time.

Given that one of the key tasks of Revelation is to offer literal description where before there was uncertainty and allusion, this passage is particularly arresting. Is it because this woman is a magical being that she has access to this special experience of time; is it because she is close to God, or is this simply revealing of an understanding open to us all, but which we fail to see?

Rather different are the explicit descriptions of eternal torment that the devil and evildoers will face on the great day (20:10–15):

> And the devil who had deceived them was thrown in the lake of fire and sulphur, where the beast and the false prophet were, and they will be tormented day and night for ever and ever [. . .] And I saw the dead, great and small standing before the throne, and books were opened, the book of life. And the dead were judged according to their works, as recorded in the books. And the sea gave up the dead that were in it, Death and Hades gave up the dead that were in them, and all were judged according to what they had done. Then Death and Hades were thrown into the lake of fire. This is the second death, the lake of fire; and anyone whose name was not found written in the book of life was thrown into the lake of fire.

Thus judgement comes to those who died before the end of days, and a verdict is found on all based on their behaviour on earth. This judgement is one that

is made on the basis of the actions of individuals in what we might call provisional, earthly time, and is the basis on which their status in permanent,
eternal, time is found. A 'second death' awaits sinners and a second, endless,
life awaits believers (21:1–6):

> Then I saw a new heaven and a new earth; for the first heaven and the first
> earth had passed away, and the sea was no more. And I saw the holy city, the
> new Jerusalem, coming down out of heaven from God, prepared as a bride
> adorned for her husband. And I heard a loud voice from the throne saying,
> 'See, the home of God is among mortals. He will dwell with them; they
> will be his peoples, and God himself will be with them; he will wipe every
> tear from their eyes. Death will be no more; mourning and crying and pain
> will be no more, for the first things have passed away.' And the one who was
> seated on the throne said, 'See, I am making all things new.' Also he said,
> 'Write this, for these words are trustworthy and true.' Then he said to me, 'It
> is done! I am the Alpha and the Omega, the beginning and the end. To the
> thirsty I will give water as a gift from the spring of the water of life. Those
> who conquer will inherit these things, and I will be their God and they will
> be my children.

Revelation allows believers, then, the chance to peer behind the doors of
mystery which are kept closed and elusive in the rest of the New Covenant.
Here we also see a reiteration of the Christian concept of the continuum of
time, with God's words 'I am the Alpha and the Omega, the beginning and
the end'.

History-writing in the Gospels

I now want to move from a general consideration of time in the New Testament
to look more closely at the manner in which the Gospels function as histories.
As I have already said, the Bible contains a considerable range of ways of
thinking about and describing the past. This pluralism has in some ways been
useful in forming a broad-ranging faith, but it has also encouraged dogmatism
and schisms as very particular modes of historicizing and understanding time
can be claimed as true by groups who appeal to different parts of the Bible.
Here I want to look both at the manner in which the Gospels provide models
of diverse ways of doing history that were used in different Christian sects, and
the way in which these modes have also served as templates for historians
more generally. Such templates have been of significance, of course, not just

for Christian communities but in more recent times for the world more generally, for the genres and tropes of Christian history came in some ways to be the means of describing the past in western history, whose influence was colossal over the production of the past globally.

What I am not claiming here, however, is that all the temporal forms that we have been looking at in this chapter have been adopted by later Christian cultures and then globalized as the foundations of a common understanding of the means by which we describe the past. What we really see is a competition between temporal modes in Christian culture and in later chapters we will need to explore why it was the case that the more radical, rupturing conceptions of temporal understanding in the Bible were not generally adopted.

The first lines of each of the Gospels give us some idea of the range of historical modes offered in the New Testament. As we have seen, the first book, Matthew, begins (1:1–6) in a fashion that must have been very familiar to readers of the Old Testament:

> An account of the genealogy of Jesus the Messiah, the son of David, the son of Abraham. Abraham was the father of Isaac, and Isaac the father of Jacob, and Jacob the father of Judah and his brothers, and Judah the father of Perez and Zerah by Tamar, and Perez the father of Hezron, and Hezron the father of Aram, and Aram the father of Aminadab, and Aminadab the father of Nahshon, and Nahshon the father of Salmon, and Salmon the father of Boaz by Rahab, and Boaz the father of Obed by Ruth, and Obed the father of Jesse, and Jesse the father of King David.

This family tree continues in fact for another eleven verses, taking in forty-two generations between Abraham and Jesus. The content of the form of this genealogical mode was evidently the assertion that Jesus is the last in the line of prophets whom God sent to the Jews. He is the spiritual heir to Abraham, but he is also his direct biological descendant, 'the son of David, the son of Abraham'. The presumed reader looms large here for we can well imagine the audience for whom this text was written, and the need such readers would have had for proof of the validity of Christ's claims and the uniqueness of his status among the many reformist Jewish sects that were offering the promise of a revival that would take their people back to the true path of the family history followed through the Old Testament.

We also see here how closely the genealogical mode is connected to the idea that histories serve particular peoples, tribes or nations, and that one of their chief functions is the establishment of legitimacy, through lineage, within groups. In itself this might be seen as inherently conservative, even more so when we reflect upon the patrilinear, patriarchal preferences of this kind of genealogy. As Valensi (1985: 57) says, 'Genealogy reveals itself not as an account of the past, but as an allegory of the present, a translation of political, religious, and matrimonial practices.'

The beginning of Mark (1:1–3) adopts a different mode of speech to achieve many of the same ends:

> The beginning of the good news of Jesus Christ, the Son of God. As it is written in the prophet Isaiah, 'See I am sending my messenger ahead of you, who will prepare your way; the voice of one crying out in the wilderness: "Prepare the way of the Lord, make his paths straight."'

Again, through the prophetic words of Isaiah here, reference is made to the traditions of the Old Testament, with the aim of establishing the legitimacy of Jesus in the line of Jewish prophets. The book of Isaiah is evidently treated as a historical source of truth, but the interesting idea, from the perspective of the modern historian, is that the truth of Isaiah comes not in his actions in the past but in the validity of his vision into what was then the future. In other words, this Christian historical mode adopts the continuum model of time as its basis. The text also signals something of a break with that stock of narratives of past times in its claim to offer 'The beginning of the good news'. This chimes with Schildgen's recent (1998: 11) assessment of the gospel of Mark as a book in which:

> Time is the perspective through which the author constructs the Gospel. He shows how the story of the mission and death of Jesus connects to his own Hebraic history. His narrative probes the meaning of this story to his own present, some thirty to forty years after, and to the future readers whom he addresses. Even more importantly, because of their relationship to the cosmic horizon, the events in the Gospel unfold in the context of eternity.

Luke's history of the events of the life of Jesus evidently reflects the later date at which it was written (1:1–1:4):

> Since many have undertaken to set down an orderly account of the events that have been fulfilled among us, just as they were handed on to us by those who from the beginning were eyewitnesses and servants of the word, I too decided after investigating everything carefully from the very first, to write an orderly account for you, most excellent Theophilus, so that you may know the truth concerning the things about which you have been instructed.

Here, he is in effect describing himself as a historian and setting out some essential details of his craft and his place in a wider guild of narrators of the past. He talks about competing versions of events, the need for an 'orderly account' of the past, the 'fulfilled' nature of events, the use of primary sources and oral traditions, the consideration of their transmission, the diligence and completeness of the approach of the true scholar, the written text as the ultimate historical form, the writing of histories for particular audiences, and the establishment of an absolute truth of the past (this assumption is made throughout the New Testament). These are building blocks for the pursuit of history that would seem fairly commonplace to the modern historian, but they were evidently in the process of coming into being in the work of a writer like Luke. Nor should we assume that such laws for the divination of the past are universal. As we shall see later, they certainly do not constitute the bases for the practice of history in other cultural traditions, and, as we are seeing here, Luke's approach is of a different generic order from that of the writers of the other Gospels.

In fact, there are aspects of Luke's methodology that are at a greater variance with the methods of modern, empirical history than might at first seem to be the case. Let us take Luke's use of the term 'fulfilled' in this passage. This verb implies predestination, that events took shape because they were meant to be. This has always been an influential idea in Christian modes of historicizing, though it is of course now generally rejected by empirical historians whose partly secularized orientation has led them away from ideas of destiny.

John's history of the life of Jesus strikes a very different tone (1:1):

> In the beginning was the Word, and the Word was with God, and the Word was God. He was in the beginning with God. All things came into being through him, and without him not one thing came into being.

Where Matthew stressed genealogy, Mark the intertext of the Old Testament, and Luke the practicalities of the writing of history, John takes a more elusive, philosophical path. He sets up a series of equivalences between God, the Word and Jesus which claim a continuum between them that is offered to the constructing reader who pieces together the logic of John's words. In their own ways Matthew, Mark and Luke had also sought to impose authority – the authority of a given truth – upon their readers, but John instead seems to present more of an offer of engagement in the making of truth with his readers. His words remind us of the cult of literacy in a later religion – Islam – which insisted that its adherents were able to read the text of the Qur'an and to engage with its ideas as individuals who made truth with the aid of a text.

Yet, there are also resonances with the writers of the other Gospels here. After all, John is writing about beginnings, as were the three other writers, and he is seeking to develop a narrative of truthful legitimacy from that point of origin. What is most strikingly different is what is left out of this account – the need for any mediation (genealogy, prophets or method) between God, Jesus and the reader (the Word).

Paul's history

Having looked at these different modes of history writing in the Gospels, I now want to move on to consider Paul's account of the history of Christianity. As we have already seen, this question is a difficult one not only because Paul seems to present contradictory views in different places (there are of course important generic reasons as to why this is the case, since Paul wrote letters to varied constituencies and it should not be surprising to us that he emphasized different things in those letters), but also because there is a case that Paul's idea of Christianity was utterly different from that presented by Jesus. As Jeremy Bentham put it in the title of his polemic work, he was for *Jesus not Paul* (see Smith 1823). In these contexts we need to ask whether we are dealing with ambiguities that can be viewed benignly as constructive or whether we read about truly divergent descriptions of the nature of Christianity. Paul's account of the past of Christianity and his own place in the developing history of the religion are of critical importance in the shaping of the faith and the development of particular ways of describing Christian time.

In order to prove his Christianity, Paul stressed the force of his Judaism in what he describes as his 'earlier life' (Galatians 1:13–14):

> You have heard, no doubt, of my earlier life in Judaism. I was violently persecuting the church of God and was trying to destroy it. I advanced in Judaism beyond many among my people of the same age, for I was far more zealous for the traditions of my ancestors.

Yet, in Acts (21:39) he still declares: 'I am a Jew, from Tarsus in Cilicia, a citizen of an important city' – a statement that makes us wonder if Paul's idea of Jewishness relates mainly to ethnic identity, or whether he conceives of his 'earlier life' being deeply embedded in the new faith he adopted after his conversion on the road to Damascus. While on trial, Paul describes Christianity as what might be called a branch of reform Judaism (Acts 24:14):

> But this I admit to you, that according to the Way, which they call a sect, I
> worship the God of our ancestors, believing everything laid down accord-
> ing to the law or written in the prophets.

While it is striking that Paul accords Christianity the singular title 'the Way', it
is just as remarkable that he declares that this sect not only worships the same
God as the Jews, but that it also adheres to the same laws and histories as
Judaism. This identification of Christianity simply with a belief in the line of
Jewish prophets reappears in a later moment of Paul's trial, in his dialogue
with King Agrippa (Acts 26:27–28): 'King Agrippa, do you believe the
prophets? I know that you believe.' Agrippa said to Paul, 'Are you so quickly
persuading me to become a Christian?'

Here Agrippa becomes the first voice in the New Testament to use the term
'Christian' to describe 'the Way', yet his primary understanding of this faith
is that it entails a belief in the Jewish prophets. One might suggest that underlying this belief is the idea that Jesus is the last of the prophets, and the one
foretold by the prophets of the Old Testament, but I think that it is equally
plausible to read Agrippa's remarks as indications of a Pauline conception of
the faith as a branch of Judaism. Elsewhere Paul seems much more decisive in
his rejection of Judaism. In Titus (1:13–14), for instance, he recommends that
the Cretans be sharply rebuked, 'so that they may become sound in the faith,
not paying attention to Jewish myths or to commandments of those who reject
the truth.'

As well as introducing terms such as 'the Way' and 'Christian', Paul also
describes 'the church' and its organization in much greater detail than the
earlier writers of the New Testament (the term itself in fact occurs only twice in
Matthew 16:18 and 18:17, Schweizer 1961: 2b), implicitly suggesting that he
is referring to a religious institution independent of the structures of the
Jewish faith. Most of his letters concern the maintenance of a particular vision
of the Way in the geographically dispersed Christian communities. Thus in 1
Timothy (3:14–16) we read:

> I hope to come to you soon, but I am writing these instructions to you so
> that, if I am delayed, you may know how one ought to behave in the house-
> hold of God, which is the church of the living God, the pillar and the bulwark
> of the truth. Without any doubt, the mystery of our religion is great . . .

While 'the mystery' of what is emphatically and singularly described as 'our
religion' may be great, Paul's own 'instructions' are designed to dispel doubt
and mystery for he is concerned to impose a certain sense of orthodoxy upon
the practices of Christians. In the letters to the Corinthians this is seen as being

of great importance because of that people's deviation from the true way as it was perceived by Paul. The problem of the Corinthians would seem to be indicative of some of the consequences that arose from the ambiguities of the early Christian faith (1 Corinthians 1:11–15):

> It has been reported to me by Chloe's people that there are quarrels among you, my brothers and sisters. What I mean is that each of you says, 'I belong to Paul', or 'I belong to Apollos', or 'I belong to Cephas', or 'I belong to Christ.' Has Christ been divided? Was Paul crucified for you? Or were you baptized in the name of Paul? I thank God that I baptized none of you except Crispus and Gaius, so that no one can say you were baptized in my name.

The lesson Paul preaches here is evidently that the true path to God is through Christ, not through Paul or other Christians, who are merely followers and interpreters of the teachings of the Son of God. Yet, later, Paul's proposed route to orthodoxy seems to contradict the logic of his critique of the practices of the Corinthians (4:14):

> I am not writing this to make you ashamed, but to admonish you as my beloved children. For though you might have ten thousand guardians in Christ, you do not have many fathers. Indeed, in Christ Jesus I became your father through the gospel. I appeal to you, then, be imitators of me.

Paul's comments here can easily be read as indicative of a cult of personality, and one that would seem to go against all his earlier teachings which minimized his own importance in Christianity as compared with Christ. Yet, if we look more closely at this passage we find even more puzzles. The language used here is that of familial time, whereby man's being is defined by the stages of life that come with family life, such as birth, childhood, marriage, parenthood and old age. We might expect Christ to play the central role in this imaginary, yet the reverse turns out to be the case. There may be ten thousand Christs watching over the people of Corinth, but there is only one father, and that is Paul. Admittedly it was through Jesus and the Gospel that Paul attained such status, but in manifold ways this passage is suggestive of the central tension of the early church, which was the question as to whether Paul's account of the meaning and practices of Christianity would be questioned.

Writing of those tensions, Sanders remarks that (1985: 172):

> Paul's letters reveal a deep and serious conflict between himself and the leaders of the Mother Church at Jerusalem. From their point of view, Paul's interpretation was not only a travesty of the true faith, of which they were the

guardians, but it had also dangerous possibilities. The logic of Paul's soteriology negated the Jewish claim to a superior spiritual status *vis-à-vis* the Gentiles. Reports reached Jerusalem that Paul was undermining the Law, while the Jewish Christians there were striving to prove their zealous orthodoxy and thus recommend their faith to their compatriots.

According to Sanders, Paul's victory in this battle of ideas only took place because of the complete victory that the Romans gained over the Jews in 66–70 C.E., which led to the destruction of both a people and their holy city. Hence (1985: 174–75), 'The fact that Christianity had stemmed from Judea, and that Jesus had actually been executed as a Jewish revolutionary, placed Christians in a potentially dangerous situation. It was urgently necessary to show that, despite its Jewish origins, Christianity was not essentially Jewish, and that Christians were in no way 'fellow-travellers with Jewish nationalism', which was of course a boon to Paul, and it was thus that Mark's Gospel (1985: 177) blamed the Jews for the death of Jesus, ahistorically implying that his faith had as much of an allegiance to Rome as it did to Judaism.

When we look at the books of the Bible that describe the life of Jesus, it is not surprising that we need the clarification of texts such as Hebrews, for it is often unclear from the Gospels what Jesus meant by Christianity. This is well illustrated by the nuanced view he espoused on evangelism. In some senses, what the Gospels describe is an evangelical life, for Christ's time on earth was spent bringing people to his truth through persuasion and his demonstration of special faculties such as miracles. Yet in other places, Christ seems to describe a faith that was essentially private, and in some cases was intended to be secret (Mark 8:27–30 and Luke 8:56):

> Jesus went on with his disciples to the villages of Caeserea Philippi; and on the way he asked his disciples, 'Who do people say that I am?' And they answered him, 'John the Baptist; and others, Elijah; and still others, one of the prophets.' He asked them, 'But who do you say that I am?' Peter answered him, 'You are the Messiah.' And he sternly ordered them not to tell anyone about him.

> [after raising a girl from the dead] Her parents were astounded; but he ordered them to tell no one what had happened.

The modesty of this faith is suggestive of a religion whose early intent was not universal, and was not based around elaborate institutions and rites designed to demonstrate in a public fashion the devout qualities of believers. As Christ says (Matthew 6:1), 'Beware of practising your piety before others in order to be seen by them; for then you have no reward from your Father in heaven.'

In Hebrews, Jesus is not only described as being the Son of God, but also as existing in a continuum with God (1:1–3):

> Long ago God spoke to our ancestors in many and various ways by the prophets, but in these last days he has spoken to us by a Son, whom he appointed heir of all things, through whom he also created the worlds. He is the reflection of God's glory and the exact imprint of God's very being, and he sustains all by his powerful word.

It is also made evident here that the message of Jesus is of greater import than that of earlier prophets, given his proximity to God. One wonders also whether the stress on his 'powerful word' is not a direct challenge to the likes of Paul who was building a religion that was argued by some to go against the teachings of Christ.

The idea of the church is present in Christ's life, but it is described primarily as a form of relationship among people and a state of being in belief, which contrasts with the development of ritual orthodoxies in the vision of Paul (Matthew 18:15 and 18:20):

> If another member of the church sins against you, go and point out the fault when the two of you are alone. If the member listens to you, you have regained that one.

> For when two or three are gathered in my name, I am there among them.

It is certainly clear that Christ saw a special place for the disciples in his church, for he says to his father (John 17:12–19):

> I guarded them, and not one of them was lost except the one destined to be lost, so that the scripture might be fulfilled. But now I am coming to you, and I speak these things in the world so that they may have my joy made complete in themselves. I have given them your word, and the world has hated them, because they do not belong to the world, just as I do not belong to the world. I am not asking you to take them out of the world, but I ask you to protect them from the evil one. They do not belong of the world, just as I do not belong to the world. Sanctify them in the truth; your word is truth. As you have sent me into the world, so I have sent them into the world. And for their sakes I sanctify myself, so that they may also be sanctified in truth.

The church implied here is certainly one that is destined to expand, for it is clear that the disciples are destined to go out into the world to spread the message of Jesus. In the later books of the New Testament we read of their work in Asia, Arabia, the Balkans, southern Europe, north Africa and the Levant. John (4:44), in fact, declares that 'Jesus himself had testified that a prophet has no honour in the prophet's own country.'

Metaphors and dreams

The New Covenant does not describe a programmatic faith with a single central authority and a code of laws; nor does it say much about rites, forms of worship and prayer. In this way Christianity is clearly distinguishable from the Jewish culture from which it emerged. Instead, its tone is often metaphorical and its parables are elliptical. Metaphors and similes were of great importance to Christians, for in many ways Christians were people who had access to a metaphorical understanding of time. Through similes and metaphors, they believed that Christ's death was like theirs and that a continuum across time was thus established in their both being in the world. In many branches of Christianity this simile is metaphorically conjured in the lives of believers through the ritual of communion where bread is felt to become the body of Christ and wine his blood. The bread and the wine retain their innateness as things but they also become something else in the bodies of believers. Importantly, this rite is used as a symbolic marker of time as adherents perceive their own journey in the world as being marked by communions.

In a simpler sense, the metaphor and the simile might be described as specific temporal forms of grammar in the manner in which they function differently from most language, for language is generally designed to convey an immediate, unthinking meaning, whereas the point of metaphor and simile is to induce a reflective delay in meaning, as sense is made of the comparisons that they make. They mesh the poetic and the spiritual in Christian grammar.

The same might also be said to be true of the Christian belief in the Trinity. As a concept, its meaning can be understood through logical exposition, but it is better comprehended in a more ambiguous, metaphorical fashion, for to believe in the Trinity, like so many aspects of Christianity, is to disbelieve the laws of the natural world one sees around one and instead to place one's faith in a hidden, metaphorical, order of things. Similarly, the role played by icons suggests a metaphorical orientation towards time and space, since the icon is a device through which believers can break free from the material world through to the deeper architecture of the space-time of Christianity.

The parable is the classic example of Christ's belief in the value of meta-phorical time. Why did Jesus use parables? Why did he not simply explain his teachings and his message in the clearest way possible? The answer to these questions is that Christ evidently believed that his teaching was often better conveyed in an oblique fashion, with a meaning that was one step removed from literal interpretation; in other words, it prized the metaphorical over the everyday. An idea could be conveyed directly, but for a believer to have faith in it meant that its meaning needed to be constructed in their mind, which was why the parable was such a powerful narrative form. We might recall here Wittgenstein's observation that the four Gospels together form something of a parable since their differences encourage a metaphorical reading of the New Testament as a whole, in which belief comes through the individual's con-struction of meaning.

Across the Gospels Christ makes it very clear that the parable is a figure of speech which is to be used to generate a particular form of meaning in the minds of potential believers (Matthew 13:10–14 and Mark 4:33–34):

> Then the disciples came and asked him, 'Why do you speak to them in parables? He answered, 'To you it has been given to know the secrets of the kingdom of heaven, but to them it has not been given. For those who have, more will be given, and they will have an abundance; but from those who have nothing, even what they have will be taken away. The reason I speak to them in parables is that "seeing they do not perceive, and hearing they do not listen, nor do they understand." '

> With many such parables he spoke the word to them, as they were able to hear it; he did not speak to them except in parables, but he explained every-thing in private to his disciples.

What Christ then says is that what people see and hear is not what is really there, for there is a radical disjuncture between the time perceived by man in life and the truth of Christian time and God's message for the world that is revealed through parables. This itself is couched in terms of the coming 'end of time' (John 16:25): 'I have said these things to you in figures of speech. The hour is coming when I will no longer speak to you in figures, but will tell you plainly of the Father.'

The parable, however, is but one branch of a broader genre of writing that is deployed in the Bible which conveys a meaning that is one step removed from the most immediately perceived material reality. The parable is related to the prophecy, to revelation and to dreams. These altered states of conscious-ness show truth without recourse to descriptions of the otherworldly. This is well described in the story of Jesus' birth, where truth is opposed to man's understanding of nature (Matthew 1:21–23):

> She will bear a son, and you are to name him Jesus, for he will save his people from their sins. All this took place to fulfil what had been spoken by the Lord through the prophet: 'Look, the virgin shall conceive and bear a son, and they shall name him Emmanuel' . . .

It would seem to be of great significance that this revelation comes to Joseph in a dream: a form of existence recognized by man both to be life and to be at one remove from the meaning of conscious existence.

Conclusion

I hope that this chapter has shown that the New Covenant reveals Christianity to be a religion obsessed with time. There are many varieties of Christianity but all depend on a stock of ideas about time which set the Christian world-view apart from that of unbelievers and adherents of other faiths: the idea of temporal continuum, the coming end of days, predestination, God's mastery of time, and the central opposition between the visible time of nature and the truth of the unseen time of God's will, which depends heavily on notions of mastery and the continuum. This instantiation of the opposition between the seen and the non-seen evidently draws on the central temporal dynamic of the Old Testament, and part of Christianity's distinctive contribution is the final resolution of this struggle in favour of time perceived by the mind over a time seen with one's eyes.

As we have seen, the New Testament makes these claims in a variety of ways, some plain-speaking and some more complex in the case of metaphors, dialectical ambiguities and parables. Throughout, it deploys utterly new forms of temporal grammar which retain their power to shock readers and to encourage them to evaluate in the most basic way the meaning of their lives and the world they see around them. Expressions of temporality provide men with the clues that can lead them to the truth which Christianity proposes.

The consideration of the work of Moltmann, Bultmann and other modern writers on Christian time was designed to show both that Christian thought is engaged in a continual project of reading and re-reading the Bible, and that Christians have by no means exhausted the possibilities of that text as a repository of ideas about time and history. This evidently owes a great deal to the fact that it is a multi-authored work and to the sense of creative ambiguity which ensues from that and other features of its textual qualities, in contradistinction, as we shall see, to a culture such as that of Islam. We shall also return to a number of the themes of this chapter in our discussion of Hume and the Enlightenment, which draws out some of the implications of ambiguity and doubt in the Bible.

Let us now turn to a temporal culture much older than that of Christianity, whose ideas of time and history are very different from those we find in the New Testament: the Australian Dreamtime. While this chapter focused almost exclusively on a reading of a single source as the key to understanding Christian ideas of time, I shall need to look more at secondary literatures in anthropology, art history and history as a means of describing the complexity of Australian temporality.

C h a p t e r   6

On dreaming time

Introduction

This chapter describes the temporal world of classical Australian culture. The term 'classical' (Sutton 1989: 7) is used here to denote that period of almost complete continental isolation from the second millennium B.C.E. until the late eighteenth century C.E., during which time Australian civilization had almost no contact with other cultures. After the invasion of the British in 1788 C.E. parts of classical Australian culture survived, though the ecology of that culture – which was founded on notions of faith, land and time – was in the main destroyed in the genocide of the nineteenth century.

All discussions of Australian history are of necessity moral enterprises. Since the inception of the British colony, a public process of negotiation has taken place whereby white settlers have attempted to describe and re-define their relations to the original peoples of Australia (and to a lesser degree, at least in published sources, Aborigines have sought to do the same). My concern in this chapter is not to set out the changing character of this historical relationship but, rather, to examine the manner in which time and history function in classical Australian religions.

In some ways this is a difficult task, for the material remains of classical Aboriginal religion seem, at first, rather slight. This was not a literate culture, so there appear to be no foundational texts. It was not a culture with an architectural heritage, so no buildings remain. While it was a faith that also functioned as law and politics, it was not a religion that developed large-scale hierarchies and institutions, for its focus was on interconnected social units of around two to four hundred people. These features of Australian religion have tended to lead to its being described as a collection of 'myths', though there seems to be scant justification for not according Australian beliefs the classification 'religion', since in terms of longevity, continuity and complexity they appear no less intricate or sophisticated than those of other faiths. At the present day, such ideas have been well expressed by the Aboriginal Legal Rights Movement, which argued (Broome 2002: 251) that 'there is a confusion of [Australian] religious beliefs with European logic. If it is not logical and not reported then it must be fabricated. This is at a time when Christians are about to celebrate the Virgin birth on Christmas Day.' It seems significant that this group identified the intersection of temporality and narrative in Christianity as the basis of their critique.

In evaluating Australian temporalities we need to adopt a truly comparative perspective which displays a self-awareness as to the constructed, rather than natural, qualities of our rationalities and histories (a recent, important, work, which contrasts western and Australian temporalities along such lines is TenHouten 2005). Lewis (1985: 100) writes of the acknowledgement of such difference in terms that include even contrasting neurological bases for cultures:

> The 'Dreamtime' rites of Australian Aborigines, the trances of Bali, the voodoo séances of Haiti, the hallucinogenic-induced visions of Meso-america or Amazonia, are expressions of panhuman capacities for altered-heightened states of consciousness. These may represent the development and cultural valuation of mental faculties – for mystical, holistic thought – which are underdeveloped and disvalued in the Western rational tradition. Many may be expressions of faculties centred in the (usually right) brain hemisphere, complementary to the one in which faculties of language and analytic logic are centred.

The historian of Australian religion is therefore forced to rely on a set of rather unusual sources and a set of conceptual tools and literatures that are largely drawn from other disciplines. The chief texts of Australian religion are oral traditions and art works, while a reconstruction of this faith requires an engagement with archaeology, anthropology, linguistics and art history. The methods and epistemologies of these disciplines vary considerably from western empirical history, so a historiographical engagement with Australian religion helps us to expand our notions of practising history in two ways: through the development of historical narratives founded on other disciplinary models, and through the consideration of a temporal culture which western historians would not instinctively see as sophisticated, nor a faith from which they feel they might learn.

I focus on this second lesson in developing a historiographical argument across this chapter which contends that one of the most important ways of denaturalizing western history is to take seriously not just other cultures' modes of apprehending time, but also the notion that western historians might produce work founded on those other temporal schemata. After all, it seems wholly natural to us that others should instinctively adopt our methods of thinking and production. Yet, we are also aware of the narrative conceit upon which these presumptions are founded and the need to critique those ideas of progress that led western Europeans to believe that they had developed a culture which was at the apex of world civilization.

It was of course in the nineteenth century, when this religio-moral myth was imbued with its greatest power, and through enterprises such as the colonization of Australia that the idea found its most perfect, practical form. If history is to be truly decolonized it will need not just to approach subjects such as Australian religion with an openness to the equal moral value of other cultures, but also a willingness to consider the reimagination of its own practice through such encounters. This chapter tries to show how such radical historiographical speculation offers great opportunities to the discipline. There is an instinctive assumption within the discipline of history that the practical offer of historiography amounts to little more than a form of scepticism which engenders minor alterations in historical writing. In looking at Australian temporalities, however, I want to show how liberatory possibilities are opened up which have the potential to alter historical practice in fundamental ways. This implies that history needs to become more genuinely comparative, more philosophically and conceptually aware, and more open to the idea that within history there may be very many methods founded upon radically different epistemologies. Such a history would also break from the constraints of assigning itself the job of recalling a lost past, and take on the role of studying time.

Anthropologizing Australians

In the nascent human sciences of the late-nineteenth-century – anthropology, sociology, psychology – the Australian Aborigine became a favoured object of study. Australian culture was of great interest to such fields for its seeming difference from the mores of the modern west and, more importantly, for its 'primitive' qualities which pointed to it as a possible laboratory for studies into the origins of human culture and religion. *Terra Australis Incognita* was seen

as 'the last continent', historically cut off from paths of progress and development, where, even as late as the 1950s, one could witness and analyse 'our
living stone age'. Two archetypal figures who were interested in Australians
were the founding fathers of, respectively, psychology and sociology, Sigmund
Freud and Emile Durkheim.

In *Totem and Taboo* Freud aimed to investigate (1955: vii) 'Some points of
agreement between the mental lives of savages and neurotics', for in Australian
culture he saw a civilization living through its moment of childhood (1955:
xiv), which could offer the psychologist clues as to the origins of the structures
of social development that could no longer be seen in the west, or, rather,
could perhaps only be found in psychiatric hospitals. Freud claimed that
(1955: 17) 'the same incestuous wishes, which are later destined to become
unconscious [in civilized society], are still regarded by savage peoples as
immediate perils against which the most severe measures of defence must
be enforced.' Yet, in Australian society Freud was not convinced that he
saw a religious culture – for he argued (Muecke 2004: 98) that 'It is quite
doubtful whether they [Australians] evince any traces of religion in the
worship of higher beings' – which unfortunately led him to miss what he might
have found most engaging in Australian culture: namely, the development
of a Freudian analysis of the 'Dreamtime' which lies at the heart of Australian
religions.

Durkheim, like Freud, concentrated on totemism in his study of Australian
culture, *Basic Structures of Religious Life*, relying heavily, as Freud had, on
the records of European ethnographers and explorers to develop a picture of
Australian religion. From these texts, what Durkheim believed he saw was
(1960: 1) 'the most primitive and simple religion currently known to man.'
Although Durkheim insisted (1960: 4) that he did not believe in developing a
moral hierarchy of religions, it is nevertheless obvious from his work that he
supposed that the 'primitive' qualities of Australian religion would allow him
access to (1960: 2) 'the religious nature of man' found in all human societies.
The discovery of these basic urges and structures was a task of great urgency
for Durkheim, for he believed that it was sociology's duty to provide the
secularizing west – particularly France – with the tools by which religious
mores might be 'translated' into secular forms of social adhesion which would
bind together post-religious western society.

Writers like Freud and Durkheim evince many of the characteristics of
colonists and other early interpreters of Australian culture. They saw in that
culture things that were of use to them in the west, fundamentally mistaking
the complexity, and character, of the society which they claimed their new
methods allowed them to describe. As Strehlow cuttingly remarks (1970: xvi)

of the ethnographic sources upon which the human sciences' view of Aborigines was founded:

> If a non-white observer, who could neither read nor understand any of the European languages, had come to Europe and had by any chance written down an eye-witness account of the symbolic actions performed in a Christian church ceremony without being able to furnish any interpretation based on the actual words used in that ceremony, we should think very poorly of his account as a piece of accurate or informative descriptive writing.

Eliade (1973: xii) rightly observes that, 'It now seems obvious that all these hypotheses, theories and "historical" reconstructions are more significant for the cultural history of the Western world than they are for the understanding of the Aboriginal religions.' It is also evident that the literatures of the human sciences provided a theoretical backdrop and a moral justification for settler colonies, akin to Said's (1979) broader analysis of European *Orientalism*.

While it was probably largely complete by the inception of the human sciences in the late nineteenth century, the historical tragedy of the Australian genocide was founded on similar grounds, for the dehumanization of Australians rested on a basic presumption of an ordering of cultures and morals. What we can now see is that the Australian encounter did not take place between two cultures at different points on a linear path of development; it simply took place between two different cultures, neither of which was equipped to understand the complexities of notions of space and time in the other's cosmology. This was of little consequence for western colonists since their political–military power negated a need for such understanding, but it was of terrible import for Australians. In return for gaining a place in the narrative of universal history, Australians saw their numbers reduced by around ninety per cent between 1788 and the 1840s (Butlin 1983: 5). It is of critical importance that we see that such events relied very heavily upon concepts of time and history, which posited a universality of linear time and did not attempt to understand Australian time.

In spatial terms the extent of this misunderstanding, and the central place of religion in the encounter, can be seen in Broome's (2002: 18) description of the spatial and political organization of the continent:

> Each tribe believed that its boundaries were fixed and validated by the stories about the movement of their ancestors, and therefore there was no reason to desire or try to possess the country of another group: it would

have seemed meaningless since their creation stories only related to their own piece of territory.

We can thus understand how simple the acquisition of land was for the colonists since they encountered a people both who did not engage in territorial disputes and for whom the acquisition of land seemed futile.

The centrality of the differences of these modes of historicizing in the stories of the lives of Australians is made plain by Eliade (1973: xv–xvi) in his celebration of *Australian Religions*, where he valorizes the Australian idea that (1973: 62) '*Living as a human being* is in itself *a religious act*.' In 1973 he wrote that:

> No contemporary ethnologist or historian of religions believes that the primitives are or have been *Naturvölker*, that they neither live in nor have been changed by History. The main difference in comparison with other types of culture consists in the fact that the primitives are not so much interested in what we call 'history,' that is, in the series of irreversible events taking place in linear, historical time. They are concerned rather with their own 'sacred history', that is, with the mythical and creative acts which founded their culture and institutions, and bestowed meaning upon human existence.

While I think Eliade is right to identify temporal misunderstanding as a central dynamic in the Australian–colonist encounter, he relies here on too simple a dichotomy between (secular) linear, historical time and sacred time. It is arguable both that the sacred has not been so effectively disembodied from western time and that such time operates in non-linear fashions, not only in religious culture but also in advanced scientific forms. This will be explored further in Chapter 9.

The history people: classical Australian culture and time

Classical Australian culture provides one of the best examples of the complexity with which humans have developed temporal cultures. Australian understandings of time are as beautiful and productive as those we see in the Book of John, the Alhambra and Zen Buddhism.

Life in classical Australian culture can be seen as a historical existence, so long as one can understand history as a concept which moves across past, present and future. At first glance, it is a culture of indistinctness, where divisions between times, between people, and between man and the land seem to be slight. Yet such indistinctness comes only from the isolation of aspects of a worldview that needs to be understood in its totality.

Although there are around five hundred separate 'tribes' in Australia – each subdivided into the more important group units, most of which have their own languages – common notions of time and history exist across the continent. It is not surprising that each of these groups should operate with a common religious worldview, since they have been involved in complicated systems of exchange across the continent for millennia. Some forms of exchange were economic (though without the use of money, since ownership of objects was disdained), though of far greater importance was the exchange of songs that described interconnected aspects of the foundational moment in the earth's history known to Australians as 'the Dreamtime'.

Australians believe that the physical shape and the living inhabitants of the earth were made during this period when god-like creatures came on the earth to give it life and its distinctive landscapes. These creatures then moved back into the earth or ascended to the skies, often leaving behind distinctive topographical features as reminders of their presence. Classical Australian religious texts focus on the events of this Dreamtime and particular social groups are responsible for the upholding of particular 'Dreamings' from this period.

Responsibility for the ownership of a dreaming is a very serious business and one's life is in many ways constructed around the maintenance and transmission of a dreaming. In a very important sense the dreaming forms one's own identity, and, as well as the continuance of group dreamings, individuals also care for dreamings which relate to the point in the world where their mother conceived.

Here it is not possible to look in detail at the narratives of the Dreamtime. Chatwin (1987) acutely called these stories the *Songlines* of Australia, suggesting that, read together, they make up a single holy text which can be sung across the continent, serving as religious narrative, an account of the land, a journey and a description of time. If the point of studying Australian religion was to accord to it a universal respect accorded to other great religions, it is this meta-narrative that might form the basis of such a study, in which the text is the world, and the word and the life of the world are like the ancestor beings. However, the focus of classical Australian culture was local (Berndt 1973: 74) and while we might now assert the existence of the Dreaming meta-text – partially reconstructed by Strehlow – we ought to remember that Australians did not need to believe in the existence of such an overarching sense of order, for the practice and meaning of faith was not found in the grand accretion of a breadth of knowledge, but through the development of a depth of understanding of that local world for which one bore responsibility.

It is for this reason that Dixon (1980: 27–28) stresses Australians' exceptional attendance to the ways in which words are things, found in the great importance given to naming objects and people. This is seen especially in the significance that is attached to the giving of names to the newborn which are seen to offer appropriate links to the world of the sacred, and in the complex systems of taboo which outlaw not just the use of the names of the recently-dead, but also words connected to their names.

In terms of approaching the texts of the Dreaming, Eliade (1973: 57) makes a very useful analogy with modernist literature:

> One must read the descriptions of Spencer and Gillen *in extenso* to understand why even the most dreary landscape is, for the aborigines, charged with awe: every rock, spring and water hole represents a concrete trace of a sacred drama carried out in the mythical times. For the Western reader, these endless wanderings and fortuitous meetings of the Dream Time Heroes seem excessively monotonous. (But then the wanderings of Leopold Bloom in *Ulysses* also seem monotonous for the admirer of Balzac or Tolstoi.)

Just as modernism required new forms of reading if one was to appreciate the novel ways in which it apprehended the modern world, Australian texts demand a willingness to read and understand differently from non-Australian readers. Eliade's analogy is an especially appropriate one since one might argue that Australian texts display precisely the kinds of temporal and spatial dislocation that troubled readers of Joyce and Eliot who had been brought up on very specific and stable forms of linear, progressive temporalities.

In some ways 'the Dreamtime' is an inappropriate translation of Australian ideas, for to live in the Dreamtime is not a life lived in a hazy world of memory and analogy, but a life of great physical immediacy, for the dreaming emanates not just from oneself and in shared teachings but also in one's apprehension of the rocks, sand, trees and the other physical features of the world. Critics such as Lewis are wrong to describe it (1985: 120) as 'a drowsy surrealistic world in which the coordinates of time and space are suspended or shifting.' In daily life one sees the routes taken by the figures of the Dreaming and the places where their stories were enacted and one orients one's own life and conversations within the community around this sacred geography and temporality. More than this, when one encounters other local groups one learns of their Dreamings – some of which relate to shared figures from the Dreamtime – and this common, interrelated knowledge is shared through the recitations of songs, while flux-time is conjured in particularly vivid forms through collective rituals, in a manner comparable to the rites of the Christian Eucharist.

It is not, then, simply the case that the individual is a fixed point in a temporal flux or continuum, for one's self is, was and will be in the Dreaming. This is what Stannard (Lewis 1985: 120) called the 'everywhen', which is of course strongly reminiscent of our earlier discussions of the ways in which Christianity deployed temporal grammar as a means of apprehending the world in complex ways. The productive qualities of the Dreaming and the duty of the individual to ensure its coming-into-being were well described by a contact of Stanner (Sutton 1989: 15):

> My father . . . said this: 'My boy, look! Your Dreaming is there; it is a big thing; you never let it go [pass it by]; all Dreamings come from there.' Does the white man now understand? The blackfellow, earnest, friendly, makes a last effort. 'Old man, you listen! Something is there; we do not know what; *something*.' There is a struggle to find words, and perhaps a lapse into English. 'Like engine, like power, plenty of power; it does hard work; it *pushes*.'

The fact that the culture of the Dreaming has existed for thousands of years and the fact that individuals are duty-bound to preserve it in as close an approximation to that which was given them has encouraged many commentators to describe Australian religion and culture (little separates these two terms) as conservative. In some ways this is correct, but in other ways it belies the complexity of Australian religion. It also reflects a culture that many would judge to have been colossally successful, in that the classical Australian world was a place of almost no organized violence, great inter- and intra-group cooperation, with a much greater proportion of life devoted to play, culture and faith than has perhaps been found in any other world culture, since work was restricted only to economic necessity rather than the sustenance of an economy of ownership and goods (Dixon 1980: 6–7). This was a society of little personal choice, but it was also a world without formal hierarchies of control over the individual, where each person remade the perfection of the Dreaming through their life.

It is worth thinking of the many things that are offered in Australian temporalities that we do not see in other cultures as a means of addressing its complexity. It is a faith where no distinction is made between religion, literature, history and law, all of which are described through song. Histories are recounted through song or art, often of a temporary nature, made on the land or painted on to bodies. These texts offer detailed temporal accounts of things that are almost absent from other historical cultures, such as mountains, seas and rivers. This implies a phenomenological intricacy which has rarely been addressed by academic literatures, for what such accounts imply is not simply that things exist both *in their thingness* but also in some wider sense as *things in time*. Thinking through this is almost beyond us. Pictures or metaphors of objects within shards of light that stretch and travel together come to mind. To use an analogy from western culture, let us imagine a situation where we are able to understand in an equally comprehensible manner the shape and meaning of both time and events as they relate to a journey we took yesterday, are taking and will take tomorrow. It is important to note here that history does not need to be permanently inscribed by man to acquire authority. Where westerners venerate the veracity of permanence and the inscription of truth in a moment, Australian histories have a much greater capacity to come in and out of being.

Todorov (1987: 69) – in whose texts histories serve philosophical analysis and philosophy serves the writing of history – is one of the very few writers to have addressed such questions. In his work on the encounter between the peoples of the Americas and Spaniards in the late fifteenth century (a situation analogous to our case, just as there is a symmetry with Todorov's method), he asks:

> Would it be forcing the meaning of 'communication' to say, starting from this point, that there exist two major forms of communication, one between man and man, the other between man and the world, and then to observe that the Indians cultivate chiefly the latter, the Spaniards the former? We are accustomed to conceiving of communication as only interhuman, for since the 'world' is not a subject, our dialogue with it is quite asymmetrical (if there is any such dialogue at all). But this is perhaps a narrow view of the matter, one responsible moreover for our feeling of superiority in this regard. The notion would be more productive if it were extended to include, alongside the interaction of individual with individual, the person and his social group, the person and the natural world, the person and the religious universe.

Todorov is surely right that the idea of communication with the world became devalued within western cultures, thus reflecting a particular form of narrowness which then informed western views in colonial encounters. Interestingly, it is precisely this field of man's communication with the world of things that served as a central problematic in the work of Heidegger, and this strand of his work has proved perhaps the most difficult in terms of its absorption within the traditions of western thought.

Eliade describes such complexity in his account of the multiple nature of existence of the ancestors of the Dreamtime (1973: 49–50):

> Another characteristic of their [Ancestors'] mode of existence is their multiplicity and their simultaneous presence on the earth. An Ancestor *exists* simultaneously: (a) under the earth, (b) in various cosmic and ritual objects (rocks, waterfalls, *tjurungas*, etc.), (c) as 'spirit children' and finally as (d) the man (or men) in which he is presently reincarnated.

Such talk may lead us back to the question of agency, for one might ask: is what we are really seeing here a culture of complete destiny where, however unspoken, powerful forces work in order to ensure that everything will be as it should be? This is not in fact the case in Australian faiths, since powerful, all-seeing Gods play little role in the religious culture. Individuals have a constant moral duty to make time in a way that accords with the narratives and norms of their culture, but there is absolutely no doubt that this is a form of invocation where failure is as possible as success. There is an Australian sense of eternal time, since it was not believed that the world itself was made in the Dreaming, for what was made there was essentially culture. The creatures of the Dreamtime ruptured this canopy of time in order to make life and it is incumbent upon all individuals that they keep rupturing time through their actions so that we retain our state of being rather than the earlier state of unbeing.

I disagree then with those who argue that Australian culture does not possess temporal distinctiveness. Stanner, for instance, (1969: 63) asserts that 'the Dreaming took little account of futurity. So far as they thought of the long future at all they seemed to suppose that it would take care of itself as a kind of everlasting present, and the present was supposed to be very like the past.' Lawlor goes beyond this (1991: 37) to claim that 'None of the hundreds of Australian languages contain a word for time, nor do the Australians have a concept of time.' Yet studies of Australian linguistics show that such claims are erroneous, for Australian languages distinguish between times through the use of qualifiers (Dixon 1980: 271), lexical roots (Dixon 1980: 283), purposive inflections and irrealis (Dixon 1980: 380), and of course systems of tenses. Study of tenses does however reveal (Dixon 1980: 380) that, while some languages possess 'past, present and future inflections', 'There are languages in which past and present, or future and present, fall together.' Quite why there should be these variations – often at very local levels where neighbouring tribes will, respectively, possess only ideas of the non-past (present-future) or the non-future (present-past) – suggests that more detailed work needs to be done in temporal aspects of Australian linguistics.

Debates also exist among linguists as to whether Australian time is revealed as cyclical through language. Stanner, for instance, suggests (Harris 1991: 56) that:

> Time as a continuum is a concept only hazily present in the Aboriginal mind. What might be called *social* time is, in a sense, 'bent' into cycles or circles. The most controlled understanding of it is by reckoning in terms of generation-classes, which are arranged into named and recurring cycles. As far as the blackfellow thinks of time at all, his interest lies in the cycles rather than in the continuum . . .

Elkin investigates Australian notions of sameness within cycles – for instance (Harris 1991: 56), the idea that 'it is ever the same sun and moon' that we see rising and falling – and the way in which some Australian kinship systems imply cyclical forms of reincarnation, such as (Harris 1991: 56) 'the four-section kinship system wherein females "return" to the subsection of their mother's mother: grandmother and grandchild are in the same subsection and have the same "skin" name.' These cyclical ideas are also borne out in the language studies of Huttar (1977) and Sayers (1977).

Harris, though, displays some doubts as to the distinctness of the differences between western time and Australian time in this respect, and I think she is right to do that, for, as we have seen, when unpacked Christian time is a far richer set of notions of linear, cycle and continuum than the simple linear model which it has been believed has prevailed in the west. Stanner, above, also points to some of the limitations of seeing Australian time merely as cyclical, for he rightly identifies this as a form of 'social' time, implying that other temporal modes exist in Australian culture. It is remarkable, in fact, how expressive of Aboriginal art are the ideas he elucidates here, and it is perhaps through art that we might be able to more successfully parse a typology of forms of Australian time and the manner in which they interact.

Seeing time

It has recently been suggested (Chaloupka 1988: 13) that rock paintings from Arnhem Land in Northern Australia may be the oldest art in the world. Whether this is the case or not, it is certainly true that Australia has the longest continuous legacy of artistic production of any world culture. These forms have not remained static, but there has been a consistency of purpose about

Australian art from its early manifestations in cave 'galleries' through to fashionable contemporary artistic production. Australian art is a social manifestation of religion, designed to transmit the truth of the Dreaming and to describe the ways in which people can engage with the Dreamtime (Berndt 1973: 31). As Berndt says (1973: 36), 'Art has to be communicated, and it has to be social [. . .] it has a language which must be learnt.' Art was designed for ceremony (Sutton 1989: 29) and the point of ceremony was education, as knowledge was passed from the old to the young. As the contemporary painter Dinny Nolan Tjampitjinpa says (Green 1988: 42), 'This is how it is – these stories are the law that controls the canvas. You have to read these paintings. These are the stories the old people knew.'

Given the non-literate character of Australian culture, art assumed a greater role in the communication of religious truth than in many cultures, though we must remember that almost all of this art was designed to be temporary and to be destroyed once its ceremonial function was exhausted. Nevertheless, it is apparent that art works which have survived, in caves and on objects, refer to the same themes and styles that were inscribed on to bodies and the land.

The question of reading Australian art is an interesting one. The first western viewers of classical Australian art had neither the visual apparatus nor the cultural knowledge to be able to understand the paintings they saw, and often chose to reject its value with claims to its lack of quality which masked their incomprehension. Modern westerners, however, are much better equipped to read Australian art, since it has always displayed two features – conceptualism and abstraction – which became norms in the art of the twentieth-century west. As Sutton (1989: 37) says:

> While the Impressionist painter sought to achieve something like a *copy of* a visual impression, the Aboriginal artist generally seeks to create reductive signs for the thing represented. In other words, the Impressionist's approach is predominantly perceptual, while the Aboriginal artist's approach is generally more conceptual.

Two of the most emblematic forms of classical Australian art which displayed this conceptualism were so-called 'X-ray paintings' and 'mimi art'. The latter style depicts movement, particularly of spirits, and therefore represents a world that cannot be seen. In X-ray paintings (Brandl 1973: 92), 'artists depict what they know about their subjects from two different viewpoints: what can be seen, and what can be inferred. Incorporated in X-ray paintings are representations of anatomical detail of animals and occasionally of human beings, for example, the backbone, heart and intestines.' Both of these forms, therefore, seek to represent that which cannot be directly observed in nature, describing conceptualized knowledge which relates to the broader questions that religion seeks to answer. They are expressive of the conceptual depth and complexity of Aboriginal cosmology.

We should not forget, though, that where western viewers see abstract beauty in Aboriginal painting, trained audiences are able to see objects, narratives and temporal description in the art. As Peter Peemuggina says (Sutton 1989: 13), ' "nothing is nothing": everything has meaning [. . .] the world is made of signs'. There is, of course, a central difference between the representation of such signs in the classical and modern Australian artistic idioms, for in the classical age one's audience was assured to be the people of one's own social grouping, whereas art is now produced for an anonymous Aboriginal and non-Aboriginal audience. Consequently, the 'secret-sacred' is written out of modern art in a way that was not the case in the classical period. The art of allusion and hinting through visual cues and clues has become characteristic of modern Australian art (the first so-called Papunya paintings included tribal secrets, which were quickly written out of paintings once it became known that this had happened).

Writing about Australians and time, Eliade (1973: 190–91) asserts that:

The definitive characteristic of Australians and other primitive peoples is not their lack of historicity but their specific interpretation of human historicity. They too live in history and are shaped by historical events; but they do not have a historical awareness comparable, say, to that of Westerners; and, because they do not need it, they also lack [191] a historiographical consciousness. The aborigines do not record things in an irreversible chronological order.

Yet, I think that it is arguable that Australian historiographical consciousness can be found in art and landscapes. A historiographical consciousness does not depend upon a teleological or progressive temporal ordering, and I think that in Australian art we see not just temporal description but also commentaries on the way that histories and earlier discussions of time are made. In its simplest and clearest fashion, this is seen in the manner in which Aboriginal art approaches the landscape, for there is little distinction between history and natural history in Aboriginal culture. Uluru is not simply a topographical, physical feature, but it is also a collection of narratives that were left in the Dreaming across the features of the rock. While western viewers might see such things as the products of natural history, to Australians they are the result of the history of their people. Australian art, therefore, acts as a commentary on the histories of the Dreamtime and a historiographical consciousness can be said to have developed in this dialogue between the landscape-art of the Dreamtime and later temporal-artistic representations of such events.

Aboriginal art has only recently been accorded the status of 'high art' in Australia. As late as 1970, Hughes' survey of the history of art in Australia ignored all Australian art and artists, in spite of the fact that Albert Namatjira had been a major figure in the 1950s, painting what was seen to be in a western idiom at the time, but which has now been re-assessed as a fusion of western forms and Australian concerns and concepts. From 1972, with the inception of the Papunya School, Australian art has arguably entered a neo-classical period, for while there are clear stylistic differences between modern art production and classical forms in terms of look, themes and concept, contemporary Australian art aims to deepen and re-view traditional knowledge. Such art is aware that its teaching role is different from that of earlier artistic production, since it addresses Australians who live as splintered minorities on land that was once harmonious and unchanging.

Neoclassical Australian art offers a deepening of traditional truth, adding complex layers of interpretation on to classical art, providing precisely the kinds of historiographical consciousness that Eliade cannot find in Australian culture. Such discussions self-consciously address the relationship between classical and neoclassical production, the possibility of accessing ancient truths in the modern world, and, therefore, the viability of Dreaming temporalities today. We should not assume that the reading of such art is a simple matter, as I hope to show in the case of Timothy Leura Tjapaltjarri and Clifford Possum Tjapaltjarri's *Napperby Death Spirit Dreaming* (the question of reading and learning a new way of reading and seeing is a useful analogy for the general study of temporalities).

The painting displays many characteristic forms of Australian art, for it (Caruana 2003: 128):

> . . . depicts the journey through the artist's life and country. The painting features a path-line meandering between circular resting places, and major Dreamings of the artist are shown in three vignettes. From left to right, these are the Old Man's Dreaming, the Yam Dreaming and the Sun and the Moon Dreaming. The spears and a boomerang indicate the presence of the great ancestral Hunter. The spirit of death, a skeleton, is shown nearing the end of the journey.

The painting then lies somewhere between the representation of a journey, around dreaming sites, and a journey in itself, since the manner in which one reads this long and complex set of narratives is to move along the journey it represents. This, then, offers the first instance of a form of temporal complexity which both replays and refines Australian temporalities, since the experience of viewing this painting, for those open to its heritage, is to be both in the *now* of the painting and in the *then*, or the *will be*, of its journey. The force of the past ruptures into the viewer's present in the way in which the earth's coming into being emerged in the Dreamtime, along with the manner in which the sanctity of daily life was revealed in classical culture as the signs of that coming into being, which were both celebrated and incorporated into the life-stories of Australians. The painting is therefore ceremonial, but of an order of complexity not seen in classical art, suggesting the need to create a reworking of traditional tropes in permanent forms on canvases in these new times.

Traditional knowledge is also replayed in an interesting form in the manner in which four Dreamings are incorporated in one art work, offering a recognition that the contemporary painting can serve to fill the role that was formerly taken whereby dreamings were shared and recounted among neighbouring tribes. The Tjapaltjarris seem to suggest that art thus possesses the possibility to re-connect the songlines across the continent, and to bring back to life a culture that was almost eradicated in the colonial period.

The architecture of the painting aims to describe the nature of a life lived in or through the Dreaming, for, while a central path is offered through the movement from corporeal life towards death, this clear track does not hold hierarchical sway over the more convoluted journeys through the bush that are suggested by the uneven edges of the sections of colour which represent both the landscapes of the desert and the meanings of those landscapes.

The painting also offers a serious defence of the validity of the Dreaming as a religious rather than a mythical culture, for its appropriation of aesthetic ideas and tropes from ancient Australian art seems to me a vindication of the truth and character of that faith. In the painting we see a skeleton reproduced in the *mimi* style, the dots and circles characteristic of the impermanent ceremonial art of the desert and (Caruana 2003: 128) spears and a boomerang indicating 'the presence of the great Ancestral Hunter'. While this art does possess a new sensibility in its ability to reference the whole history of forms in Australian art, it offers no implication that the nature of Australian faith ought to change, for it finds greatest meaning in the restatement of the oldest truths.

Art such as this needs no validation in the form of comparisons with western painting, yet we might note the parallels with a painting such as Gauguin's *Where do we come from? What are we? Where are we going?*, which sought out the traditional art forms of the Pacific as a means of being able to tell a religious story about the nature of existence in a narrative and aesthetic form that bears close connections to the works of Tjapaltjarris, though one might suggest that their work came before his.

There is much else that one could say about this painting and the manner in which it acts as a summation of Australian culture, and temporal culture in particular. It is a conceptual painting, an account of a creation story, a history of the natural world, a work deeply imbued with its locality and local meaning, a work of duty to the Dreaming, a natural history in which the lives of men are set alongside the lives of plants, rocks and the earth. It is a painting of physical immediacy in the manner in which it recalls the natural world, yet of pheno-menological intricacy in the manner in which it weaves suggestions as to the organization of such things in time. It expresses the idea that narration is a way of being, while truth is arrived at through abstraction rather than the literal representation of things.

In Australian culture, history does not need to be permanently inscribed by man to acquire authority. Western empiricism offers the idea that man is able to sketch an objective account of truth atop the nature of things and that this sketch calcifies into a truth which, while lost, can be accessed in later times. Since Australian culture does not possess such stern notions of temporal breaks, the true nature of things has the potential to disappear and reappear, in the works of man but also in the manner in which man engages with landscapes and the traditional narratives. This, then, as the Napperby Spirit Dreaming shows us, is a life lived much more deeply in time than western lives. Where time is the great unsaid in the modern west, Australians have an invocation to make time and to live their lives as open orientations towards time. The Tjapaltjarris paint-ing is at once an account of a day's journey, that of a lifetime and of all time.

Caterpillar dreaming

'The Milky Way is stretched out across the centre of the sky and I see what is mine laid out on the long path. Route walked along many times by us in other times, past the green-grey rocks which tell a story close to this one. Those fellas weren't to know how mashed-up their path would get. Special care needed for us to stay on the way been as they don't sing that story's connection to us no more.

'First signs of grey in the east, before their earth come up and long after ours come through. Praps don't realise how much is coming in those ruby rocks. Day begins to glimmer and the old ways and the new times come smashing right together as the unmaking 'comes the making of the ways round here. That fella sees his story making, but he don't see mine, and now I seen too good where his story goes. Lots of reasonable talking takes us places we don't all wanna go.

'The birds begin to sing, then the red morning sky, not sure if it all holds together, but only way of seeing is doing and trying. Can't be that whole world will go and fall into their story. Singing back the always ways with a hammer and a lot of talk coming back to me from the old ones. Yellow tool for a white fella for green paper all mashed up in an orange sand.

'Eastern sky aflame with the fingers of the sun, right good feeling of being on our own and of joining with the old ones. Caterpillar always was a story of justice, 'bout the ways that people sung together. Need a lotta memories to make it in the same ways, and to keep it coming.

'Caterpillar was the only grub they found that day and they knew this one was no good, made you right sick, but they'd promised they'd find the witchety grubs for him, and they hadn't, and she was still with him, they'd better not scarper, but head back to the smooth stones and give him the caterpillars, sick or no sickness. Not so much of a choice, but they won't know that, will they? He ate them anyway of course, and they're watching, hoping.

'Sun burning down in all its heat and brightness.

'Not quite there now, but quite there too, cos the sun's too strong to go on, so we rest up a while in a place which has a lot of force and where the memories of all the times come through. Not so clear like, but soon the sun is low in the western sky, so got to keep on moving, not make it all in the ways that they used to.

'Big pattern of shadows all over the earth, back to some places where he and I were born. Lots of spiniflex there, dancing its way through some stories that we stayed to watch in the long leaves and told on the ground, and then we watch the wind take them, when the sun is sinking fast.

'Evening sky is aflame with red and yellow. Hoping it was a full-story which they told, not just halves in a world split apart. Worth remembering that they had always seen outside, even if it was not around with the sureness of these days. Java hadn't stopped no dreaming.

'Then the time when the tufts of grass could no longer be distinguished apart. A caterpillar gone back to dreaming and the land looking like it had for all that time.'

Conclusion

The caterpillar dreaming tries to answer the question of whether the Dreaming is dead as a mode of historical understanding. It asks whether it could only ever function as a form of replayed ritualized myth of a civilization's origins or whether it could be deployed as a form of narrative in which later events could be described. Could the Dreamtime refer to anything other than the memories of its own culture, or could we imagine that it could be used as a way of seeing others? However complicated and uncertain, the answer to these questions is ultimately that it is not dead and that it is available to others as a means of writing time, as I think neoclassical Australian art has proven.

It is now exceptionally difficult to imagine quite how the Dreaming could be used, but the narrative above incorporates references to late Aboriginal culture's engagement with Europeans with the tropes of the classical language of the Dreaming. This evidently requires a certain degree of reflexivity in the writing as means of reflecting upon different times, but it would be wrong to presume that such notions were absent from classical narratives. As has been said, Australian culture was not unchanging – even if it was stable – and there are interesting examples of Dreamings from Australia's coasts which incorporate accounts of engagements with other people and the cultural borrowing that ensued.

Another reason for believing that such an exercise is not futile is found in the work of W.G. Sebald (2002). His work merged memoir, history, myth, philosophy and art in an attempt to explore other ways of apprehending time, and, while Sebald was specifically interested in the culture of the modern west, there is much in his method that is reminiscent of temporal schemata such as the Dreaming. The writing of Walter Benjamin – who announced (1989: 176) that 'Every epoch not only dreams the next, but while dreaming impels it towards wakefulness. It bears its end within itself.' – with its stress on the manner in which we create worlds of dreams, also suggests that there are perhaps deeper structures of dreaming emplotted into cultures in and outside the west.

The caterpillar dreaming is structured around temporal distinctions used by the Aranda, identified by Strehlow (1970: 706–08), as a means of demonstrating the capacity of the simplest linguistic temporal distinctions being used as a means to accessing others' ways of understanding the world. There have been very few texts published by Australians that have sought to offer descriptions of their modern experience, based upon and through the classical narratives of their culture, but this is not to say that such texts have not existed outside the published realm.

The Australian case studied in this chapter is important in and of itself, but it is also important because it makes the point that history is a repository of others' truths. To many this may sound a facile point, but the slightest escape from an envelopment of rationality reveals its centrality to the possibility of truly comparative historical consciousness.

Just as there is an increasing awareness that minority languages are in need of ecological protection, the same is also true of modes of historical thinking. Coombs (1978: 31) recalls a meeting which Stanner had in this regard:

> In the Boyer Lectures [...] Stanner tells the sad story of an elderly Aboriginal whose tribe had been scattered, who saw the links which bound him to the land being broken, who felt himself to be cut off from the sources of his own life and from the continuities of his people. He was aware that everything that he had loved and everything with which he was familiar was in ruins around him and that he must come to terms with the alien white man's civilization. When he was about to leave his country to seek a place within that white man's civilization, Stanner found him burning something in a fire and asked him what he was doing. And the old man replied quietly and unemotionally: 'I am burning my dreaming'.

It was thus that an ecology of time was ruptured, for the flux of being that was, is and should be was destroyed. Paul Kropinyeri described the move to a new time of life: (Harris (Ian Charles) 1991: 51):

> Then I had the shock of starting to live by time – three meals a day, get up in the morning at the same time, go to bed by the clock. Before, it was if you're hungry you eat, if you're not you don't, if you're sleepy you sleep, if you feel good you do what you feel like you're doing. Then all of a sudden you come into a world where you're controlled by the clock.

Yet, ecologies of time and of historical consciousness are arguably more recoverable than other forms of human culture. Processes of recovery imply some recognition of the idea that people live in different times, but the range of areas of human culture in which temporal modes are embedded – language, literature, art, religious texts, histories – suggests that Dreamings ought no longer be burnt.

Moving on to look at Islam in the next chapter, we shall see that in questions of time and history, just as in relation to theology, philosophy and art, Islam tried to adapt and advance the ideas of the ancient Jews and Christians to the new realities of the early medieval world. In many ways it is arguable that Islam was a much more natural successor to Judaism than it was to Christianity, for we shall see that it too was riven by divisions over time, where Christianity was ultimately able to resolve most aspects of its temporal edifice.

Chapter 7

The Islamic synthesis

Introduction

This chapter is slightly different from those on Judaism and Christianity. While it too focuses on exemplary texts – which reveal much about the connections between time, faith and history in a major world religion – it deliberately addresses a much broader span of time than those earlier chapters. It concerns itself not primarily with the point of origin of a religion, but with its development in a particular geographical region over a number of centuries. It also looks at the manner in which historical narratives about that period are later deployed for political and theological purposes. In this sense, the chapter is somewhat more historiographical in its analysis of a range of sources, rather than an exercise in historical theory or research focused on a single key text.

It begins by looking at ideas of time and history in the Qur'an and the early Islamic centuries before moving on to consider 'al-Andalus', the term used by Islamic historians to describe the Iberian Muslim state which existed, in a variety of forms, from 711 C.E. until 1492 C.E. This state came into being almost eighty years after the death of the Prophet Mohammed, and about one hundred years after the formation of an organized Islamic religion. Its life coincided almost exactly with what became known as the *classical* era of Islamic culture and history, and many of the most emblematic figures of that culture came from al-Andalus, including Ibn Rushd, Ibn Khaldūn, Wallāda and Ibn Hazm. Chapter 9 of this book will consider the ideas of Ibn Rushd and Ibn Hazm in more detail in a discussion of the Islamic roots of the European Enlightenment.

In 622 C.E. Mohammed and his followers began the *Hijra*, or flight, from Mecca to Medina. He bore with him the message of a new faith for the peoples of the Arabian peninsula, which, in less than two generations, had moved thousands of miles eastwards and westwards. In doing so it absorbed and synthesized aspects of existing Mediterranean and Asian religions and mythologies, but the new time of Islam was enshrined for Muslims in a calendar whose first year began in the Gregorian year 622 C.E. The breadth and speed of the development of this new religious empire encouraged the formation of very particular local Islamic cultures, and this chapter deals with the practice of Islamic culture at the western edge of the Muslim world.

Andalusi culture was politically divorced from the caliphate – the religio-political entity which notionally unified the Islamic world after the death of Prophet Mohammed – from 756 C.E. when al-Andalus was perceived as existing as an independent entity within the *umma*, the Muslim world community. In this, al-Andalus was actually representative of the development of Islamic culture, rather than being an anomaly, for, if Islam ever truly existed as a single, unified political-religious state, it was only in the first century of its existence. In the medieval era it is more accurate to talk of 'a polyfocal Islamic world' (Robinson 2002: xviii) or (Robinson 2002: xxi) an 'Islamic commonwealth of states', rather than *the Islamic world*.

Islam has always been remarkable in terms of its decentred character. While it does possess a sacred geography, with Mecca at its heart, there is no ultimate power structure in Islam, no hierarchical prelature, no central bodies of learning and doctrine (al Azhar in Cairo comes closest), and no central co-ordination of the expression of ideals and dicta. This situation reflects the historic division of Islam along geographical and ideological lines while also sustaining such separation, though many would interpret this localism as strengthening the underlying unity of the *umma*.

This chapter also addresses central questions of historiography as they pertain to a discussion of religion and history. It looks at the nature of historical production at five key phases in the history of al-Andalus, not only as a means of unpicking the connections between time and faith in historical writing, but also to show the manner in which religious histories function not as narratives that are divorced from the present, but as powerful texts that impel paths of political, religious and cultural action. Two of the most important texts I want to consider are buildings – the Great Mosque of Cordoba and the Alhambra – so as to extend the range of this book's discussion of historical texts, while also drawing on discussions of the central place buildings play in the lived and textual worlds of religions.

In choosing to focus on al-Andalus, I am of course claiming some special status for that culture within the history of Islamic civilization, and suggesting that situations can be described there that are emblematic of wider debates within Islam. While I am not of course claiming that medieval Islam developed only in Iberia, I am suggesting that some of its most symbolic texts and situations can be found there. For instance, a central feature of all Islamic histories and cultures is a stress on tensions that have existed between Islam as it is practised in rural locales and the development of the faith in the world of large cities. Writing about Iberia, Ibn Khaldūn, the Andalusi-Maghrebi critic described by many as the first great philosopher of history, argued that the history of the faith was destined to be characterized by cycles of struggle in which rural tribes conquered urban centres, claiming both booty and the reclaiming of the soul of their faith, which they suggested had been lost in cities. Such groups thereafter themselves inevitably fell into the same pattern of development as their forebears, and were thus overthrown once they had themselves created complex, urban civilizations. Ibn Khaldūn's observation on the mechanics of Islamic history was in many ways a precursor to the idea of the dialectic which drove the work of Hegel.

The history of al-Andalus is not a story disconnected from other worlds of faith, since for centuries Muslims were a minority on the Iberian peninsula, and a theme that runs through this chapter will be the consideration of the ways in which Muslim culture dealt on a very local level with Christians and Jews in Iberia, and also how this affected Islamic thought more generally. As the Qur'an constantly stresses, Islam was born into a world dominated by Judaism and Christianity.

Islam and time

Islam was the third of the great Abrahamic religions to emerge, some two thousand years after the advent of Judaism and more than six hundred years after the inception of Christianity, and Mohammed believed that he stood as the last in the line of God's great prophets (Qur'an 2:135), which had included Abraham, Moses and Jesus. Early Muslims were deeply conscious of their faith's continuation of Judaeo-Christian history and the Qur'an (2:61) stresses Islam's recognition of fellow 'peoples of the Book', 'Believers, Jews, Christians and Sabaens – whoever believes in God and the Last Day and does what is right – shall be rewarded by their Lord; they have nothing to fear or regret.' In addressing early Muslims, the Qur'an announces (2:38) 'Children of Israel, remember the favour I have bestowed upon you. Keep your covenant, and I will be true to mine.' This is accompanied by a great stress on duty, ritual and punishment in a manner that appears to implicitly select a continuance of the Jewish culture of the Torah as against later Jewish or early Christian cultures (though one might note the Arabian context of the Qur'an's appearance with regard to polygamy). Admonitions are framed in temporal terms familiar from the Jewish law, such as the caution (2:234) that widows should stay away from other men for four months and ten days. The concept of a sacred month is added to that of a Sabbath day and there is great stress on the failure of Jews who broke away from their own rituals in order to worship in other fashions. Particular stress is accorded to (7:151) 'Those that worshipped the calf incurred the anger of the Lord and disgrace in this life', reinforcing the Jewish fear of the (temporal) power of nature cults.

Believers of other, non-Abrahamic religions were not accorded this respect, and one of the chief tasks of early Muslims was the recruitment of those who had been lost to polytheistic and 'pagan' faiths, though it has been noted (Bashaear 1997: 94–111) that the eschatological forms that Islam borrowed from Christianity and Judaism were themselves adapted from myth-based cultures. Islam's monotheism was intellectually strengthened through its encounter with Neoplatonic philosophy as it expanded westwards from Arabia through cities such as Alexandria, the former home of Plotinus and the location of a vibrant Greek philosophical culture.

Its eschatology – with an end of days described (4:87) as 'the Day of Resurrection' – was arguably much clearer than that essayed in Judaism or early Christianity. Tiwari (1997: 208) describes it as 'the most straightforward' of eschatologies and it is apparent that this was another theological area where Muslims had learned a great deal from existing faiths (though it would not stop the later fragmentation of Islamic eschatological traditions: see Sachedina 1981). In part, this connection to Jewish and Christian eschatology emerged from the fact that early Muslims faced many of the same battles with non-believers as those we read about in the Bible. As Haddad and Smith (1981: 1) remark, 'Disbelief, rejection and ridicule – thus the Qur'an portrays the response of the Meccan community to the message delivered by Prophet Mohammed concerning the day of resurrection and the universal judgement', noting the importance of the Qur'an's remarks that (16:38) 'They swear by God to the very limit of their oaths that God will not raise him who dies' and (79:10–12) 'They say, Are we to be returned to our former state when we have become decayed bones? They say, that would be a detrimental return!' In this sense Islam most certainly bore the legacy of challenging the popular stress on nature as the overarching temporal order.

Islamic time was in some sense a reaction to the ideas of temporality that prevailed among the tribes of the Arabian peninsula at the time of Prophet Mohammed. As Goodman notes (2003: 138):

To the Arabic poets of the pre-Islamic age, time was fate or destiny, often complained against as the source of human misfortunes, personified it apostrophed as a malign or corrosive influence, emblematic of change, loss and death.

In a broader geographical region dominated by monotheistic faiths, the temporal offer of Islam needed to be less fatalistic, more optimistic and of an order of conceptual complexity that could effectively compete with the time cultures of Judaism and Christianity. This latter target was achieved in a remarkable fashion between the eighth and thirteenth centuries, though, as Goodman observes (2003: 139–40), the questing, scientific, logical bent of Islamic thought sometimes took it to places which it had not originally imagined visiting, as seen in the conflict between the schools of *kalam* (knowledge, of a theological kind) and *falasifa*, or philosophy:

> In the schools of dialectical theology, *kalam*, that grew up in the garrison cities of Basra and Kufa in Iraq and elsewhere in the Islamic empire, time now became problematic in ways that would have seemed abstract and alien to the original audience of the Prophet. One concern of the *mutakallimun*, or practitioners of *kalam*, was to demonstrate God's creation of the world. But the effort was rendered difficult, as Maimonides [. . .] explains: Endeavors to prove that God created the world often proved too much because they rely on the idea that God's creation is necessary: in the case of the *falasifa*, Muslim philosophers in the tradition of Neoplatonic Aristotelianism, the tendency is towards the notion of a necessary and therefore eternal universe. Necessary creation yields the idea of eternal creation, an unwelcome outcome for those who held that God created the universe *in the beginning*, that is, that the cosmos has a temporal origin.

The underlying problems with debates between *kalam* and *falasifa* were that one was predicated on doubt and the other on certainty, one on relentlessly seeking out the chinks in the logic and epistemology of Islam (as a means of perfecting the religion), the other wishing to draw a line in the sand, to say that speculation could become an indulgence that took men away from their chief task of obedient belief. This debate was emphatically won by the theologians over the philosophers in the twelfth and thirteenth centuries, and, as Goodman observes (2003: 161–62), a simpler and more manageable account of Islamic time began to prevail, in which 'Time lost its bite, its teeth were drawn, when it was moralized – domesticated, as it were – subjected to God's purpose. That purpose was judgement, and it was for the sake of judgement that time had first been created.' We ought not to think that this clash between logic and faith in the realm of time was a novel development that came into being with Islam, for similar tensions had earlier existed in Christianity, with Toulmin noting that (1965: 68) 'the more the Christian message came to depend on prophecies, portents and revelations, the more difficult it was for Christianity to coexist with the rationalistic elements in Greek science and philosophy.' Equally it was not necessarily so apparent that Goodman's account of moralizing and God's mastery of time reflected a wholly unambiguous picture of time found in the Qur'an. After all, God's lordship of time is at one point expressed in a manner reminiscent of Peter's (2 Peter 3:8) relativization of time in which 'with the Lord one day is like a thousand years, and a thousand years are like one day' or as the Qur'an reads (2:259):

> Or of him, who, when passing by a ruined and desolate city, remarked 'How can God give life to this city, now that it is dead?' Thereupon God caused him to die, and after a hundred years brought him back to life.
>
> 'How long have you lingered?' asked God.
>
> 'A day,' he replied, 'or part of a day.'
>
> 'Know, then,' said God, 'that you have stayed away a hundred years. Yet look at your food and drink: they have not rotted. And look at your ass. We will make of you a sign for mankind: see how We will raise the bones and clothe them with flesh.'
>
> And when it had all become manifest to him, he said: 'Now I know that God has power over all things.'

God then is arguably a master of times rather than a master of time.

Islam was then a self-consciously *synthetic* religion, but we need to be very careful in our understanding of this term. It is in no way pejorative, and we must not think that the term *synthesis* simply implies in this case that Islam amounted to the *sum* of a set of ingredients borrowed from other religions. The genius of Islam was that it was able to celebrate its relative lateness and to create a religious culture which critically examined core beliefs from both theological and secular traditions, for example in the manner in which (2:177) it was able to see the Bible as 'The Book', rather than the disparate collection of texts it had amounted to in earlier cultures. Islamic thinkers never simply accepted beliefs from other cultures; rather, they worked with them, asked how they could be advanced, how they fitted together with key ideas in other traditions, and interrogated them in the deepest fashion possible. While Islamic sources often stress the literary beauty of classical Arabic in Islam, for outsiders it is often the content of the religion more than its form that impresses most.

At times the Islamic conception of synthesis can be frustrating for modern scholars for one encounters a culture in which the dividing lines between disciplines, fields of study and enquiry are simply not found in the positions that have come to seem natural in the modern (western) academy. Yet, this is, of course, a source of liberation for those interested in denaturalizing the modern western way of seeing the world, for classical Islam offers historians and historiographers utterly new ways of conceiving of studies of time. Al Kāfiyajī, the author of what is arguably the first Islamic monograph on historiography, contends that the study of the past is divided into those who are 'transmitters of tradition' and those who are 'historians', with rather more prestige attached to the former profession than the latter. As he says (Rosenthal 1968: 254), 'The same four qualifications which are required for transmitters of traditions are also required for the historian. He is required to be intelligent, accurate, a good Muslim, and fair.'

Islam quickly developed a deeply historical culture, but it cannot be overemphasized both how productive and disorienting Islamic syntheses of religion, science, politics and culture can be to those working outside the Islamic tradition. The development of the synthetic mode required the formulation of styles of enquiry that were linguistic and epistemological, for, if bodies of knowledge were to be combined and re-thought, then they needed to be reconsidered in their most basic forms, in language. This philological approach infused all aspects of Islamic learning, which shared a common interest in linguistic classification, the study of genre, and a self-consciousness as to the linguistic production of knowledge. Such an approach is evident in the interrogation of the linguistic idea of time in Al Kāfiyajī's *Short Work on Historiography* (Rosenthal 1968: 250) and many other classical Islamic texts:

> Now, linguistically, (the words) time-section (*zamān*) and time (*waqt*) are identical. Time is a generally known (concept). (The word) *mīqāt* (derived from *waqt*, 'time') has a wider range than time. The time appointed for a certain activity, such as the time of the pilgrimage, or of prayer, and so on, is called *mīqāt*. In addition, *mīqāt* is used for the place designated for something. The *mīqāt* of the Syrians is the point where they have to enter into the *īhram*, that is al-Juhfah; the *mīqāt* of the Yemenites is Yalamlan; that of the 'Irāqians Dāt al-'irq, and so on.

Interestingly, time here is understood not only through language, but also through practice and the different regional understandings of temporal ideas, which bears some connection to Martin Heidegger's investigation into time, being and the world. It is worth adding that such discussions were also a function of the logical manner in which so-called classical Arabic developed, for all words in Arabic are formed from three root-letters, with later words and ideas drawing on these root concepts, thus allowing etymologists very clear lines of enquiry as they track the progress of ideas through language.

The epistemological character of Islamic history, and its location of temporality at the heart of historiographical debate are also seen in the work of al-Tabarī, the first of the great Islamic historians (Humphreys 1991: 73). It seemed obvious to al-Tabarī (1989: I, 169) that his epic history of Islam should begin with a conceptual discussion of time:

> First, however, I shall begin with what for us comes properly and logically first, namely the explanation of
> What is time?
> How long is its total extent?
> Its first beginning and final end.
> Whether before God's creation of (time) there was anything else.

Such questions were of critical importance to al-Tabarī because they served to provide not only a reliable method for historical work, but also a form of justification or motivation which located historical study within God's universe (Al-Tabarī was well aware of the manner in which such questions had been answered in other religions). As the very first lines of his study begin (1989: I, 165) 'Praise be God, first before any first and last after any last, enduring without cease and persevering in everything without moving away. [. . .] He remains after everyone infinitely without term.' Understandings of history, God and oneself flowed together in a consideration of the nature of time, for (1989: I, 166) 'In this fleeting world [. . .] He is the Creator of all eternal and temporal time.' God, then, is the provider of a variety of times, through which he orders things, and time functions as a form of religious semiotics (1989: I, 167), 'distinguishing the signs for people who know.' This variety of times through which God orders the world is made plain by al-Tabarī in the following description (1989: I, 167):

> And We have made the night and the day two signs. We have blotted out the sign of the night, and We have made the sign of the day something to see by, so that you may seek bounty from your Lord and so that you may know the number of years and the reckoning. For everything, We have made clear distinctions.' [Qur. 17:12] And so that they may achieve knowledge of the times – the hours of night and day, the months and the years – when the religious duties God has imposed upon them are to be fulfilled, such as prayer, charity, pilgrimage, fasting, and their other religious duties, as well as the time for settling their debts and their claims . . .

God therefore uses time as a means of offering men a life of 'clear distinctions' and righteous men have then adopted time as the grammar of their secular and religious lives as a means of embedding a knowledge and faith in God in all aspects of their existence.

The repository or archive of the root-words of classical Arabic is, of course, the Qur'an, whose linguistic and philosophical ideas are perhaps of more interest to the historiographer than its discussions of history, many of which are familiar to students of Judaism and Christianity. As a prophetic faith in the Hebraic tradition, there is an emphasis on an 'end of days', at which (2:89) 'Ignominious punishment awaits the unbelievers', and throughout there is a strict emphasis on the contrast between the duality of time for men (our material existence, and the true life to come) as compared with God's singular understanding of time (Roberts 1986: 3). It is arguable that the Qur'an does not possess the creative ambiguity of the New Testament, for from its very beginning it is forceful in its conviction that (2:1) the 'Book is not to be doubted. It is a guide for the righteous.'

The clarity of the Qur'an's message as compared with those found in the Old and New Testaments is also a function of its composition, for whether one believes the Qur'an's claims that it was dictated by God, through Gabriel, to Prophet Mohammed, there is evidently a much higher degree of textual unity to a relatively short text composed in one locale over a matter of decades, than the centuries or millennia across which the New and Old Testaments were written by a varied cast of authors. It was also a reaction based upon a reading of Jewish and Christian histories which saw the Old and New Testaments (and in subsequent developments) as describing a continual fall and rise of the communities of the faithful, and a splintering of religious communities. Where the Old Testament Judaism of Job and Ecclesiastes and the New Testament of the four Gospels were framed around questions of doubt, Islam needed to be centred upon the great certainty of the singularity and divine character of its holy book. In a sense the Bible had revealed itself too easily to be a textual production and a compilation of sources, inviting forms of fragmentation that Islam saw as inappropriate to a faith with universal aspirations (for the Qur'an rejects Biblical readings that would see Judaism or Christianity as universal offers). The Qur'an describes a world (3:20) in which 'God is watching all his servants.'

In fact, an important conceit of the Qur'an, which would by no means have been agreed to in all contemporary Arabian Jewish and Christian communities, was the idea that the Bible was a single text, in which Christianity emerged seamlessly from the Jewish tradition. The purpose of this reading of biblical history was evidently to prove that Islam was the continuation and culmination of the Abrahamic faiths, but it is also explained by the fact that the Prophet Mohammed and the early Muslims almost certainly knew of the Bible only through oral traditions (Wessels 2000: 2), which stressed continuities and connectedness, where there may have been none to Jewish and Christian scholars (this also explains the anachronisms found in the Qur'an).

It is notable that when the Qur'an refers to the Bible it usually mentions only the Torah and the Gospels, though it is true that other biblical figures (usually prophets) make appearances. The Qur'an asks (2:84), 'Can you believe in one part of the Scriptures and deny another?', yet from Jewish and Christian perspectives it is arguably a text which denies significant parts of a Bible which it sees as an inviolate textual unity. What is more, Jews and Christians are asked to see the Bible as a living text which is completed by the inclusion of its final chapter, the Qur'an. Referring to Jews and Christians, the Qur'an states (2:91) that 'When they are told: "Believe in what God has revealed," they reply: "We believe in what was revealed to *us*." But they deny what has since been revealed, although it is the truth, corroborating their own scriptures', so this question of the textual status of the Testaments of the Bible with regard to the Qur'an was evidently of critical importance in relations between Muslims and non-Muslims.

Reading the Qur'an, it is arguable that its chief theme is in fact this historiographical-theological reading of Biblical culture, for Islam was wholly dependent on its reception as the closing chapter in a narrative of moral and religious progress. This also explains Seale's note (1978: 71) that:

> Moses looms large in the Qur'an where much is made of the opposition he encountered in his career: evidently the Prophet saw here a parallel with the persecution he himself suffered at the hands of the Meccans and the unbelief he met with.

Yet, there are also evident shifts in the position of Mohammed towards Jews and Christians which reflected the early history of Islam described in the Qur'an. I should note here that in some senses I have perhaps over-simplified the character of the Qur'an in that it switches between biblical narratives, accounts of early Islamic battles and a limited amount of world historical contextualization. This is further complicated by the fact that most editions of the text are compiled with the chapters (*sura*) arranged according to length rather than chronology. Nevertheless it is apparent that across the text there is a shift from early Islam, where Muslims initially prayed towards Jerusalem (Wessels 2000: 123), and the increasingly hostile rhetoric towards Jews that coincided with the decline in relations between Mohammed and the Jewish tribes of Arabia in the period after the *hijra* (Wessels 2000: 129). We read (3:109) that

'Had the People of the Book accepted the Faith, it would surely have been better for them. Some are true believers, but most of them are evil-doers' and that (5:13) 'They have tampered with words out of their context and forgotten much of what they were enjoined. You will ever find them deceitful, except for a few of them. But pardon them and bear with them.' What is more, the Jews are castigated for denying (4:157) 'the truth' of Christ and the virgin birth, and for having 'put to death the Messiah'. There is therefore a sense that the Qur'an chooses very particular aspects of Jewish and Christian history and its representation in the Bible, while imposing a very clear sense of narrative unity and meaning on this historical representation.

With regard to Christians, an analogous textual move can be seen in the concentration upon supposed references in Christian culture to the idea that Jesus had predicted he would be followed by another prophet (Wessels 2000: 140). In this case, and with regard to other historical writing in the Qur'an such as the accounts of the battles of Badr and Uhud, Wessels notes (2000: 2–3), that 'the reporting in the Qur'an is fragmentary', which he suggests has less to do with a paucity of sources (for Muslims could have written very detailed accounts of the battles they fought) and more to do with a conviction that the purpose of historical narration was the generation of meaning that would advance the 'will of God' and the historical mission incumbent on the early Muslims. A continuation of that message can be found in contemporary scholarship such as that of Draz (2000: 136):

> The same procedure which is used to reconcile, or arrange in a hierarchy, the four Gospels, should be applied to the ensembled religious heritage which the messengers of God have left us. All, for us, are saintly and holy. In spite of the distance which separates them in time and space, in spite of their differences in language and racial source, they are evidence of the same experience of the Divine. The concordance of their testimony about what is essential should open the eyes of the profane to the truth of the teachings which describe to us the true nature of the supreme Reality under its various aspects.

Although the crucifixion and Jewish attitudes towards Jesus are used as a means to criticize Judaism, it is also the case that the Qur'an offers very strong criticisms of Christian beliefs in both the idea that God appeared as the Messiah (5:17) and therefore notions of the Trinity (and the metaphorical and symbolic cultures of Judaism and Christianity are arguably more generally ignored or rejected). In one remarkable passage (5:114) a counterfactual historical conversation between God and Jesus is imagined:

Then God will say: 'Jesus son of Mary, did you ever say to mankind: "Worship me and my mother as gods besides God?"'

'Glory be to You,' he will answer, 'I could never have claimed what I have no right to. If I had ever said so, You would surely have known it. You know what is my mind, but I do not know what is in Yours. You alone know what is hidden.'

The issue of the differentiation of Islam is paramount here, but it is imperative to see that this is founded upon a particular recounting of the biblical historical narrative.

As Khalidi explains (1994: 68–69), the Qur'an also draws on conceptions of cyclical time from the Abrahamic tradition:

> The historical sections of the Qur'an are largely devoted to the histories of prophets, Biblical and non-Biblical. These histories, as we saw earlier, are basically stories *retold* to fit into a pattern made up of a prophetic mission, with basically the same invitation to people to submit to the One God, the rejection of the mission by the high and haughty, and the disaster which finally overtakes the *umma* of each prophet. Prophecy in the Qur'an is thus a cyclical phenomenon, doomed to a failure from which it can only be rescued by a final revelation. The Muhammadan experience is at once the exemplar and the triumphant completion of that futile experience.

The cyclical conception of time is combined with God's singular understanding of time to describe a circular temporality that would be instinctively familiar to audiences aware of the rejection of linear understandings of time in Christianity, for in the Qur'an we read that (21:33) 'He is the One who created night and day, the sun and the moon. All swim in a sphere'. Such notions, and the language through which they are formed, are of interest to us in developing an intellectual history of Islam, but we should also remember that Islam demanded a new approach to faith from its adherents, for, since the language of the Qur'an came directly from God, Muslims were compelled to engage with its teachings in its original, classical Arabic form, no matter where they were from in the Islamic world. This injunction arguably established a competitive advantage for Islam in the medieval period, where rates of literacy were of course far, far greater than in the spheres of any other religious culture.

The sense of novelty and difference in Islam was also developed through a new grammar of time, with its calendar which started from the point of the *hijra*. As Ibn al-Athir argued in the twelfth century (Robinson 2002: 21), 'Muhammad's emigration is the divide between truth and falsehood' and, as the popular maxim went (Margoliouth 1930: 41), 'Islam cancels all that was before it'. Before there was the *Jāhiliyya* (time of ignorance) and, after, the time of Islam. Khalidi (1994: 162) offers an interesting comparison with the broader Ismaili belief in the idea that 'Time has two principal eras, the Era of Concealment and the Era of Disclosure'. The new calendar, based on lunar cycles, was promoted by the state through coinage and official documents.

Islamic history

Classical Islam developed both an extensive range of historical modes and a raft of philosophies of history and historiographical tools. In some ways these developments were more remarkable than other fields of Islamic learning, for Islamic history drew sparsely on traditions of Greek or Persian history and there had been relatively little pre-Islamic Arabian history (Margoliouth 1930: 22). On the Arabian peninsula, most history had come in the form of genealogical oral traditions, whose (Robinson 2002: 10) 'content [could] be adapted to the changing requirements of tribal societies, where one's identity [was] determined principally by perceived bonds of kinship. In very schematic terms, a tribesman rationalise[d] his social and economic ties to contemporaries by creating or severing ties between supposed forefathers.'

Colossal numbers of historical manuscripts survive from the classical Islamic period, many of them still unpublished, and we are fortunate to possess a modern historiographical movement which has undertaken a detailed study of this field, carefully delineating the changing character of historical production from the seventh until the fifteenth centuries. Much of this scholarship has been written with a knowledge of both the classical Islamic and modern western traditions, which allows its authors to see both of these forms of temporalizing as inherently strange and unnatural.

One such area is the question of the professional purpose of history, for it is evident that much classical Islamic history served religious and legal purposes. Robinson (2002: 187–88) contends that:

> Historiography and historians stood on the margins of an academic establishment designed by and for lawyers. Rather than generate truths, it [history] could only reflect or exemplify truths already made manifest by God [. . .] Its function was accordingly restricted to instructing, moralizing, entertaining and archiving.

Such a picture is given credence by texts such as that of Al Kāfiyajī, which argue (Rosenthal 1968: 252) that 'the knowledge of history is a community duty, because it presents the best available method of establishing the chronology of the whole course of human affairs, including the other life.' Yet, even such claims have the potential to unnerve the historian from another tradition, for how, we might ask, can chronological history serve to offer us understanding of 'the other life' to come?

In fact, one might argue that the independence, syntheses and language of classical Islamic history constitute a form of temporal investigation that lies both outside the western tradition and in some way beyond functionalist interpretations which seek to see history only as a branch of theology. One area in which we see this is in the colossal number of distinct historical genres that were generated at this time (analogous developments also took place in literature). A short list of the most important would include *khabar* (the historical as opposed to the legal past), *isnād* (proofs of transmission), *hadith* ('report of the words or deeds of a religious authority', and, as Khalidi (1994: 17–18) says, 'In the Qur'an *hadith* has two basic meanings. In Meccan verses, especially the *hadith* of Moses or of Pharaoh, for example, it means 'story' or, better still, 'parable'. In Medinese versions, *hadith* tends to mean 'speech' or 'report'), *ta'rīkh* (dates or dating), *al-khulafā* ('history organized by caliphal reigns') (Robinson 2002: xii–xiii), *sīra* ('the way of proceeding') (Robinson 2002: 29), *tabaqāt* ('compilations of biographical material organized chronologically'), *tafsir* (Qur'anic exegesis), genealogies, biographies, prosopographies and chronographies. Khalidi has identified what he believes to be a path of development through these genres, in which a series of (1994: xii) 'epistemic canopies' succeeded each other from the seventh until the fifteenth centuries (1994: 232–33):

> History was looked upon from four major points of view. History as *Hadith* meant the preservation of the sacred and secular past of the community with the emphasis falling upon the modes of transmission of historical reports rather than on their intrinsic probability. History as *Adab* meant history as a narrative record of human civilization where patterns may be detected as guides to political and ethical conduct. History as *Hikma* meant a more rigorous attention to the workings of nature and rationality in the acceptance of historical reports, largely perhaps in order to prune religion of legend. History as *Siyasa* meant history as an imperial bureaucratic chronicle, authoritative, comprehensive, and primarily designed for administrative use.

Robinson (2002: 61), meanwhile, claims to identify a consolidation of historical genres in the mid-ninth century as the Abbasid caliphate instituted imperial control over the production of historical knowledge, so as to erase

'Unpleasant and controversial history' from the records, most notably the Abbasid's own slaughter of the Umayyad house, whose caliphate the Abbasids had usurped. The point is extended in Humphreys (2002: 92) to a more general claim that 'splits in early Islam promoted the collection of histor-ical material and the creation of factional histories'. El-Hibri's recent work (Robinson 2002: 42) takes a very different approach, with its contention that even the most partisan histories often found subtle ways of critiquing their political present through the contextualization of that present within a universal history, which afforded a covert means of questioning the moral character of contemporary rule.

The historical genre that has been most debated in the past hundred years has been the *hadith*. Traditionally the *hadith* were unquestioningly treated as holy texts, second only to the Qur'an in their authenticity and the moral truth of their messages, but more recently doubts have been cast on the dating and veracity of many *hadith*. As Hoyland puts it (1997: 2):

> Islamicists, who once rejoiced that their subject 'was born in the full light of history' have recently been discovering just how much apparent history is religio-legal polemic in disguise, some even doubting whether the host of Arab historical works that appear in the late eighth and early ninth centuries contain any genuine recollection of the rise and early growth of Islam. The *hadith* are in many ways a perfect example of Islamic synthesis, for although they are being discussed here as forms of history, for the manner in which they report on the actions of the prophet and his companions, they can just as easily be viewed as laws (for they serve as one of the bases for *shar'iā* law), politics (for they act as guides to behaviour in the public sphere) or religion (for they act as moral teachings too).

For Islamic scholars the *hadith* are of importance in and of themselves, but also because they form part of a wider structure of belief founded on holy texts. In this respect, it is the *isnād*s, or mode of transmission, which is crucial. Each *hadith* is accompanied by an *isnād* which indicates not only the provenance of each particular saying, but also the chain of provenance through which it has passed before acquiring its definitive, written form. As Khalidi says (1994: 23), 'the *isnād*s came to resemble pyramids of authority, the apex being the substance (*matn*) of the *hadith* in question and the sides and base a slowly increasing company of narrators.' It was the veracity of the *isnād*s that was called into question by Julius Wellhausen and Ignaz Goldziher, which in turn led Schacht to develop his two critical theses (Humphreys 1991: 73): '(1) that *isnād*s going all the way back to the Prophet only began to be widely used around the time of the Abbasid Revolution – i.e. the mid-second/eighth century; [and] (2) that, ironically, the more elaborate and formally correct an *isnād* appeared to be, the more likely it was to be spurious.'

Such claims raise a series of questions, some specific to Islamic history and some of more general historiographical interest. How might history look, for instance, if one adopted Schacht's approach to *isnād*s to argue that the more reliable and perfect a source seemed, the less likely it was to be reliable? Why have textual challenges such as that of Schacht been perceived as being of more general damage to Islam than has been the case with Christian theological studies, which have tended to cohere around a biblical chronology which sites most of the composition of the New Testament outside the life of Christ? Some answers to this latter question have been provided in the description of the deeply textual character of Islam. The *hadith* are part of a textual edifice which has the Qur'an at its heart, and an attack on one part of that structure is necessarily a questioning of the integrity of the most sacred and unchallenged site in Islam. More recently, writers such as Wansbrough, Cook and Crone have moved on from Schacht's work to contend that much of the Qur'an itself was written in the centuries following the death of Mohammed, which of course directly contradicts Muslims' basic belief that the Qur'an was narrated by God, through Gabriel, to his emissary Mohammed.

Andalusi time: the conquest

The question of the construction of Islamic history – perhaps even of history more generally – is well illustrated in accounts of the conquest of Iberia in the early eighth century. As an 'event', the conquest of Iberia serves as an almost perfect case study for deconstructionist historiographers, for we know of no contemporaneous sources from the years 711 or 712 C.E. In other words those *primary sources* which empirical historians claim as the building blocks of their reconstructive texts are utterly absent in this case. It would then seem harder than is usually the case to contest here Munslow's description (2003: 2) of the historical field as 'a mind- and discourse-dependent performative literary act', for there is an inevitability about the literary quality of histories in this instance.

The divergence of the available sources on the key questions of what happened in 711 C.E. and why it happened – the two central questions posed, and often confused or conflated, in histories – is illustrative of the discursive, literary and positioned qualities of these texts. Such narratives are obviously constructed from inferences about the later shape of the state of al-Andalus and the positioning of the authors. The greatest differences between such accounts can be seen in their descriptions of whether or not the invasion of Iberia was a bloody one. The Anonymous Christian chronicler of 754 C.E. (Constable 1997: 29–32) emphasizes the great violence of the Muslim invasion while many early texts in Arabic stress the relatively limited resistance that was offered by the politically and religiously divided Gothic rulers of the peninsula. Some, such as Ibn 'Abd al-Hakam's ninth-century 'Narrative of the Conquest of al-Andalus' (Constable 1997: 32–36), even go on to claim that Tāriq bin Ziyād and his troops were invited on to the peninsula in order to settle a dynastic dispute that had been taking place within the ruling Gothic clans in the south of Iberia. While later historians have tended to emphasize the suspicious narratological coherence of this tale, it has also influenced contemporary historians such as Olagüe (1969) and Armour (2002).

Earlier evidence, in the form of peace treaties made between Iberian communities and the invading armies (Constable 1997: 37–38), has been used to reinforce the idea of a relatively peaceful 'conquest', though such notions are taken to a more extreme point in the many later, often populist, Arabic histories of 711 C.E., such as Tariq Mohammed al-Swidan's *Tārīkh al-Andalus al-Mafqūd* (n.d.), which uses the term *futūhāt* or 'opening' to describe what took place in Iberia in that year. The use of such a term reflects a conscious choice to avoid the implied conflict of *ghazawāt* ('conquest') or *ijtiyāh* ('invasion'), and to minimize the significance of any violence through the establishment of a causal connection between conquest and the introduction of Islam to the Iberian peninsula. Relatedly, there was also a crucial set of legal issues at play in the eighth century with regard to the manner in which a radical distinction had been established in Islamic law between the so-called *dar al-harb* (the 'place of war') and the *dar al-Islam* (the place of Islam, or peace). Muslim armies gained much more significant rights over the property of those who were conquered through war, and were obliged to offer more substantial packages of rights to those who peacefully submitted to them. There are many different interpretations (Kennedy 1996: 8–9) that could be placed on the designation of much of Iberia as a *dar-al-Islam*, and there is some irony in the fact that Islamic accounts of the conquest became more peaceful over time, as later generations had nothing to gain from describing the conquest as a bloody struggle and a greater moral desire to cast Islam as a religion of peace.

The use of the term *futūhāt* simultaneously answers the question as to what happened, and why it happened, and, as one might expect, the religious explanation predominates in later Islamic explanations of why these events took place. Such accounts invariably invoke religion as the principal or single cause of these events in contrast to other histories that stress military-strategic rationales, economic explanations and the weakness of Gothic Iberian society. Military-strategic accounts (Makki 1992: 6–7) are inherently connected to religious explanations as they underline the importance of Iberia's place in guarding the expanding Islamic world from northern and western Europe, the 'natural' frontier of the Pyrenees and the importance of control of the entrance to the Mediterranean. This last factor is also intimately related to economic interpretations (Watt 1965: 4) of the conquest which stress both the richness of Iberian natural resources and the trade benefits that came from control of the entrance to the Mediterranean (which would of course later lead Henri Pirenne to develop his famous thesis that the medieval Mediterranean became a relatively impoverished 'Muslim lake'). Finally, other narratives stress the internal weaknesses, both political and religious, within Iberian Gothic society, and one finds accounts which stress the moral laxity of the Goths in both Christian and Islamic sources. Kennedy (1996: 13) notes that from the ninth century onwards 'the most plausible explanation [offered by Christian historians for the fall of the Gothic kingdom] was that the Goths were immoral and had disobeyed God's commandments.'

While modern, empirical histories of the conquest draw heavily on these explanations as to how and why the Islamic invasion occurred, they are of course much more attendant to the aim of many early histories to glorify a particular religion, nation or group, and the difficulty entailed in separating out the religious and historical impulses of both Islamic and Christian accounts. From a historiographical point of view, however, there is some irony in the fact that the convincing qualities of these different and divergent narratives of the conquest (and of course historical narratives are intrinsically convincing texts for most of us when we read them) exist in spite of the complete lack of extant eyewitness or primary source material. In a sense this lack of sources is part of the explanation as to why such divergent historical accounts of the period exist.

Andalusi time: the Umayyads

The dynastic founders of al-Andalus were the Umayyad clan of Damascus who were also the caliphs of the Muslim world in the first decades of the eighth century. That broader dominion ended in 750 C.E. when the Umayyads were usurped by the Abbasid grouping who came from what is today Iraq. The Abbasids invaded Damascus and, in taking control of the centre of the Umayyad empire, they slaughtered almost every male member of the caliphal clan. The only important figure to survive was the young 'Abd al-Rahmān, grandson of the caliph Hishām, who fled Damascus, moving quickly through territories still loyal to his family in North Africa to reach al-Andalus in 756 C.E. Against considerable odds, 'Abd al-Rahmān managed to assert his own political authority over competing figures in al-Andalus, thence declaring the formation of an independent Umayyad Iberian Islamic emirate which was to stand as a counterpoint to the new Abbasid caliphate. If this account sounds rather too much like a legend or a fairy story in its satisfying completeness, readers should certainly consider consulting the extensive historiographical literature on the Umayyads (Hawting 1986: 126).

In order to cement his religio-political authority, 'Abd al-Rahmān began a programme of mosque-building across al-Andalus, the centre-piece of which was the new Great Mosque of Cordoba. While the architecture of the mosque was designed to reflect this new authority, it was also intended to function as a historical text that evoked very specific memories for its readers. First, it was built on a site that had previously hosted a cathedral, and 'Abd al-Rahmān was careful to incorporate into his mosque styles and motifs that recalled the Gothic and Roman Christian cultures which had preceded the arrival of Muslims in Iberia. This was most evident in the so-called 'forest of arches' which dominates the interior of the mosque, where a sense of height was achieved through the effect of layering row upon row of arches on top of each other. The particular arch that was selected for the mosque was the horseshoe arch, favoured by the Goths, and the arrangement of these arches evoked memories of Roman aqueducts, while also referencing Christian Byzantine culture in its alternating red and white brickwork. This feature also expressed the second main point of reference in the mosque: to the Great Mosque of Damascus, the holiest of buildings erected by the Umayyads, which had borrowed from the Byzantine Christian culture of Syria in which the Umayyads had risen to prominence. The building was then also designed to tell a particular story about the past to the people of al-Andalus, 'Abd al-Rahmān's kinsmen, and to the ruler himself. It established a trope of nostalgia and memorialization which was to characterize much of Umayyad and Andalusi culture, not least its buildings.

The Great Mosque of Cordoba served as material proof of the adaptive qualities of Islam and its capacity to adjust itself in new lands through the development of synthetic cultural forms. This synthetic culture came to characterize all the major faith groups in Umayyad al-Andalus. Christians and Jews, who were protected as the *dhimmi* – fellow peoples of the Book – utilized this freedom to create cultures which mirrored the eclecticism and confidence of the Umayyads. Many Christians, for instance, came to be known as Mozarabs, for the fact that they abandoned almost all aspects of their previous culture, other than their faith, choosing to dress, eat, speak and think like their new Muslim political rulers. Similarly, Jews began to build synagogues which reflected the particular *mélange* of the Great Mosque of Cordoba, to the extent that buildings such as the Synagoga del Transito in Toledo are almost indistinguishable from Andalusi mosques. In cities such as Toledo worshippers of the Abrahamic faiths even practised their faiths in each others' houses of worship.

The cultural confidence of Umayyad rulers and the growth of Islam in al-Andalus were reflected in the series of expansions of the Great Mosque which were planned by a series of emirs. These culminated in the major additions of 'Abd al-Rahmān III and his son al-Hakam II in the tenth century. 'Abd al-Rahmān III was the first Umayyad ruler to break with the convention of describing himself merely as an emir, choosing to proclaim himself to be the caliph, and therefore the political-spiritual head, of the entire Islamic world. This grandiosity was mirrored in his construction of a new royal city ten miles outside Cordoba, Madinat al-Zahrā', which signalled the movement of the new caliph beyond the local affairs of his own province and the new station he had seen for himself in life. The city-complex at Madinat al-Zahrā' was in many ways an architectural hymn to the design tropes and motifs of the Umayyads, as the arches and distinctive features of the Great Mosques of Damascus and Cordoba were endlessly replayed.

Al-Hakam II went even further in his alteration of the Great Mosque of Cordoba than his father. He built a courtyard and further extensions which echoed the Damascene precedent (Hillenbrand 1992: 130), while also extending the *qibla* wall. This has always been one of the most controversial aspects of the design of the building, since 'Abd al-Rahmān I had constructed a *qibla* (which orients the believer's direction of prayer) not eastwards towards Mecca, but southwards towards Ghana. The logic of this position was that this mirrored the southward-facing *qibla* found in Damascus, but it also suggested what for some Muslims was a worrying stress on the precedence of Umayyad royal power over Islamic orthodoxy. This tendency was pushed even further by al-Hakam II who extended the *qibla* to construct for himself a private *mihrab*. The *mihrab* had traditionally been a small niche built in the *qibla* wall, but in al-Hakam II's vision the *mihrab* became a private prayer chamber in which the ruler would worship ahead of his people. This was in some ways more heretical even than 'Abd al-Rahmān I's innovations, for it contradicted the central architectural feature of mosques, which was the democracy of the rectangular space, which ensured that no believer was offered a more privileged form of access to God than any other. This order was later defaced in a still more spectacular fashion when the aesthetic unity of the mosque was destroyed on its appropriation by the Catholic church. The democratic space of the interior was ruptured through the placing of a Christian chapel at the heart of the building.

Perhaps unsurprisingly, the rule of 'Abd al-Rahmān III and al-Hakam II represented both the cultural apogee of Umayyad al-Andalus and also the beginning of the Iberian Umayyad state's rapid demise. By the late tenth century, Madinat al-Zahrā' was in ruins, having been sacked by the Umayyad's Berber clients who resented the centralization of political and military authority, and the whole of the Iberian caliphate was on the verge of disintegrating into scores of competing city-states (the so-called *ta'ifas*). This collapse ensued partly from the poor quality of the political instincts of the late Umayyad rulers and partly from their vivid desire to write central roles for themselves and the Umayyad house in the history of Islam.

Andalusi time: the Alhambra

In terms of the architectural history of al-Andalus, the Alhambra (literally 'the red one', referring to its red, castellated walls) is regarded as Granada's great counterpart to Cordoba's Umayyad Mosque. The Alhambra is not, however, a religious building in itself (though it did contain a mosque, which has since been destroyed), for it was constructed as a palace complex by the Nasrid rulers of Granada during the last centuries of Islamic rule on the peninsula, when the kingdom of al-Andalus had shrunk from controlling most of Iberia to a small area around a single city in the south of the country. Yet, the Alhambra is incontrovertibly an Islamic building and text, which proposes a unique statement of Islamic history and temporality, as well as offering aesthetic beauties so great that it was rapaciously coveted by Christian Iberian rulers such as Ferdinand and Isabella.

After the fall of the Umayyads and the disjointed *ta'ifa* period, the Andalusi state had been successively conquered by Berber Muslim tribes from North Africa (the Almoravids from 1085–1147, who, in turn, were defeated by the Almohads, 1147–1232). While successful in re-establishing the territorial unity of the Iberian Islamic state, the Almoravids and Almohads also lost a great deal of land to the increasingly confident Christian kingdoms of northern Iberia. This so-called *Reconquista* eventually led to al-Andalus's consisting simply of the small Nasrid kingdom of Granada, which survived as an Islamic emirate for two hundred and sixty years as its rulers cleverly played off the rival Christian states which surrounded them on the peninsula.

On one level, the Alhambra was designed as an emblem of the synthetic power of Islam, for it aspired to describe primal connections between man and nature, man and God, logic and belief, science, art and God, and the oneness of Muslim time. If such claims sound overly abstract in theory, let us look at the practice of some parts of the building to better understand these ideas. The unity of man in the face of God is seen throughout the building in the repeated inscription 'There is no God but God and all men stand before him', which stresses the commonalties of all Muslims, rather than the privileged status of the Alhambra's builders. This stands in marked contrast to the crass Christian additions to the building which see the names of Ferdinand and Isabella plastered over the walls of the building, unknowingly debasing themselves in their expression of royal power and their status at the apex of Spanish Catholicism. Brothers (1994), indeed, offers a detailed study of the manner in which Christian attempts to appropriate the Alhambra played a role in the Morisco revolt of 1568.

The oneness of science, art and God is expressed through the use of designs that merge Qur'anic calligraphy with geometric patterns of stunning complexity. Geometry was considered as much an artistic pursuit in Islam as a scientific investigation, for through artistic geometry came the possibility of man's representing those basic structures of nature that had been gifted to man by God (thus also avoiding the iconic representation of human or holy forms, which was disparaged in most Islamic cultures). Such decoration also led believers from a study of logic, as it was expressed in geometry, to a consideration of man's place on earth and the concomitant inevitability of belief. These ideas were further enhanced through the use of courtyard architecture, gardens and pools, which expressed not only approximations of paradise on earth but also the opportunity for the individual believer to situate himself in such a fashion that religious meditation came through the contemplation of the endless skies above and the envelopment of sacred architecture all around. Grabar (2006: 142) has also suggested that a complex mythology of Solomon was used to frame this discussion of man's access to the divine through architecture, design and gardens (see also Irwin 2004).

The Alhambra also functioned as a historical text and a discussion of time for its contemporary readers in a number of other ways. The heterogeneity and complexity of its design styles reflected its status as a palace of refugees, for Granada had become a last redoubt for many Iberian Muslims, who brought their distinct craft traditions and styles from across the peninsula (see also Grabar 2006: 138). It was also designed as a building oriented towards the future as well as the past, displaying what might be called a *premonitory nostalgia*. Any study of the political history of al-Andalus in the late medieval period would have led to the conclusion that the Nasrid kingdom would eventually be conquered by Christian rulers, just as had been the case with the rest of al-Andalus. Yet, the Nasrids devoted colossal economic and psychic resources to the construction of a building with the exterior of a fortress and a fantastically palatial interior. They did this, then, not simply for Muslims in their own time but also for future generations of Muslims and, indeed, non-Muslims. The wistful desire to reflect the glories of Andalusi Islam was brilliantly realized, and this is of course reflected in the massive historiography devoted to the interpretation and reception of the Alhambra. Ruggles' (2003) study of the gardens of al-Andalus, for instance, sees a great contrast in the gardens from the Umayyad to the Nasrid periods: where earlier they were designed to evoke royal power, they later came to serve as memory statements. He writes that (2003: 222):

> As the size of Muslim-ruled al-Andalus shrank and confidence in Muslim rule began to wane, the patrons of architecture clung to the forms and motifs of the Umayyad period, regarded as a golden age of Muslim ascendance on the Iberian Peninsula. The repertoire of architectural forms did not change significantly, but the meanings and the perceptions of them did. The most striking example of this is the mirador, which changed from a signifier referring to the active relationship of the powerful, sovereign viewer to his territory of gardens and endless vistas, to a signifier referring to the memory of that relationship.

We might also note the powerful influence of the Alhambra as both a set of styles and aesthetics in post-1492 Spain, and as a structuring idea in 'buildings as time statements', such as Seville's Alcazar (begun in 1364), where the Alhambra's valorization of nostalgia is warped into a melancholic longing for that earlier nostalgia (which could never return because Muslims were now being expelled from Iberia).

The historical-architectural text of the Alhambra finds its historiographical counterpart in the work of the contemporaneous Ibn Khaldūn, who was born in the Maghreb but lived for long periods in Iberia, basing much of his *Muqaddima* and *History* on the Andalusi past. He is variously claimed as the first world historian, the first sociologist and the author of the first great work in the modern philosophy of history. Khalidi's description (1994: 223) of his work is revealing of the underlying connections of the synthetic method in Islamic culture:

> In many ways the *History* of Ibn Khaldūn resembles a Mamluk architectural monument. The powerful scale of the exterior merges slowly into the

delicacy of the interior detail, just as the grand panorama of great contemporaneous states is worked out on a smaller scale by their numerous
off-shoots and branches.

While Khalidi here compares Ibn Khaldūn's work with Mamluk architecture,
the comparison might just as easily be made with the Alhambra, for it too
strove to narrate a history of Islam which crossed time and which incorporated
unified Islamic understandings through its form.

Andalusi time: 1492

For many Muslims, the final days of the Nasrid kingdom are encapsulated in
the words reputedly uttered by Aisha, mother of the last Nasrid ruler, to her
son, Boabdil, 'Weep like a woman for what you could not defend like a man!'
The loss of al-Andalus has been felt very deeply by Muslims across the world
since 1492 C.E. It was one of the few Islamic states which then reverted to
non-Islamic rule and until very recent times it was the only state from which
Muslims were ethnically cleansed, along with Iberia's Jews. This sense of loss
– which is as apparent in histories as it is in fictions and theological works – was
accentuated (Jayyusi 1992: xvii–xix) by the romantic cast that was put on the
material and religious glories of Andalusi Islamic culture. In other words, a
particular 'Andalusi narrative' has served as a trope in the Islamic historical
imaginary, with a set of lessons and inferences designed to be drawn from
this tale.

The clarity and strength of this narrative was also critical because it was
designed to compete with another extremely powerful history of 1492 C.E.:
that of the victorious Spanish crown, which rapidly set about designing a
version of events which saw their expulsion of Muslims from the peninsula as
(divinely) preordained. This argument developed an appropriate historical
form that came to be known as the 'continuity narrative' of Spanish history.
Both of these concepts were constructs, though they came to be naturalized to
some degree over time within Iberian culture.

The continuity narrative, as exemplified by a writer such as Sanchez-
Albornoz (1975), suggested that Ferdinand and Isabella were continuing to
uphold Iberia's inherent Christian character, and that the period from the
defeat of the Goths until 1492 C.E. was not one that had significantly affected
the character of the Iberian culture or people, for Iberia's Muslim rulers had
been outsiders, and foes of Christianity (thus we see how such a narrative also

had a productive political purpose in justifying the expulsion of Muslims and Jews). Such an outlook was tenuous in the extreme in the fifteenth century for much of Iberian culture was Arabized and Islamized – food, language, philosophy, literature and political forms for example – and new symbols of 'Spanishness' had yet to be constructed: before 1492 C.E. there was no Spanish language, no capital in Madrid, no common religion across the peninsula, and no tradition of a centralized political authority. All of these things were created from the late-fifteenth to the seventeenth centuries as Spain became arguably the first country to constitute itself as a nation state, with appropriate historical forms that stressed the ethnic, religious and political unity of the Spanish nation and people.

While religion clearly played a critical part in these Islamic and Spanish histories, it may be more useful to contend that two political communities saw advantages in interlocking narratives about the past in which one side argued that religious truth and destiny provided a basis for military victory, whilst its *other* side suggested that it was the specific religious and moral weaknesses of particular rulers that had allowed its foes to take control. The moral power of these arguments, and their strong appeal to their respective audiences, ensured the manner in which they served as the basic structure of emplotment of both Spanish and Islamic histories of al-Andalus for centuries. It should not escape our notice that such histories also of course replayed, in reverse fashion, the Islamic and Christian tropes which had been developed in the eighth century to explain Muslim destiny and Christian weakness (in the period of the Reconquista there is also considerable textual evidence that Christian accounts of 'holy wars' borrowed heavily from archetypal Islamic accounts of *jihād*).

Yet, there are many other Islamic and Spanish histories of al-Andalus, leaving aside those accounts of the past from other, less partisan positions. There are the stories of the Muslim refugees from Iberia who settled across the Mediterranean, taking with them a distinct culture which can be seen in the names of the towns called Andalus across North Africa, just as Andalusi Jews developed a distinct Sepphardic culture whose influence became global in their faith community. There was also the question of the manner in which the story of the Andalusi Muslims became a part of larger historical accounts such as the narrative of the Crusades. In recent years revisionist historians have undertaken a project of unpicking and dissociating al-Andalus from the Crusades, for, while there is an agreeable simplicity about the connection of broader late Medieval Christian–Muslim struggles with events in Iberia, there is very little evidence that the so-called 'Reconquista' was religiously motivated. Instead, it was driven by political expansionism within a world of competing northern Iberian kingdoms. Calls for religious wars may have sometimes been used as forms of propaganda, but the realities of the intimate ties between Christians and Muslims in and outside those kingdoms – at popular cultural and elite diplomatic levels – gave the lie to the idea that Iberian 'Crusades' took place.

More recently, accounts of the late Nasrid period and first centuries of the Spanish state have tended to concentrate on the role played by Iberia as the incubator and developer of Classical ideas, in fields such as philosophy, art and medicine, which were to act as the intellectual motor for both the European Renaissance and the Enlightenment (Gutas 1998, Imaddin 1965, Lasater 1974, O'Learey 1922, Brotton 2002, Dionisus and Hitchcock 1994, Lopez-Baralt 1992 and Boase 1992). Detailed studies of the work of writers such as Defoe and Dante have identified clear Andalusi Islamic antecedents, while scholars concerned with the philosophical question of the doubting of God have tracked the influence of the thought of writers such as Ibn Rushd in European centres, such as Paris, which centuries later were to become centres of the Enlightenment. Such texts have also led to a reappraisal of the character of the late Andalusi period, which is now much less often read as a tragedy in both western and Islamic histories.

Andalusi time today

In recent decades there has been an upsurge in interest in the history of al-Andalus with narratives about Islam, Spain and history being deployed for very specific purposes inside and outside the Iberian peninsula.

The renewal of Spanish interest in al-Andalus was intimately connected with the processes of democratization and regional devolution that followed the death of Franco in 1972. Since Francoist ideology was deeply attached to all aspects of the continuity narrative, it was natural that progressive forces in Spanish society would look to the past for other histories that might legitimate their own description of peninsular identity and nationhood. Popular and academic texts (Herbert 2002, Boycott 2001) found in al-Andalus an idea of Spain which was complex, multicultural, multi-faith, multilingual and associated with cultural success, where Francoism had been associated with the most rigid form of culturally conservative Spanishness which stressed central control, dictatorship, a single shared language and a single common faith. This revived idea of Spain also became a crucial tool in the nation's development of tourism as a major economic sector and in its broader attempts to represent itself in a new light to the world.

The discontinuity narrative came therefore to be used as an ethical resource and archive for those who championed the revival of regional identities and governance in Catalonia, the Basque Country, Galicia and Andalucia itself. Yet, there were tensions attached to this political deployment of historical narrative. Socialists such as Felipe Gonzales could comfortably reference al-Andalus in his description of a new Spain which, for the first time since the early seventeenth century, included a significant Muslim population, and in his championing of Spain as the logical location for peace talks between Palestinians and Israelis. For other 'progressive' constituencies, however, the conjunction of Arab-Muslim culture and Iberia was a more problematic idea. Nowhere was this more evident than in Catalonia, which was on the one hand a driving force behind the political deployment of discontinuity narratives, and an instinctive critic of the notion that Islam and Arab culture had any influence on Catalan identity. In these new times, an old form of racism emerged where Catalans, from the President downwards, began to claim that an essential difference between Catalan and Spanish languages and cultures lay in the latter's Arabization and the former's continuance of an unbroken Latin heritage.

In some ways it may seem unduly harsh to concentrate on Spain in this regard, for this general question of the recognition of Islamic pasts is a troubled one in Europe which has perhaps been dealt with more openly in Spain than has been the case in Portugal, Sicily, Greece, Hungary, Russia and much of the Balkans. It seems notable that in 2004 the tense negotiations surrounding the historical preamble that was to accompany the European constitution were polarized between religious figures who favoured making reference to Europe's Christian heritage and those who advocated the excision of references to religion, either on secularist grounds or on the basis of respect for religious, primarily Muslim, minorities currently living in Europe. Few made the case for a constitution that acknowledged the influence of all three Abrahamic faiths upon European history.

The significance of the Andalusi story has also been much discussed by both academic historians and other writers in recent years. For some it has provided an opportunity to describe an open, liberal, tolerant version of Islam. Since September 11 such texts (Menocal 2002 is the best example) are as likely to be directed to non-Muslim audiences as they are to the *umma*. There has also been a revisionist trend in Islamic intellectual history (Jayyusi 1992: xviii) which has begun to dismantle the 'Andalus as tragedy' narrative, and in its place to develop an account which stresses both the strengths and dynamism of Andalusi culture, and its contributions to European culture.

Yet, al-Andalus has also regained a central place in the Islamist and *jihādist* historical imaginary. Where liberal Muslims saw in al-Andalus a cosmopolitan model of Islam's co-existence with other religious communities, Islamists see instead a historical justification for a programme of just, imperial reconquest. In 'Defending the Land of the Muslims' Abdallah Azzam (Burke 2003: 69) demands of jihādists that their:

> Duty will not end with victory in Afghanistan; jihād will remain an indi-vidual obligation until all other lands that were Muslim are returned to us so that Islam will reign again: before us lie Palestine, Bokhara, Lebanon, Chad, Eritrea, Somalia, the Philippines, Burma, southern Yemen, Tashkent and Andalusia.

Yet, Azzam, Osama bin Laden and other *jihādists* make such claims about the 'return of Andalusia' while rejecting all but the very earliest Islamic history for, as Burke notes (2003: 78), they see 'The culture and sophistication of the Umayyads and the Abbasids, the architecture and the poetry, the philosophy and the lore of the Muslim world [. . .] as tainted by weakness and corrupted by failure.' Bin Laden in fact recalls the tragic motif found in many Islamic his-tories of al-Andalus: 'Let the whole world know that we shall never accept that the tragedy of Andalusia would be repeated in Palestine. We cannot accept that Palestine will become Jewish.' Something of the wilful ahistoricism of this approach is conveyed in the conflation at work here, but we also see the manner in which the Andalusi story comes to underpin a very particular political version of contemporary Islam. The Palestinian connection which bin Laden makes here has been a common trope in the post-war period, most evident in the work of Palestinian poets such as Mahmoud Darwish who have sought to add historico-cultural strength to the Palestinian cause (Jayyusi 1992: xviii).

Conclusion

This chapter has sought to describe the historical and historiographical cul-ture of Islam, both in the foundational texts from the birth of the faith, and in a specific Islamic culture. Islamic philosophies of history are clearly connected to the temporal traditions of the Mediterranean world, yet they are very differ-ent from Christian and Jewish historiographies in significant ways. The shift from complex and plural temporal and historical modes in the foundational texts of Judaism and Christianity to simpler, blunter and more operable forms in the medieval period contrasts with the Islamic experience where the relatively plain and clear temporalities of the Qur'an were complicated in medieval Islamic cultures. The distinctiveness of the Islamic synthesis can only truly be appreciated through an abandonment of a series of structures (disciplinary, temporal, religious) which are deeply embedded within western culture, but once gained it offers a tool which is of use as a point of comparison in the analysis of all Islamic cultures. Such cultures never lose their epistemo-logical focus and a productive dynamic is engaged through epistemological questioning of a common set of historical texts across the Islamic world.

An exemplary case of such questioning which has enjoined massive debate at popular and academic levels in recent years has been the development of Islamic gender history, in which competing positions have been developed that rely on textual and historical analysis in the formation of contemporary social theory. In part this has entailed a return to classical models, as seen in the work of Fatima Mernissi (1996: 92), who has noted that:

> Contrary to widespread belief, early Muslim historians gave considerable exposure to women in their writings. They did not, as might be expected, talk about them only as the mothers and daughters of powerful men. General history books, genealogies and chronicles identified women as active participants and fully involved partners in historical events, includ-ing the crucial emergence of Islam. In religious histories describing events which took place from the Prophet's birth to his death, as well as in religious texts themselves, such as Hadith repertories or Qur'an Tafsir, women are acknowledged and their contributions generously praised as both dis-ciples of the Prophet during his lifetime and as authors of Hadith after his death. In fact, more than ever before, historical argument seems to be crucial concerning the rights of women in Muslim theocracies.

While forms of secular feminism exist in the Islamic world, most notably in the work of Nawal el Saadawi (1984), writers such as Mernissi, Hambly (2000) and Daftary (Hambly 2000) stress the need to develop new appreciations of gender from ideas that are already present in foundational texts and the classical moment in Islamic history. The Andalusi case has again served as an exemplar in this respect, for debates (Viguera 1992: 709) have formed around the question of the relatively high levels of freedom accorded to women in Andalusi society, and the origins of this way of life. Specific figures, such as Wallāda bint al-Mustakfi – the Cordoban princess who wrote poems which articulated a fiercely independent sense of selfhood and sexual identity – move easily in contemporary debates, for the archive of Islamic history is at the same time a language available for contemporary social and political discussion.

Time and untime – Buddhism

Introduction

This chapter looks at ideas of time in Buddhism. Its unusual organization attempts to mirror the fragmented character of Buddhist culture. Some contemporary scholars are reluctant to describe Buddhism as a single religion, preferring to speak of 'Buddhisms' as a means of describing the sects that have emerged since the death of Gotama, the figure conventionally known as the Buddha. The structure I have adopted here represents an attempt to negotiate a balance between stressing the unifying aspects of different branches of the faith and the avoidance of the creation of false commonalties between these different schools.

It is imperative that this chapter offers a clear understanding of Buddhist culture, but it also demands of its readers a willingness to think in new ways and to adapt to language and ideas being used in ways that wrench them from our conventional understandings. Buddhism is perhaps the most epistemologically oriented of all world religions since it is relentlessly concerned with questioning the bases of our understanding of the world. It offers not only answers that lead us to abandon many of our preconceived ideas, but also sets of questions that induce even deeper forms of change. Buddhists, above all, seek to be awakened, for the term Buddhist comes from the root *budh*, meaning to wake up, yet we ought not to assume that Buddhism allows us to awake from a dream-state to the real world.

Buddhism is at once two things: it is a set of simple practices and it is a form of theology or philosophy which conceptualizes the world. It is a system of complex classification – where all things are enumerated and ordered and it is a call to go beyond our systematization of the world. There is a Buddhism centred on ritual as the meaning of life (see for example McDermott 1984: 145) and there is a Buddhism which rejects both ritual and the idea of life itself, contending that reality and meaning cannot be apprehended in the world we experience. In such a view, the space and time of the world are loaded with illusory forms of meaning that prevent us from seeing the virtues of an existence without reality, meaning or truth: the un-space, un-time, un-being of nirvana.

There appear to be contradictions within Buddhist culture here, but, as we saw in the case of the New Testament, religions need ambiguity as much as they need certainty, since belief is often forged in the moment of choice that is made in the evaluation of ambiguities. Buddhism too is founded on the notion that individuals face choices, and that chief among these choices is the question of whether one simply accepts one's view of the world as it seems, or whether one strives to find another standpoint. More accurately, there is a Buddhism that consists of work on the self and there is the prevailing Buddhist idea that selves do not exist. This second position quickly leads us to other questions – are there also no things? If there are no things or selves, can we have histories? – which are characteristic of the Buddhist method of opening up a space of uncertainty in our 'natural' view of the world and the probing of its assuredness.

This rejection of 'natural' views of time is well expressed in the *Visuddhi Magga* where the method called the 'fivefold questioning' of time is enumerated (Warren 1922: 243). This consists of interrogating the key aspects of time and existence in, respectively, the past, the future and, as seen here, the present:

> 'Am I?
> Am I not?
> What am I?
> How am I?
> Whence came this existing being?
> Whither is it to go?'

There may be something reassuring to the western sensibility about these questions and the manner in which they cohere with foundational modes of interrogation in other religions and cultures, but the setting out of these questions in Buddhism is not to establish them as the bases of Buddhist culture, but merely to abandon them. All such questions are discarded, for they represent the roots of a false picturing of the world, in which ultimate truths could be ascertained through the extension of an understanding of the self to the comprehension of the world. The extent of this rejection can be gleaned from Chao-chou's (Suzuki 1970a: 150) response to the question: 'What is the answer to history, the one thing which will open the door?' when he replied, 'Have a cup of tea!' This rejoinder is both humorous and serious, but perhaps best described as being ridiculous for it reveals Chao-chou's disdain for the logic which informs the original question that had been posed.

There is no other religious culture as centred on discussions of time as Buddhism. Its major doctrinal splits are based on different conceptions of temporal order, founded on the struggle between history and no-history, time and un-time, the cycle of life and nirvana, which ends time. In this chapter I shall attempt to skate between observations on how these discrete claims might affect the way that non-Buddhists practise history and my broader aim of piecing together a Buddhist philosophy of history. The account offered draws freely on different Buddhist traditions, but most especially on the Mādhyamika, Yogācāra, Ch'an and Zen branches of the Mahāyāna.

Gotama's invocation to his priests

The priest who does not look back to the past or look forward to the future, having known that all this in the world is false, gives up Orapára [his ability to be reborn], as a snake (casts off its) decayed, old skin.

(Coomára Swámy 1874: 4)

– The Buddhist, then, gives up the past?
– And the future.
– But does the past exist?
– The past is not looked back-upon.
– But is the past false, or merely the present apprehension of it?
– The present is false.
– So the present is not a special case?
– Think of the truth of the snake before you.
– And think of the truth of its skin.
– The skin has no truth.
– Not even of the past?
– The skin is no longer a part of the snake's being.
– But how far are we from a discussion of non-being?
– We need to go back to find the larger message of joy here.

Meditation on time

In discussing Buddhism, we must be very careful in two ways. First, to distinguish between what might be called the Buddhist *imaginary* and the Buddhist *description* of the world, for, while it is arguable that the former offers a wilder and more radical picture of things, it may be that more prosaic *descriptions* of things seen and experienced, rather than things *imagined*, form the bases of much of Buddhism (in this book I am more interested in the first of these two fields). Secondly, and conversely, we need to take the idea of Buddhist temporality seriously. Even if Buddhist ideas of time have not generally been used in the generation of narratives which we would call histories, we need to accept the idea that Buddhist notions of temporality might force us into fundamental reconsiderations of the nature of history. The apperception of these ideas does not come easily; as well as acquiring knowledge we need to work hard at questioning the bases of our own thinking.

It is clear that from its earliest days Buddhist thought engaged with empiricism of a kind which is similar to that which informs modern western historical thinking and the modern west more generally. Buddhism emphatically rejected the empirical method, so part of the challenge entailed in a reconstruction of a Buddhist philosophy of history is to follow the divergent paths Buddhism took once it had rejected the empirical basis on which we centre our own understanding of the world.

Gotama showed us what this work looked like while in a meditative trance in which he saw his buddhahood within the line of buddhas (Warren 1922: 11):

> And strenuous effort made I there,
> The while I sat, or stood, or walked;
> And ere seven days had passed away,
> I had obtained the Powers High.
> When I had thus success obtained
> And made me master of the Law,
> A Conqueror, Lord of all the World,
> Was born, by name Dīpamkara
>
> What time he was conceived, was born,
> What time he Buddhaship attained,
> When first he preached – the Signs appeared.
> I saw them not, deep sunk in trance.

Time is made central to Buddhism here. While lost in trance, Gotama is able to read the drama of time, but not in an omniscient fashion for even with the great powers of buddhahood he is only able to find meaning rather than precision. This, curiously, is because he is both in the time of Dīpamkara and in the time of his trance, for in the connected-selfhoods of Buddhist cyclical time Gotama and Dīpamkara are both one and not one. The great vision of time which this affords is by no means a goal within Buddhism for it is a part of *Samsara*, the endless cycle of suffering through which we all live, and, whereas other faiths operate with a sense of the future conditional which is oriented towards an impending personal fulfilment, Buddhism seeks to finally end the sense of personhood, consciousness and the individual experience of time. Nirvana, as we shall see, is a time rather than a place, but it is better still described as an un-time.

We must also acknowledge that Buddhists' ideas on time evidently drew on notions current in Hindu, Jain and other religious modes of thought in India. Vedic thinking allowed for a very wide range of conceptualizations of time, which included (Pande 1993: 183) theistic accounts in which gods directed events, atheistic representations of time, 'which regarded time as a real but passive substance necessary for action but not determining it' and in which nothing changed in time, and the absolutist conception of time as unreal. Different branches of Buddhism were to adapt these three archetypes in very different ways, with schools such as the Yogācāras and the Madhyāmakas (Klostermaier 1999: 70) questioning all time beyond momentariness, and the Madhyāmaka philosopher Nāgārjūna denying the 'existence of past, future, and present.'

If we compare Nāgārjūna's 'Examination of Time' with that of Gotama cited above, we can see the way in which the Madhyāmakas delighted in unpicking the logic of existing philosophical systems in order to reveal new epistemological realities which needed to be confronted (Garfield 1995: 50–51):

If the present and the future
Depend on the past,
Then the present and the future
Would have existed in the past.

[…]

If they are dependent upon the past,
Neither of the two would be established.
Therefore neither the present
Nor the future would exist.

[…]

A nonstatic time is not grasped.
Nothing one could grasp as
Stationary time exists.
If time is not grasped, how is it known?

If time depends on an entity,
Then without an entity how could time exist?
There is no existent entity.
So how can time exist?

All forms of Buddhism were heavily dependent upon ideas of causation, for the so-called wheels of the faith needed to turn, yet the radical shift proposed by Nāgārjūna – in opposition to both Gotama and empiricism – is that an examination of causation leads us to deny the existence of time. As Keenan writes (Griffiths 1989: 3): 'In Mahāyāna Buddhist thinking all things arise in interdependence and there is nothing that exists apart from its causes and conditions.' Time dissolves not only as a metaphysical or conceptual category but also as a form of shorthand that distinguishes between past, present and future. As Nāgārjūna implies, the idea of time is inherently appealing to us but, so long as we cannot establish that the present and the future exist as dependent entities within the past, then we are unable to rely on such a mode of thought as a means of structuring our apprehension of the world.

Six early questions for the empirical historian

i.   If the world is not real, can we have history?
ii. And if there is no time?
iii. Could truth still be a facet of historical narratives?
iv. How can a faith so entranced by ideas of time be said to be a religion of no-history?
v.   What should Buddhist history and a Buddhist philosophy of history look like?
vi. If we were to live without hindsight and prophecy, where would we be?

Buddhist historiography

In order to try to understand Buddhist philosophies of history, there are two genres that we might investigate: traditional Buddhist texts which describe themselves as 'histories' and contemporary work which draws on Buddhism to develop new approaches to the past.

We might distinguish between two forms of traditional Buddhist history. The first type consists of the stories, myths and accounts of important figures in the development of branches of Buddhism, which together make up the background (literally in terms of art, figuratively in terms of these narratives' place in ritual) for the practice of Buddhism, most especially in monasteries. These histories are unexceptional for they tend to perform simple cultural and educative functions, often meshing with similar folk traditions in the many local cultures into which Buddhism travelled. In many cases their form and epistemological grounding bear little relation to the broader, and more radical, Buddhist cosmology. The second form of Buddhist history does draw on the Buddhist world-picture in a more coherent fashion, and can be found in texts such as the *Anāgata-Vamsa*, the History of Future Events, which rupture empirical understandings of time.

There is a far greater number of the first of these two brands of Buddhist history, many of which have now been subjected to historiographical analysis as a means of describing the manner in which such texts reveal the broader preoccupations of the Buddhist cultures in which they were written. A good example of such an investigation is Newman's (1998) study of the role of eschatology in the *Wheel of Time Tantra*. This Indian Buddhist innovation, which is only regarded as coming from Gotama's time in Tibet and Central Asia (Newman 1998: 284), borrowed from Hindu mythology to create an eschatological narrative that saw Buddhism and Hinduism allied in a common, apocalyptic struggle against Islam, which was cast as a religious intruder on the subcontinent. Newman adjudges that the primary purpose of this temporal innovation (the wheel of time) was the sanctification of violence in the struggle for territory and legitimacy in the face of the rapid expansion of Islam in lands that had previously been dominated by Hinduism and Buddhism.

It seems surprising how little Buddhist thought has informed western historiography, given its complex treatment of themes that have preoccupied western students of historical theory. The one major exception to this sparse engagement is the work of David Loy, which has attempted to reveal the originality of Buddhist thought to the social sciences generally (1986) and to history in particular (2002). In *A Buddhist History of the West: Studies in Lack*, Loy attempts to imagine a reconstruction of history after an engagement with Buddhism, and it is this conceptual enterprise which is of as much interest as Loy's specific critique of modern western culture from a Buddhist perspective. It is crucial that we see the most basic aspect of Loy's book as one of its major achievements: namely, the insertion into the western historical and historiographical canon of the idea that histories need not be based upon empiricism, but can legitimately be drawn from other conceptual traditions.

The break with western orthodoxy is found in both the content and the form of Loy's history. His work is based on the idea that the history of the west has been characterized by a succession of cultures' attempts to deal with a sense of *lack* which has been felt by individuals and the societies they constitute. Successive ages (2002: 1) have been defined by the manner in which they attempted to deal with the sense of lack that we derive from our unconstructed selfhoods. Additionally (2002: 2), 'the history of the West, like all histories, has been plagued by the consequences of greed, ill will, and delusion.'

Loy's ironic claim, which seems obvious when made from a Buddhist perspective, is that westerners should not be worried about the sense of lack embedded in their history and should certainly not devote more energy to trying to solve this supposed deficiency. In fact, the sense of lack at the core of western culture ought to be celebrated for it could act as a spur to a form of enlightenment. Lack, after all, is synonymous with development in Buddhist traditions which attempt to diminish the individual's belief in their existence as autonomous selves and the concept that the social and moral world should be framed around the rights and needs of a self-ruling agency.

There is also a formal critique of western history at work here, for Loy implicates the empirical technique with the questing, progressive mode which characterizes cultures that are driven by a desire for completeness and the resolution of lack (as much in the vain task of the description of the past as in the summation of absolute self-knowledge in the life of the individual). What is more, the empirical mode is useless from a Buddhist perspective since there is no need to look outwards in time or space (as though such things were unconnected from our own ideas of our being), for moral transformation will not be engendered through such investigations. Instead we ought to see that we are spread in space and time: that we have a sense of fullness almost diametrically opposed to that illusion of lack which has come to dominate western consciousness. All we now need to do is find a path away from our quest for fullness and move further towards lack.

The second jewel: the dharma

Early Buddhism described itself as being focused on three 'jewels': the Buddha, the sangha (monastic communities) and the dharma (or 'dhamma', meaning works). The last of these three jewels is the hardest to define for the dharma includes works of theology and philosophy, man's works in his daily life (which ought to accord with Buddhist norms and scriptures), and the constituent units of reality: what scientists might call molecules, and the rest of us 'things'. The power of these connected ideas of the dharma comes across in the work of the thirteenth-century Japanese monk, Enni (Bielefeldt 1998: 204):

> Suppose there is a dark cave, into which the light of the sun and the moon does not reach, yet when we take a lamp into it, the darkness of long years is naturally illuminated. [. . .] The dharmas of the mind are like this: when beings lost in the dark of ignorance and afflictions encounter the light of wisdom, they are naturally purified without changing body or mind.

We are naturally people living in 'the darkness of long years' but as bearers of dharma we also carry within ourselves the potentiality of 'the light of wisdom' that Buddhism offers. The dharma then is founded on an idea of time, for the darkness of the cave and the mind are a form of both stasis and becoming. As Williams says (2000: 114), 'the "doctrine that all exist" is specifically the doctrine that if a dharma is a future, a present, or a past dharma it nevertheless still exists.'

Yet, why, one might ask oneself, should a dharma centred on enlightenment play such an important role in Buddhist thought given our knowledge that enlightenment in the sense of the illumination of the dark cave of life is merely an extension of man's suffering? How would the dharma lead us to nirvana? The answer to this question is explained in the *Abhidhamma*, the canon of foundational texts which set out the philosophical basis of Buddhism. The 'dharma theory' (*dhammavada*) of the *Abhidhamma Pitaka* distinguishes between two forms of dharmas (Bodhi 1993):

> The unconditioned dhamma, which is solely Nirvana, and the conditioned dhammas, which are the momentary mental and material phenomena that constitute the process of experience. The familiar world of substantial objects and enduring persons is, according to the dhamma theory, a conceptual construct fashioned by the mind out of the raw data provided by the dhammas. The entities of our everyday frame of reference possess merely a consensual reality derivative upon the foundational stratum of the dhammas.

The lighting of the darkness of the cave opens, therefore, a perspective on one of the realities that we as humans have the potential to understand. Yet, there is a second, unconditioned reality that can only be reached in nirvana.

Pande (1993: 204) stresses the importance of Gotama's idea that reality operated on two levels – 'a contingent flux superimposed on eternal quiescence' – and the manner in which different schools took this observation:

The focus of his vision is on the timeless reality of *Nirvāna*, the experience of flux being contingent on Nescience or *Avidyā*. Activity and change, the contingent process of existence and non-existence in time, are necessary features, not of reality, but of appearance or phenomena described as 'conditioned elements', the deepest condition being Nescience or *Avidyā*. The finite entities are real only as they occur in time, which presupposes the force of *karma*. Whether the conditioned elements in themselves are to be attributed to a timeless reality, ideal or noumenal [Vaibhāsika Sarvāstivādins and Theravādins], or whether reality is to be restricted to momentary phenomena [Sautrāntikas], or to momentary noumena underlying the empirical phenomena [neo-Sautrāntika-Yogācāras], are questions to which different schools have given different answers but the principal thrust of the tradition is to restrict conditioned reality to the momentary phenomena of which time is a necessary aspect. The tradition, however, is equally definite that there is a timeless reality. At least *Nirvāna* is accepted as an unconditioned entity by all Buddhist schools. It is only the Sautrāntikas who conceive *Nirvāna* negatively but by doing so they clearly flout the Buddha's rejection of nihilism.

Karma

Before we could hope to understand the concept of nirvana we need to see that it is one part of a causal triad which lies at the heart of Buddhist belief: that of karma, samsara and nirvana. Karma describes both the morality of behaviour and the legacy of that behaviour as an accretive layer of judgement which we build upon ourselves. This is destined to follow us in the future forms in which our karma lives, not that we are reincarnated as individuals or souls, for Buddhism disdains few things more than the idea of the soul. It is a form of negotiating system in time, for it serves to connect and order the way things are across time.

Samsara is the system of rebirth, in which Buddhists believe we are destined to live. This is a cyclical system founded on suffering, for there is no joy in rebirth. The wheel of samsara is one which those who seek peace wish to leave, but the opportunities for escape are limited. Only humans are able to break the cycle of samsara, for only self-consciousness can lead us to karmic redemption. In the moment of potentiality as a human it is one's karma that determines the possibility of this escape. Only through good dharma, and therefore karma, in the conditional world does one introduce the possibility of entry into the unconditioned dharma. As the *Samyutta-nikāya* proclaims

(Conze 2002: 80), 'The being is bound to samsara, karma is his (means for) going beyond.'

We can see here the appeal of the idea of the wheel and the cycle to Buddhists, for, as Gotama said (Coomára Swámy 1874: 139): 'The world exists by cause; all things exist by cause; and beings are bound by cause (even) as the rolling cart by the pin of an axletree.' Karma is a system of causation in time and, as we shall see, nirvana is an end of causation. As Yasutani says (Kapleau 1972: 8), in this system, 'What we call life is no more than a process of transformations', while Chuang-tzu noted, 'Birth is not a beginning; death is not an end.' This has major implications in terms of our understanding of ideas of selfhood, which is something I will come to later.

Nirvana

If samsara is the cycle of life and death it does not lead to an eschatological end in the Christian manner. The fullness of the Christian end, with the promise of lives of joy or pain for those who are judged, contrasts with the emptiness of the Buddhist end-point, where the fullness of a life lived many times over is replaced with no-thing. As Gotama put it (Kapleau 1972: 7):

> Where obsessive desire is absent, there is neither coming nor going, and where coming and going have ended there is no death, no birth; where death and birth do not exist there is neither this life nor an afterlife, nor any in between – it is, disciples, the end of suffering.

We should not, however, think of nirvana as either another place (Snelling 1992: 55) or as nothingness. Its character is simply not something that we can perceive, though we can gain greater understanding through the use of meditation and other tools which open us to the connections between the Buddhist worldview and the coherence of its ideas about time which otherwise escape us.

Gotama also described the manner in which those who would find nirvana might begin to comprehend it in their lives (Coomára Swámy 1874: 103):

> That priest conducts himself well whose ideas of things as past or future have ceased, who is endowed with sacred knowledge, and who having overcome (the three times) is not subject to any future state.

Nirvana is, then, very much an overcoming of the sense of time and, in particular, that sense of time that we derive from the natural world which encourages us to believe that there are three temporal modes that govern our existence. Looking at such claims we can understand how it is quite possible to see Buddhist thought of the most radical sort originating with Gotama, and not simply reflecting developments in later Buddhist cultures.

The Theravada

Like all widespread faiths, Buddhism broke into distinct schools of thought, the most important of which are the Theravada, the Mahayana and the Vajryana. The character of these schools was greatly affected by their engagement with other faiths in south and east Asia, from organized religions such as Hinduism to engagements with less systematized local beliefs.

The Theravada tradition bases itself most strongly on the teachings of Gotama and the 'basket' of texts that make up the Pali Canon, the earliest surviving collection of Buddhist teachings. Here the notion of nirvana appeared in a rather less abstract form than I described above (Coomára Swámy 1874: 100):

> I ask the wise sage who has crossed (the flood of existence), gone over to the other side, attained tranquillity, and is firm-minded: How should a priest, flinging his desires away, (and) abandoning a household life, conduct himself well in the world?

'The other side' is described as a place to which one can travel, where tranquillity may be found, which implies a certain continuity in the idea of the movement of selfhood across 'the flood of existence'. It is arguable that this clarity and simplicity is sacrificed for greater levels of conceptual complexity in later Buddhism.

Scales and varieties of time are set out in Theravada texts. Gotama asserts (Keown 1996: 31) that he could remember back 'as far as ninety-one eons', with an 'eon being roughly equal to the lifespan of a galaxy'. He, like us, had within him many times, but his being was not primarily defined by the excavation of meaning from those times (it would be the ending of this process that resolved matters). The extent of Gotama's great memory across time was, however, described as being insignificant next to the lives of gods, planets and other parts of the universe, for (Keown 1996: 36) such figures measured time in billions of years, which could only be understood in a relative fashion by humans. There is a connection here between the great lengths of time in the world of the gods and the cyclical character of their time-experience. That their time is experienced in this fashion is not to deny the possibility of time seeming linear to others operating in mere fragments of the time of gods, but it allows those who live in linear time to break free from the idea that that must be the only form of temporal arrangement in the universe.

In the Buddhist imaginary, therefore (Keown 1996: 36), 'a human lifetime, for example, seems like a day to the gods at the lower levels' (recalling 2 Peter's remark that 'with the Lord one day is like a thousand years, and a thousand years are like one day'). This relativism was not a notion of convenience but an idea which allowed the temporal system of Buddhism to cohere in a manner which was consistent yet undogmatic and flexible. A religion such as Christianity needed to create a new language of poetic temporality in order to distinguish its textual offer from earlier faiths, but relativism has provided Buddhism with a core belief of a kind which served as well in the time before Christ as it does in the scientific world of the present. It is a relativism founded upon the central premise that the universe is not centred around the lives of discrete individuals, and that any given moment of perspective on time lies relative to other sets of temporalities.

The Mahayana

The Mahayana, or 'Great Vehicle' school of Buddhism radically reinterpreted Buddhism from the third century C.E. as the religion spread farther into East Asia. It was in part a social movement, driven by constituencies who felt that Buddhism had become diminished and derailed from its original public purpose in its monastic centres. It also offered radically different interpretations of core Buddhist beliefs, such as the status of buddhas (which would be extended still further in the Vajrayana movement). As Keown (1996: 64) says:

> The major Mahāyāna *sūtras*, such as the *Lotus Sūtra* (200 C.E.) embark on a drastic revisioning of early Buddhist history. They claim, in essence, that although the historical Buddha had appeared to live and die like an ordinary man, he had, in reality, been enlightened from time immemorial.

In Gotama's time he was only able to teach people the basics of the Buddhist creed, since that was all they were ready for at that moment, but now a time had come when more complex teachings could emerge. One seemingly striking change was the coining of the idea of the *bodhisattva*, the human who in his or her own lifetime could become a Buddha. As we read in the *Ratnagotravibhāga*, from the New Wisdom School of the Mahayana (Conze 2002: 181):

> Because the Buddha-cognition is contained in the mass of beings,
> Because it is immaculate and non-dual by nature,
> Because those who belong to the Buddha's lineage go towards it as their reward,
> Therefore all animate beings have the germ of Buddhahood in them.

Yet, it could be argued that this extension of buddhahood in scale and time did not deviate from the principles of the Theravada. We must remember that Gotama himself was not *the* Buddha, but one figure in a chain of the enlightened, who never sought to set himself up as a unique link in that chain. While it is true that he did not envisage his followers becoming buddhas in their lifetimes, he did believe that they might eventually attain nirvana, which is after all more critical to a buddha or a bodhisattva than their karmic existence.

The Mahayana movement fostered a series of branches of Buddhism which adapted the foundational teachings further, among which the Chinese school of Ch'an is one of the most conceptually interesting (later called Zen when it was exported to Japan). Before moving on to look at Zen, let us briefly consider the equally influential Mādhyamika (best represented in the work of Nagarjuna) and the Yogācāra (as seen in Asanga). Looked at from outside the Buddhist tradition one might argue that the differences between these two schools are rather less than they may appear within it (Nagaboshi 1994: 410; Harris (Pam) 1991).

Conze (1993: 50) writes that:

> The Mādhyamika philosophy is primarily a logical doctrine which aims at an all-embracing scepticism by showing that all statements are equally untenable. This applies also to statements about the Absolute. They are all bound to be false and the Buddha's 'thundering silence' alone can do justice to it. Soteriologically, everything must be dropped and given up, until absolute Emptiness alone remains, and then salvation is gained.

This phase of thought was regarded by some later Yogācārins as being a way-station – the second of the 'three turnings of the Wheel of Dharma' (Tilikaratne 1993: 43) – in the movement to the Yogācāra, in which Buddhist philosophy moved through realist (Gotama), critical (Mādhyamika) and idealist (Yogācāra) moments.

The Yogācāra was a form of 'mind only' Buddhism in which (Conze 1993: 50) 'consciousness creates its objects out of its own inner potentialities' and 'Salvation is won when we can produce in ourselves an act of thought which is "Thought-only", pure consciousness, and altogether beyond the division between subject and object.' In an initial stage, the ego and the mind are therefore separated in the act of yogic meditation, for (Ridgeon 2003: 83) we come to see that 'The assumption of the "I" and the world is an error'. We might reflect on how such ideas would seem to completely disassemble the predicates of Ricœur's picture of the world, but we can see that in a Buddhist sense (Ridgeon 2003: 83) they are profoundly hopeful for they express the idea that meditation has the capacity to diminish the unhelpful assumption of selfhood.

The extent to which these ideas are foreshadowed in the Mādhyamika (Murti 1960: 199) can be seen in Nāgārjuna's *Precious Garland of Advice for the King [Rājaparikathā-ratnamālā]* (1975: 111):

> In liberation there is no self and are no aggregates.
> If liberation is asserted thus,
> Why is the removal of the self
> And of the aggregates not like you?
>
> If nirvāna is a non-thing,
> Just how could it have thingness?
> The extinction of the misconception
> Of things and non-things is called nirvāna.

Zen

Zen extends the concept of personal buddhahood to contend that all meaning can be located in the moment, and most particularly in the practice of *zazen* rituals in the present (although there are important strands of Zen which reject a devotion to ritual). Such devotions effectively offer the possibility of access to a temporal continuum between unconditioned/earthly and conditioned/ nirvana existence. As the *Kenbutsu* says (Watts 1990: 179), 'The so-called past is the top of the heart; the present is the top of the fist; and the future is the back of the brain.' Thus we find an extension of the original ideas of the karmic cycle to its end-point where all time is potentially contained in all beings.

The Japanese monk Dogen's *Shobogenzo* (Watts 1990: 142–43) offers us a vivid picture of Zen's broadening of Buddhism's relativization of time:

When firewood becomes ashes, it never returns to being firewood. But we should not take the view that what is latterly ashes was formerly firewood. What we should understand is that, according to the doctrine of Buddhism, firewood stays at the position of firewood . . . There are former and later stages, but these stages are clearly cut. It is the same with life and death. Thus we say in Buddhism that the Un-born is also the Un-dying. Life is a position of time. Death is a position of time. They are like winter and spring, and in Buddhism we do not consider that winter *becomes* spring, or that spring *becomes* summer.

Here the earlier Theravada logic of causality is wholly abandoned. The karmic triad is also discarded, for the movement of karma through bodies until its eventual redemption in nirvana is sacrificed in favour of an emphasis upon stasis and the achievement of enlightenment through meditation in the present. Where both systems coincide, however, is in their overt insistence that Buddhism depends upon a meditation on, and orientation towards, time. As Dogen says so pithily, 'Life is a position of time'.

The need for history disappears in such a system. For Zen, (Snelling 1992: 442) even 'the historicity of the early patriarchs is irrelevant, since the authenticity of the enlightenment experience, which can be easily tested by an enlightened master, is the matter of primary concern.' In the manner in which earlier Buddhists described a fleeing of corporeality and consciousness in the transition from being to non-being in nirvana, the Zen Buddhist seeks to introduce this flight from apperception into the life of the now. As Enni put it (Bielefeldt 1998: 205), 'when we are truly on the way of no-mind, there are no three realms [of existence] or six paths [of rebirth], no pure lands or defiled lands, no buddhas, no beings, not a single mind'; in other words, the foundational precepts of Therevadan Buddhism disappear in this interpretation.

In an early history of Zen – *The Secret Message of Bodhidharma or the Content of Zen Experience* – the author (Suzuki 1970b: 227) remarks that a leading figure's 'landing on the southern shore of China is recorded as taking place in the first year of P'u-t'ung (A.D. 520)', but he then observes that 'the question has nothing to do with these things. Zen is above space–time relations, and naturally even above historical facts.' Even if empirical history could be said to be realizable, it has no real point in such a worldview. This recalls Dogen's remark (Suzuki 1970b: 19) that Buddhism 'is a doctrine that from the beginningless beginning has never been easily learned', with its temporal implication that the search for origins and fixity in time is to move away from the very ethos of Zen Buddhism.

Zen contradicts the idea that spiritual discovery must be a form of progressive journey. Instead, it debates within itself the question as to whether enlightenment might better be arrived at through a concentration on Zen ritual and the study of the conceptual world of Buddhism, or whether it is more likely to be achieved through the practice of daily life and the loss of a sense of selfhood that comes through a life of action. Both approaches rely upon the idea that the enlightenment process is engendered by a move away from existence as consciousness to a realization that within our unconscious being lies the truth of the de-individuated self; that, as Suzuki says (Suzuki 1970a: 107), 'The Unconscious does not seem to lie too deeply in our homely consciousness.'

A Zen history would, then, be an interesting thing. Other histories seek knowledge, understanding, analysis, perspective, detail and narrative in attempting to explain the uniqueness of both things and times. A Zen history might try to do the reverse of each of these things. It would oppose the idea of movement in time and it would abandon the mania for description and thought that it perceived in empirical history. Its literary purpose would also be rather different from those histories we know, for it could not be an entertainment, nor a contribution to our collective stock of knowledge (for that is of irreality). Instead, it would serve as a form of incantation that would mesh with a driven spirit to take a believer away from things to no-thing.

The darkness of long years

The darkness of long years

The darkness of long years

The darkness of long years

The darkness of long years

The darkness of long years

The darkness of long years

The darkness of long years

The darkness of long years

The darkness of long years

The darkness of long years

The darkness of long years

The darkness of long years

The darkness of long years

The darkness of long years

Which is to say that Zen need not ignore earlier Buddhist traditions, for there are concepts to be retrieved there.

An accidental Buddhist history

Digging, keep on digging, beginning to forget dinner and family and the other things, keep on digging. And then death took him at the moment of digging, this Buddha.

Selves and selflessness

Caught up in many of the discussions essayed thus far in this chapter have been contrasting ideas of the self and selflessness in Buddhism. When we begin to reflect upon these things we also enter into a meditation upon the role of the self in other historical and temporal systems. We realize, for example, that western empirical history is predicated on the Renaissance-era idea of the unique, undivided self, and that to abandon this epistemological presumption would be to lose the very grammar with which we do history in the modern west. Could we, for instance, imagine writing a history in which the karmic flows in Henry VIII's life were traced back and forward into time as a means of comprehending his 'life', or, by contrast, a Zen history of the Boer War in which we abandoned our quest for understanding and meaning?

Given its stress on the karmic cycle, we should not be surprised at Theravadan Buddhism's deprecation of singular selfhood. In the Milindapañha, a king named Milinda learns from a monk (Warren 1922: 127) that 'There is no Ego', deploying a form of logical analysis that would be familiar to linguistic philosophers, for he equates the self with the idea of a chariot, contending that, just as the component parts of chariots do not themselves make something that we can call a chariot, we cannot enumerate aspects of selfhood in order to claim a uniqueness to individual selves.

Things are not quite as apparent as we might first think from our use of language, as Wittgenstein would later agree. Yet, there are tensions here within Theravadan Buddhism, as Warren (1922: 209) makes plain:

> The Buddhists [. . .] resolve the human being into a number of elements called *dhammas* which possess no permanent existence, and they say that on account of this transitoriness no one of these can be considered as the individual, the Ego, the 'self.' There is therefore here nothing to be reborn – nothing to transmigrate. How then is it, that when he has thus denied all substantive existence to everything which the Occidental thinker appears to possess the greatest reality, the Oriental should attribute to karma this faculty of being reborn indefinitely?

The answer of course is that the 'self' is not the self we imagine; precisely because of the karmic cycle, we are both ourselves and not ourselves. We are only ourselves in a very limited sense in that we are self-conscious bearers of karma, who possess within our human forms the potential to escape the karmic cycle, but, if we do not make that flight, we do not become another form in time; we are not remade. The movement of karma and the lack of movement of selves or consciousness are another reminder to us of our lack of importance in the Buddhist universe. In a Buddhist view, it follows that most other human cultures situate themselves at the heart of the universe, but if no idea of selfhood is believed in then there is no need to adopt that particular conceit.

Such ideas reach even clearer conclusiveness in Zen, for as Enni says (Bielefeldt 1998: 204):

> When we have awakened to the fact that from the beginning the one mind neither arises nor ceases, then there is no distinction between self and other, there is no good or bad, no love or hatred; we are completely no-thought and no-mind.

There is a connection here, therefore, between the Mahayana notion of the bodhisattva, with the possibility of attaining states of nirvana on earth, and the insistence upon an eternal present, from which we cannot escape if we hope to speak meaningfully about the world. 'What', as Snelling (1992: 7) says, 'is the essence of Buddhism?' Is it, as he says, 'the great question of who or what we are, right here, now, at this very moment', or do we recognize here an easier form of logic which accepts the primacy of the present without feeling the need to abandon ideas of selfhood?

Ultimately, the leap to the double conception of conjoined-existence and no-existence is necessary to begin to understand the Buddhist rejection of the ego.

The Buddhist dialectic

We now ought to see that much Buddhist thought is driven by a distinct form of dialectical reasoning. I use the term 'distinct' in a precautionary fashion, since we must not see the Buddhist dialectic as being equivalent to the modern, western understanding of the term. Where the latter is centred on notions of movement and progress, the Buddhist dialectic's drive is towards no-movement and stasis.

The Buddhist dialectic is something whose work we have already seen in practice, but it is worth considering its operations in more detail. In a practical sense it refers to Gotama's desire for Buddhism to pursue a 'Middle Way' between the prevailing religious modes of asceticism and ceremony which he found in the Indian culture in which he lived. Its metaphysical implications are far greater, however, for Buddhism aspires to develop a culture where there can be no discrimination between self and other, subject and object, birth and death, the now and the then.

As Chih says (Suzuki 1970a: 79), in Buddhism 'The duality of subject and object is gone – which is called the seeing into Self-nature.' This is far from being nihilistic, but it risks being interpreted in that fashion because it rests on a complex of views about the world whose sense is diminished when they are isolated and compared with the totality of other worldviews. Indeed, the Yogācārin and other Buddhist schools stressed that their identity was founded on an opposition to nihilism and the potential for nihilism which they saw in competing brands of Buddhist thought. As Willis writes of the key concept of śūnyatā in the work of Asanga and Nāgārjuna (Arva Maitreya and Asanga 1979: 13–14):

> Śūnyatā as 'emptiness' points to the absence of intrinsic reality, of an abiding self or essence in all phenomena of the relative world, whether of people or things. Persons and things are in truth devoid of self and devoid of essence. Śūnyatā does not mean nothingness, however, but that no thing exists of its own, in its own right.

The Buddhist dialectic is therefore founded on what we might call an ontology of no-being. This was revealed by the early Zen writer Hui-neng (Suzuki

1970a: 22) in the first line of his great work, where he announced 'From the first not a thing is', effectively summing up the idea that a dialectic might help us to work not towards a synthesis of rationality and progressive understanding, but as a radical injunction to abandon such ideas if we wished to see that no-understanding trumps understanding.

Buddhist epistemology is therefore based on a rejection of all that seems clearest to us in our most basic apprehension of the world, that which we can see and the rationalizations that we make on the basis of sight and sound: the distinction between self and other, for instance. As Suzuki (1974: 62) remarks:

> When all these [Dhyanas – types of meditation] are tossed aside and there is a state of imagelessness, then a condition in conformity with Tathata [suchness] presents itself; and the Buddhas will come together from all their countries and with their shining hands will stroke the head of this benefactor.

The state of 'imagelessness' allows us therefore to begin to abandon the picture of the world we develop, whose stress on distinction leads not just to the generation of ourselves as things, but others too (Suzuki 1974: 63), for:

> Immeasurable is our deep-seated attachment to the existence of all things the significance of which we try to understand with words. For instance, there are the deep-seated attachments to signs of individuality, to causation, to the notion of being and non-being, to the discrimination of birth and no-birth, to the discrimination of cessation and no-cessation, to the discrimination of vehicle and no-vehicle, of Samskrita and Asamskrita, of the characteristics of the stages and no-stages. There is the attachment to discrimination itself, and to that arising from enlightenment the attachment to the discrimination of being and non-being on which the philosophers are so dependent, and the attachment to the triple vehicle and the one vehicle, which they discriminate.

Again we see the manner in which Zen seeks to abandon much of the practical architecture of Buddhist belief, in the name of developing those aspects of Buddhist thought which are most distinctive, and which may lead those of us who study the past to reflect on the connections that exist between the things we see and the histories we write, and perhaps even whether a sense of imagelessness might lead us towards the production of no-histories.

The dry-landscape garden of Ryōgen-in

If we accept the idea that Zen offers clear, and sometimes extended, notions of Buddhist time, then we ought to be especially interested in its gardens, which are perhaps the greatest expression of Zen culture. It should not seem surprising to us that Zen was particularly attracted, in art as well as gardens, towards non-verbal representations of its ideas. The notion that a garden can be a history, or even offer a philosophy of history, is familiar to us from Islamic architecture in al-Andalus, and I think there is a set of useful parallels, in our approach and their content, between the Zen gardens of Kyoto and the gardens of the Alhambra.

In what sense, then, can we say that this is a history? It is a history because it is clearly an exploration of time, which in its originary and linguistic sense is what histories are about (and not the narration of the truth of past times). Zen gardens are an invitation to explore the temporality of the Buddhist universe, and in particular the negotiation of the dualities that need to be overcome if we are to understand the Buddhist sensibility. In the garden we see both nature and the representation of nature, for the garden is full of rocks and moss, but they have artfully been placed there to offer a distillation of nature's character. In the garden we view time and a representation of time, for, while the act of contemplation is an entry into a particularly privileged form of *zazen* time, we also understand that these are texts about time. Reference is made to the natural cycles of time that we see around us, for these are places we are expected to see at different times of year, but we also understand that an attempt at transcending such forms of time is to be attempted.

There is both conditioned and unconditioned reality placed right there before us (the is and the isn't). The gardens are nirvana-movements; they are abstractions that take us on the path to no-thing for it is as though the universe fragments when we contemplate them. Their abstraction is an expression of their epistemological character as they strive to serve as bridges to a broader understanding of things as our ideas of selfhood dissolve in the manner in which nature begins to break up in the garden.

The garden is a place of joy and beauty but it is also a place of duty, for its simplicity is deceptive: just as the Buddhist soul needs much work over time to come close to nirvana, the Zen garden needs to be cared for in a devoted fashion. It should also be said that many such gardens also connect to broader narratives, such as natural histories which explain the origins of things in the world, but my feeling is that the garden should be seen primarily as a site for contemplation rather than explanation.

Conclusion: principles of Buddhist time

Buddhism, then, can hardly be said to be a natural place for the empirical historian to look for support for her methods and worldview. While divided by a central split between the Theravada and the Mahayana, all Buddhism is predicated on openness to a discussion of time which is antithetical to historical study. Buddhists need to orient themselves in time and to devote their lives to a consideration of time in a conceptual and a practical sense. If successful, this meditation leads not to revelation, truth and perspective but to a sense of transiency which might move into an understanding of un-time and un-being, which we can only really appreciate if we have grasped the radical epistemology of time present in Buddhism. Traditional western historians of religion saw the rejection of time in Buddhism and other eastern religions as evidence of a form of primitive mysticism, as seen in McTaggart (1908: 23), but I hope that this chapter has shown how considered and rich such ideas are in Buddhism.

The last Buddha – Gotama – articulated a sense of time heavily grounded in causality – noting (Conze 1957: 19) 'We are the heirs of our actions' – but later Buddhists began to unpick the unhelpful predicates they believed such a view was based upon. Such constructive dismantling reached an end-point in Zen texts where Buddhist epistemology was allowed to reach its logical conclusion. As Watts (1990: 179) said:

> All time is here in this body, which is the body of Buddha. The past exists in its memory and the future in its anticipation, and both of these are now, for when the world is inspected directly and clearly past and future times are nowhere to be found.

Just as there is no self in the now, there is no time in the now, for if nirvana is here there can be no selves and no time – there is only the un-time and the un-being, whose histories are yet to be written, if they can ever be described.

If, therefore, we take Buddhist cosmology and ideas about selfhood seriously there are many aspects of history and biography – as they are empirically understood – that need to be abandoned. I said in the introduction to this chapter that Buddhism is perhaps the most epistemologically oriented of all major world religions, and we see this in the manner in which it offers an evaluation of the very building blocks of empirical thought: of causality, time, being, experience, reality and meaning. Each of these unspoken predicates which cohere to form the empirical perspective is broken down in Buddhism, their logic interrogated, and ultimately rejected.

When asked how the world began, Gotama responded that time should not be wasted on such questions for it could be devoted to attempting to escape samsara. It seems inadequate to speak of Buddhist forms of history, historiography or a Buddhist philosophy of history. To do so is to use words and concepts that are antithetical to the Buddhist tradition, and, just as it had to coin new language, ideas and paths of thought to describe itself, it would seem more realistic to close an appreciation of Buddhist temporality with a stress on the centrality of un-time.

Chapter 9

Modern times

Introduction

Rather than looking at time and history in a single religious culture, this final chapter asks what has become of these things in the modern world. Its theses are simple, but the journey it takes to reach them is rather complicated. I argue that 'modern', western notions of time and history are founded upon Newtonian ideas which are considerably less complex and rich than the temporal cultures we found in classical religious cultures. This is significant not just for religions and the discipline of history, but for all of us, for our lives are as defined by our ruling temporal order as were the lives of Christians in the second century or pre-conquest Australians. The second part of my argument is that modern temporality is in the process of collapsing, for, just as the Newtonian paradigm in science was replaced by Einstein's re-description of the world, notions of relativity are also complicating our understanding of time.

There is a neat circularity here, for I shall also propose that Einsteinian time is in many ways similar to ideas which we find in classical religious cultures. In this view, modern western time – which describes itself as being rational, observational, chronological, universal, unambiguous, fixed, natural, constant, and an expression of common-sense – is seen to be an historical anomaly in human culture. It is this form of time that has been used as a basis for the discipline of history. This provokes interesting questions when we reflect upon the fact that the two bases of western time have collapsed: its scientific basis was disproved by Einstein, and its universality is undermined by the plurality of other times we find in religious cultures. Historians betray their lack of self-consciousness as to their own epistemological groundings when they argue that relativism is a dangerous, unscientific corruption, rightly identifying the dangers it poses, but failing to recognize that relativistic ideas have supplanted the Newtonian scientific worldview upon which history itself was founded. What is more, relativism has become the new orthodoxy not only in scientific theory, but also in scientific and technological practice, most especially in the making of clocks and the measurement of time.

To use the title of the first volume in this series, while history was Newtonian, the *New History* is Einsteinian. In order to substantiate this claim, I want to piece together five sections of a narrative about attempts to adapt to, and describe, modern times. We begin with ideas of Reformation and Enlightenment in Islam and Christianity, move on to the counter-Reformation of the Wahhabi desert clerics, the foundation of the modern discipline of history, Wittgenstein's critique of the crudeness of Newtonian time, and, finally, we will look at Einstein's thought.

In moving from the late medieval world to the present, this chapter also addresses modern ideas of secularization and the Death of God, arguing that we can see a useful parallel between Newtonian time and the idea of secularization. Both concepts are of critical importance in the history of ideas, but their failing lies in the manner in which they come to see themselves as irreplaceable orthodoxies, where they might better be seen as competing worldviews in a market of ideas. It is therefore no surprise that the contemporary world has seen a coincidence of the collapse of absolutist Newtonian concepts with a revival of spirituality, faith, religion and enchantment, which is perhaps merely a return to the pluralistic, complex culture of time which men knew in earlier days.

Reformation and enlightenment

In a broad history of religion and time such as this one, the Reformation, which traditionally serves as a centrepiece in histories of the west, matters little. It was simply another schism of a kind that had periodically divided Christians since the death of Christ. It is true that the nature of many of the doctrinal disputes in the Reformation is intrinsically interesting to my argument, for temporal disputation played an important role in the division of the western church. In particular, time figured centrally in discussions of wealth accumulation and transubstantiation where Catholics and Protestants clashed. The direction of Christianity's temporal complexity was at stake here, for Protestants argued that this could be found as much outside the church as in it – in, for instance, the accumulation of wealth, with its celebration of risk, borrowing and the potentiality of capital in time – whilst Catholics defended the literal quality of rites such as transubstantiation, which argued for the presence of complex time in the Christian act of worship.

Some would therefore argue that the Protestant Reformation served as a forerunner of the Enlightenment, for it established the possibility of there being two earthly realms – the sacred and the secular – where previously the church had contended that there was simply God's domain on earth. There is evidently a connection between such ideas and the Enlightened notion that the world need not be explained through recourse to Christian teachings, but such claims were by no means unique to western Protestantism; six hundred years earlier Muslim philosophers had begun an analogous project.

Medieval Islamic philosophers such as Ibn Rushd (Averroes in the western canon) and Ibn Tufayl (Abubacer) were deeply religious writers, yet they were also committed to the proof of religious truth through the questioning of the central tenets of their faith. What they asked – in Ibn Rushd's 'Double Truth Theory of Knowledge' and Ibn Tufayl's *Hayy Ibn Yaqdan*, a forerunner to Defoe's *Robinson Crusoe* – was whether man might arrive at an understanding of the world only through the study of religious teachings or whether such things might also be reached through the application of human reason. In some ways this method was less unusual than might be thought, since reason and scientific thought were deeply embedded within classical Islamic culture, yet there was no doubt that both Ibn Rushd and Ibn Tufayl wanted to make a very clear distinction between religious wisdom and man's questioning. Both concluded that truth could be reached by either method, and that religion was not therefore intrinsically superior as a mode of analysis. This was most dramatically enacted in Ibn Tufayl's work, where a man stranded on a desert island is presented as living in a state of abstraction from conventional human life. His hero concludes that both reason and religion take man to the same place – a belief in God – but both Ibn Tufayl and Ibn Rushd had opened possibilities that were well understood by their more conservative critics within Islam. They crystallized a conflict between philosophical and theological approaches in Islam, in spite of their beliefs that their work bridged those two methods.

In many ways the provisional and tentative manner in which Ibn Rushd and Ibn Tufayl moved in such a way so as to suggest the possibility of diminishing the central position of God from within religious culture is remarkably similar to the western Enlightenment five hundred years later. Western culture was so deeply imbued in the Judaeo-Christian heritage that it proved impossible for early radicals to state bluntly that God was dead. When such claims were later made they were seen as terrifying, for it was widely felt that social chaos might ensue from such assertions, as evinced by the work of Durkheim with its desperate attempts to construct a new morality for a post-religious age. We might also view Durkheim's position with some irony, however, not only because religions did not die, but also because Durkheim's position was a 'functionalist' one, which is to say that Durkheim did not work from the premise that the nature of being had been religious in previous times, merely that religion had served as an organizational architecture of social life in the pre-modern period. It was not the truth of religion that mattered, or its message, but its effect in successfully underpinning generally stable and functioning societies.

Yet, this book has argued that time, as expressed through religion, is the locus of human being, and not simply a functionalist veneer lying atop a life of practice and experience. Studies of a range of religious communities have suggested that temporal notions become deeply embedded in language and that through language and texts they are successfully transmitted across space and time. This was very well understood by some of Durkheim's French forebears in the Revolutionary period when the ending of the classical *Ancien Régime* was accompanied not only by attempts to transfer popular affection from the Catholic Church to 'substitute religions' – which retained the structure and forms of Christianity – but also by a fundamental restructuring of the language of time. The world began again with Year Zero and the structuring of daily life was altered through the creation of new days of the week and a new system of months (later recalled in the opening line of Orwell's *1984*: 'It was a bright cold day in April and the clocks were striking thirteen.')

While we might say that the programme of Enlightened philosophy came to propose man's disengagement of his beliefs from organized religion, we might also note that Enlightenment philosophers were right to feel sceptical as to how greatly the world would change in this regard. In the case of western Europe, the ideas, forms and temporal modes of established Christianity simply moved from organized religion to a series of 'secular' social spheres. This is especially evident in fields such as the development of mass politics in the nineteenth century (Sironneau 1982), particularly those of a messianic zeal, but also to be found in science, the arts, literature and architecture. How often the train stations, department stores, factories, public monuments and sports arenas of that time are identified as 'cathedrals of the modern age'.

An additional consequence of this migration of religious forms from Christianity to secular society was that it ultimately served to revive western Christianity, for, when the 'civil' and 'substitute' (Charlton 1963) religions of the nineteenth century collapsed one after another from the 1800s onwards, the institutions that benefited most from this phenomenon were the established churches. Nowhere was this more apparent than in the churches' reaction to the work of Darwin, for, while the churches retained their core clients through a strategy of ridiculing Darwin's work, they were also able to accommodate Darwin's worldview within Christian theology in a remarkably short space of time. Theologians contended that the geological view of time was one that could accord with biblical teachings, where the Bible was seen as a home of rich metaphor, once Darwin's teachings were seen as part of a process of modernizing Christianity. There is good reason for thinking that Darwin saw his work as contributing to this modernization.

After Islam's enlightenment

A similar process of counter-enlightenment took place in the Islamic world in the form of Wahhabism, a revivalist branch of Islam construed in the eighteenth century, which for many has come to be seen as an original and uncorrupted version of the faith, in spite of its arguable lack of historical antecedents. Like the Prophet Mohammed, Mohammed ibn Abd al-Wahhab was a religious reformer from the Arabian Peninsula who vowed to end his people's state of *jahiliya* (ignorance). In the case of Prophet Mohammed, people had needed to be shown the path to one true God, away from their polytheistic and animist practices, whilst Abd al-Wahhab was centrally concerned with purifying Arabian Islam of polytheistic and ritualized practices which he believed had diverted it from the core of its monotheistic message.

In spite of the presence of the holy cities of Mecca and Medina, Arabia seemed an unlikely location for a revolution in eighteenth-century Islamic thought. From the period of the death of Prophet Mohammed onwards, the political, theological and intellectual centre of Islam had moved among the great cities of that central strip of the world which cuts across continents as it runs from Spain to India – Damascus, Baghdad, Cordoba, Cairo, Fez, Isfahan, Delhi, Constantinople – but it had never lain in what one might have presumed to be Islam's geographical heartland (Kepel 2004: 170).

Abd al-Wahhab's location was symbolic of a return to Islam's origins and, in beginning his mission to revive a notionally pure form of Islam, Abd al-Wahhab was making both a political and a theological statement about the geographical character of the Islamic world. Theologically, he asserted that the fracturing of Islam into a series of sects – many of which had purportedly been influenced by other religions – had acted to deny the oneness of the faith, while his coded political message was that the religious practices of the Ottoman rulers, who controlled much of Arabia at that time, were inimical to the unity of Islam. In other words, Wahhabism represented a form of anti-imperialism (Vassiliev 1998: 79–80), a brand of 'Arab nationalism', and a more general conviction that the balance between *amir* (political leaders) and *imam* (religious leaders) in the Islamic polity had moved too far in favour of the former over the latter.

This was not to say that Abd al-Wahhab proposed a pure form of theocracy where Muslims would be led by clerics, for he is, of course, now remembered as the figure whose alliance with the al-Sa'ud dynasty provided that family with the theological legitimacy that allowed them to create the first successful nation state on the Arabian peninsula. As Abd al-Wahhab announced to Mohammed ibn Sa'ud (Hopwood 1982: 27), 'I bring you good news of glory and power. Whoever holds to and works by the word of *tawhid* [the oneness of God] will rule through them lands and men.' The Sa'udi state, which emerged through Abd al-Wahhab's sanction of *jihads* with dual political and religious motives and his assertion of the destiny of the al-Sa'uds, was not secure in its initial form, but it is notable that each of the three formations of a Sa'udi state have been centrally founded on the notion of an alliance between the al-Sa'ud family and the followers of the teachings of Abd al-Wahhab (DeLong Bas 2004).

Wahhabism is of interest in the context of a discussion of time, enlightenment and history for the manner in which it abandoned Islam's traditional flexibility, which allowed for the accommodation of rapid social, scientific and intellectual change, in favour of a rigid insistence of the moral value of things being determined by the literal texts of the Qur'an and the *hadith*. Abd al-Wahhab was determined to impose a single view of Islam on a faith community that had flourished precisely because of plurality and the lack of a hierarchical structure with a dogmatic centre. This leads us to the idea that Christianity and Islam found themselves diametrically opposed in approach at this time, for the Reformation had of course been designed to produce a decentred theological structure closer to that which had traditionally been found in the Islamic world. A helpful comparison might also be made in noting that Abd al-Wahhab re-established the virtues of the theological state at precisely that moment when it was being broken down in the west. When writers, generally from the west, ask how different the Islamic world might have been had it had its own Enlightenment, one might argue that Islam was indeed enlightened for much of its history, but that, through modern revivalist movements such as Wahhabism, the always present forces of counter-Enlightenment seized control of much of the faith.

A major change instituted by Wahhabism was a gradual narrowing of the optic of Islamic history, for, while history had always served political purposes in the Islamic world, Wahhabism essentially negated the value of Islamic civilization and history in the period from the death of the Prophet to the eighteenth century (including of course Islamic law, which in many ways served as the fabric of Islamic life, marrying religion and politics – DeLong-Bas 2004: 29). Just as we read of Spanish 'continuist' historians who alleged that the Islamic presence in Iberia had not had long-term effects on Spanish and Portuguese culture and identity, Abd al-Wahhab's own continuist narrative contended that much of the period between the eighth and the eighteenth centuries was a wayward deviation from the true path of the collective Islamic temporal narrative. This was of course not uncontested in the eighteenth century and it has remained a central divide between, on the one hand, Wahhabism and other Salafi Sunni revival movements and, on the other, the great plurality of forms of Sunni and Shi'a Islam. This debate pits the idea of greatness in unity against greatness in diversity and it has a very strong temporal element, as seen in the celebration or denigration of key moments in the Islamic calendar such as the birthday of Prophet Mohammed, Ashura (the memorialization of the death of Hussein, grandson of Prophet Mohammed, which also marks the day that Noah left the ark and Moses was saved in Egypt), and the celebration of the ascension of Prophet Mohammed.

This narrowed temporal focus was also of practical importance in terms of the management of daily life. As DeLong-Bas remarks (2004: 11), Wahhabis were angered by the fact that their fellow Muslims did not distinguish between the scriptures and their interpretations (2004: 12):

> The reformers believed that this practice was inappropriate. They pointed to the fact that interpretations and commentaries often reflected the context in which they were written, both geographical and political, rather than the context in which the scriptures were revealed and originally understood.

In other words, good eighteenth-century Muslims ought to imagine themselves living in the eighth century, for to be a true Muslim was to live in a temporal continuum where the revealed truth of faith could not change. Abd al-Wahhab also (DeLong-Bas 2004: 13) 'rejected imitation of the past (*taqlid*) in favour of fresh and direct interpretation (*ijtihad*) of the scriptures and Islamic law by contextualising them and studying their content', and we might question how these two temporal aspirations were to be run together. Wahhabism after all was especially weakened by its literalism and its rejection of poetic and metaphorical forms of belief – such as the many forms of intercession that had developed in Islam – which it believed denied the unity of the individual's relationship with God.

As is the case with all puritanical faith movements, there have been great splits within Wahhabism, which are nowhere more evident than in contemporary Sa'udi Arabia, the state which embodies Wahhabism in its own history and identity. While the modern world and the hegemony of western temporality are held at bay through the ubiquitous use of the Islamic calendar in the Kingdom, oil wealth and its management have provided dilemmas and temptations that could never be reconciled within Wahhabi Islam. In many ways the Sa'udi state has been remarkably successful in managing a form of religio-political identity crisis which has arrived with westernized modernity, but at the expense of deep fissures within Salafi Islam, for it has proved inevitable that the House of Sa'ud are identified with precisely the kind of *jahiliya* that motivated the missions of the Prophet Mohammed and Abd al-Wahhab. The pressure of trying to maintain a society grounded in the moral norms of the eighth century is becoming increasingly difficult to bear in the twenty-first century.

Disciples

In the contemporary west we accept a situation where there is competition in ideas, where our instincts lead us as individuals to construct different combinations of belief and time. We see this as a world of interaction, coexistence and choice, yet in many ways this end-point offers an utterly false picture of the intellectual struggles that took place in the post-Enlightenment period. This is nowhere more evident than in the case of the formation of the discipline of history, where a process of collective forgetting has allowed historians to construe utterly fantastic ideas as to their discipline's origins.

History was a classic Enlightenment field of enquiry in the sense that it emerged as an organized field of academic study – a discipline with a particular place in the university – in early-nineteenth-century Europe. This is not to say that histories had not been written before that point, but simply to observe that this was the beginning of a professionalized field of history in the west which developed a set of practical and theoretical collective norms. In the early days of the discipline these norms were not, of course, self-evident. They emerged from often bitter battles between theorists from rival ideological positions, and I do not think it is unreasonable to suggest that the formation of history in an atmosphere of philosophical disputation in the first half of the nineteenth century can serve as a symbol of the impact of Enlightenment thought on western man's construction of knowledge more generally.

It is never said, but another reason why history might serve as the emblem of the incorporation of the Enlightenment into western culture is of course that, while historians often claimed to represent progressive social tendencies (i.e. those associated with the Enlightenment), their methods drew just as much from the philosophical outlook of the *Ancien Régime*. Indeed, one might argue that the discipline of history that eventually emerged was completely inimical to Enlightened philosophy. The true philosophical struggle which took place in the early years of the nineteenth century – which is almost absent from our histories of history – was between what ought to be called theological and Enlightened modes of history.

By theological history, I mean a way of looking at the past which, like religion (and specifically Christianity), was essentially founded upon the notion of *faith*: faith that the truth of the past can be known, faith that man can reproduce operable versions of historical truth through his studies, and a faith that such history serves a broader social purpose. Enlightened history, in contradistinction, is founded around the philosophical virtue of *doubt*: doubt whether men can really know the truth of the past, doubt whether men's descriptions of the past have any credibility as descriptions of the way things were, and a doubting of men's motives in developing particular narratives of the past. In taking the theological route, historians explicitly rejected the path of epistemological scepticism. This is seen in an extreme fashion in the figure of David Hume, for his histories clearly followed the theological path, ignoring the import of his sceptical philosophical writing. Histories became sure descriptions of the world, like sermons, rather than conjectures as to the nature of things or explorations of doubt, like philosophical treatises.

When thinking about the formation of their discipline, historians came to believe that the central epistemological struggle which had taken place in the nineteenth century was between idealist historians (such as Hegel and Marx) and empiricists (such as Ranke), with the latter camp eventually winning out, and idealist history migrating to philosophy and political theory. Yet, that disagreement was essentially a prosaic one over scale, with the former camp contending that the historian's unit of investigation could range from the local to the global, and the latter grouping asserting the superiority of micro-history.

This local disagreement was of only minor epistemological import as compared with the possibility that history might have taken an Enlightened path, adopting a radically sceptical approach to our ability to know past times. We know this from our reading of texts such as Richard Whately's *Historic Doubts Relative to the Existence of Napoleon Bonaparte* (originally published in 1819, but revised and reissued through the following decades). Whately's text had a satirical purpose, but its form is hugely revealing of the true character of epistemological discussions on history in the early-nineteenth century. As the title of the pamphlet suggests, Whately's work posited the idea that perhaps Napoleon had never existed; that he had been a fiction, cynically imagined by politicians and newspaper editors. As such, it seemed to fully express an historical version of the scepticism of the Enlightened critique of theological modes of thinking.

Whately goes on to set out a logical case for doubting Napoleon's existence which draws on a detailed knowledge of Enlightened philosophy to assert that the bases of our knowledge of the past lie insufficiently questioned, that epistemological presumptions utterly define the production of knowledge, and that we need to look sceptically at the literary character of the production of historical knowledge. Let us look in more detail at the final section of Whately's critique of Napoleon's existence as a way of seeing the elegance and depth of his case (1985: 16):

> Let us, then, consider what sort of a story it is that is proposed to our accept-ance. How grossly contradictory are the reports of the different authorities, I have already remarked: but consider by itself the story told by any one of them; it carries an air of fiction and romance on the very face of it. All the events are great, and splendid, and marvellous: great armies, great victories, great frosts, great reverses, 'hairbreadth 'scapes,' empires subverted in a few days; everything happened in defiance of political calculations, and in opposition to the experience of past times; everything upon that grand scale so common in epic poetry, so rare in real life; and thus calculated to strike the imagination of the vulgar, and to remind the sober-thinking few of the Arabian Nights. Every event, too, has that roundness and completeness which is so characteristic of fiction; nothing is done by halves; we have complete victories, total overthrows, entire subversion of empires, perfect re-establishments of them, crowded upon us in rapid succession. To en-umerate the improbabilities of each of the several parts of this history would fill volumes; but they are so fresh in every one's memory, that there is no need of such a detail.

Whately's roll-call of questions posed to historical knowledge will be familiar to historiographers acquainted with the linguistic turn in postmodern phil-osophies of history, yet it is of critical importance that these questions come not from recent writing but from the time of the very origins of the discipline. Whately himself was a theologian – who later became Archbishop of Dublin – and the point of his satire was to demonstrate the logical end-points of Enlightened philosophers' doubting of the narratives of the Bible and other accounts of the past, but in the very act of writing this text Whately provided us with not only a full picture of the potentiality of Enlightened history but also an understanding of the divisive intellectual atmosphere of the Enlightenment. History in the west absorbed far more from theological reasoning than it did from Enlightenment critique and one might argue that radical historiography today is simply an extension of debates from the early-nineteenth century.

God reviewed

In an epistemological sense one might say that the last forty years in the academy have involved the learning of a sense of irony to replace the certainty of nineteenth-century intellectuals. This is seen nowhere more clearly than in discussions of secularization. Where this term had, for a hundred and fifty years, been used to describe a process of the waning of religious belief across the world, from the middle of the twentieth century it came to be used as an expression of complexity, as a means of accounting for a world where religious and non-religious worldviews co-existed and competed with each other. Nineteenth-century secularism not only described the retreat of religion but tended to advocate a purging of its roots from modern cultures, whereas recent writing on secularization has tended to display a respect towards classical religious cultures on the basis of their curious longevity.

As was the case in many things, Wittgenstein provided an acute understanding of the central importance of this shift in understandings of secularization in western culture, though he was well aware that his analysis was one that was in the process of coming into being, rather than emerging fully formed. Wittgenstein criticized the Newtonian worldview from two positions: from Einsteinian relativism and from a religious standpoint. His remarks, then, are of a special prescience because, whereas most of Wittgenstein's intellectual peers were able to critique Newton through Einstein, few imagined the possibility of an analytical narrative which joined together contemporary scientific relativism with readings from classical religious texts. For Wittgenstein the relativity and complexity of time was as evident in the Bible as it was in Einstein.

We should not forget, however, that Wittgenstein was very much a figure on the cusp of great changes: he tended to critique all science on the basis of its Newtonian temporal narrowness, and could not fully articulate the lessons of relativity, which nevertheless informed his philosophy. Instead, it is primarily religion which is charged as a form of opposition to science.

The themes of religion, time and history were of interest to Wittgenstein across his work, in part because they enabled discussions which allowed him to try to access the core of his own project: to find clarity and to interrogate uncertainty. In setting up such discussions, Wittgenstein, I believe, also established a compelling critique of empirical history and a case for seeing history as a cross-cultural investigation into modes of temporalizing. Through the idea of time, he was able to develop ideas which meshed religion with a critique of Newtonian science.

Wittgenstein asserted (1980: 22e) that philosophers tended not to notice that temporality was 'embedded in their grammar'. This led him to begin to question the assuredness of these embedded temporal notions which lay outside the canon of philosophical discussion. He noted (1979: 13) that:

> When people talk about the direction of time, precisely the analogy of a river is before them. Of course a river can change its direction of flow, but one has a feeling of giddiness when one talks about time being reversed. The reason is that the notion of flowing, of *something*, and of the direction of the flow is embodied in our language. Suppose that at certain intervals situations repeated themselves, and that someone said time was circular. Would this be right or wrong? Neither. It would only be another way of expression, and we could just as well talk of circular time. However, the picture of time as flowing, as having a direction, is one that suggests itself very vigorously.

In other words, we are possessed, through language, of a sensation that linearity is the natural state of time, but we should be open to the possibility that time might operate in other ways. Wittgenstein generalizes his own 'giddiness' to his readers as a mode of accessing another way of viewing things which we do not usually see or question. This nascent loss of faith in linearity is connected to Wittgenstein's broader critique of ideas of scientific progress and their ubiquity in the modern west, while readers will also be reminded of the manner in which Wittgenstein's alternatives to linearity are of course familiar from our study of religious temporalities.

As he begins to interrogate the concept of 'time' and our use of it, Wittgenstein starts to draw out more and more of our assumptions and their predicates (1979: 22):

> Why does one feel tempted to say, 'The only reality is the present'? The temptation to say this is as strong as that of saying that only *my* experience is real. The person who says only the present is real because past and future are not here has before his mind the image of something moving past →

present → future. This image is misleading, just as the blurred image we would draw of our visual field is misleading inasmuch as the field has no boundary.

Wittgenstein is concerned here to deal with time in a way that connects with other parts of his worldview. Time is compared with language, and notions of the uniqueness of the individual experience of time are rejected in the manner of the refutation of the private language argument. In one of his most striking metaphors Wittgenstein says that a linear view of time 'is misleading, just as the blurred image we would draw of our visual field is misleading inasmuch as the field has no boundary.' We do not trouble ourselves with this limitation on a daily basis – for we see what we see – but Wittgenstein is determined to establish equivalence between the temporal and spatial limits to our apprehension of the world.

Wittgenstein also references his own ideas regarding positioning, for, if our individual experience of time in the present is necessarily limited, and that limit is blurred (presumably with the purpose of enabling us to get on with life), we might also wonder how historians believe that they can extend this temporal frame and use their sense of 'perspective' and 'hindsight' to talk authoritatively about others' experiences in the past. A useful analogy here is with the operations of the cinema. When we watch films we are offered perspectives on realities that we would not otherwise experience. This is true in a narrative sense – in that we are asked to go to places we have never been and to identify with the lives of others – but it is also true in a technical and an optical sense, because the camera can show us more than would be possible to see with our eyes alone. Our visual field is extended by the movie camera so, for example, we can see in deep focus, our field of vision is extended to up to 180 degrees, and in many other ways films are designed to give viewers a sense of omniscience. We also, of course, apprehend time in radically different ways from those that we commonly experience, and we often codify films according to the different systems of the editing of time that they present us with (Eisensteinian montage, continuity editing and the institutional mode of representation, the jump-cut and the Nouvelle Vague).

Now, if films extend the visual and temporal field for their viewers, isn't this the kind of thing that histories do for the temporal field, and, just as there are detailed and evolving encodings of the narrative and visual techniques used to generate such experiences in film, should historians not be attempting to develop the temporal equivalents of such typologies? One might say that this is precisely what historiography has been doing for the past one hundred and fifty years, yet, if this were really the case, we might ask why the question of time is so absent from such discussions – certainly as compared with the centrality of classifications of time, as well as visual codes and narratives, in the study of film.

Wittgenstein moved beyond his questioning of the assuredness of linear temporality in a speculative fashion which I think could be useful to historians (1979: 14):

> If I asked for a description of yesterday's doings and you gave me an account, this account could be verified. Suppose what you gave as an account of yesterday happened *tomorrow*. This is a possible state of affairs. Would you say that you *remembered* the future? Or would you say instead that you remembered the past? Or are both statements senseless?

The importance of such theorizing in the modern west was that it confronted the monolithic reliance on linear time in Newtonian science, which Wittgenstein saw as a great danger to the world (and we should remember here that Deeds Ermarth and others have shown that empirical history was drawn from the same epistemological roots as Newtonian science). Wittgenstein feared (1980: 63e) that 'perhaps science and industry, having caused infinite misery in the process, will unite the world – I mean condense it into a *single* unit, though one in which peace is the last thing that will find a home', a world in which (1980: 60e) '*One* particular method elbows all the others aside.'

For Wittgenstein the temporal cultures of classical religions – Judaism and Christianity in particular – were of renewed critical importance for they offered a potential mode of resistance to what Wittgenstein perceived as the homogeneity of western scientific time. Religion offered a way of seeing and understanding which connected an understanding of the empirical, physical realities of the world directly to an assuredness as to the coherence of things, along with a sense that values such as justice and truth could exist in such a world. As Wittgenstein says (1980: 64e) of religion, 'It strikes me that a religious belief could only be something like a passionate commitment to a system of reference. Hence, although it's a *belief*, it's really a way of living, a way of assessing life.'

The fact that religious experience and practice constantly mediated between inner feelings and the description of the world through language clearly held an innate appeal to Wittgenstein, as did the therapeutic qualities of religion. He believed that its aims and its moral purpose could not be further away from those of modern science, and part of his concern with religion was to show its extensiveness in the modern world: to stress that accounts of its death were exaggerated. Such an aim was of course rather different from that of most philosophy and academic work at the time at which he wrote. Much of the ambiguity regarding Wittgenstein's ideas outside philosophy can be accounted by the fact that Wittgenstein looked back to the early-nineteenth century for two different things: for the liberating qualities of Enlightenment, and for the assurance of religion.

Wittgenstein's writing on Christianity is particularly interesting as it is here that he develops his most detailed treatment of history. His particular concerns are the question of belief, the variety of historical language games (which express a form of relativism, as Wittgenstein stresses different humans' commitment to different language games), the function and form of historical narratives and the place that history plays in religion and in men's lives.

Many of these themes and the question of the messages of history appear in Wittgenstein's remarks on Kierkegaard and the Bible (1980: 31e):

> Kierkegaard writes: If Christianity were so easy and cosy, why should God in his Scriptures have set Heaven and Earth in motion and threatened *eternal* punishments? – Question: But in that case why is this Scripture so unclear? If we want to warn someone of a terrible danger, do we go about it by telling him a riddle, whose solution will be the warning? – But who is to say that the Scripture really is unclear? Isn't it possible that it was essential in this case to 'tell a riddle'? And that, on the other hand, giving a more direct warning would necessarily have had the *wrong* effect. God has *four* people recount the life of his incarnate Son, in each case differently and with inconsistencies – but might we not say: It is important that this narrative should not be more than quite averagely historically plausible *just so that* this should not be taken as the essential, decisive thing? So that the *letter* should not be believed more strongly than is proper and the *spirit* may receive its due i.e. what you are supposed to see cannot be communicated even by the best and most accurate historian; and *therefore* a mediocre account suffices, is even to be preferred. For that too can tell you what you are supposed to be told. (Roughly in the way a mediocre stage set can be better than a sophisticated one, painted trees better than real ones, – because these might distract attention from what matters.)

In other words, if we think about the Bible as a text with which readers need to engage – where the strength and meaning of religion takes place in the individual's dialogue with the spirit – it makes much more sense for the Bible to consist of four inconsistent narratives than one more 'historically plausible' record.

The implications of this for history are considerable because the value of descriptions of the past comes to be seen much more in the way that they are consumed than in the skill of the producer. Histories here described are moral, religious or political texts whose effects should be central to our under-standing of their worth. Histories are narrative experiences whose explicit purpose and apparent meaning carry with them a certain spirit that is grasped through the individual experience of engaging with the narrative.

We might also say that such comments liberate us from the idea of the need to connect history to some idea of universal truth (rather than *believed* truth), and they posit a much more central role for historiography within the disci-pline of history, for it is historiography that studies the narrativization of the past and its effects. Historiography not only regains the centrality that its epistemic investigations deserve, but we can see the way in which a work such as White's *Metahistory*, which is focused on historical effects, could be seen as central to the purpose and definition of history.

Wittgenstein (1980: 32e) does go on to clarify that for him the Bible's historical narrative is rather different from other narratives:

> Christianity is not based on a historical truth; rather, it offers us a (histor-ical) narrative and says: now believe! But not, believe this narrative with the belief appropriate to a historical narrative, rather: believe, through thick and thin, which you can only do as a result of a life. *Here you have a narrative, don't take the same attitude to it as you take to other historical narratives!* Make a *quite different* place in your life for it. – There is nothing *paradoxical* about that!

The more Wittgenstein elaborates on this theme, the more it becomes clear that he develops a critique of empirical history, even if this was not his chief intent. Wittgenstein (1980: 32e) questions the idea that there is any unified linguistic investigation that we can call history, suggesting that there are always plural ways of looking at the past, with different narrative structures and purposes. Returning to the Bible, he remarks (1980: 32e):

> Queer as it sounds: The historical accounts in the Gospels might, histor-ically speaking, be demonstrably false and yet belief would lose nothing by this: *not*, however, because it concerns 'universal truths of reason'! Rather, because historical proof (the historical proof-game) is irrelevant to belief. This message (the Gospels) is seized on by men believingly (i.e. lovingly). *That* is the certainty characterizing this particular acceptance-as-true, not something *else*.

> A believer's relation to these narratives is *neither* the relation to historical truth (probability), *nor yet* that to a theory consisting of 'truths of reason'. There is such a thing.

In other words, when we think about the past, and when we look at the way others approach the past, we should be aware that we will find a variety of 'proof-games', which we would imagine function in a rather similar fashion to language games. The 'historical proof-game' is one among many, and we should only look to it for certain kinds of understanding from the past. While it might offer what Wittgenstein calls 'probability', other narratives of the past have a purpose and function of faith, and they offer a different kind of truth. Central to this pluralizing of the past, and the analysis of its genres, is a consideration of the readers of the past, and their positioning, or as Wittgenstein says here their 'relation to these [different] narratives'.

Another way of saying this might be to follow Wittgenstein's assertion that 'We have quite different attitudes even to different species of what we call fiction!', to contend that we should have quite different attitudes to different species of what we call history! The philosophical impact of Einstein's relativism on Wittgenstein's thought is quite evident here.

The new science

Today it is much harder to make the claim that science relies utterly on the basest forms of linear time. This may be true of commercialized technologies, but it is arguable that the theoretical sciences now operate with as broad a set of temporalities as those we found in classical religions such as Christianity. We may even say that modern science provides rich new temporal grammars which offer alternatives to pre-existing temporal modes in a manner similar to the way in which Jewish temporalities replaced myth- and nature-based conceptions of time. Such a contention also suggests that a resolution of the Enlightenment project could be construed through the social impact of an understanding of pluralized temporalities which can be found in modern science.

It was Einstein who revealed these new possibilities, for, while thinkers such as Newton had seen time as an uncomplicated singularity, Einstein pluralized and troubled the idea of time. Newton (Davies 1995: 30–31) had described 'absolute, true and mathematical time [which] of itself, and from its own nature, flows equably without relation to anything external.' As Davies says (1995: 32), this 'concept of time invites us to chop it up into past, present and future in an absolute and universal manner'. This tidy image of time as defining a succession of universal present moments has important implications for the nature of reality, for in the Newtonian worldview only what happens *now* can be said to be truly real. This, of course, is a form of temporal description which meshes neatly with the principles of an empirical history which insists on rigid distinctions between three forms of time, and a special place for the trained historian of the now in the analysis of the past. Wilcox also points out (1987: 8) that it was by no means coincidental that a new system of dating accompanied the Newtonian revolution:

> The bond between the modern dating system and Newtonian time are not simply conceptual: they are historical. The system was devised and implemented during the same century in which the ideas were formulated that led to Newton's great work. A Jesuit scholar named Domenicus Petavius published the key work setting out the B.C./A.D. system in 1627. [. . .] The B.C./A.D. dating system allows us to quantify the relationship between any two events with a precision no ancient historian could imagine, and to express this precision with a single number.

The limits of this model are revealed in Davies' remark (1995: 32) that:

> Newton's time had endured for two centuries and was scarcely questioned by Westerners, though it had always rested uneasily alongside Eastern thought, and is alien to the minds of indigenous peoples in America, Africa and Australia. [. . .] Newton's time is the time of 'common sense'.

The time of 'common sense' is therefore the time of a very specific form of geographically restricted imaginary, for Davies' remarks about Australians chime with what we have seen of the radical difference of an Australian time-being, which is as founded upon common-sense in its context as is Newtonian time-being.

Einstein's special theory of relativity destroyed almost all of the ruling premises of Newtonian time: its universality, its constancy and its status as an accurate, scientific description of the behaviour of things. As Galison has shown, Einstein's revolutionary ideas drew on a number of areas of thought to undermine Newton: from Einstein's work in the Bern patent office, where he was exposed to the latest mechanical technologies; from his reading of Mach, Minkowski and others working on time; through his experience of seeing unsynchronized time (in Bern, he was able to see not just clocks with international times, but those that gave the times for villages whose different time he could see with his own eyes); and the impact of Enlightened philosophy, especially the work of Hume. Einstein's theory of relativity was in many ways a classic moment of Enlightened science, for it drew on insights of scientists and philosophers of the eighteenth century – which were ideas that could only begin to come into being at that earlier point – and allowed him to accept the logical inferences of those ideas. The end-point that Einstein reached, as he described it (Davies 1995: 70), was that 'The distinction between past, present and future is only an illusion, even if a stubborn one.'

Yet, like the Enlightened thinkers of the late-eighteenth century, it was not immediately apparent as to how Einstein's paradigm would change things. Bertrand Russell (Durrell 1931: iii) suggested that, 'When the ideas involved in Einstein's work have become familiar, as they will do when they are taught in schools, certain changes in our habits of thought are likely to result, and to have great importance in the long run.' While this has certainly been the case in science, it has not been true of history, in spite of the fact that our view of the central object of historical investigation (time) had been changed so radically by Einstein.

In fact, most historians chose to bind themselves to more and more stringent forms of Newtonian absolute time, at precisely that point when scientists were abandoning this paradigm (Gaddis 2002: 76–77). A minoritarian relativist historical tradition did emerge in the work of American writers of the 1930s such as Carl Becker and Conyers Read, but this movement absorbed relativism in only one discrete sense: through the notion that all individuals must have their own senses of time and therefore their own, different, true pictures of the world. For Becker, 'everyman' became 'his own historian', whilst Read described the growing 'relativity of all history' (Marwick 1989: 79). Influential later theorists such as E.H. Carr (1987: 164) and Aron (1959: 289) were able to find agreement with this use of relativist thought as a corrective to common-sense reasoning.

Yet, the work of such theorists hardly seems to answer the question as to what a post-Einsteinian history might look like. The theory of relativity, as physicists understood, was not conceived as a corrective, but as the revelation of a striking new way of seeing the world. It was epistemological in the manner that it demanded the uprooting of central propositions of the old worldview and the construction of a redescribed picture of the world faithful to new epistemic truths. How, then, could we imagine such a process operating in history?

There are two answers to this question that I should like to consider. The first is to say that postmodern historiographers such as Jenkins and Munslow are finally implementing a relativist project in the discipline. 'Relativism' is a belief for which they are often castigated, but those with any notion of the idea's intellectual history would be aware of the irony that pseudo-scientific empiricists are engaged in a battle over theory with postmoderns, whose scientific credentials are far more respectable than their own. A second answer is to say that the relativization of time offers historians the framework through which they might construct a discipline founded on pluralized notions of (foregrounded) time, rather than a single, absolute and unspoken Newtonian time. The duty of the historian is not then simply to the truth of the past but to the truths of the times of the peoples of the past. History becomes a discipline of rich, productive, philosophical possibilities, and, critically, one whose method is globalized, rather than being centred on the western academy.

After Einstein, we can say quite comfortably that we all live in a variety of times. The identification of our time modes, their interaction and the differences between people and places remain to be studied (the discipline of anthropology has made the best start in this field). Post-Einsteinian science offers a rich fund of language and ideas for the study of time and the eventual delineation of our states of concurrence. In brief, there is the notion of space-time, which claims the indivisibility of these variables; there is the notion of 'imaginary time' (Hawking 1988: 143), through which one might move forwards and backwards; there are thermological, entropic and cosmological 'arrows of time', which operate in different ways (Hawking 1988: 145); and there is a new grammar of time which emerges from the novel questions opened up after Einstein.

Such grammars, of course, are critical not only as ideas but, as we have seen in the Christian example, for the manner in which they form the bases of human lives. Hawking, recalling Wittgenstein (1988: 144), asks, 'Where does this difference between the past and the future come from? Why do we remember the past but not the future?' If, as Hawking contends (1988: 144), 'The laws of science do not distinguish between the past and the future', what can this mean for historians? Going back to the earlier quotation from W.G. Sebald, I would suggest that what this means for history is that we should recognize that new states of time-being are emerging all around us, in the manner that religious cosmologies appeared in earlier civilizations. A seeming difference between our world and earlier cultures is that our civilization is much less discrete than cultures of the past, so flows of ideas of time are more malleable and rapid. All live with a plurality of times, and relativist ideas underpin the limitless possibilities of combinations of times. Just as physicists such as Davies (Rawlence 1985: 188) find themselves 'trying to formulate a scientific language that doesn't depend on the space and time concepts', historians need to deploy a similarly epistemological approach to asking both what kinds of time underpin our practices, and what alternative temporalities might be reconfigured in language and in texts.

The relativization of time presents us with the duty of seeing other cultures' temporal modes as being of equal value to our own and as intrinsically valuable parts of human culture. The universal discipline and method of history no longer exists, yet it obtains the potential to become something much greater than this for, if other temporalities (and the complex epistemologies and methods with which they are associated) can be imagined as bases for history, the value of history increases just as its old certainties diminish. Such claims imply a much broader role for history and the production of work which goes well beyond the fulfilment of a contested set of narratives which together amount to an archive of truth. Or perhaps, so long as we could see the archive in the productive fashion imagined by Australians, or as a refuge from which we should seek to escape in Buddhism, this is all history should be.

For Einstein, the realization that sparked his new thinking was the notion that (Deeds Ermarth 1992: vii), 'Until at last it came to me that time was suspect'. Historians need to ask themselves what they no longer question, what they never suspect. The answer, I have suggested, is that here too it is time that deserves troubling. What is more, the resources for such a project lie not only in fields such as modern physics, but in the cultures of the world's religions, all of which located an orientation towards time as a central feature of their belief systems. As we have seen, the centring of faith on approaches to time has led different religious cultures towards very different senses of time and varied ideas of what might constitute a text about time, or a history. Let us now recover those lost times.

Chapter 10

Conclusion

I have tried to argue that historians have a great deal to gain by thinking more carefully about time. The first part of this book set out the current state of play in discussions of time in both history and a series of other disciplines. It became clear that, in spite of the fact that time lies at the heart of the historical enterprise, theoretical literatures on time in historiography and the philosophy of history are much less well developed than discussions that we find in disciplines such as anthropology, sociology, philosophy and theology. Using debates from some of these subject areas – as well as considering interdisciplinary scholars such as Ricœur and Deeds Ermarth – I tried to show that the discipline of history needs to confront time in a more open fashion.

I went on to suggest that a key reality that is currently occluded in most historical and historiographical writing is that time is not a singular, natural and uncontested entity, but is viewed outside the discipline as both plural and as being constructed in varied manners in different cultures. Two of the most critical insights of modern anthropology have been the observations that the subjects of ethnographic study lived in many different kinds of time cultures and also that modern anthropologists themselves inadvertently revealed a great deal about the temporality of the modern west in their own writing.

In order to try to induce a similar kind of realization of the pluralization of time, I decided to use religious cultures as a means of illustrating the manner in which complex and very different understandings of time have emerged in world history. Just as importantly, these ideas of time were not simply formative in terms of the generation of theologies and rituals, but also in the formation of distinct forms of historical cultures.

There were a number of strategic reasons that underlay that decision to look at religious cultures as a means of developing my argument. First, those cultures offer the historian a set of primary sources that can be easily accessed and compared, as well as rich secondary literatures in theology and other fields of study which are alive to the importance of ideas of time and history in the development of religions. Second, religions have traditionally dominated the formation of ideas and the intellectual history of most human cultures. Third, religions offered both a way of tracking alterations in temporal cultures in faiths which are related (such as Judaism, Christianity and Islam) and also a means to recognizing the great difference and range of such cultures in religions such as the Australian Dreamtime and Buddhism. This is not to say that I have claimed that the former faiths represent a norm against which others are measured, for one of my secondary arguments has been that historians have not been cognizant enough of the possibilities that exist for the production of histories founded on the temporalities of non-western religions. Fourth, the study of religions made great sense in the context of this particular series of books on 'History: Concepts, Theories and Practices', for religions offer very clear instances of how concepts and theories relate to practices, whether it be in the Christian continuum of time and the rites and texts which express that idea or the manner in which the concept of nirvana leads Buddhists to compose historical texts which seek to flee from meaning, detail and other principles that form the basis of historical cultures such as we find in the modern west.

I shall now try to summarize what was most distinctive in each of the temporal cultures studied in this book, before closing by asking what these observations might imply for the study and teaching of history, and in which directions the study of time and history might fruitfully move forwards.

We saw that the identity of Jewish time and specifically Jewish philosophies of history is complicated by the character of the Old Testament of the Bible. Yet, the fact that that compilation of texts was gathered from writings from more than two thousand years of history and from across the Middle East cannot obscure the central temporal premises of the ancient Jews. Chief among these was the idea that the order of time was controlled by God and not by natural forces. It was therefore inappropriate, and regarded as primitive, to venerate the natural cycles of time of harvests and seasons (though some of these cycles were incorporated into Jewish rites), and across the text of the Old Testament we saw the great struggles the Jews' God had with his people in his attempts to make them believe in his lordship of time. This temporal schema also put man in a special place for humans lay between God and nature, capable and duty-bound both to make their own history and to rule over the natural world.

History therefore became an act of recording men's fulfilment of their duties to their God, though the horizon towards which these histories gazed changed as Jewish culture developed. In early Judaism there was a great focus on notions of race, purity, law and obedience, so that the Jews might deserve their constitution as a special chosen people, and genres such as genealogy and chronicles were deployed as a means of recording this coming into being of a people obediently living in the path directed by their Lord. Later biblical Judaism, by contrast, displayed evidence of the influence of Greek forms of thought (most especially Stoicism and scepticism as seen in the books of Job and Ecclesiastes) and eschatological leanings, which seem to have originated in attempts at rationalizing the splintering of the Jewish people.

Christianity continued the messianic and late eschatological traditions of diasporic Judaism and it centred the human experience of time in the universe in the life of Christ, sent by God with a new covenant which extended well beyond the Jewish people. A number of very different interpretations can be made of the New Covenant but what unites them is a concern with questions of time and history. Each of the Gospels' lives of Christ (which themselves were chosen from a broader set of gospels) offers a different picture of time and history, which in turn influenced the development of an institutional faith after the death and resurrection of Jesus. This pluralism was both extended and contained by the early evangelists, most notably Paul, for in the later letters and books of the New Testament we see the development of church orthodoxy across the eastern Mediterranean. It seems quite clear that that teaching was focused on an eschatological picture of time (vividly described in the Revelation to John), which saw history as a process of imminent judgement, and recent theology has stressed the importance of this promised end of times, exploring both its literal and metaphorical connotations.

History in the Christian Bible needed to appeal to both the mind and the soul, for it strove to prove that Christ had walked the earth (constantly demonstrating his status by warping time through miracles and the resurrection) and that meaning in the universe was to be determined by this life in which adherents needed to believe with all their hearts. Life and history were but provisional stages that might lead to the new times promised by Christianity which came after death in an ascension to heaven. So, just as Judaism sought to develop an idea of faith and history as being dependent as much on things not seen as those that were visible to man, Christianity extended such ideas to assert that accounts of time as different as those of Luke (which concentrated on historical practice) and John (which stressed philosophical meaning) served the same higher purpose.

While it is clear that the most sophisticated Jewish and Christian ideas of time are found in the Bible, and are still being found there, it is arguable that Islam's most sacred text, the Qur'an, served only as the prelude to, and

incubator of, Islamic ideas of time and philosophies of history in the later
medieval period. This should not seem surprising since the Qur'an preceded
the development of complex, urban Islamic civilizations and it was centrally
concerned with relating the message of the Prophet Mohammed to the offers
of the competing faiths of Judaism, Christianity and brands of paganism into
which it was born on the Arabian peninsula.

Medieval Islamic ideas of time are characterized by their complexity,
intricacy and (global) ambition, evidenced also in the historical texts which
developed from such ideas: in monuments such as the Alhambra as much as
the first world histories written by Ibn Khaldun and Rashid al-Din Tabib.
They successfully incorporated ideas from across a rapidly acquired global
empire that stretched from east Asia to western Europe, though it is quite clear
that variants of Greek, Persian, Indian and Judaeo-Christian thought were the
chief influences upon 'the Islamic synthesis'. Perhaps as a consequence of this
complexity, early Muslims developed a huge range of differentiated historical
and historiographical genres, and, in common with Islamic culture generally,
they fused areas which might have been seen as distinct in other human cultures; thus we have forms of history which are legal codes, histories which are
artworks and buildings, histories which are philosophies, and, of course,
histories which are theologies.

The Australian Dreamtime is probably the oldest religious culture studied
in this book, though there is some inexactness in critical writing owing to the
fact that it was not a literate culture. Artworks, from ancient and modern times,
serve as the most important source for both religious and historical ideas.
While ethnographers traditionally saw Australian cultures as primitive forms
of humanity whose thought was static and characterized by a dependence on
myth – which was contrasted with the higher order concept of history – more
recent scholarship has exploded such claims. The Dreamtime is no more
mythical than the resurrection of Christ or the transmission of the Qur'an to
Prophet Mohammed by the angel Gabriel.

The Dreamtime describes a process by which the world came into being in
the distant past and the manner in which Australian cultures need to live their
own lives in tribute to this gift of life. In some ways this is practised through
lives of complete religious devotion, in which all life, being and place is sacred
so as to engender a temporal continuum in which men might constantly reflect
on their being in the continuum. Yet, it is not the case that this temporal culture is one without agency, for what men do in their lives is to constantly
remake the originary moments of the Dreamtime through their practices and
their creative works, in which oral traditions, art works and ceremonies are
designed to offer fragments of the universal history to other groups who in

turn share their understandings of the world. Histories are therefore loaded with symbolism so as to reflect the importance of landscape in this belief system (for when the gods returned after making the earth, they left behind distinct landscapes as they ruptured the crust of the earth) and were originally characterized by their temporariness, for the central necessity of the Dream-time was that it be re-made over and over for all time and not frozen in the moment as it would then lose its meaning in the lives of its adherents.

Whereas most historical cultures are concerned with the accumulation of detail and the attempt to recover a past which seems real, Buddhists regard such aims as distracting and illusory. While it is true that conventional forms of Buddhist history exist, it is perhaps better to see them as Thai, Indian and Chinese histories that emerged in Buddhist cultures, for Buddhism itself disdains ideas of sense-making through reflection upon history. Instead, it is focused on a mechanism of transformation in which the emptiness of life – samsara – is reproduced in a system of karmic regeneration. The aim of Buddhism therefore is not to make or study history but to escape it, though to quite what one escapes is difficult to comprehend, for even tentative ap-proaches towards the concept of nirvana involve the abandonment of logics and structures that we would otherwise take for granted.

Buddhism is therefore deeply epistemological and in branches of the Mahayana tradition such as the Yogācāra and Zen we are able to study texts on time which vary in form from philosophical treatises to monastic gardens. In both cases our aim is to meditate on the character of these things and in so doing to come to some greater sense of enlightenment as to what the un-time and un-being of nirvana might constitute. As people, we are in a unique posi-tion to end suffering because of the agency that is attached to our human form, but the battle towards nirvana can often seem either too complex or too simple to be grasped. If histories exist their task is to offer moments of revelation which enhance the possibility of nirvana, but Buddhists must be very careful to avoid the kinds of narratives of progression that have characterized my own description of Buddhism in these two paragraphs.

In a discussion of Einstein and relativity in Chapter 9 we saw that modern science was another field to which this book could appeal in its claim regard-ing the pluralization of time and the existence of a series of historical cultures based upon different epistemological conceptions of time. This also entailed trying to tie up the theoretical concerns and subject matter of this study in dis-cussing the manner in which Einstein himself recognized that religions (most especially Buddhism) had earlier illustrated a number of aspects of his relat-ivization of time. For Einstein the Newtonian picture of time was an important one in the history of temporal cultures, but it was deeply flawed as compared with many earlier understandings of time because it lacked the kind of self-consciousness which would have allowed it to see that it was not necessarily a natural and uniquely powerful means of seeing the world.

One of the central binds of modern history has been the manner in which it, generally unconsciously, adopted both the Newtonian picture of time and its lack of self-consciousness as to the cultural particularity of that description of the world. In Chapter 9 I therefore also appealed to another critical figure in the history of modern thought who had insisted on the continuing relevance of understanding the radical difference of earlier religious modes of conceptualizing the world – a figure who stressed the need to occupy ourselves with questioning certainty. What I suggested Wittgenstein meant by this was the need to question the un-reflexive Newtonian picture of the world and the means by which we might think beyond that picture. He himself struggled with this notion for the length of his career, but what is striking is the manner in which he saw that religion played an important role in potentially thinking beyond the Newtonian constraints we have placed upon ourselves in the modern west. In this sense, Wittgenstein allows me to return to the early theoretical chapters of this work, for what he said was very similar to the thought of someone like Wilcox who argued that we might wrestle free from the constrictions of empirical time as easily through a consideration of the works of Suetonius and Bede as through an engagement with any modern theorist.

There is of course an irony here for, in following Wilcox's advice and choosing to look, in my case, at the writings of Enni and Job as a means of thinking beyond the temporal dilemma which I believe we have created for ourselves in the discipline of history, I am contending that doing history becomes the means by which we resolve the lacunae of history. In a sense, though, this is to draw on some of the most basic principles which are believed in by historians of all hues: that we do not go to the past to find people who look and think like ourselves and that we need to carefully attend to the radical difference of the cultures of the past. So one might say that a simple means of expressing a key part of my case is that historians need to transfer more of the assumptions of their own practices into the theories and concepts that they use to describe their discipline.

The arguments and case studies of this book will, I hope, offer some pause for reflection for both students and teachers of history, as well as producers and consumers of historical narratives outside the academy. In universities we construct degrees in history which are related to the social and political circumstances of our cultures, so that it seems unsurprising that, for example, Rankean, Marxist and gender-based approaches have had especial appeal at particular moments in time. Yet, what such trends have not tended to do is to

alter the epistemological basis for doing history and indeed to address
questions of epistemology at all. While there is no doubt that the discipline of
history has broadened considerably in the two centuries or so in which it has
been taught in universities, one might question the extent to which it has been
deepened over time. Even avowedly theoretical sub-fields such as historiography and the philosophy of history have tended to take a certain number
of basic assumptions about history as givens and in those areas we cannot
identify a figure comparable to Wittgenstein whose generalized epistemological
doubt induced a rich series of changes in (and outside) philosophy.

At our present time it would rightly be observed that one of the ways in
which historical education has changed in the past forty years is that it has
been globalized. It would now be impossible to take a degree in history which
avoided the history of the world outside the west. There are many instances of
successful courses and departments that specialize in extra-European history,
just as there are notable institutes and degrees in countries such as Japan and
India that concentrate on the history of the west. In broad terms this globalization of the curriculum evidently coincided with the post-colonial moment
in world history as European political empires collapsed and were defeated.
Yet, there has been a distinct difference in post-colonial work in history as
compared with a number of academic fields, most notably literary studies.
Where historians have seized upon the post-colonial moment as a means to
broaden their field of study, literary scholars have also asked whether it
presents an opportunity to alter their theories, concepts and practices. It is
true that some of the positive responses to that challenge – such as the use of
subaltern approaches to texts after the work of theorists such as Spivak (1990,
1994, 1999) and Nandy (1983, 1987) – have migrated from literary studies to
history, but in general historians have not seen post-colonialism as offering a
questioning or pluralization of the historical method. It was for this reason
that I described the work of Young in my third chapter for he is above all concerned with the question, first raised by thinkers such as Fanon and Césaire,
of what history might look like if it was able to conceive of new methods and
rationales that came from outside the west. The illustrative chapters of this
book were intended to provide tentative answers to those questions, though
it is evident that a great deal more work needs to be done on the question of
how history can be rethought from other places and times. Such a claim also
returns us to the purpose of this series and the work of historiographers such
as Munslow, Jenkins and Rosenstone to undertake, using the titles of their
books and journals, 'The New History', the act of 'Rethinking History', the
production of 'Experimental History' and to ask again the question 'Why
History?'

A final set of questions emerges then as to what new lines of enquiry tentatively opened up by this work need to be looked at in greater detail. One answer to this question is to point out that there are a series of areas of this study that have of necessity been rather brief discussions, where historiographers might gain from deeper engagements. I am sure I have not managed to convey the richness of Jewish and Christian theological literatures on the temporal cultures of the Bible and there would also be a great deal of scope for engaging in the temporal and historical cultures of medieval Judaism and Christianity. Deeper gains can be made, I suspect, with regard to Buddhism for the extent of western historiography's engagement with Buddhist cultures has been negligible. My own instinct was to sketch the importance of a small set of Mahayana traditions from India, China and Japan, but a good case could be made for studying Thai, Tibetan and Sri Lankan Buddhism and for interrogating much more carefully both the Theravadan and Vajryanan traditions. Then there is the question of religions not covered here such as Zoroastrianism, Hinduism and traditional African and American faiths, and of temporal spheres outside religion in fields such as literature, art and work. The guide to key reading which follows offers some suggestions of where interested readers might begin studies of these areas.

Guide to key reading

There are relatively few books and articles that address the question of time from a historiographical perspective, but we are fortunate that a number of these works are of the highest quality. Chief among them are three books: Donald J. Wilcox, *The Measure of Times Past: Pre-Newtonian Chronologies and the Rhetoric of Relative Time* (Chicago: University of Chicago Press, 1987), G.J. Whitrow, *Time in History: The Evolution of Our General Awareness of Time and Temporal Perspective* (Oxford: Oxford University Press, 1988) and David Carr, *Time, Narrative and History* (Bloomington: Indiana University Press, 1987). Each of these works shows a deep awareness of debates on time across the academy and they all display an instinctive openness to the idea that there are plural times. Wilcox is of especial interest for the manner in which he demonstrates the great sophistication of pre-Newtonian modes of temporal thought, including religious thinking. A comparable willingness to think in world historical terms is apparent in the important essay by John T. Marcus, on 'Time and the Sense of History: West and East' in *Comparative Studies in Society and History*, 1961, 3: 123–39.

Two recent collections edited by Heidrun Friese – *The Moment: Time and Rupture in Modern Thought* (Liverpool: Liverpool University Press, 2001) and *Identities: Time, Difference and Boundaries* (New York: Berghahn, 2002) – also contain a number of essays which show an awareness of debates on time in philosophy and critical theory, though they tend rather more towards the abstruse and the circular than the works cited above. Rather more effective is the work of Nathan Rotenstreich and two works, separated by almost thirty years in their publication dates, give a good picture of his work: *Between Past and Present: An Essay on History* (Port Washington: Kennikat Press, 1958) and *Time and Meaning in History* (Dordrecht: D. Reidel, 1987). Norbert

Elias's *Time: An Essay* (Oxford: Blackwell, 1992) offers an insight into debates on time from within the field of the philosophy of history and Reinhart Koselleck's *Futures Past: On the Semantics of Historical Time* (Cambridge, Mass.: MIT Press, 2004) is useful in the manner in which it connects time debates to discussions of modernity and modern German thought. Penelope J. Corfield's *Time and the Shape of History* (Yale: Yale University Press, 2007) promises to be the disciplinary starting point on its subject.

The work of three authors on the culture of time in past civilizations stands out: Donald E. Brown, *Hierarchy, History and Human Nature: The Social Origins of Historical Consciousness* (Tucson: University of Arizona Press, 1988), Jacques Le Goff, *Time, Work and Culture in the Middle Ages* (Chicago: University of Chicago Press, 1980) and Eviatar Zerubavel, 'The French Revolutionary Calendar: A Case Study in the Sociology of Time', *American Sociology Review*, 1977, 42: 868–77. Le Goff and Zerubavel have written widely on, respectively, the shaping of medieval and modern time, with both writers displaying an ability to apply sociological thought to historical discussions.

The leading figure in the interdisciplinary field of time studies is the sociologist Barbara Adam. A number of her works are listed in the bibliography and a good place to start to engage with her thought is *Time* (Cambridge: Polity, 2004). Another vital reference point in this area is Samuel L. Macey's *Encyclopedia of Time* (New York: Garland, 1994), as is Kristen Lippincott's edited collection *The Story of Time* (London: Merrell Holberton, 1999). The latter text is a beautiful edition based upon a major exhibition on time at the Royal Observatory. Its essays on clocks and chronography across the globe are useful and complement Anthony F. Aveni's brilliant *Empires of Time: Calendars, Clocks and Cultures* (London: I.B. Tauris, 2000). Aveni is the place to begin any study of time in the Americas and his work is especially strong on Incan and Mayan time. A book which takes the study of time back to prehistory and which displays a strong awareness of scientific debate is Stephen Toulmin and June Goodfield's *The Discovery of Time* (London: Penguin, 1965). Two rather more specialized but important works are John Baillie's *The Belief in Progress* (Oxford: Oxford University Press, 1950) and J.M.E. McTaggart, 'The Unreality of Time', *Mind: A Quarterly Review of Philosophy and Psychology*, 1908, 17: 456–73. The former book is very strong on Christian ideas of time and the latter essay was of seminal importance in terms of the connections it made between eastern religion and western philosophy. As I suggested earlier, the novels of W.G. Sebald – *The Emigrants, Rings of Saturn, Austerlitz, Vertigo* (London: Vintage, 2002) – all offer a subtle introduction to the varieties of time. Sebald's 'novels' are in fact hybrid texts that mix fiction, poetry, photography, history and travel writing, though they have not yet excited much interest within history.

The subject of religion and time is analysed best in two works: S.G.F. Brandon, *History, Time and Deity: A Historical and Comparative Study of the Conception of Time in Religious Thought and Practice* (Manchester: Manchester University Press, 1965) and Anindita Niyogi Balslev and J.N. Mohanty (eds) *Religion and Time* (Leiden: E.J. Brill, 1993). The former book is especially strong on Christianity and Judaism, while the latter collection contains important essays on eastern religions. Also strong on Judaeo-Christian time are Colin Brown's edited collection *History, Criticism and Faith: Four Historical Studies* (London: IVP, 1976) and Van Austin Harvey's *The Historian and the Believer: The Morality of Historical Knowledge and Christian Belief* (London: SCM Press, 1967). Those seeking a clear and recent introduction to theological debates about world religions are directed towards Lloyd V.J. Ridgeon's *Major World Religions* (London: Routledge, 2003). Also of general interest, especially for those instinctively suspicious of the ability of western scholars to offer authentic readings of non-western 'religions', is Daniel Dubuisson's *The Western Construction of Religion. Myths, Knowledge & Ideology* (Baltimore: The Johns Hopkins University Press, 2003).

Anthropology as a discipline offers a wide range of important texts on time, many of which show admirable reflexive qualities. While the work of Durkheim and other early social scientists still retains relevance, the two authors with whom any student of the subject should begin are Johannes Fabian and Alfred Gell. Fabian's chief works are the collection *Time and the Work of Anthropology: Critical Essays 1971–1991* (Amsterdam: Harwood, 1992) and *Time and the Other: How Anthropology Makes its Object* (New York: Columbia University Press, 2002), while Gell's key work is *The Anthropology of Time: Cultural Constructions of Temporal Maps and Images* (Berg: Oxford, 1992). Also useful is Nicholas Thomas, *Out of Time: History and Evolution in Anthropological Discourse*, 2nd edn (Michigan: University of Michigan Press, 1996).

Another discipline where discussions of time have been worth historians' following is linguistics. William E. Bull's *Time, Tense and the Verb: A Study in Theoretical and Applied Linguistics with Particular Attention to Spanish* (Berkeley: University of California Press, 1968) offers a good grounding in the concerns of experts in the field, while more recently Suzanne Fleischman's *Tense and Narrativity: From Medieval Performance to Modern Fiction* (London: Routledge, 1990) is a quite brilliant, and at times rewardingly complex and difficult, linguistic study applied to literary texts. Historians could learn a great deal from Fleischman.

Sociological debates on time are well covered in two quite recent works: John Hassard (ed.) *The Sociology of Time* (London: Macmillan, 1990) and Warren TenHouten, *Time and Society* (Albany: SUNY Press, 2005). Sociological discussions also form one aspect of debates on capital and time, and those interested in following up on this area should consult David Nugent (ed.) *Locating Capitalism in Time and Space: Global Restructurings, Politics, and Identity* (Stanford: Stanford University Press, 2002).

The last set of disciplinary approaches to time that merits attention is that of philosophy, and it makes sense to begin a study of this area with Robin Le Poidevin and Murray MacBeath's *The Philosophy of Time* (Oxford: Oxford University Press, 1993). A logical move would be then to consult the work of Charles M. Sherover, *The Human Experience of Time: The Development of its Philosophic Meaning* (New York: New York University Press, 1975) and *Are We in Time? And Other Essays on Time and Temporality* (Evanston: Northwestern, 2003). Those who wish to follow up my interest in Wittgenstein's ideas about time are well advised to begin with a reading of the collection of work from across his career compiled as *Culture and Value* (Oxford: Basil Blackwell, 1980) before moving on to his great, late work *The Philosophical Investigations* (Oxford: Basil Blackwell, 1972).

Before progressing to look at specific studies of time in different religious traditions, and indeed the major theological texts pertaining to those religions, it may be worth briefly running through some of the key authors in the canons of historiography and the philosophy of history, a number of whom have appeared throughout this book. A solid place to begin would be Georg G. Iggers' recent work *Historiography in the Twentieth Century* (Middletown: Wesleyan University Press, 2004), while classic works by Aron, Collingwood, Carr and Bloch still have a wide readership within the discipline: Raymond Aron, *Introduction to the Philosophy of History: An Essay on the Limits of Historical Objectivity* (London: Weidenfeld & Nicolson, 1948), R.G. Collingwood, *The Idea of History* (Oxford: Oxford University Press, 1946), E.H. Carr, *What is History?*, ed. R.W. Davies, 2nd edn (London: Penguin, 1987) and Marc Bloch, *The Historian's Craft* (Manchester: Manchester University Press, 1954). Those who are interested in the irresolvable disputes between so-called 'traditionalists' and so-called 'postmoderns' would do well to read Evans and Marwick, from the former camp, and follow that with some Munslow and Jenkins, from the latter: Richard J. Evans, *In Defence of History* (London: Granta, 1997), Arthur Marwick, *The Nature of History*, 3rd edn (London: Macmillan, 1989), Alun Munslow, *The New History* (London: Longman, 2003) and Keith Jenkins, *Why History? Ethics and Postmodernity* (London: Routledge, 1999). Those who have looked at authors such as

Wilcox, Gell and Wittgenstein mentioned in this guide to key reading will quickly realize that, whatever the respective merits of the two aforementioned camps' positions, Munslow and Jenkins have opened themselves to the wider academy and to modern thought, while Evans and Marwick promote an insular account of history.

Further evidence of the importance of historical and historiographical thought's engagement with the broader academy can be seen in the work of Hayden White (which innovated in part through its borrowing from literary studies and philosophy) and Paul Ricœur (which occupies a space across history, theology, philosophy and literary studies). White's key text is *Metahistory: The Historical Imagination in the Nineteenth-Century* (Baltimore: The Johns Hopkins University Press, 1973), while Ricœur's is the three-volume study *Time and Narrative* (Chicago: University of Chicago Press, 1984–90). The bibliography lists a selection of other valuable works by Ricœur, and those seeking a guide to his work would be well advised to begin with David Wood's edited collection *On Paul Ricœur: Narrative and Interpretation* (London: Routledge, 1991). Coming from a similar interdisciplinary trajectory, Elizabeth Deeds Ermarth's monographs are two of the most critical works on time and history: *Realism and Consensus in the English Novel: Time, Space and Narrative* (Princeton: Princeton University Press, 1983) and *Sequel to History: Postmodernism and the Crisis of Representational Time* (Princeton: Princeton University Press, 1992).

Post-colonial historical theory possesses a similar great work in Robert Young's *White Mythologies: Writing History and the West* (London: Routledge, 1990). Before tackling this book, it may be worth beginning with Peter Burke's essay 'Western Historical Thinking in a Global Perspective', in Jörn Rüsen's *Western Historical Thinking: An Intercultural Debate* (New York: Berghahn, 2002: 15–30). Like Munslow's *The New History*, cited above, Barbara Bush's *Imperialism and Postcolonialism* (London: Longman-Pearson, 2006) is also in the same series as this work, and it offers a great resource to students of this subject. Those wishing to go directly to works from subaltern studies are advised to look at the following two books: Ashis Nandy, *The Intimate Enemy: Loss and Recovery of Self under Colonialism* (Delhi: Oxford University Press, 1983) and Gayatri Chakravorty Spivak, *The Post-Colonial Critic: Interviews, Strategies, Dialogues*, ed. by Sarah Harasym (London: Routledge, 1990).

This book looked only at a limited number of time cultures. Those interested in exploring other such cultures are advised to begin by using Aveni, cited above, and, if especially interested in either North American or African conceptions of time, the following works are recommended: Benjamin Whorf,

'An American Indian Model of the Universe', *International Journal of American Linguistics*, 16, 1950: 67–72, Peter Nabokov, *A Forest of Time: American Indian Ways of History* (Cambridge: Cambridge University Press, 2002), John S. Mbiti, *African Religion and Philosophy* (London: Heinemann, 1969) and K. (J.E.) Wiredu, 'How Not to Compare African Thought with Western Thought' in Richard A. Wright (ed.) *African Philosophy: An Introduction*, 3rd edn (Lanham: University Press of America, 1984: 149–62). Greek, Roman and Near Eastern accounts of time are well covered in John F. Callahan, *Four Views of Time in Ancient Historiography* (Cambridge, Mass.: Harvard University Press, 1948), Steven L. McKenzie and Thomas Römer (eds), *Rethinking the Foundations: Historiography in the Ancient World and in the Bible* (Berlin: Walter de Gruyter, 2000) and John Van Seters, *In Search of History: Historiography in the Ancient World and the Origins of Biblical History* (New Haven: Yale University Press, 1983).

With regard to Judaism and Christianity the key primary source is evidently the Bible, with the *New Revised Standard Bible* (Oxford: Oxford University Press, 1995) being used in most recent scholarship. The best works on ancient Jewish time are the following: Gershon Brin, *The Concept of Time in the Bible and the Dead Sea Scrolls* (Leiden: Brill, 2001), Simon DeVries, *Yesterday, Today and Tomorrow: Time and History in the Old Testament* (London: SPCK, 1975), Christopher North, *The Old Testament Interpretation of History* (London: Epworth Press, 1946), Knud Jeppesen and Benedikt Otzen (eds), *The Production of Time: Tradition History in Old Testament Scholarship* (Sheffield: Almond Press, 1984), Sacha Stern, *Time and Process in Ancient Judaism* (Oxford: The Littman Library, 2003) and Yosef Hayim Yerushalmi, *Zakhor: Jewish History and Jewish Memory* (Washington: University of Washington Press, 1982). Those with an interest in medieval Jewish temporal thought are directed towards: Tamar Rudavsky, *Time Matters: Time, Creation and Cosmology in Medieval Jewish Philosophy* (Albany: SUNY Press, 2000) and Elie Kedourie, *The Jewish World: Revelation, Prophecy and History* (London: Thames and Hudson, 1979). There are of course a considerable number of important works devoted to specific books of the Old Testament. The following three texts are interesting in themselves but should also provide helpful bibliographic resources to those who wish to look at recent Old Testament scholarship in more detail: Leslie S. Wilson, *The Book of Job: Judaism in the 2nd Century BCE: An Intertextual Reading* (Lanham: University Press of America, 2006), Tremper Longman III, *The Book of Ecclesiastes* (Grand Rapids: William B. Eerdmans, 1998) and J.G. McConville and J.G. Millar, *Time and Place in Deuteronomy* (Sheffield: Sheffield Academic Press, 1994).

Of the many editions of early Christian literatures not included in the Bible, perhaps the most important is J.K. Elliott's edited *Apocryphal New Testament: A Collection of Apocryphal Christian Literature in an English Translation* (Oxford: Clarendon Press, 1993). Although now rather dated, another key resource is Richard Bauckham and David Bebbington's *History and Christianity: A Bibliography* (Leicester: UCCF, 1977). There have been a number of reasonably distinct phases in modern Christian theology, beginning with literatures on 'the Historical Jesus' from the late-nineteenth- and early-twentieth-century, moving on to classic studies of Christian time and history in the 1940s, a hermeneutic turn, under the influence of German Protestant theology in the 1960s, and, more recently, a new pluralism in terms of approaches adopted and subject matters chosen. The first of these moments is well represented by Martin Kähler, *The So-Called Historical Jesus and the Historic Biblical Christ*, Philadelphia: Fortress Press, 1964 [1896]) and Albert Schweitzer, *The Quest of the Historical Jesus: A Critical Study of its Progress from Reimarus to Wrede* (London: Adam and Charles Black, 1910). Among the best works of the second phase are: C.H. Dodd, *History and the Gospel* (London: Nisbet, 1938), Reinhold Niebuhr, *Faith and History: A Comparison of Christian and Modern Views of History* (London: Nisbet, 1949), Herbert Butterfield, *Christianity and History* (London: G. Bell and Sons, 1949) and R.L.P. Milburn, *Early Christian Interpretations of History* (London: Adam and Charles Black, 1954). The hermeneutic turn can be found in Carl Braaten, *New Directions in Theology Today, Volume II: History and Hermeneutics* (London: Lutterworth Press, 1968), while an influential linguistic study from that time is James Barr's *Biblical Words for Time* (London: SCM Press, 1962). A good example of contemporary interdisciplinary approaches to Biblical questions is Jeremy Begbie's *Theology, Music and Time* (Cambridge: Cambridge University Press, 2000).

Underpinning modern Christian theology has been a restatement of the importance of eschatology, most especially in the work of Bultmann and Moltmann. Among these two authors' many works, the following are especially recommended: Rudolf Bultmann, *History and Eschatology* (Edinburgh: Edinburgh University Press, 1957), Jürgen Moltmann, *The Coming of God: Christian Eschatology* (London, SCM Press, 1996) and Jürgen Moltmann, *The Trinity and the Kingdom of God*, London, SCM Press, 1981). Good guides to the thought of these two key figures can be found in: John Painter, *Theology as Hermeneutics: Rudolf Bultmann's Interpretation of the History of Jesus* (Sheffield: The Almond Press, 1987) and Richard Bauckham, *Moltmann: Messianic Theology in the Making* (Basingstoke: Marshall Pickering, 1987). A recent collection edited by James L. Buckley and L. Gregory Jones

– Theology and Eschatology at the Turn of the Millennium (Oxford: Blackwell, 2001) – offers a comprehensive picture of trends in recent eschatological study. Those wishing to find a good guide to Augustine's writing on time would do well to consult T.E. Mommsen, 'St Augustine and the Christian Idea of Progress', *Journal of the History of Ideas*, 12, 1951: 346-74.

As I explained in the text, there are few written collections of Australian Dreamtime texts, though one critical study, which includes large numbers of transcriptions of oral traditions, stands out as the great work of the field: T.G.H. Strehlow's *Songs of Central Australia* (Sydney: Angus & Robertson, 1970). Strehlow's masterpiece is now a very hard book to find because since it was written a new mood has emerged in Australia, where it has come to be seen to be unethical to publish and record religious ceremonial material which was never intended to be inscribed in books and articles. In part because of this, there is now a rather nuanced view of Strehlow in the field, though to my mind such ambiguity ill serves the skill and monumental quality of his work, and his great attendance to the needs of his subjects, among whom he lived his whole life. A sympathetic portrait of Strehlow is offered by Bruce Chatwin, *The Songlines* (London: Vintage, 1998). A number of excellent studies of Australian art offer both sources and important interpretative essays: Ronald M. Berndt (ed.), *Australian Aboriginal Art* (New York: Macmillan, 1964), Peter Sutton (ed.), *Dreamings: The Art of Aboriginal Australia* (New York: Viking, 1989), Wally Caruana, *Aboriginal Art*, 2nd edn (London: Thames & Hudson, 2003) and Howard Morphy, *Aboriginal Art* (London: Phaidon, 1998). The best linguistic studies are those by S.A. Wurm, *Languages of Australia and Tasmania* (The Hague: Mouton, 1972), Colin Yallop, *Australian Aboriginal Languages* (London: André Deutsch, 1982) and R.M.W. Dixon, *The Languages of Australia* (Cambridge: Cambridge University Press, 1980). The best introductions to Australian religions and philosophy are probably Mircea Eliade, *Australian Religions: An Introduction* (Ithaca: Cornell University Press, 1973) and Tony Swain, *A Place for Strangers: Towards a History of Australian Aboriginal Being* (Cambridge: Cambridge University Press, 1993). Another crucial writer on Australian culture who should not be ignored is W.E.H. Stanner, whose *After the Dreaming: The 1968 Boyer Lectures* (Sydney: Australian Broadcasting Corporation, 1969) gives a very clear picture of the methodological and moral issues at stake in the study of Australian history.

Muslim ideas of time are best approached first in a reading of *The Koran* in the edition edited by N.J. Dawood (London: Penguin, 1990), while the massive early Islamic historical project can be studied, very selectively, in the thirty-nine volumes of Muhammad ibn Jarīr Al-Tabarī's *History*, edited and translated by Franz Rosenthal (Albany: State University of New York, 1990). Two recent works are especially recommended as guides to reading the Qur'an: Anton Wessels, *Understanding the Qur'an* (London: SCM Press, 2000) and M.A. Draz, *Introduction to the Qur'an* (London: I.B. Tauris, 2000). The modern literature on early Islamic history and historiography is very extensive and any of the following eight works would make a good starting point in this area: A.A. Duri, *The Rise of Historical Writing among the Arabs*, ed. and tr. by Lawrence I. Conrad (Princeton: Princeton University Press, 1983), T. El-Hibri, *Reinterpreting Islamic Historiography* (Cambridge: Cambridge University Press, 1999), Tarif Khalidi, *Arabic Historical Thought in the Classical Period* (Cambridge: Cambridge University Press, 1994), R.S. Humphreys, *Islamic History: A Framework for Enquiry*, 2nd edn (Princeton: Princeton University Press, 1991), M.G. Rasul, *The Origin and Development of Muslim Historiography* (Lahore: Sh. Muhammad Ashraf, 1968), Chase F. Robinson, *Islamic Historiography* (Cambridge: Cambridge University Press, 2002), Franz Rosenthal, *A History of Muslim Historiography*, 2nd edn (Leiden: E.J. Brill, 1968) and Albrecht Noth and Lawrence Conrad, *The Early Arabic Historical Tradition: A Source-Critical Study*, 2nd edn (Princeton: Darwin Press, 1994). Most scholarly enquiries in Islamic studies begin with a consultation of the authoritative *Encyclopedia of Islam*, edited by P.J. Bearman and others, 12 vols (Leiden: E.J. Brill, 1960–2005). Another critical figure in the field whose work must be considered is Dimitri Gutas. His books include *Greek Thought, Arabic Culture: The Graeco-Arabic Translation Movement in Baghdad and Early Abbasid Society* (London: Routledge, 1998).

In contrast to the other religions studied, the Buddhist canon of primary sources is huge. A good starting point is the classic collection *Buddhism in Translations: Passages Selected from the Buddhist Sacred Books*, edited by Henry Clarke Warren (Cambridge, Mass.: Harvard University Press, 1922). Another good collection is *The Wheel of Death: Writings from Zen Buddhist and Other Sources*, edited by Philip Kapleau (London: George Allen & Unwin, 1972). Gotama's teachings can be approached in: M. Coomára Swámy (ed.), *Sutta Nipáta or, Dialogues and Discourses of Gotama Buddha* (London: Trübner, 1874). The writing of Asanga, Nāgārjuna and Dōgen, all studied in this book, can be found in: Nalinkasha Dutt (ed.), *Bodhisattvabūmih, Being the XVth Section of Asanga's Yogācārabhūmih* (Patna: K.P. Jayaswal Research Institute, 1978), Jay L. Garfield (ed.), *The Fundamental Wisdom of the Middle Way: Nāgārjuna's Mūlamadhyamakakārikā* (Oxford: Oxford University Press, 1995) and Reihō Masunaga, *A Primer of Sōtō Zen: A Translation of Dōgen's Shōbōgenzō's Zuimonki* (London: Routledge, 1972).

Secondary literatures of the highest quality on Buddhism also abound. A good starting point would be Edward Conze's *Short History of Buddhism* (Oxford: Oneworld, 1993), perhaps followed by a consideration of the work of Paul Williams: *Buddhist Thought: A Complete Introduction to the Indian Tradition*, with Anthony Tribe (London: Routledge, 2000) and his multi-volume edited collection for Routledge on *Buddhism: Critical Concepts in Religious Studies*. Three other texts which should be of general interest, and which offer a good guide to modern Buddhist studies, are: David J. Kalupahana, *A History of Buddhist Philosophy: Continuities and Discontinuities* (Honolulu: University of Hawaii Press, 1992), Donald S. Lopez (ed.), *Buddhism in Practice* (Waterloo: Laurier Books, 1998) and Andrew Skilton, *A Concise History of Buddhism* (Birmingham: Windhorse, 1994). With regard to specific traditions, Zen is best interpreted by D.T. Suzuki (see *Essays in Zen Buddhism*, first series, (London: Rider, 1970) and many other books listed in the bibliography), while Alan Watts (*The Way of Zen*, London: Arkana, 1990) offers a very clear picture of Zen designed specifically for western readers; Nāgārjuna's thought is successfully placed in its social context by Joseph Walser in *Nāgārjuna in Context: Mahāyāna Buddhism and Early Indian Culture* (New York: Columbia University Press, 2005); Yogācāra is situated in the history of Buddhist philosophy in Ian Charles Harris, *The Continuity of Madhyamaka and Yogacara in Indian Mahayana Buddhism* (Leiden: Brill, 1991); and Mādhyamika is well analysed in T.R.V. Murti, *The Central Philosophy of Buddhism: A Study of the Mādhyamika System* (London: Mandala Books, 1960). The best guide to Buddhist temporalities is H.S. Prasad, whose *Essays on Time In Buddhism* (Delhi: Sri Satguru, 1991) is a brilliantly conceived project in which secondary works from across the modern history of Buddhism are set aside one another. The application of Buddhist philosophical ideas to history is wonderfully realized in David Loy's *Buddhist History of the West: Studies in Lack* (Albany: State University of New York Press, 2002). Loy's text has its weaknesses, but it merits praise for its originality and its imagination of the possibility of Buddhism offering entirely new insights into western history and culture.

Questions of time in modern science are best approached in guides to Einstein's thought and intellectual histories of the Einsteinian revolution in physics. Two books, in particular, stand out: Paul Davies, *About Time: Einstein's Unfinished Revolution* (London: Penguin, 1995) and Peter Galison, *Einstein's Clock, Poincaré's Maps: Empires of Time* (London: Sceptre, 2003). Those with an interest in following up temporal developments in modern physics are directed towards the rather difficult Stephen Hawking, *A Brief History of Time: From the Big Bang to Black Holes* (London: Guild, 1988) and

Jennifer Trusted, *Physics and Metaphysics* (London: Routledge, 1994). The three best studies of secularization, which concentrate, in turn, on modernity, civil religions and theology, are: James A. Beckford, *Religion and Industrial Society* (London: Unwin Hyman, 1989), D.G. Charlton, *Secular Religions in France, 1815–1870* (London: Oxford University Press, 1963) and David Martin, *The Religious and the Secular: Studies in Secularization* (London: Routledge and Kegan Paul, 1969).

Bibliography

Adam, Barbara (1990) *Time and Social Theory*, Cambridge: Polity.

Adam, Barbara (1995) *Timewatch: The Social Analysis of Time*, Cambridge: Polity.

Adam, Barbara (1998) *Timescapes of Modernity: The Environment and Invisible Hazards*, London: Routledge.

Adam, Barbara (2004) *Time*, Cambridge: Polity.

Agius, Dionisus A. and Richard Hitchcock (eds) (1994) *The Arab Influence in Medieval Europe*, Reading: Ithaca Press.

Alberktson, Bertil (1967) *History and the Gods: An Essay on the Idea of Historical Events as Divine Manifestations in the Ancient Near East and in Israel*, Lund: Gleerup.

Al Qardawi, Yusuf (2000) *Time in the Life of a Muslim*, London: Taha.

Al-Swidan, Tariq Mohammed (n.d.) *Tārīkh al-Andalus al-Mafqūd*, audio-tape collection, Riyadh: Qurtuba lil Intāj al-Fannī.

Al-Tabarī, Muhammad ibn Jarīr (1989) *The History*, edited and translated by Rosenthal, Franz, 39 vols, Albany: State University of New York.

Ankersmit, F.R. (1986) 'The Dilemma of Contemporary Anglo-Saxon Philosophy of History', *History and Theory*, Beiheft 25, 1–27.

Ankersmit, F.R. (1994) *History and Tropology: The Rise and Fall of Metaphor*, Berkeley: University of California Press.

Armour, Rollin S. (2002) *Islam, Christianity and the West: A Troubled History*, New York: Orbis.

Aron, Raymond (1948) *Introduction to the Philosophy of History: An Essay on the Limits of Historical Objectivity*, London: Weidenfeld and Nicolson.

Aron, Raymond (1959) 'Relativism in History', in Meyerhoff, Hans (ed.) (1959) *The Philosophy of History in our Time*, New York: Doubleday, 153–61.

Arva Maitreya and Asanga (1979) *The Ultimate Mahayana Explanatory Text on The Changeless Nature (The Mahayana Uttara Tantra Shastra)*, Eskdalemuir: Karma Drubgyd Darjay Ling.

Aveni, Anthony F. (2000) *Empires of Time: Calendars, Clocks and Cultures*, London: I.B. Tauris.

Baillie, John (1950) *The Belief in Progress*, Oxford: Oxford University Press.

Balslev, Anindita Niyogi and J.N. Mohanty (eds) (1993) *Religion and Time*, Leiden: E.J. Brill.

Barr, James (1962) *Biblical Words for Time*, London: SCM Press.

Barth, Karl (1956–77) *Church Dogmatics*, 5 vols, Edinburgh: T&T Clark.

Barth, Karl (2002) *Protestant Theology in the Nineteenth Century: Its Background and History*, Grand Rapids: William B. Eerdmans.

Bashaear, Suliman (1997) *Arabs and Others in Early Islam*, Princeton: Darwin Press.

Bauckham, Richard and David Bebbington (1977) *History and Christianity: A Bibliography*, Leicester: UCCF.

Bauckham, Richard (1987) *Moltmann: Messianic Theology in the Making*, Basingstoke: Marshall Pickering.

Bauckham, Richard (1993) *The Climax of Prophecy: Studies on the Book of Revelation*, Edinburgh: T&T Clark.

Bauckham, Richard (2002) *God and the Crisis of Freedom: Biblical and Contemporary Perspectives*, Louisville: Westminster John Knox Press.

Baur, Ferdinand Christian (1968) *Ferdinand Christian Baur on the Writing of Church History*, New York: Oxford University Press.

Bearman, P.J. *et al.* (eds) (1960–2005) *Encyclopedia of Islam*, 2nd edn, 12 vols, Leiden: E.J. Brill.

Beckford, James A. (1989) *Religion and Industrial Society*, London: Unwin Hyman.

Beckford, James A. (1997) 'The disenchantment of postmodernity', *New Blackfriars*, 78–913, 121–28.

Begbie, Jeremy S. (2000) *Theology, Music and Time*, Cambridge: Cambridge University Press.

Benjamin, Walter (1983) *Charles Baudelaire: A Lyric poet in the Era of High Capitalism*, London: Verso.

Benjamin, Walter (1989) *Paris: capitale du XIXe siècle: Le livre des passages*, Paris: Les Éditions du Cerf.

Bentley, Michael (ed.) (1997) *Companion to Historiography*, London: Routledge.

Berg, Sandra Beth (1980) 'After the Exile: God and History in the Books of Chronicles and Esther', in Crenshaw, James L. and Samuel Sandmel (eds) *The Divine Helmsman: Studies on God's Control of Human Events, Presented to Lou H. Silberman*, New York: Ktav, 107–27.

Bergant, Diane (1982) *Job, Ecclesiastes*, Wilmington: Michael Glazier.

Berndt, Ronald M. (ed.) (1964) *Australian Aboriginal Art*, New York: Macmillan.

Berndt, Ronald M. and E.S. Phillips (eds) (1973) *The Australian Aboriginal Heritage: An Introduction through the Arts*, Sydney: Australian Association for Education through the Arts.

Beyer, Stephan (1974) *The Buddhist Experience: Sources and Interpretations*, Encino: Dickinson.

Bickerman, Elias (1967) *Four Strange Books of the Bible: Jonah, Daniel, Koheleth, Esther*, New York: Schocken.

Bielefeldt, Carl (1998) 'A Discussion of Seated Zen' in Lopez, Donald S. (ed.) *Buddhism in Practice*, Waterloo: Laurier Books, 197–206.

Bin Laden, Osama, speech www.dynamist.com/scene/oct01.ht – accessed 01.11.06.

Black, Jeremy and Donald D. MacRaild (2000) *Studying History*, 2nd edn, London: Macmillan.

Bloch, Marc (1954) *The Historian's Craft*, Manchester: Manchester University Press.

Boase, Roger (1992) 'Arab Influences on European Love Poetry', in Jayyusi, Salma, *The Legacy of Muslim Spain*, Leiden: E.J. Brill, II, 457–82.

Bodhi, Bikkhu (1993) *A Comprehensive Manual of Abhidhamma: The Abhidhamatta Sangaha of Acariya Anuruddha*, Kandy: Buddhist Publication Society – web edition: www.accesstoinsight.org/lib/bps/misc/abhiman.html – accessed 01.11.06.

Boycott, Owen (2001) 'Spain succumbs to new Moorish invasion', *The Guardian*, 1 March.

Braaten, Carl (1968) *New Directions in Theology Today, Volume II: History and Hermeneutics*, London: Lutterworth Press.

Braaten, Carl E. and Robert W. Jenson (eds) (2002) *The Last Things: Biblical and Theological Perspectives on Eschatology*, Grand Rapids: William B. Eerdmans.

Brandl, Eric J. (1973) 'The Art of the Caves in Arnhem Land', in Berndt, Ronald M. and E.S. Phillips (eds), *The Australian Aboriginal Heritage: An Introduction through the Arts*, Sydney: Australian Association for Education through the Arts, 92–107.

Brandon, S.G.F. (1965) *History, Time and Deity: A Historical and Comparative Study of the Conception of Time in Religious Thought and Practice*, Manchester: Manchester University Press.

Brettler, Marc (2004) 'Cyclical and Teleological Time in the Hebrew Bible' in Rosen, Ralph M. (ed.), *Time and Temporality in the Ancient World*, Philadelphia: University of Pennsylvania Museum of Archaeology and Anthropology, 111–28.

Brin, Gershon (2001) *The Concept of Time in the Bible and the Dead Sea Scrolls*, Leiden: Brill.

Broome, Richard (2002) *Aboriginal Australians: Black Responses to White Dominance 1788–2001*, 3rd edn, Sydney: Allen & Unwin.

Brothers, Cammy (1994) 'The Renaissance Reception of the Alhambra: The Letters of Andrea Navagero and the Palace of Charles V', *Muqarnas: An Annual on Islamic Art and Architecture*, Leiden: Brill.

Brotton, Jerry (2002) *The Renaissance Bazaar: From the Silk Road to Michelangelo*, Oxford: Oxford University Press.

Brough, John Barrett and Lester E. Embree (eds) (2000) *The Many Faces of Time*, New York: Springer.

Brown, Alan (ed.) (1986) *Festivals in World Religion*, London: Longman.

Brown, Colin (ed.) (1976) *History, Criticism and Faith: Four Historical Studies*, London: IVP.

Brown, Colin, 'History and the Believer', in Brown, Colin (ed.) (1976) *History, Criticism, Faith*, Leicester: Inter-Varsity Press, 147–224.

Brown, Donald E. (1988) *Hierarchy, History and Human Nature: The Social Origins of Historical Consciousness*, Tucson: University of Arizona Press.

Bruce, F.F. (1978) *The Time is Fulfilled: Five Aspects of the Fulfilment of the Old Testament in the New*, Exeter: Paternoster Press.

Brundage, B.C. (1954) 'The Birth of Clio: A Résumé and Interpretation of Ancient Near East Historiography', in Hughes, H. Stuart (ed.) *Teachers of History: Essays in Honor of Lawrence Bradford Packard*, Ithaca: Cornell University Press.

Buckley, James L. and L. Gregory Jones (eds) (2001) *Theology and Eschatology at the Turn of the Millennium*, Oxford: Blackwell.

Bull, William E. (1968) *Time, Tense and the Verb: A Study in Theoretical and Applied Linguistics, with Particular Attention to Spanish*, Berkeley: University of California Press.

Bullock, Alan (1951) 'The Historian's Purpose: History and Metahistory', *History Today*, 5–11.

Bultmann, Rudolf (1957) *History and Eschatology*, Edinburgh: Edinburgh University Press.

Bultmann, Rudolf (1984) *New Testament and Mythology and Other Basic Writings*, Philadelphia: Fortress Press.

Burke, Jason (2003) *Al-Qaeda: Casting a Shadow of Terror*, London: I.B. Tauris.

Burke, Peter (1969) *The Renaissance Sense of the Past*, London: Edward Arnold.

Burke, Peter (2000) 'The Web and the Seams: Historiography in an Age of Specialization and Globalization' in Stuchtey, Benedikt and Peter Wende (eds) *British and German Historiography 1750–1950: Traditions, Perceptions, Transfers*, Oxford: Oxford University Press, 401–09.

Burke, Peter (2002) 'Western Historical Thinking in a Global Perspective', in Rüsen, Jörn, *Western Historical Thinking: An Intercultural Debate*, New York: Berghahn, 15–30.

Burrows, Millar (1955) 'Ancient Israel', in Bainton, Roland *et al. The Idea of History in the Ancient Near East*, New Haven: Yale University Press, 99–131.

Bury, J.B. (1920) *The Idea of Progress: An Inquiry into its Origins*, London: Macmillan.

Bush, Barbara (2006) *Imperialism and Postcolonialism*, London: Longman-Pearson.

Butlin, Noel (1983) *Our Original Aggression: Aboriginal Populations of Southeastern Australia 1788–1850*, Sydney: Allen & Unwin.

Butterfield, Herbert (1949) *Christianity and History*, London: G. Bell and Sons.

Butterfield, Herbert (1951) *History and Human Relations*, London: Collins.

Callahan, John F. (1948) *Four Views of Time in Ancient Historiography*, Cambridge, Mass.: Harvard University Press.

Caponigri, A. Robert (2004) *Time and Idea: The Theory of History in Giambattista Vico*, New Brunswick: Transaction.

Capra, Fritjof (1983) *The Tao of Physics: An Exploration of the Parallels between Modern Physics and Eastern Mysticism*, 2nd edn, London: Flamingo.

Carr, David (1987) *Time, Narrative and History*, Bloomington: Indiana University Press.

Carr, E.H. (1987) *What is History?*, ed. R.W. Davies, 2nd edn, London: Penguin.

Caruana, Wally (2003) *Aboriginal Art*, 2nd edn, London: Thames & Hudson.

Chaloupka, George (1988) 'Rock art of the Northern Territory', in West, Margie K.C. (ed.) *The Inspired Dream: Life as art in Aboriginal Australia*, South Brisbane: Queensland Art Gallery, 13–19.

Charlton, D.G. (1963) *Secular Religions in France, 1815–1870*, London: Oxford University Press.

Chatwin, Bruce (1987) *The Songlines*, London: Vintage.

Christianson, Eric S. (1998) *A Time to Tell: Narrative Strategies in Ecclesiastes*, Sheffield: Sheffield Academic Press.

Clark, Gordon H. (1971) *Historiography: Secular and Religious*, Nutley: Craig Press.

Clements, R.E. (1989) *The World of Ancient Israel: Sociological, Anthropological and Political Perspectives*, Cambridge: Cambridge University Press.

Codomannus, L. (1590) *Chronographia: A Description of Time from the Beginning of the World until the Year of our Lord, 137, Divided into Six Periods, Wherein the Several Histories, both of the Old and New Testament are Briefly Compiled and Placed in their Due Order of Years*, 2nd edn, London: Richard Field.

Cohen, C. (1965) *Introduction to the History of the Middle East: A Bibliographical Guide*, Berkeley: University of California Press.

Cohen, Sande (1986) *Historical Culture: On the Recoding of an Academic Discipline*, Berkeley: University of California Press.

Coleman, David (2003) *Creating Christian Granada: Society and Religious Culture in an Old-World Frontier City*, Ithaca: Cornell University Press.

Collingwood, R.G. (1946) *The Idea of History*, Oxford: Oxford University Press.

Constable, Olivia Remie (1997) *Medieval Iberia: Readings from Christian, Muslim and Jewish Sources*, Philadelphia: University of Pennsylvania Press.

Conze, Edward (1957) *Buddhism: Its Essence and Development*, 3rd edn, Oxford: Bruno Cassirer.

Conze, Edward (1993) *A Short History of Buddhism*, Oxford: Oneworld.

Conze, Edward (ed.) (2002) *Buddhist Thought in India: Three Phases of Buddhist Philosophy*, New Delhi: Munshiram Manoharlal.

Cook, Michael and Patricia Crone (1980) *Hagarism: The Making of the Islamic World*, Cambridge: Cambridge University Press.

Coomára Swámy, M. (ed.) (1874) *Sutta Nipáta or, Dialogues and Discourses of Gotama Buddha*, London: Trübner.

Coombs, H.C. (1978) *Kulinma: Listening to Aboriginal Australians*, Canberra: Australian National University Press.

Corbin, Henry (1973) 'Cyclical Time in Mazdaism and Ismailism', in Campbell, Joseph (ed.) *Man and Time: Papers from the Eranos Yearbooks*, Princeton: Princeton University Press, 115–72.

Corbin, Henry (1983) *Cyclical Time and Ismaili Gnosis*, London: Kegan Paul.

Corfield, Penelope J. (1996) *Naming the Age: History, Historians and Time*, Egham: Royal Holloway.

Corfield, Penelope J. (2007) *Time and the Shape of History*, Yale: Yale University Press.

Corngold, Stanley (1994) *The Fate of the Self: German Writers and French Theory*, Durham: Duke University Press.

Cotton, John (1654) *A Brief Exposition with Practical Observations upon the Whole Book of Ecclesiastes*, London: Anthony Tuckney.

Crawford, I.M. (1968) *The Art of the Wandinja*, Melbourne: Oxford University Press.

Crenshaw, James (1980) 'The Birth of Skepticism in Ancient Israel', in Crenshaw, James L. and Samuel Sandmel (eds) *The Divine Helmsman: Studies on God's Control of Human Events, Presented to Lou H. Silberman*, New York: Ktav, 1–19.

Cullmann, Oscar (1962) *Christ and Time: The Primitive Conception of Time and History*, 3rd edn, London: SCM Press.

Curtis, John B. (1963) 'A Suggested Interpretation of the Biblical Philosophy of History', *Hebrew College Annual*, 34.

Davies, Paul (1995) *About Time: Einstein's Unfinished Revolution*, London: Penguin.

Deeds Ermarth, Elizabeth (1983) *Realism and Consensus in the English Novel: Time, Space and Narrative*, Princeton: Princeton University Press.

Deeds Ermarth, Elizabeth (1992) *Sequel to History: Postmodernism and the Crisis of Representational Time*, Princeton: Princeton University Press.

DeLong-Bas, Natana J. (2004) *Wahhabi Islam: From Revival and Reform to Global Jihad*, Oxford: Oxford University Press.

Den Boer, W. (1968) 'Graeco-Roman Historiography in its Relation to Biblical and Modern Thinking', *History and Theory*, 7, 60–75.

DeVries, Simon (1975) *Yesterday, Today and Tomorrow: Time and History in the Old Testament*, London: SPCK.

Dickie, James (1976) 'The Islamic Garden in Spain' in MacDougall, E.B. and R. Ettinghausen (eds) *The Islamic Garden*, Washington: Dumbarton Oaks, 89–105.

Dinkler, Erich (1955) 'Earliest Christianity', in Bainton, Roland *et al. The Idea of History in the Ancient Near East*, New Haven: Yale University Press, 169–214.

Dionisus, A. and Richard Hitchcock (eds) (1994) *The Arab Influence in Medieval Europe*, Reading: Ithaca Press.

Dixon, R.M.W. and Barry J. Blake (eds) (1979) *Handbook of Australian Languages*, Amsterdam: John Benjamins.

Dixon, R.M.W. (1980) *The Languages of Australia*, Cambridge: Cambridge University Press.

Dodd, C.H. (1938) *History and the Gospel*, London: Nisbet.

Dodd, C.H. (1963) *The Apostolic Preaching and Its Developments: Three Lectures, with an Appendix on Eschatology*, London: Hodder & Stoughton.

Donfried, Paul (2006) *Who Owns the Bible? Towards the Recovery of a Christian Hermeneutic*, New York: Crossroad.

Doniger, Wendy (ed.) (1999) *Merriam-Webster's Encyclopedia of World Religions*, New York: Merriam-Webster.

Dray, W.H. (1964) *Philosophy of History*, Englewood Cliffs: Prentice-Hall.

Draz, M.A. (2000) *Introduction to the Qur'an*, London: I.B. Tauris.

Dubuisson, Daniel (2003) *The Western Construction of Religion. Myths, Knowledge & Ideology*, Baltimore: The Johns Hopkins University Press.

Duméry, Henry (1975) *Phenomenology and Religion: Structures of the Christian Institution*, Berkeley: University of California Press.

Duri, A.A. (1983) *The Rise of Historical Writing among the Arabs*, ed. and tr. by Lawrence I. Conrad, Princeton: Princeton University Press.

Durkheim, Emile (1960) *Les Formes Élémentaires de la Vie Religieuse: Le Système Totémique en Australie*, 4th edn, Paris: Presses Universitaires de France.

Durkheim, Emile (1963) *L'Éducation Morale*, Paris: Presses Universitaires de France.

Durkheim, Emile (1973) *Le Suicide: Étude de Sociologie*, Paris: Presses Universitaires de France.

Durrell, Clement V. (1931) *Readable Relativity*, London: G.Bell.

Dutt, Nalinkasha (ed.) (1978) *Bodhisattvabūmih, Being the XVth Section of Asanga's Yogācārabhūmih*, Patna: K.P. Jayaswal Research Institute.

El-Hibri, T. (1999) *Reinterpreting Islamic Historiography*, Cambridge: Cambridge University Press.

El Saadawi, Nawal (1984) *Woman at Point Zero*, London: Zed Books.

Eliade, Mircea (1973) *Australian Religions: An Introduction*, Ithaca: Cornell University Press.

Elias, Harry Chacalos (1989) *Time and Change: Short but Differing Philosophies*, Rockville: Potomac Press Circle.

Elias, Norbert (1992) *Time: An Essay*, Oxford: Blackwell.

Elliott, J.K. (1993) *The Apocryphal New Testament: A Collection of Apocryphal Christian Literature in an English Translation*, Oxford: Clarendon Press.

Ellul, Jacques (1972) *The Politics of God and the Politics of Man*, Grand Rapids: Eerdman.

Evans, Richard J. (1997) *In Defence of History*, London: Granta.

Fabian, J. (1992) *Time and the Work of Anthropology: Critical Essays 1971–1991*, Amsterdam: Harwood.

Fabian, J. (2002) *Time and the Other: How Anthropology Makes its Object*, New York: Columbia University Press.

Favre, Yves-Alain (ed.) (1990) *Horizons d'Edouard Glissant*, Pau: J&D Editions.

Finley, M.I. (1990) *The Use and Abuse of History*, 2nd edn, London: Penguin.

Fischer-Schreiber, Ingrid *et al.* (eds) (1994) *The Encyclopedia of Eastern Philosophy and Religion*, Boston: Shambaala.

Fleischman, Suzanne (1990) *Tense and Narrativity: From Medieval Performance to Modern Fiction*, London: Routledge.

Fox, Michael (1999) *A Time to Tear Down and a Time to Build Up*, Grand Rapids: William B. Eerdmans.

France, R.T. (1976) 'The Authenticity of the Sayings of Jesus', in Brown, Colin (ed.) *History, Criticism, Faith*, Leicester: Inter-Varsity Press, 101–43.

Fraser, J.T. (ed.) (1966) *The Voices of Time: A Cooperative Survey of Man's Views of Time as Expressed by the Sciences and by the Humanities*, New York: George Braziller.

Fraser, J.T. (1975) *Of Time, Passion and Knowledge*, Princeton: Princeton University Press.

Freud, Sigmund (1955) *The Complete Psychological Works Volume XIII: Totem and Taboo and Other Works*, London: The Hogarth Press.

Freud, Sigmund (1967) *Moses and Monotheism*, New York: Vintage.

Friese, Heidrun (ed.) (2001) *The Moment: Time and Rupture in Modern Thought*, Liverpool: Liverpool University Press.

Friese, Heidrun (ed.) (2002) *Identities: Time, Difference and Boundaries*, New York: Berghahn.

Fuller, Daniel P. (1968) 'The Fundamental Presupposition of the Historical Method', *Theologische Zeitschrift*, 24–44.

Gaddis, John Lewis (2002) *The Landscape of History: How Historians Map the Past*, Oxford: Oxford University Press.

Galison, Peter (2003) *Einstein's Clock, Poincaré's Maps: Empires of Time*, London: Sceptre.

Gallagher, Mary (2003) *Soundings in French Caribbean Writing 1950–2000*, Oxford: Oxford University Press.

Garfield, Jay L. (ed.) (1995) *The Fundamental Wisdom of the Middle Way: Nāgārjuna's Mūlamadhyamakakārikā*, Oxford: Oxford University Press.

Gell, Alfred (1992) *The Anthropology of Time: Cultural Constructions of Temporal Maps and Images*, Berg: Oxford.

Gilderhus, Mark T. (2000) *History and Historians: A Historiographical Introduction*, 4th edn, Upper Saddle River: Prentice Hall.

Glick, Thomas F. (1979) *Islamic and Christian Spain in the Early Middle Ages*, Princeton: Princeton University Press.

Goetz, Hans-Werner (2002) 'The Concept of Time in the Historiography of the Eleventh and Twelfth Centuries' in Althoff, Gerd, Johannes Fried and Patrick J. Geary (eds) *Medieval Concepts of the Past: Ritual, Memory, Historiography*, Cambridge: Cambridge University Press, 139–66.

Gohari, M.J. (2000) *Islamic Judaism: An Account of References to Jews and Judaism in the Quran*, Oxford: Logos Press.

Goodman, Lenn (2003) *Islamic Humanism*, Oxford: Oxford University Press.

Gorman, Frank H. (1990) *The Ideology of Ritual: Space, Time and Status in the Priestly Theology*, Sheffield: Sheffield Academic Press.

Grabar, Oleg (2006) *Islamic Art and Beyond: Constructing the Study of Islamic Art*, Aldershot: Ashgate.

Green, Anna and Kathleen Troup (1999) *The Houses of History: A Critical Reader in Twentieth-Century History and Theory*, Manchester: Manchester University Press.

Green, Ian (1988) ' "Make 'im flash, poor bugger": Talking about men's painting in Papunya', in West, Margie K.C. (ed.), *The Inspired Dream: Life as art in Aboriginal Australia*, South Brisbane: Queensland Art Gallery, 41–47.

Green, William Henry (1999) *Conflict and Triumph: The Argument of the Book of Job Unfolded*, Edinburgh: Banner of Truth.

Griffiths, A. Phillips (ed.) (1991) *Wittgenstein Centenary Essays*, Cambridge: Cambridge University Press.

Griffiths, Jay (1999) *A Sideways Look at Time*, New York: Tarcher/Putnam.

Griffiths, Paul J. and Noriaki Hakamaya (eds) (1989) *The Realm of Awakening: A Translation and Study of the Tenth Chapter of Asanga's Mahāyānasangraha*, Oxford: Oxford University Press.

Griffiths, Paul J. (2001) 'Nirvana as the Last Thing? The Iconic End of the Narrative Imagination', in Buckley, James L. and L. Gregory Jones (eds) *Theology and Eschatology at the Turn of the Millennium*, Oxford: Blackwell, 17–36.

Guiart, Jean (1963) *The Arts of the South Pacific*, London: Thames & Hudson.

Guichard, Pierre (1974) 'Les arabes ont bien envahi l'Espagne', *Annales*, 6, 1483–1513.

Gunn, J. Alexander (1929) *The Problem of Time: An Historical and Critical Study*, London: Allen & Unwin.

Gurvitch, Georges (1964) *The Spectrum of Social Time*, Dordrecht: D. Reidel.

Gutas, Dimitri (1998) *Greek Thought, Arabic Culture: The Graeco-Arabic Translation Movement in Baghdad and Early Abbasid Society*, London: Routledge.

Gyatso, Tenzin (1975) *The Buddhism of Tibet*, London: Allen & Unwin.

Haddad, Yvonne and Jane Smith (1981) *The Islamic Understanding of Death and Resurrection*, Albany: SUNY Press.

Hambly, Gavin (ed.) (2000) *Women in the Medieval Islamic World*, London: Palgrave.

Haneef, James Oliver (2002) *The 'Wahhabi' Myth: Dispelling Prevalent Fallacies and the Fictitious Link with Bin Laden*, Toronto: Trafford.

Harris, Ian Charles (1991) *The Continuity of Madhyamaka and Yogacara in Indian Mahayana Buddhism*, Leiden: Brill.

Harris, Pam (1991) *Mathematics in a Cultural Context: Aboriginal Perspectives on Space, Time and Money*, Geelong: Deakin University Press.

Harrison, Peter (1990) *'Religion' and the Religions in the English Enlightenment*, Cambridge: Cambridge University Press.

Harvey, Van Austin (1967) *The Historian and the Believer: The Morality of Historical Knowledge and Christian Belief*, London: SCM Press.

Hassard, John (ed.) (1990) *The Sociology of Time*, London: Macmillan.

Hawking, Stephen (1988) *A Brief History of Time: From the Big Bang to Black Holes*, London: Guild.

Hawting, G.R. (1986) *The First Dynasty of Islam: The Umayyad Caliphate AD 661–750*, London: Croom Helm.

Hayes, Zachary (2000) *Visions of a Future: The Study of Christian Eschatology*, Collegeville: Liturgical Press.

Hays, Richard B. (2001) ' "Why do you stand looking up toward heaven?" New Testament eschatology at the turn of the millennium', in Buckley, James L. and L. Gregory Jones (eds) *Theology and Eschatology at the Turn of the Millennium*, Oxford: Blackwell, 113–33.

Hazlitt, Henry (1986) *Time Will Run Back: A Novel About the Rediscovery of Capitalism*, 2nd edn, Lanham: University of America Press.

Heidegger, Martin (2004) *The Phenomenology of Religious Life*, Bloomington: Indiana University Press.

Herbert, Jean-Loup (2002) 'Spain: al-Andalus revived', *Le Monde Diplomatique*, 12 November, 12–13.

Herman, A.L. (1983) *An Introduction to Buddhist Thought: A Philosophic History of Indian Buddhism*, Lanham: University Press of America.

Hervieu-Léger, Danièle (1987) *Vers un nouveau christianisme? Introduction à la sociologie du christianisme occidental*, 2nd edn, Paris: Cerf.

Heschel, Abraham Joshua (1976) *God in Search of Man: A Philosophy of Judaism*, New York: Farrar, Straus and Giroux.

Hick, John (1976) *Death and Eternal Life*, London: Collins.

Hillenbrand, Robert (1992) ' "The Ornament of the World": Medieval Cordoba as a Cultural Centre', in Jayyusi, Salma (1992) *The Legacy of Muslim Spain*, Leiden: E.J. Brill, 112–35.

Hodges, Richard and David Whitehouse (1983) *Mohammed, Charlemagne and the Origins of Europe: The Pirenne Thesis in the Light of Archaeology*, Ithaca: Cornell University Press.

Hodgson, Peter C. (1966) *The Formation of Historical Theology*, New York: Harper & Row.

Hoogland, Jan (1996) 'The necessity of intercultural philosophy' in Tiemersma, D. and H.A.F. Oosterling (eds) *Time and Temporality in Intercultural Perspective*, Amsterdam: Rodopi, 25–41.

Hopwood, Derek (1982) 'The Ideological Basis: Ibn Abd al-Wahhab's Muslim Revivalism', in Niblock, Tim (ed.) *State, Society and Economy in Saudi Arabia*, London: Croom Helm, 23–35.

Houtepen, Anton (ed.) (1995) *The Living Tradition: Towards an Ecumenical Hermeneutics of the Christian Tradition*, Utrecht: Interuniversitair Instituut voor Missologie en Oecumenica.

Hoyland, Robert G. (1997) *Seeing Islam as Others Saw It: A survey and evaluation of Christian, Jewish and Zoroastrian writings in early Islam*, Princeton: Darwin Press.

Hughes, Robert (1970) *The Art of Australia*, 2nd edn, London: Penguin.

Humphreys, R.S. (1991) *Islamic History: A Framework for Enquiry*, 2nd edn, Princeton: Princeton University Press.

Humphreys, R.S. (2002) 'Turning Points in Islamic Historical Practice' in Wang, Q. Edward and Georg G. Iggers (eds) *Turning Points in Historiography: A Cross-Cultural Perspective*, Rochester: University of Rochester Press, 89–100.

Huppert, George (1970) *The Idea of Perfect History: Historical Erudition and Historical Philosophy in Renaissance France*, Urbana: University of Illinois Press.

Huttar, G.L. (1977) 'World views, intelligence and cross-cultural communication', *Intercultural Studies*, 1–3, 24–35.

Iggers, Georg G. (1968) *The German Conception of History: The National Tradition of Historical Thought from Herder to the Present*, Middletown: Wesleyan University Press.

Iggers, Georg G. (1975) *New Directions in European Historiography*, Middletown: Wesleyan University Press.

Iggers, Georg G. (2004) *Historiography in the Twentieth Century*, Middletown: Wesleyan University Press.

Imaddin, S.M. (1965) *Some Aspects of the Socio-Economic and Cultural History of Spain 711–1492 A.D.*, Leiden: E.J. Brill.

Irwin, Robert (2004) *The Alhambra*, Cambridge, Mass.: Harvard University Press.

Izutsu, Toshiko (1978) 'The Field Structure of Time in Zen Buddhism', *Eranos Yearbook*, 47, 309–40.

James, Wendy and David Mills (eds) (2005) *The Qualities of Time: Anthropological Approaches*, Oxford: Berg.

Javary, Michèle (2002) *The Economics of Power, Knowledge and Time*, Cheltenham: Edward Elgar.

Jayyusi, Salma (1992) *The Legacy of Muslim Spain*, Leiden: E.J. Brill.

Jenkins, Keith (1995) *On 'What is History?': From Carr and Elton to Rorty and White*, London: Routledge.

Jenkins, Keith (1999) *Why History? Ethics and Postmodernity*, London: Routledge.

Jeppesen, Knud and Benedikt Otzen (eds) (1984) *The Production of Time: Tradition History in Old Testament Scholarship*, Sheffield: Almond Press.

Johnson, Martin (1944) *Time, Knowledge and the Nebulae*, London: Faber and Faber.

Kähler, Martin (1964) *The So-Called Historical Jesus and the Historic Biblical Christ*, Philadelphia: Fortress Press.

Kalupahana, David J. (1976) *Buddhist Philosophy: A Historical Analysis*, Honolulu: University of Hawaii Press.

Kalupahana, David J. (1992) *A History of Buddhist Philosophy: Continuities and Discontinuities*, Honolulu: University of Hawaii Press.

Kapleau, Philip (ed.) (1972) *The Wheel of Death: Writings from Zen Buddhist and Other Sources*, London: Allen & Unwin.

Käseman, Ernst (1964) *Essays on New Testament Themes*, London: SCM Press.

Kearney, Hugh F. (1949) 'Christianity and the Study of History', *The Downside Review*, 67, 62–75.

Kedourie, Elie (1979) *The Jewish World: Revelation, Prophecy and History*, London: Thames & Hudson.

Keesing, Roger M. (1981) *Cultural Anthropology: A Contemporary Perspective*, 2nd edn, Fort Worth: Harcourt Brace.

Kennedy, Hugh (1996) *Muslim Spain and Portugal: A Political History of al-Andalus*, London: Longman.

Keown, Damien (1996) *Buddhism: A Very Short Introduction*, Oxford: Oxford University Press.

Kepel, Gilles (2004) *The War for Muslim Minds: Islam and the West*, Cambridge, Mass.: Harvard University Press.

Khalidi, Tarif (1994) *Arabic Historical Thought in the Classical Period*, Cambridge: Cambridge University Press.

Klostermaier, Klaus K. (1999) *Buddhism: A Short Introduction*, Oxford: Oneworld.

Knight, Douglas (2000) 'Jenson on Time' in Gunton, Colin E. (ed.) *Trinity, Time and the Church: A Response to the Theology of Robert W. Jenson*, Grand Rapids: William B. Eerdmans, 71–79.

Knysh, Alexander (2000) *Islamic Mysticism: A Short History*, Leiden: Brill.

Komatsu, Chiko (1989) *The Way of Peace: The Life and Teachings of the Buddha*, Kyoto: Hozokan.

The Koran (1990) ed. by Dawood, N.J., London: Penguin.

Koselleck, Reinhart (2004) *Futures Past: On the Semantics of Historical Time*, Cambridge, Mass.: MIT Press.

Kritzer, Robert (1999) *Rebirth and Causation in the Yogācāra Abidharma*, Vienna: Arbeitskreis für Tibetische und Buddhistische Studien Universität Wien.

Kümmel, Werner Georg (1973) *The New Testament: The History of the Investigation of Its Problems*, London: SCM Press.

LaCapra, Dominick (1998) *History and Memory after Auschwitz*, Ithaca: Cornell University Press.

Lacey, Robert (1981) *The Kingdom*, London: Fontana.

LaCocque, André and Paul Ricœur (2003) *Thinking Biblically: Exegetical and Hermeneutic Studies*, Chicago: University of Chicago Press.

Lasater, Alie A. (1974) *Spain to England: A Comparative Study of Arabic, European and English Literature of the Middle Ages*, Jackson: University of Mississippi Press.

Latourette, K.S. (1949) 'The Christian Understanding of History', *The American Historical Review*, 54, 259–76.

Lawlor, Robert (1991) *Voices of the First Day: Awakening in the Aboriginal Dreamtime*, Rochester: Inner Traditions.

Layton, Robert (1989) *Uluru: An Aboriginal History of Ayers Rock*, Canberra: Aboriginal Studies Press.

Leff, Gordon (1969) *History and Social Theory*, London: Merlin Press.

Legget, Trevor (1978) *Zen and the Ways*, London: Routledge & Kegan Paul.

Le Goff, Jacques (1980) *Time, Work and Culture in the Middle Ages*, Chicago: University of Chicago Press.

Le Goff, Jacques (1991) *Medieval Civilization 400–1500*, Oxford: Blackwell.

Le Poidevin, Robin and Murray MacBeath (1993) *The Philosophy of Time*, Oxford: Oxford University Press.

Lévinas, Emmanuel (1987) *Qui êtes-vous?*, Paris: La Manufacture.

Lewis, I.M. (1985) *Social Anthropology in Perspective: The Relevance of Social Anthropology*, 2nd edn, Cambridge: Cambridge University Press.

Linehan, Peter (1993) *History and the Historians of Medieval Spain*, Oxford: Clarendon Press.

Lippincott, Kristen (ed.) (1999) *The Story of Time*, London: Merrell Holberton.

Longman III, Tremper (1998) *The Book of Ecclesiastes*, Grand Rapids: William B. Eerdmans.

Lopez, Donald S. (1995) *Religions of India in Practice*, Princeton: Princeton University Press.

Lopez, Donald S. (ed.) (1998) *Buddhism in Practice*, Waterloo: Laurier Books.

Lopez, Donald S. (1998) 'A Prayer for the Long Life of the Dalai Lama' in Lopez, Donald S. (ed.), *Buddhism in Practice*, Waterloo: Laurier Books, 170–75.

Lopez-Baralt, Luce (1992) 'The Legacy of Islam in Spanish Literature' in Jayyusi, Salma, *The Legacy of Muslim Spain*, Leiden: E.J. Brill, II, 505–52.

Löwith, Karl (1949) *Meaning in History: The Theological Implications of the Philosophy of History*, Chicago: University of Chicago Press.

Loy, David (1986) 'The Mahayana Deconstruction of Time', *Philosophy East and West*, 36.1, 13–23.

Loy, David (2002) *A Buddhist History of the West: Studies in Lack*, Albany: State University of New York Press.

Lucas, J.R. (1993) 'The Temporality of God', in Russell, Robert John, Nancey Murphy and C.J. Ishan (eds) *Quantum Cosmology and the Laws of Nature: Scientific Perspectives on Divine Action*, Vatican: Vatican Observatory Publications, 235–46.

Lundin, Roger (ed.) (1997) *Disciplining Hermeneutics: Interpretation in Christian Perspective*, Grand Rapids, William B. Eerdmans.

Lüthi, Bernhard (ed.) (1993) *Aratjara: Art of the First Australians*, Düsseldorf: Kunstsammlung Nordrhein-Westfalen.

Macey, Samuel L. (1994) *Encyclopedia of Time*, New York: Garland.

Maier, Charles S. (1997) *The Unmasterable Past: History, Holocaust, and German National Identity*, 2nd edn, Cambridge, Mass.: Harvard University Press.

Makki, Mahmoud (1992) 'The Political History of al-Andalus' in Jayyusi, Salma (1992) *The Legacy of Muslim Spain*, Leiden: E.J. Brill, 3–87.

Marcel, Gabriel (1973) *Tragic Wisdom and Beyond, including Conversations between Paul Ricœur and Gabriel Marcel*, Evanston: Northwestern University Press.

Marcus, John T. (1961) 'Time and the Sense of History: West and East', *Comparative Studies in Society and History*, 3, 123–39.

Margoliouth, D.S. (1930) *Lectures on Arab Historians*, Delhi: Idarah Arabiyat i Delhi.

Marines, Alejandra Galindo (2001) *The Relationship Between the Ulama and the Government in the Contemporary Saudi Arabian Kingdom: An Interdependent Relationship?*, University of Durham PhD dissertation.

Markus, R.A. (1970) *Saeculum: History and Society in the Theology of St Augustine*, Cambridge: Cambridge University Press.

Marrou, Henri-Irénée (1954) *De la connaissance historique*, Paris: Editions du Seuil.

Marrou, Henri-Irénée (1968) *Théologie de l'Histoire*, Paris: Editions du Seuil.

Martimort, Aimé Georges (1986) *The Liturgy and Time*, London: Geoffrey Chapman.

Martin, David (1969) *The Religious and the Secular: Studies in Secularization*, London: Routledge & Kegan Paul.

Marwick, Arthur (1970) *The Nature of History*, London: Macmillan.

Marwick, Arthur (1989) *The Nature of History*, 3rd edn, London: Macmillan.

Massignon, Louis (1973) 'Time in Islamic Thought', in Campbell, Joseph (ed.) *Man and Time: Papers from the Eranos Yearbooks*, Princeton: Princeton University Press, 108–114.

Masunaga, Reihō (ed.) (1972) *A Primer of Sōtō Zen: A Translation of Dōgen's Shōbōgenzō's Zuimonki*, London: Routledge.

Maughan, Janet and Jenny Zimmer (eds) (1986) *Dot and Circle: A Retrospective of the Aboriginal Acrylic Paintings of Central Australia*, Melbourne: Royal Melbourne Institute of Technology.

Mbiti, John S. (1969) *African Religion and Philosophy*, London: Heinemann.

Mbiti, John S. (1991) *Introduction to African Religion*, 2nd edn, London: Heinemann.

McConville, J.G. and J.G. Millar (1994) *Time and Place in Deuteronomy*, Sheffield: Sheffield Academic Press.

McDermott, James Paul (1984) *Development in the Early Buddhist Concept of Kamma/Karma*, New Delhi: Munshiram Manoharlal.

McKenzie, Steven L. and Thomas Römer (eds) (2000) *Rethinking the Foundations: Historiography in the Ancient World and in the Bible*, Berlin: Walter de Gruyter.

McTaggart, J.M.E. (1908) 'The Unreality of Time', *Mind: A Quarterly Review of Philosophy and Psychology*, 17, 456–73.

Menocal, Maria Rosa (2002) *The Ornament of the World: How Muslims, Jews and Christians Created a Culture of Tolerance in Medieval Spain*, Boston: Little Brown and Company.

Mernissi, Fatima (1996) *Women's Rebellion and Islamic Memory*, London: Zed Books.

Mernissi, Fatima (1997) *The Forgotten Queens of Islam*, Minnesota: University of Minnesota Press.

Meyer, Michael A. (ed.) (1987) *Ideas of Jewish History*, Detroit: Wayne State University Press.

Meyerhoff, Hans (ed.) (1959) *The Philosophy of History in our Time*, New York: Doubleday.

Milburn, R.L.P. (1954) *Early Christian Interpretations of History*, London: Adam and Charles Black.

Moltmann, Jürgen (1981) *The Trinity and the Kingdom of God*, London, SCM Press.

Moltmann, Jürgen (1991a) *History and the Triune God: Contributions to Trinitarian Theology*, London: SCM Press.

Moltmann, Jürgen (1991b) *Theology of Hope: On the Ground and the Implications of a Christian Eschatology*, San Francisco: Harper.

Moltmann, Jürgen (1996) *The Coming of God: Christian Eschatology*, London, SCM Press.

Momigliano, A.D. (1966) *Studies in Historiography*, London: Weidenfeld & Nicolson.

Mommsen, T.E. (1951) 'St Augustine and the Christian Idea of Progress', *Journal of the History of Ideas*, 12, 346–74.

Morgan, D.O. (ed.) (1982) *Medieval Historical Writing in the Christian and Islamic Worlds*, London: SOAS.

Morphy, Howard (1998) *Aboriginal Art*, London: Phaidon.

Muecke, Steven (2004) *Aboriginal Australians: First Nations of an Ancient Continent*, London: Thames & Hudson.

Müller, Klaus E. (2002) 'Perspectives in Historical Anthropology', in Rüsen, Jörn, *Western Historical Thinking: An Intercultural Debate*, New York: Berghahn, 33–52.

Munslow, Alun (2003) *The New History*, London: Longman.

Muntz, Peter (1977) *The Shape of Time: A New Look at the Philosophy of History*, Middletown: Wesleyan University Press.

Murti, T.R.V. (1960) *The Central Philosophy of Buddhism: A Study of the Mādhyamika System*, London: Mandala Books.

Nabokov, Peter (2002) *A Forest of Time: American Indian Ways of History*, Cambridge: Cambridge University Press.

Nagaboshi, Tomio S. and Shifu Terence Dukes (1994) *The Bodhisattva Warriors: The Origin, Inner Philosophy, History and Symbolism of the Buddhist*, New York: Weiser.

Nāgārjuna (1975) *The Precious Garland of Advice for the King [Rājaparikathā-ratnamālā]* in Gyatso, Tenzin *The Buddhism of Tibet*, London: George Allen and Unwin, 105–206.

Nagel, Ernst (1963) 'Relativism and some problems of working historians', in Hook, Sidney (ed.) *Philosophy and History: A Symposium*, New York: New York University Press, 76–91.

Nandy, Ashis (1983) *The Intimate Enemy: Loss and Recovery of Self under Colonialism*, Delhi: Oxford University Press.

Nandy, Ashis (1987) *Traditions, Tyranny and Utopias: Essays in the Politics of Awareness*, Delhi: Oxford University Press.

Nattier, Jan (1998) 'A Prophecy on the Death of the Dharma' in Lopez, Donald S. (ed.), *Buddhism in Practice*, Waterloo: Laurier Books, 249–56.

Negri, Antonio (2003) *Time for Revolution*, New York: Continuum.

Neusner, Jacob (2003) *The Idea of History in Rabbinic Time*, Leiden: Brill.

Newman, John (1998) 'Eschatology in the Wheel of Time Tantra', in Lopez, Donald S. (ed.) *Buddhism in Practice*, Waterloo: Laurier Books, 284–89.

New Revised Standard Bible (1995) Oxford: Oxford University Press.

Newsom, Carol A. (2003) *The Book of Job: A Contest of Moral Imaginations*, Oxford: Oxford University Press.

Niebuhr, Reinhold (1949) *Faith and History: A Comparison of Christian and Modern Views of History*, London: Nisbet.

North, Christopher (1946) *The Old Testament Interpretation of History*, London: Epworth Press.

Noth, Albrecht and Lawrence Conrad (1994) *The Early Arabic Historical Tradition: A Source-Critical Study*, 2nd edn, Princeton: Darwin Press.

Nugent, David (ed.) (2002) *Locating Capitalism in Time and Space: Global Restructurings, Politics, and Identity*, Stanford: Stanford University Press.

O'Donnell, John J. (1983) *Trinity and Temporality: The Christian Doctrine of God in the Light of Process Theology and the Theology of Hope*, Oxford: Oxford University Press.

Olagüe, Ignacio (1969) *Les Arabes n'ont jamais conquis l'Espagne*, Paris: Flammarion.

O'Learey, De Lacey (1922) *Arabic Thought and Its Place in History*, London: Routledge.

Painter, John (1987) *Theology as Hermeneutics: Rudolf Bultmann's Interpretation of the History of Jesus*, Sheffield: The Almond Press.

Pande, G.C. (1993) 'Time in Buddhism', in Balslev, Anindita Niyogi and J.N. Mohanty (eds) *Religion and Time*, Leiden: E.J. Brill, 182–207.

Pannenberg, Wolfhart (1970–71) *Basic Questions in Theology*, 2 vols, London: SCM Press.

Pannenberg, Wolfhart (2000) 'Eternity, Time and the Trinitarian God', in Gunton, Colin E. (ed.) *Trinity, Time and the Church: A Response to the Theology of Robert W. Jenson*, Grand Rapids: William B. Eerdmans, 62–70.

Parker, Christopher (2000) *The English Idea of History: from Coleridge to Collingwood*, Aldershot: Ashgate.

Patrides, Constantinos A. (1972) *The Grand Design of God: The Literary Form of the Christian View of History*, London: Routledge & Kegan Paul.

Patte, Daniel (1995) *Ethics of Biblical Interpretation: A Reevaluation*, Louisville: Westminster John Knox Press.

Patterson, L.G. (1967) *God and History in Early Christian Thought: A Study of Themes from Justin Martyr to Gregory the Great*, London: Adam and Charles Black.

Peters, Ted (1997) 'The Trinity in and Beyond Time', in Russell, Robert John, Nancey Murphy and C.J. Ishan (eds) *Quantum Cosmology and the Laws of Nature: Scientific Perspectives on Divine Action*, Vatican: Vatican Observatory Publications, 263–91.

Philipse, Herman (1998) *Heidegger's Philosophy of Being: A Critical Reinterpretation*, Princeton: Princeton University Press.

Pitkin, Hanna Fenichel (1972) *Wittgenstein and Justice: On the Significance of Wittgenstein for Social and Political Thought*, Berkeley: University of California Press.

Plumb, J.H. (1969) *The Death of the Past*, London: Macmillan.

Pollard, Sidney (1968) *The Idea of Progress: History and Society*, London: C.A. Watts.

Pomian, Krzystof (1984) *L'ordre du temps*, Paris: Gallimard.

Powell, J.M. and M. Williams (1984) *Australian Space, Australian Time: Geographical Perspectives*, Oxford: Oxford University Press.

Powers, John (1991) *The Yogācāra School of Buddhism: A Bibliography*, Metuchen: Scarecrow Press.

Prasad, H.S. (ed.) (1991) *Essays on Time In Buddhism*, Delhi: Sri Satguru.

Prasad, H.S. (1996) 'Time in Buddhism and Leibniz: An Intercultural Perspective', in Tiemersma, D. and H.A.F. Oosterling (eds) *Time and Temporality in Intercultural Perspective*, Amsterdam: Rodopi, 53–64.

Rapaport, Herman (1989) *Heidegger and Derrida: Reflections on Time and Language*, Lincoln: University of Nebraska Press.

Rasul, M.G. (1968) *The Origin and Development of Muslim Historiography*, Lahore: Sh. Muhammad Ashraf.

Rawlence, Christopher (ed.) (1985) *About Time*, London: Jonathan Cape.

Read, Peter (2000) *Belonging: Australians, Place and Aboriginal Ownership*, Cambridge: Cambridge University Press.

Rée, Jonathan (1998) *History and Truth in Being and Time*, London: Phoenix.

Reid, W. Stanford (1973) 'The Problem of the Christian Interpretation of History', *Fides et Historia*, 5.

Reill, Peter H. (1975) *The German Enlightenment and the Rise of Historicism*, Berkeley: University of California Press.

Ricci, Gabriel (2002) *Time Consciousness: The Philosophical Uses of History*, New Brunswick: Transaction.

Richardson, Alan (1964) *History Sacred and Profane*, London: SCM Press.

Ricœur, Paul (1965) *History and Truth*, Evanston: Northwestern University Press.

Ricœur, Paul (1979) 'The Human Experience of Time and Narrative', *Research in Phenomenology*, 9, 17–34.

Ricœur, Paul (1980) *The Contribution of French Historiography to the Theory of History*, Oxford: Clarendon Press.

Ricœur, Paul (1981) *Hermeneutics and the Human Sciences: Essays on Language, Action and Interpretation*, Cambridge: Cambridge University Press.

Ricœur, Paul (1984–90) *Time and Narrative*, 3 vols, Chicago: University of Chicago Press.

Ricœur, Paul (1994) *Oneself as Another*, Chicago: University of Chicago Press.

Ricœur, Paul (1999) 'The Contribution of French Historiography to the Theory of History', in Clark, Stuart (ed.) *The Annales School: Critical Assessments*, London: Routledge, 47–95.

Ricœur, Paul (2003) *The Rule of Metaphor: The Creation of Meaning in Language*, London: Routledge.

Ridgeon, Lloyd V.J. (2003) *Major World Religions*, London: Routledge.

Ritter, David (2004) 'The Judgement of the World: The Yorta Yorta Case and the 'Tide of History', *Australian Historical Studies*, 123, 106–21.

Ritter, Harry (1986) *Dictionary of Concepts in History*, New York: Greenwood.

Roberts, Joseph Bradin (1986) *Early Islamic Historiography: Ideology and Methodology*, PhD dissertation, Ohio State University.

Robinson, Chase F. (2002) *Islamic Historiography*, Cambridge: Cambridge University Press.

Robinson, James M. (1959) *A New Quest of the Historical Jesus*, London: SCM Press.

Robinson, Richard H. and Willard L. Johnson (1982) *The Buddhist Religion: An Historical Introduction*, 3rd edn, Belmont: Wadsworth.

Rosenstone, Robert A. (2006) *History on Film/Film on History*, London: Longman-Pearson.

Rosenthal, Franz (1968) *A History of Muslim Historiography*, 2nd edn, Leiden: E.J. Brill.

Ross, John (1993) *Chronicle of Australia*, Ringwood: JAL.

Rotenstreich, Nathan (1958) *Between Past and Present: An Essay on History*, Port Washington: Kennikat Press.

Rotenstreich, Nathan (1960) *History and Time: A Critical Examination of R.G. Collingwood's Doctrine*, Jerusalem: Hebrew University of Jerusalem.

Rotenstreich, Nathan (1987) *Time and Meaning in History*, Dordrecht: D. Reidel.

Rudasvsky, Tamar (2000) *Time Matters: Time, Creation and Cosmology in Medieval Jewish Philosophy*, Albany: SUNY Press.

Rudman, Dominic (2001) *Determinism in the Book of Ecclesiastes*, Sheffield: Sheffield Academic Press.

Ruggles, D. Fairchild (2003) *Gardens, Landscape and Vision in the Palaces of Islamic Spain*, University Park: Penn State Press.

Rüsen, Jörn (2002) 'Introduction: Historical Thinking as Intercultural Discourse', in Rüsen, Jörn (ed.) *Western Historical Thinking: An Intercultural Debate*, New York: Berghahn, 1–11.

Russell, Robert John, Nancey Murphy and C.J. Ishan (eds) (1993) *Quantum Cosmology and the Laws of Nature: Scientific Perspectives on Divine Action*, Vatican: Vatican Observatory Publications.

Sachedina, Abdulaziz Abdulhussein (1981) *Islamic Messianism: The Idea of Mahdi in Twelver Shi'ism*, Albany: SUNY Press.

Said, Edward (1979) *Orientalism*, London: Penguin.

Sanchez-Albornoz, Claudio (1975) *Spain: A Historical Enigma*, 2 vols, Madrid: Fundación Universitaria.

Sanders, E.P. (1985) *Jesus and Judaism*, London: SCM Press.

Sayers, B.J. (1977) 'Aboriginal world view and tense, mood and aspect in Wik-Munkan', *Workpapers in Papua New Guinea Languages*, 20.

Schauss, Hayyim (1996) *The Jewish Festivals: History and Observance*, New York: Schocken Books.

Schildgen, Brenda Deen (1998) *Crisis and Continuity: Time in the Gospel of Mark*, Sheffield: Sheffield Academic Press.

Schoonenberg, Piet (1964) *God's World in the Making*, Dublin: Gill and Son.

Schoonenberg, Piet (1970) 'Historicity and the Interpretation of Dogma', *Theology Digest*, 18.

Schweitzer, Albert (1910) *The Quest of the Historical Jesus: A Critical Study of its Progress from Reimarus to Wrede*, London: Adam and Charles Black.

Schweizer, Eduard (1961) *Church Order in the New Testament*, London: SCM Press.

Seale, M.S. (1978) *Qur'an and Bible: Studies in Interpretation and Dialogue*, London: Croom Helm.

Sebald, W.G. (2002a) *The Emigrants*, London: Vintage.

Sebald, W.G. (2002b) *Rings of Saturn*, London: Vintage.

Sebald, W.G. (2002c) *Austerlitz*, London: Penguin.

Sebald, W.G. (2002d) *Vertigo*, London: Vintage.

Seixas, Peter (ed.) (2004) *Theorizing Historical Consciousness*, Toronto: University of Toronto Press.

Sharma, Arvind (1995) *The Philosophy of Religion*, Delhi: Oxford University Press.

Shaw, Bruce (1981) *My Country of the Pelican Dreaming: The Life of an Australian Aborigine of the Gadjerong, Grant Ngabidi, 1904–1977*, Canberra: Australian Institute of Aboriginal Studies.

Sherover, Charles M. (1975) *The Human Experience of Time: The Development of its Philosophic Meaning*, New York: New York University Press.

Sherover, Charles M. (2003) *Are We in Time? And Other Essays on Time and Temporality*, Evanston: Northwestern.

Sider, Ronald J. (1972) 'The Historian, the Miraculous and Post-Newtonian Man', *Scottish Journal of Theology*, 25, 309–19.

Silva, Moisés (1995) *Biblical Words and Their Meaning: An Introduction to Lexical Semantics*, 2nd edn, Grand Rapids: Zondervan.

Sironneau, Jean-Pierre (1982) *Sécularisation et religions politiques*, La Haye: Mouton Editeur.

Sirriyeh, Elizabeth (1999) *Sufis and Anti-Sufis: The Defence, Rethinking and Rejection of Sufism in the Modern World*, London: Curzon.

Skilton, Andrew (1994) *A Concise History of Buddhism*, Birmingham: Windhorse.

Skinner, Quentin (1968) 'Meaning and Understanding in the History of Ideas', *History and Theory*, 7, 3–53.

Smart, Ninian (1970) *Buddhism and the Death of God*, Southampton: University of Southampton Press.

Smart, Ninian (1996) *Dimensions of the Sacred*, London: HarperCollins.

Smith, Gamaliel (1823) *Not Paul but Jesus*, London: John Hunt.

Snelling, John (1992) *The Buddhist Handbook: A Complete Guide to Buddhist Teaching and Practice*, 2nd edn, London: Rider.

Sorel, Georges (1969) *The Illusions of Progress*, Berkeley: University of California Press.

Soulsby, Marlene J. and J.T. Fraser (2001) *Time: Perspectives at the Millennium/The Study of Time*, Westport: Bergin and Garvey.

Spengler, Oswald (1961) *The Decline of the West*, London: Allen & Unwin.

Spivak, Gayatri Chakravorty (1990) *The Post-Colonial Critic: Interviews, Strategies, Dialogues*, ed. by Sarah Harasym, London: Routledge.

Spivak, Gayatri Chakravorty (1994) *In Other Worlds: Essays in Cultural Politics*, London: Routledge.

Spivak, Gayatri Chakravorty (1999) *A Critique of Postcolonial Reason: Towards a History of the Vanishing Present*, Cambridge, Mass.: Harvard University Press.

Stanner, W.E.H. (1969) *After the Dreaming: The 1968 Boyer Lectures*, Sydney: Australian Broadcasting Corporation.

Stern, Sacha (2003) *Time and Process in Ancient Judaism*, Oxford: The Littman Library.

Stone, Jackie (1998) 'Original Enlightenment in the Nichiren Tradition [Lotus Sūtra]' in Lopez, Donald S. (ed.) *Buddhism in Practice*, Waterloo: Laurier Books, 228–40.

Strehlow, T.G.H. (1970) *Songs of Central Australia*, Sydney: Angus & Robertson.

Surtz, Ronald E., Jaime Ferrán and Daniel P. Testa (eds) (1988) *Américo Castro: The Impact of His Thought – Essays to Mark the Centenary of His Birth*, Madison: The Hispanic Seminary of Medieval Studies.

Sutton, Peter (ed.) (1989) *Dreamings: The Art of Aboriginal Australia*, New York: Viking.

Suzuki, D.T. (1969) *The Zen Doctrine of No Mind*, London: Rider.

Suzuki, D.T. (1970a) *Essays in Zen Buddhism*, first series, London: Rider.

Suzuki, D.T. (1970b) *Essays in Zen Buddhism*, second series, London: Rider.

Suzuki, D.T. (1974) *Manual of Zen Buddhism*, London: Rider.

Swain, Tony (1993) *A Place for Strangers: Towards a History of Australian Aboriginal Being*, Cambridge: Cambridge University Press.

Tambiah, S.J. (1970) *Buddhism and the Spirit Cults in North-East Thailand*, Cambridge: Cambridge University Press.

Tanabe, George J. (1998) 'Myōe's Letter to the Island', in Lopez, Donald S. (ed.), *Buddhism in Practice*, Waterloo: Laurier Books, 88–91.

Tanabe, George J. (1998) 'The Matsumoto Debate' in Lopez, Donald S. (ed.), *Buddhism in Practice*, Waterloo: Laurier Books, 241–48.

Tanaka, Stefan (2004) *New Times in Modern Japan*, Princeton: Princeton University Press.

Taylor, Charles (1989) *Sources of the Self: The Making of the Modern Identity*, Cambridge: Cambridge University Press.

Taylor, Mark C. (1975) *Kierkegaard's Pseudonymous Authorship: A Study of Time and the Self*, Princeton, Princeton University Press.

TenHouten, Warren (2005) *Time and Society*, Albany: SUNY Press.

Thomas, Alain (1996) *Paul Ricœur, une poétique de la morale: aux fondements d'une éthique herméneutique et narrative dans une perspective chrétienne*, Leuven: Leuven University Press.

Thomas, Edward J. (1951) *The History of Buddhist Thought*, 2nd edn, London: Routledge and Kegan Paul.

Thomas, Nicholas (1996) *Out of Time: History and Evolution in Anthropological Discourse*, 2nd edn, Michigan: University of Michigan Press.

Tidball, Derek (1998) *That's Just the Way it is: A Realistic View of Life from the Book of Ecclesiastes*, Fearn: Christian Focus.

Tilakaratne, Asanga (1993) *Nirvana and Ineffability: A Study of the Buddhist Theory of Reality and Language*, Kelaniya: Institute of Pali and Buddhist Studies.

Tillich, Paul (1968) *A History of Christian Thought*, London: SCM Press.

Tiwari, Kedar Nath (1997) *Comparative Religion*, Delhi: Motilal Banarsidass.

Todorov, Tzvetan (1987) *The Conquest of America: The Question of the Other*, London: HarperCollins.

Topolski, Jerzy (1994) *Historiography between Modernism and Postmodernism*, Amsterdam: Rodopi.

Tornikotis, Panayotis (2001) *The Historiography of Modern Architecture*, Boston: MIT Press.

Torrance, Thomas F. (1976) *Space, Time and the Resurrection*, Edinburgh: The Handsel Press.

Tosh, John (ed.) (2000) *Historians on History*, London: Longman.

Toulmin, Stephen and June Goodfield (1965) *The Discovery of Time*, London: Penguin.

Toynbee, Arnold (1979) *An Historian's Approach to Religion*, 2nd edn, Oxford: Oxford University Press.

Tracy, David (1994) *On Naming the Present: Reflections on God, Hermeneutics and the Church*, New York: Orbis.

Troeltsch, Ernst (1972) *The Absoluteness of Christianity and the History of Religions*, London: SCM Press.

Trompf, G.W. (1979) *The Idea of Historical Recurrence in Western Thought: From Antiquity to Reformation*, Berkeley: University of California Press.

Troup, Calvin L. (1999) *Temporality, Eternity and Wisdom: The Rhetoric of Augustine's Confessions*, Columbia: University of South Carolina Press.

Trusted, Jennifer (1994) *Physics and Metaphysics*, London: Routledge.

Tupper, E. Frank (1974) *The Theology of Wolfgang Pannenberg*, London: SCM Press.

Turner, H.E.W. (1963) *Historicity and the Gospels: A Sketch of Historical Method and its Application to the Gospels*, London: Mowbray.

Tuveson, Ernest L. (1949) *Millennium and Utopia: A Study in the Background of the Idea of Progress*, Berkeley: University of California Press.

Tytler, Ernest J. (1975) *The Story of Time*, London: Educational Productions/Rolex.

Valensi, Lucette (1985) *Tunisian Peasants in the Eighteenth and Nineteenth Centuries*, Cambridge: Cambridge University Press.

Van Seters, John (1983) *In Search of History: Historiography in the Ancient World and the Origins of Biblical History*, New Haven: Yale University Press.

Vassiliev, Alexei (1998) *The History of Saudi Arabia*, London: Saqi.

Vermes, Geza (1973) *Jesus the Jew: A Historian's Reading of the Gospels*, London: Collins.

Viguera, Maria J. (1992) 'On the Social Status of Andalusi Women', in Jayyusi, Salma (1992) *The Legacy of Muslim Spain*, Leiden: E.J. Brill, 709–24.

Von Denffer, Ahmad (1979) *Christians in the Qur'an and Sunna: An Assessment from the Sources to Help Our Relationship*, Leicester: The Islamic Foundation.

Von Rad, Gerhard (1962 and 1965) *Old Testament Theology*, Edinburgh: Oliver and Boyd.

Walser, Joseph (2005) *Nāgārjuna in Context: Mahāyāna Buddhism and Early Indian Culture*, New York: Columbia University Press.

Walsh, W.H. (1967) *An Introduction to the Philosophy of History*, London: Hutchinson.

Wansbrough, John (1977) *Qur'anic Studies: Sources and Methods of Scriptural Interpretation*, Oxford: Oxford University Press.

Ward, C.H.S. (1947, revised edn) *Buddhism – Hinayana*, 2nd edn, London: Epworth Press.

Warren, Henry Clarke (1922) *Buddhism in Translations: Passages Selected from the Buddhist Sacred Books*, Cambridge, Mass.: Harvard University Press.

Watt, W. Montgomery (1965) *A History of Islamic Spain*, Edinburgh: Edinburgh University Press.

Watts, Alan (1990) *The Way of Zen*, London: Arkana.

Welbon, Guy Richard (1968) *The Buddhist Nirvāna and its Western Interpreters*, Chicago: University of Chicago Press.

Wenham, Gordon (1976) 'History and the Old Testament', in Brown, Colin (ed.) *History, Criticism, Faith*, Leicester: Inter-Varsity Press, 13–75.

Wessels, Anton (2000) *Understanding the Qur'an*, London: SCM Press.

West, Margie K.C. (ed.) (1988) *The Inspired Dream: Life as Art in Aboriginal Australia*, South Brisbane: Queensland Art Gallery.

Westermann, Claus (ed.) (1963) *Essays on Old Testament Interpretation*, London: SCM Press.

Whately, Richard (1985) *Historic Doubts Relative to the Existence of Napoleon Bonaparte*, ed. by Ralph S. Pomeroy, Berkeley: Scolar Press.

White, Hayden (1973) *Metahistory: The Historical Imagination in the Nineteenth-Century*, Baltimore: The Johns Hopkins University Press.

White, Hayden (1991) 'The Metaphysics of Narrativity', in Wood, David (ed.) *On Paul Ricœur: Narrative and Interpretation*, London: Routledge.

Whitrow, G.J. (1988) *Time in History: The Evolution of Our General Awareness of Time and Temporal Perspective*, Oxford: Oxford University Press.

Whittaker, Molly (1984) *Cambridge Commentaries on Writings of the Jewish and Christian World 200 BC to 200 AD, volume 6: Jews and Christians: Graeco-Roman views*, Cambridge: Cambridge University Press.

Whorf, Benjamin (1950) 'An American Indian Model of the Universe', *International Journal of American Linguistics*, 16, 67–72.

Wilch, John R. (1969) *Time and Event: An Exegetical Study of the Use of ʿēth in the Old Testament in Comparison to Other Temporal Expressions in Clarification of the Concept of Time*, Leiden: E.J. Brill.

Wilcox, Donald J. (1987) *The Measure of Times Past: Pre-Newtonian Chronologies and the Rhetoric of Relative Time*, Chicago: University of Chicago Press.

Wildon Carr, H. (1918) *'Time' and 'History' in Contemporary Philosophy; with special reference to Bergson and Croce*, London: The British Academy.

Williams, Paul and Anthony Tribe (2000) *Buddhist Thought: A Complete Introduction to the Indian Tradition*, London: Routledge.

Williams, Paul (ed.) (2005) *Buddhism: Critical Concepts in Religious Studies*, vol 5, *Yogācāra, the epistemological tradition and Tathāgatagarbha*, London: Routledge.

Williams, Peter (2002) *From Despair to Hope: Insights into the Book of Job*, Epsom: Day One.

Wilson, Leslie S. (2006) *The Book of Job: Judaism in the 2nd Century BCE: An Intertextual Reading*, Lanham: University Press of America.

Wilson, Robert R. (1980) *Prophecy and Society in Ancient Israel*, Minneapolis: Fortress Press.

Windschuttle, Keith (2004) 'Historical Error versus Historical Invention: A Reply to Stuart Macintyre and Patricia Grimshaw on The Fabrication of Australian History', *Australian Historical Studies*, 124, 375–82.

Wiredu, K. (J.E.) (1984) 'How Not to Compare African Thought with Western Thought', in Wright, Richard A. (ed.) *African Philosophy: An Introduction*, 3rd edn, Lanham: University Press of America, 149–62.

Wittgenstein, Ludwig (1969) *Zettel*, Oxford: Basil Blackwell.

Wittgenstein, Ludwig (1971) *Tractatus Logico-Philosophicus*, 2nd edn, London: Routledge and Kegan Paul.

Wittgenstein, Ludwig (1972) *The Philosophical Investigations*, Oxford: Basil Blackwell.

Wittgenstein, Ludwig (1974) *On Certainty*, Oxford: Basil Blackwell.

Wittgenstein, Ludwig (1979) *Lectures on Philosophy: Wittgenstein's Lectures 1932–35*, ed. by Alice Ambrose, Oxford: Blackwell.

Wittgenstein, Ludwig (1980) *Culture and Value*, Oxford: Basil Blackwell.

Wolfers, David (1995) *Deep Things out of Darkness: The Book of Job*, Grand Rapids: William B. Eerdmans.

Wolin, Richard (1995) *Labyrinths: Explorations in the Critical History of Ideas*, Amherst: University of Massachusetts Press.

Wood, David (ed.) (1991) *On Paul Ricœur: Narrative and Interpretation*, London: Routledge.

Wood, David (2001) *The Deconstruction of Time*, 2nd edn, Evanston: Northwestern University Press.

Woolf, D.R. (ed.) (1998) *A Global Encyclopedia of Historical Writing*, 2 vols, New York: Garland.

Wurm, S.A. (1972) *Languages of Australia and Tasmania*, The Hague: Mouton.

Yallop, Colin (1982) *Australian Aboriginal Languages*, London: André Deutsch.

Yerushalmi, Yosef Hayim (1982) *Zakhor: Jewish History and Jewish Memory*, Washington: University of Washington Press.

Young, Robert (1990) *White Mythologies: Writing History and the West*, London: Routledge.

Zaehner, R.C. (1972) *Drugs, Mysticism and Make-Believe*, London: Collins.

Zerubavel, Eviatara (1977) 'The French Revolutionary Calendar: A Case Study in the Sociology of Time', *American Sociology Review*, 42, 868–77.

Zerubavel, Eviatar (2004) *Time Maps: Collective Memory and the Social Shape of the Past*, Chicago: University of Chicago Press.

Index